Creativity and the Arts with Young Children

Join us on the web at

EarlyChildEd.delmar.com

Creativity and the Arts with Young Children

Rebecca T. Isbell, Ed. D.
Director, Center of Excellence in Early Childhood Learning and Development
Professor of Early Childhood Education
East Tennessee State University

Shirley C. Raines, Ed. D.
President
Professor of Curriculum and Instruction
University of Memphis

THOMSON
DELMAR LEARNING

Australia Canada Mexico Singapore Spain United Kingdom United States

THOMSON

DELMAR LEARNING

Creativity and the Arts with Young Children
Rebecca T. Isbell & Shirley C. Raines

Executive Director:
Susan L. Simpfenderfer

Executive Editor:
Marlene McHugh Pratt

Acquisitions Editor:
Erin O'Connor Traylor

Senior Development Editor:
Melissa Riveglia

Editorial Assistant:
Ivy Ip

Executive Production Manager:
Wendy A. Troeger

Production Editor:
J.P. Henkel

Technology Project Manager:
Joe Saba

Executive Marketing Manager:
Donna J. Lewis

Channel Manager:
Nigar Hale

Cover Design:
Tom Cicero

Library of Congress Cataloging-in-Publication Data
Isbell, Rebecca T.
  Creativity and the arts with young children / Rebecca T. Isbell, Shirley C. Raines.
    p. cm.
Includes bibliographical references and index.
  ISBN 0-7668-2033-5
  1. Arts--Study and teaching (Early childhood) 2. Creative ability in children. I. Raines, Shirley C. II. Title.
  LB1139.5.A78 I73 2002
  370.15'7--dc21
                              2002019304

NOTICE TO THE READER

Contents

Chapter 1
Creativity

Chapter 2
The Creative Teacher with Creative Children   35

Chapter 3
The Important Role of Play   63

Chapter 4
The Many Forms of Art   97

Chapter 5
Music: It Begins in Infancy   141

Chapter 6
Creative Movement: More
Than the Hokey Pokey   173

Chapter 7
Creative Drama in the
Early Childhood Classroom   195

Chapter 8
Creativity across the Curriculum and throughout the Classroom   227

Chapter 9
The Expressive Arts in the Early Childhood
Classroom and Curriculum   257

Foreword

Rebecca T. Isbell and Shirley C. Raines have presented us with a wonderful book on creative arts with young children. As they state, the creative arts are a powerful tool when used with young children. It accommodates to their needs and means of instruction. I do not know why we have had so little of this kind of education. When I was in Japan in 1979 and 1980, I visited some 25 preschools where the curriculum was built on the arts: music, literature, drama, folktales, and the like. While the curriculum in the primary schools was less creative, the evidence showed that children maintained the creativity that had been cultivated in the early years.

Another important point that the authors make is that creativity and the arts are not alone for the gifted and talented, but are for all children. As I have studied creativity, I have become aware that some children of only ordinary intelligence are highly gifted in one or more of the arts, and this fuels their learning.

The authors have had rich experiences in working with the creative arts and draw on this broad experience to give us a very worthwhile book. As children themselves, they experienced plays, drama, dance, and music, and were entertained and enriched by this. They also found that they could introduce creative ideas into the regular curriculum in science, social studies, and the language arts.

The authors use separate chapters in addressing specific areas of the creative arts: art, music, movement, drama, and literature. They use inspiring quotations from artists, philosophers, and creative teachers throughout the book to promote new ways of thinking about creativity in the arts. They also use pictures, open-ended activities, and children's literature to stimulate creativity and imagination. I feel confident that readers in the early childhood education field will find many helpful ideas in this book for developing creativity.

E. Paul Torrance
Georgia Studies of Creative Behavior

Preface

Introduction

It is both an exciting and challenging time to be an early childhood teacher. So much is known about how young children learn and develop. National and international interest in the capabilities of young children, and the impact of the environment on their development, is at an all-time high. Never before has there been such a need for creative thinking as we participate in the 21st century filled with new problems, global issues, and expanding technology. Today's teachers must make learning meaningful as they compete for the attention of young children living in a world filled with flashing visual images and high-impact drama. Early childhood classrooms must be supportive places, filled with meaningful experiences, compelling materials, alluring songs, and opportunities to think in creative ways. A new kind of early childhood educator is needed to meet these challenges, one who understands the holistic nature of young children's development.

The world is often seen at its best when people are playing, painting, singing, designing, and pretending. The important parts of civilization and culture are preserved in imaginative literature, art, drama, music, and dance. These areas that were so important in ancient times, should continue to be powerful influences in the lives of young children. The arts remain a basic and essential form of human communication. The arts help us make meaning out of our deepest feelings and share our most significant thoughts. The arts permeate our lives and provide an avenue for joyful participation.

The creative arts is a powerful tool for inviting young children to use their knowledge, work cooperatively, and make connections across content areas. Participation in the arts gives young children the opportunity to discover the world around them as well as expanding into new worlds. This textbook is designed to be a resource for teachers as they integrate the arts into their early childhood classrooms.

The Value of the Arts

Like Shirley, the arts have been an integral part of my life since childhood. From a very early age, music filled my home and sparked a lifelong interest in music. Throughout my years in school, I participated in madrigal groups, choral ensembles, dramatic productions, and creative endeavors. It was in these areas that I blossomed and built a positive image of my capabilities. During the first five years of my teaching career, I taught music to K–5 children. These were wonderful years filled with singing, moving, and creating music.

Later, I worked with "gifted and talented" children, and again, I found creative thinking and the arts were essential. During this entire period, I was interested in how to develop and nurture creativity in young children. How could I help them develop a love for the arts that would follow them throughout their lives? I knew that the arts would enrich their lives, make them better persons, and provide a healthy outlet for their creative energies. I have experienced this personally and with thousands of children.

When I began teaching at the university level, I found that there were few courses that focused on the creative arts or included these areas of study. In response to this need, I developed a course on creativity and the arts. Refinement of this course over the past ten years has provided the foundation for this textbook. I have had the pleasure of watching early childhood teachers rekindle their creative fires. They have become excited and capable of designing wonderful programs for young children that include the arts. Creative classroom environments begin with the teacher who can ignite an effective program for young children.

Rebecca Isbell

Like Rebecca, I have had the joy of teaching children and teaching adults who will eventually teach children. Few experiences can compare to the creativity of the young child and the ingenuity of those who teach them. My years of study and work in the field of early childhood education have convinced me that the ways we organize classrooms, provide materials, and open our minds to children's inventiveness are key factors in fostering creativity.

Growing up in a rural community with a large extended family, I learned that music was a link to our shared heritage, and a fun way to spend Sunday afternoons with guitars, piano-playing, and family members singing harmony. No one had to convince me of the value of music: I lived it. Play, drama, dance, and using one's imagination entertained me, and occupied the attention of my cousins and the younger children.

As a teacher, my classroom became alive with activity when children were free to choose their own expressive arts, and when I added creative ideas to the regular curriculum in science, social studies, and language arts. Children thrive in classrooms where the arts are a way of life. Invitations to be creative have structures beneath them such as resources, time, and ways of engaging children's thinking. The delight in the arts begins with the young child and lasts for a lifetime.

My husband is an artist and sees the world through an artist's eyes. His stained glass art in several churches and his paintings are evidence of the artistic process, but the great joy of his artistic life is much like what I feel when I see children painting, making collages, or dancing. The ability to express one's self and to enjoy the process of creating has applications to the artist's life, but it also has applications to life in general. Children and adults compose their lives. I am still in the process of the composition but I am enjoying the music. This book is jointly composed, but it is Dr. Isbell who is the maestro. I have learned a great deal from her about how one supports creativity because my colleague has supported me in my own composition.

Shirley Raines

How to Use This Book

This text is a practical introduction to the creative arts in early childhood. It is designed to nurture the creativity of new or experienced early childhood teachers. The first chapter provides the background for understanding creativity. It includes theories, research, and environmental issues that help recognize the significance of the creative process. Chapter two explores the potential for creativity that exists in each person. The focus is on the creative possibilities that are within each early childhood educator. The next chapter examines the importance of play in the development of young children and its relationship to creativity. Teachers can design play environments that will nurture young children's creative endeavors in the early childhood classroom.

The chapters that follow address specific areas of the creative arts such as art, music, movement, and drama. Each chapter will include what, why, and how the art form should be included in early childhood programs, and give specific ways to enrich their development. Chapters eight and nine provide insight into the meaningful integration of the arts across the curriculum. These chapters include developmentally appropriate approaches for making the arts an important component of the classroom content.

Special Features

Creative Episodes and Reflective Questions. Each chapter begins with the description of an experience that demonstrates the creative child or adult, doing his best work. The episode is followed by a discussion of what can be learned from observing creative moments that occur throughout the day. At the end of each chapter, questions are posed to assist readers in reflecting on the episode and identifying the creative aspects of their observations.

Quotes. The powerful words of artists, philosophers, and creative teachers provided throughout the book promote new ways of thinking about creativity and the arts. These quotations provide inspiration to teachers for including the arts in programs for young children.

Pictures and Drawings. For many people, visual images provide important connections for learning. Throughout this book, wonderful images of children and adults are included that demonstrate active participation in the arts. In addition, specific examples of children's work are included to show the range of creative possibilities across the early childhood period. These provide another way of understanding the creative potential of young children.

Possibilities for Adult Learners. At the end of each chapter, there are several examples of activities that can be used with adults. These activities provide opportunities for students in college courses to experience the power of the arts and the creative process for themselves. Adults learn and enjoy active participation almost as much as young children. The activities that are included should be expanded and enriched to match the needs of the specific class and the interest of the adult students.

Open-ended Activities for Young Children. Each chapter includes open-ended activities for young children. Examples are provided for both Pre-K–K and primary grades so adult students can recognize opportunities for the creative arts across the early childhood developmental span. The focus of these activities is on diverse and unique responses instead of on "cute products." None of the activities are meant to be prescriptive or replicated. Teachers should adapt and shape the ideas for their specific group of children, and add their own creative touch.

Additional Reading. This section at the end of each chapter provides references for additional reading on the chapter's topic. These sources are for students who want to expand their knowledge of a subject or search for additional information on these topics.

Children's Literature. Children's books are a resource that provides additional support for learning about the arts and creative thinking. Each chapter includes recommended books to extend children's understanding and provide a literary connection to the arts. An annotation is included so the teacher can make appropriate selections for the specific needs of children in the classroom.

Helpful Web Sites. A listing of Internet resources is included at the end of each chapter. These online resources can provide additional information related to the content of each chapter and identify other avenues for obtaining current information. Due to the dynamic nature of the Internet, remember that Web sites are subject to change at any time. For updated information, log on to http://Child.ETSU.edu and select Creativity Book Web sites under the resources tab.

Online Resources™
The Online Resources™ to accompany *Creativity and the Arts with Young Children* is your link to early childhood education on the Internet. The Online Resources™ contain many features to help focus your understanding of creative arts for young children. You can find the Online Resources™ at http://www.earlychilded.delmar.com

Appendices.   The appendices are extensive and provide a great deal of practical information for the teacher to use in early childhood classrooms. The busy student-teacher or experienced teacher often does not have time to find recipes, songs, or finger plays that they would like to use. The appendices also provide stories for dramatizing and creative units to demonstrate some unique possibilities. The National Standards for Arts Education: *What Every Young American Should Know and Be Able to Do in the Arts*, developed by the Consortium of National Arts Education Associations, provides guidelines for program design in the areas of art, music, theater, and dance. The appendices are a resource for educators and provide new materials that will enrich classroom offerings.

Key Terms and the Glossary.   When a new term or concept is introduced in the text, it will appear in color print. The bolded terms are listed at the end of each chapter and defined in the glossary at the back of the book. Terms used by artists in their field also are included. These terms and definitions can be used to expand the vocabulary of early childhood teachers and may be used with children as they participate in the arts.

Ancillaries

Instructor's Manual

The instructor's manual includes questions for review and discussion, multimedia resources, and other references to support instruction.

Acknowledgments

This book was created with the support of many different people having a wide range of capabilities and talents. Stacy Larsen has been the essential person in making sure that the early childhood content was accurate, current, and appropriate. Throughout the process, she has retained her sense of humor and continued to make creative suggestions that have had a positive impact on this book. Sarah Hackney assisted in the final stages of the project to refine and check details to improve the book. Michael Talley has worked diligently to get just the right picture that effectively demonstrates the young child in creative activities; a very difficult job that he has accomplished with great skill. Su Lorencen has contributed many of the wonderful photos of very young children. Her eye for observing and recording children's creative moments has added a special view into the world of infants and toddlers. Mary Myron, Susan Lachmann, and Stacey Larsen also contributed some photographs. Sheila P. Smith has worked with us on each step of the manuscript process, editing with a focus on details and making sure that the work followed the established guidelines. Her contribution has been invaluable.

Many of the photographs have been taken in the Child Study Center, a component of the Center of Excellence in Early Childhood Learning and Development on the campus of East Tennessee State University in Johnson City, Tennessee. The director, teachers, and children allowed us to observe, photograph, and retake pictures. They have welcomed us into the center, even at the most inopportune times. We thank them for collaborating with us and supporting our efforts to include visuals that effectively represent the creative children in their environment.

Most photographs of primary children were taken at the University School located on the campus of East Tennessee State University. The principal and talented early childhood teachers welcomed us into their classrooms to observe and record the many creative happenings that occur in these settings.

During some of the difficult moments encountered in the writing of a textbook, we have had supportive family and friends who have assured us repeatedly that we could make it happen. We could not have created this book without their personal support and tolerance.

For over 20 years, we have had the joy of working with many amazing early childhood students. Our experiences with them in creative arts classes, and later in their early childhood classrooms, have convinced us that it is possible to become more creative and to use these approaches with young children. These interactions with creative teachers have helped us continue to grow and to challenge the limitless possibilities that creative thinking provides. It is our hope that this textbook will help you enrich your own creativity, and that you will pass it on to all the children that you inspire.

Rebecca T. Isbell
Shirley C. Raines

Reviewers

The authors and Delmar Learning would like to thank the following reviewers for their valuable comments and suggestions.

Linda Aulgur, Ph.D.
Westminister College
Fulton, Missouri

Julie Bakerlis
Becker College
Leicester, Massachesetts

Pamela Davis
Henderson State University
Arcadelphia, Arkansas

Jill E. Fox, Ph.D.
Virginia Commonwealth University
Richmond, Virginia

Theresa Frazier
Thomas Nelson Community College
Hampton, Virginia

Sue Grossman, Ph.D.
Eastern Michigan University
Ypsilanti, Michigan

Karen Liu, Ph.D.
Indiana State University
Terre Haute, Indiana

Leila Christie Mullis, Ed.D.
State University of West
   Georgia/Dalton
Ringgold, Georgia

To Ben and Bob,
our husbands whose creativity
and love of beauty
have brought joy to our lives.

About the Authors

Dr. Rebecca Isbell is Director of Tennessee's Center of Excellence in Early Childhood Learning and Development, and professor of Early Childhood Education at East Tennessee State University where she received the Distinguished Faculty Award for Outstanding Teaching.

She is a former teacher of preschoolers and gifted–talented children in elementary school, and has been a director of programs for young children. Dr. Isbell has developed undergraduate and graduate programs in Early Childhood Education that have received NAEYC approval. Her specific areas of interest are creativity, environments, and literacy development. Dr. Isbell has authored a number of books including *The Complete Learning Center Book* and co-authored *Stories: Children's Literature in Early Education*.

Dr. Shirley Raines is President of the University of Memphis, and professor of Education. She is past President of the Association for Childhood Education International (ACEI), and a former classroom teacher, Head Start director, and child care center director. Dr. Raines has taught undergraduate and graduate courses in the creative development of young children at a number of universities and colleges. She has been a strong advocate for quality programs for all young children. Dr. Raines has many publications including the *Story S-t-r-e-t-c-h-e-r-s* series for preschool and primary children, and co-authored *Stories: Children's Literature in Early Education*.

Chapter 1

Creativity

This chapter explores creativity and the importance of the creative arts in early childhood education. Theories that relate to young children's creative development will be examined including constructivism, multiple intelligences, and humanism. The inclusion of creativity and the arts during the early years of a child's life is seen in relation to the development of the "whole child."

Creative Episode

Jonathan was in the art area of his kindergarten class. He was cutting tiny pieces of construction paper to add to the mosaic he was creating. Jonathan was very intent on the task although it was difficult for him to cut the tiny pieces of fabric he wanted. He had decided to create an ornate design by attaching many pieces to a cardboard base. When his teacher began singing the "clean-up" song, Jonathan was concerned. He called out to his teacher, "I can't stop now. My head is too full of ideas!" His teacher recognized his intense interest in the project and allowed Jonathan time to continue his work. After a period of time, he declared, "I'm done," as he proudly showed his intricate mosaic. Sufficient time, unique materials, and a sensitive teacher allowed Jonathan to create an amazing mosaic.

Introduction

The world is changing at an incredible pace and is filled with new technologies. This expansion of knowledge has brought about a great deal of discussion concerning preparing today's children for the future. Many educators, scientists, and philosophers have recommended that today's children should learn to be thinkers. Specific facts and memorized information that have long been major components in the educational system are no longer useful to children who will live their lives in this expanding world. Rather, children must be able to solve problems, be flexible in their thinking, and be willing to venture into new areas of study that have yet to be discovered. Today's children must be creative thinkers.

As we begin our study of creativity, it is important to build a framework for understanding the nature of this complex process. What is creativity? Who has it? Can it be taught or nurtured? Can it be identified in young children? These are recurring questions asked by those seeking to understand the creativity process, and the answers to these and other questions can provide information for those venturing into the land of creativity as they chart a new course for themselves and the children whose lives they touch.

Infant expanding his world through interactions with a responsive caregiver. (Photo by Su Lorencen)

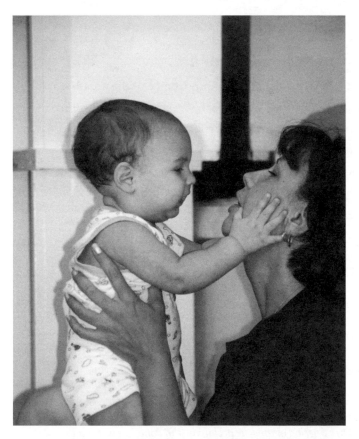

In this chapter, you will examine factors that help explain the creative process. You also will learn how specific theories and models assist in understanding the intricate operations that are at work during creative thinking. And you will investigate the unique features of the creative development of young children. Chapter two explores creative teachers and the critical influence they have on the development of young children. The chapters that follow focus on the creative arts and the important connections to these areas that should be established during the early years of children's lives. The creative process is interwoven with the arts and the integrated curriculum that is appropriate for young children.

What is Creativity?

There are many different ways to define **creativity** and the definitions are as varied as the people who developed them. Some say creativity is doing things in a unique way. Others believe that creativity requires the person to move out of a pattern of sameness. Creativity has been described as "thinking outside the box." Some believe that creativity is flexible thinking whereas others see it as a special type of problem-solving. Still others believe that creativity must generate a useful or appropriate product. And creativity has been described as the production of novel thoughts, solutions, and/or products based on previous experience and knowledge (Hendrick, 1986). These definitions do not explain fully the intricate nature of the creative process or list ways to determine when creativity has occurred. Therefore, you must examine all the components of creativity to find a clearer view. In 1992, E. Paul Torrance's artistic definition of creativity stated that:

> Creativity is digging deeper.
> Creativity is looking twice.
> Creativity is crossing out mistakes.
> Creativity is talking/listening to a cat.
> Creativity is getting in deep water.
> Creativity is getting out from behind locked doors.
> Creativity is plugging in the sun.
> Creativity is wanting to know.
> Creativity is having a ball.
> Creativity is building sand castles.
> Creativity is singing in your own way.
> Creativity is shaking hands with the future. (p. 5)
> (Courtesy of Dr. E. Paul Torrance)

Creativity and Young Children

In the massive amount of literature on creativity, young children frequently are mentioned as examples of creative thinkers because they play with ideas and exhibit characteristics often found in creative individuals. Albert Einstein (Schilpp, 1949), the renowned scientific thinker, said he was most creative as a young child when he played with ideas.

E. Paul Torrance (1964) said we are most creative at four years of age. If this is true, it might be interesting to examine the characteristics of young children

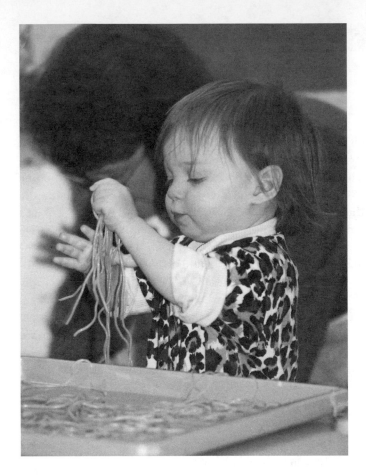

that demonstrate they are creative. What special qualities do they possess that can help us understand their unique way of experiencing the world?

Many four-year-old children are:
- independent
- curious
- uninhibited
- interested in learning new things
- active participants
- playful
- adventurous

Many young children, who have lived their first years in supportive environments, naturally exhibit the characteristics of creative individuals. However, by adulthood, many have learned to camouflage these qualities and perform in more expected ways to conform to the expectations of the society in which they live. Their early creative abilities seem to have been lost in an environment that does not value doing things differently.

If young children are naturally creative, how can the environment be designed to support this ability? How can creativity be nurtured so it is maintained throughout their lives? Perhaps a good starting point is to develop an awareness of the complex process of creative thinking. Creativity is very difficult to understand. It often is unobservable and may not have a finished product to evaluate. For these reasons, it is necessary to look at the components of creativity and identify observable features.

Dimensions of Creativity

In an attempt to understand creativity, four specific dimensions are frequently studied.

1. The creative person.
2. The creative process.
3. The environment that nurtures creativity.
4. The product of the creative act.

The study of each of these dimensions has contributed to our knowledge of creativity. It is important to remember that most of these aspects have been investigated as they relate to adults. This information, however, can be transferred into what is known about young children and their creative activities. At the beginning of each chapter, you will find specific creative episodes, including adults and young children, which demonstrate children's development and help establish a relationship with the creative process.

The Creative Person

Many believe that creativity is a gift only a few people possess. Highly creative individuals have had a tremendous impact on our world. Ben Franklin's work with electricity, Galileo's study of astronomy, Picasso's use of cubes, and Frank Lloyd Wright's architectural designs are examples of the work of creative geniuses. They are only some of the creative people who have had a tremendous impact in their field and on our way of thinking.

In the past, investigations have focused on highly creative adults who have produced great works of art, designed unique buildings, or made important scientific discoveries. Determining the common characteristics of creative people has provided insight into personal traits and attributes that frequently occur within this special group.

Although studies are interesting and provide insight into the uniqueness of creative adults, they do not truly define what creativity is, especially as it relates to young children. It is interesting to note, however, that many of the characteristics of creative adults are the same as those identified by Torrance and are recognizable in young children (Table 1–1).

Case studies of creative individuals provide a framework for seeing creativity in a more personal way. In addition, teachers can begin to identify some of these characteristics in people and perhaps recognize them in themselves. It is helpful to make the distinction between cultural creativity and personal creativity to begin to recognize that creativity is possible for both adults and children, and is not limited to a few talented people whose contributions have changed the world.

Table 1–1 Comparison of Creative Adults and Young Children

Characteristics of Creative Adults	Characteristics of Many Four-Year-Olds
Curious	Curious
Expressive	Language explosion
Spontaneous	Uninhibited
Self-confident	Independent
Playful	Playful
Adventurous	Adventurous
Open-minded	Curious
Intrinsically motivated	Active participants

Cultural Creativity

Cultural creativity is seen as an act, idea, or product that impacts the world or how it is viewed. This type of creativity is rare and happens infrequently. For example, 20th-century creative thinkers would include physicist Albert Einstein, social reformer Mahattma Gandhi, modern dancer Martha Graham, composer Igor Stravinsky, and writer Virginia Wolf (Fowler, 1990). These creative people thought in new ways and challenged others to question traditional thinking in their fields. Most created an exceptional product, and their creativity influenced their fields of expertise as well as the thinking of a broader group of people and society.

Only a few highly talented individuals, whose innovative ideas have challenged traditional views, have accomplished cultural creativity. Often, they were viewed as weird and their ideas were ridiculed by their peers. They met this adversity and continued to work in new ways. These creative people and their ideas, literally, changed the world.

Personal Creativity

Personal creativity is doing something new; something he has never done before. This type of creativity can be seen in everyday events and accomplished by ordinary people. Examples of personal creativity include making a flower arrangement, adding different ingredients to a casserole, or finding a new route to a friend's house. Personal creativity is expressed when doing new or different things. David Perkins (1981), author of *The Mind's Best Work*, explains that creativity is not some peculiar gift or mysterious process, but is best understood in terms of everyday experiences.

The concept of personal creativity is especially valuable in the world of young children. For example, the first time a young child paints the traditional symbol for a tree, he is being creative. He never had drawn two sticks for the trunk of a tree or a circle for the branches before. This is new for him. The teacher who has observed many children **painting** a tree in this way may overlook the "new" representation for this child. However, this painting of the tree is significant for this child and is a personally creative act.

This view of personal creativity also can be applied to the work of a teacher. For example a teacher may choose to cover his blackboard with woven fabric so there is more **display** area for the children's work. Although this may have been done in other classrooms, it is the first time this teacher has tried the technique. An interesting fabric is chosen and creative problem-solving is used to determine how to attach the material to the board.

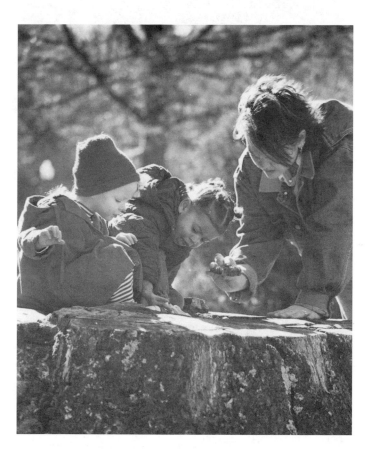

Teacher and toddlers creating rubbings of a tree stump. (Photo by Su Lorencen)

The Creative Process

The **creative process** refers to a creative act, and the methods or procedures that are used during this activity. When the process is valued, a person can be engaged in the creative act even when there is no final product (Schirrmacher, 2002). The emphasis is on the thinking and doing during the creative experience. Often, when young children are exploring materials and techniques, there is no finished product. The creative process mesmerizes them. Tasha, using white glue, is involved in the creative process. She focuses on the properties of the glue and the changes that occur when it is piled high. She explores the unique physical properties of the glue such as its smoothness and responsiveness. When she finishes her adventure with the glue, it dries to a clear, invisible form and no product exists. But observations of Tasha during the process clearly demonstrate that she has been creative in her experimentation with glue.

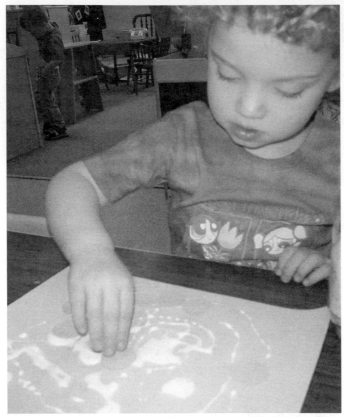

In the study of creativity, many writers and researches have described the creative process as developing in steps. Insight into these steps is another way to understand the complex workings that occur during creative thinking.

The Wallas Model.　The traditional model developed by Wallas (1926) defines four steps in the creative process (Table 1–2).

Note that these steps are similar to those used by researchers in scientific studies. A scientist identifies a problem and after some time, forms a hypothesis that is then tested and verified. The same procedures are used in the early child-

Table 1–2　Four Steps in the Creative Process

Preparation	Exploring and looking for the real problem. This can include gathering information, finding available resources, and getting acquainted with the problem or issue.
Incubation	During this step, the problem is not considered; instead there is a period of abstinence from mental work.
Illumination	This is often described as the moment of "Aha!" or "Eureka!" A new idea or combination appears that meets the requirements of the problem. This step is also referred to as the "light bulb" effect.
Verification	Trying out the solution and determining if the idea will work.

hood classroom. For example, the problem might be, "How do you display the natural materials collected during a walk?" Possibilities are discussed and explored with the children. The next day, a decision is made to place the items in plastic bags and hang them on a display board. Together, the children determined how the natural items would be displayed. Using this systematic approach, the students found a creative solution to the problem.

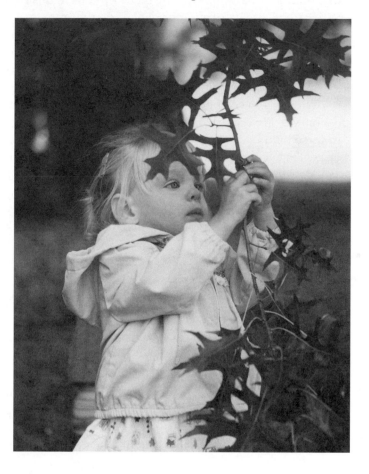

A Young child enjoys collecting natural materials. (Photo by Su Lorencen)

Creative Problem-Solving

Another way of explaining the creative process was developed by Osborn (1963) and Parnes (1967). They spent many years studying and teaching creativity in workshops, seminars, and college classes. Their **Creative Problem-Solving (CPS) model** focuses on the generation of creative ideas.

A unique feature of the CPS model is its emphasis on **divergent thinking**. For many years, education has focused on getting the right answer through **convergent thinking**. For example, when a teacher asks, "What color is this apple?" he is expecting to hear the answer "Red." The CPS model stresses the need to produce many ideas or divergent thinking. Instead of asking about the apple, the question might be, "How many different colors do you see on the apple?" Open-ended questions encourage a variety of responses and ideas. By using divergent questions and open-ended activities, the teacher allows children to think in different ways instead of trying to figure out the "correct" answer. Many possibilities exist when questions are posed in a manner that encourages diverse responses.

Brainstorming

Osborn also developed procedures for **brainstorming**. This technique is widely used today as a way of producing many options in business, education, and scientific study. Brainstorming provides an environment where all ideas are accepted and judgment is deferred during the generation process. Only later are the ideas critiqued and/or selected for implementation. This free-flowing process provides unique ideas that might not have been contributed if evaluated during brainstorming.

Brainstorming can be used in early childhood classrooms to produce many possibilities. For example, a parent brings in a large bag of paper towel rolls. How can these be used in the classroom? Children can come up with unique suggestions when encouraged to brainstorm ideas. Some suggestions for the rolls might include adding them to the art area, building with them along with the blocks, attaching them to space helmets, cutting them into smaller pieces for jewelry, and making tunnels for the guinea pig. Participation in the process gives children empowerment as well as an experience that demonstrates their ideas are valuable.

Torrance's View of the Creativity Process

E. Paul Torrance (1964, 1969), one of the most prolific writers on creativity in education, identified four components of the creative process.

1. **Originality** The idea that is truly unique. It is not like any other product; it is a one-of-a-kind idea.

2. **Fluency** The generation of many different ideas. The emphasis here is on the number of ideas produced.

3. **Flexibility** The ability to change direction or think in another way.

4. **Elaboration** Taking an idea and expanding it to make it more intriguing and complex.

Originality can be observed as a young child builds a structure from pieces of cardboard cutouts. In each of the circular openings, he glues brightly colored tissue paper. On the top are flags made out of pieces of colorful fabric. He names his interesting structure, "the house of colored lights." Although many children have built cardboard structures before, this is an original interpretation using a variety of materials.

Young children also elaborate on the ideas of others. Jessica is making a paper chain out of construction paper. Leonard, seeing this chain, proceeds to make a chain from strips of ribbon left from holiday wrapping. He has taken an idea and elaborated on it to produce a different kind of chain. A teacher also elaborates, or piggybacks, ideas when he takes the idea of another teacher and does it a different way. Angie adds real musical instruments to the classroom center. Lucretia sees the real musical instruments in the classroom and this inspires her to bring in her kalimba and some music recordings. Sometimes, this

> *"The best way to have a good idea is to have a lot of ideas."*
>
> L. Pauling, 1961[1]

elaboration is not considered creative; "I got the idea from Angie." But Lucretia added her own interpretation and included an instrument that had not been in her classroom previously.

The Environment That Nurtures Creativity

Although these views of the creative process focus on an organized approach to thinking, they can be applied to young children as they investigate problems and find solutions. The teacher can use them as he plans, selects materials, and designs the classroom environment. Theories and models also can assist in the design of an environment that will nurture young children in their creativity.

The Product of the Creative Act

One way of examining creativity is to focus on what is created, or the final product. The creative product could vary from a shaded watercolor painting to a musical composition or dramatic performance. It is possible to evaluate the creative product by determining its uniqueness or usefulness. For the product to be truly creative, it must be different, original, or use innovative methods.

Emphasizing the end product of creativity may limit, or even exclude, the work of young children. During the early years, most young children show little interest in the final product; they are focused on the process of creation. The young child is more interested in mixing colors than the final hue that appears on the paper. They want to explore how glue works instead of how the picture looks when they are finished attaching cutouts to the panel.

In the primary grades, some children become interested in the final product and want to represent their ideas realistically. Older children may want to make

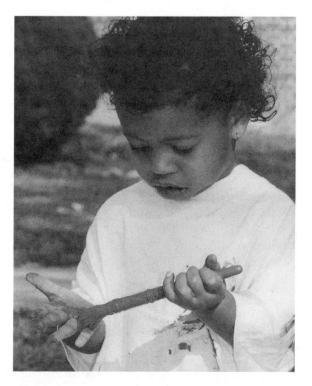

When a toddler experiments with paint, it includes painting one's hand. (Photo by Su Lorencen)

their clay models look like real horses. But the transition from process orientation to product focus should follow the developmental interest of the child, and not be imposed by adults or teachers. Early emphasis on the product can discourage the creative efforts of young children. Amabile (1989), in her book *Growing Up Creative*, cautions that "children's motivation and creativity can be destroyed if evaluation, reward, and competition are misused" (p. 69).

Theories and Models

Theories and models can provide other ways to understand creativity. A number of theorists have discussed the process of creative thinking. The next section will discuss these theories and describe their application to young children and their teachers.

Psychoanalytic Theory

One early theorist who discussed creativity was Sigmund Freud (1964). He believed that creativity was the result of a subconscious conflict between the sexual urges (libido) of the id and the influences of the social conscience (superego). He also suggested that childlike regression and free play are creative activities. There have been several interpretations of this **psychoanalytic theory**, each with its own variation. But the interpretations each share the common belief that conflict and difficulties provide motivation for creative acts. The manner in which subconscious thought influences creativity and the illumination of wonderful ideas is still debated.

Behaviorist Theories

Behaviorist theories provide little insight into an understanding of creativity. Behavioral theorists believe in the importance of reinforcement (reward) in learning responses to particular stimuli. Behaviorists also offer different interpretations of the effects of reward on behavior or the nature of the stimulus-response (S-R) relationship. For example, Skinner (1971) explained that the behavior of a creative person is the product of his genetic and environmental history. This view sees the environment as a critical element that reinforces creative activity or diminishes the possibility that it will occur.

According to the behaviorist interpretation, in a creative environment where making music is rewarded, young children will be more interested in participating in musical activities. The teacher, a musical person, uses music throughout the day and rewards children who display special musical talent. Music becomes very important in this classroom environment and musical talent is encouraged. When the parent or teacher values the creative arts, the young child will be rewarded for his effort. Of course, when the adult values conformity and strict compliance to rules, the young child may be rewarded only when this behavior is exhibited. Therefore, the child will be less likely to try creative activities because these are not rewarded. He will attempt to act in the way that produces a positive response and avoids negative consequences.

The behaviorist theory also emphasizes the importance of the adult "model." Children who observe influential adults involved in creative arts are more likely to imitate this behavior, particularly if it is encouraged. A mother who is an artist may set up an easel for her son beside her own easel. The teacher who creates an attractive display of the children's work allows his students to see that aesthetics are valued in his classroom. Both are powerful role models for the children with whom they work.

Psychologically Safe Environment

Carl Rogers (1962) and Abraham Maslow (1970) believed that creativity was obtainable for most people. Rogers described the ability to be creative as an attribute that every individual possesses but which may be buried under layers of psychological defense. Rogers and Maslow's work contributed to the concept of the **psychologically safe environment** that is so important during the early years of children's development. This is where there is freedom to think creatively and take intellectual risks. In such an environment, individuals are accepted unconditionally and allowed to follow specific interests. The psychologically safe environment is a critical feature of programs that serve young children. Early childhood classrooms must meet the child's basic needs, support ideas, and respect individual differences. It is an environment where risk can be taken and interesting materials explored without fear of criticism or ridicule. This psychological safeness is an essential ingredient of an environment designed to nurture children's cognitive and social-emotional development, as well as their creative abilities.

Humanistic Theory

In the **humanistic theory**, the creative person is viewed as a self-actualized person. He uses his talents to become a fully functioning and mentally healthy person. Self-actualization is seen as the highest level of personal development that can be reached only after basic needs are met (physiological needs, safety needs, the need for love and belonging, and self-esteem). Maslow's pyramid (Figure 1–1) illustrates the basic needs that form the foundation necessary to move to higher levels of personal fulfillment (Maslow).

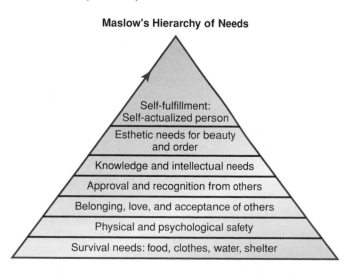

Maslow's Hierarchy of Needs

Figure 1–1 Maslow's Hierarchy of Needs

Maslow's information on needs-based motivation suggests that children who are hungry or worried about their home life will have difficulty engaging in art activities that focus on higher level esthetic needs. Understanding this means the teacher of young children must consider if these basic needs are being met. If a child arrives at school hungry, it is important to provide breakfast or a snack. Physical and psychological safety can be met by establishing an environment that respects children, accepts mistakes, provides choices, and supports all levels of accomplishment. In the arts, where doing things differently is valued, children must feel safe to try new things and to venture into unexplored territory.

Maslow defines the **self-actualized** person as becoming what one is capable of being. It is interesting to note that a goal of most early childhood program is to "help each child reach his or her potential." For many children, the nurturing of creativity and enrichment with the arts may be the best way to reach this important goal. It may be the spark that lights the interest of a child or helps find a new possibility for joyful participation.

Maslow further explains that self-actualized people often live productive lives and tend to do things in a more creative manner. He explains that art education is important, not so much to develop an artist or a product, but to develop better people. For children to become full human beings, they have to move toward actualizing their potential. Education, through the arts, works to meet these goals. Instead of being regarded as a frill, art education should be taken seriously and recognized as the way to develop educational potential (Maslow).

Carl Rogers (1962) added some important conditions that are believed necessary for creativity to occur.

1. Psychologically safe environment. This is an atmosphere where ideas are accepted and people are respected.

2. Internal locus of evaluation. This refers to the personal characteristics of self-confidence and independence. The individual makes a decision and is willing to accept responsibility for the outcome.

3. A willingness to play with ideas and possibilities. This characteristic allows the individual to demonstrate playfulness.

4. Openness to experience. This is seen as an attraction to new experiences and receptiveness to new ideas.

The humanistic theory provides insight into environments that encourage creativity in young children. Such environments must be psychologically safe to support the efforts of each individual. This theory also identifies the need for the individual to become self-confident and independent. Included in this interpretation is the need to be playful and participate in new experiences. Although these conditions are necessary for becoming self-actualized adults, they also support the development of psychologically healthy children.

Constructivist Theory

The **constructivist theory**, postulated by Jean Piaget (1960), focuses on the development of cognition. According to the constructivist theory, individuals are active participants in the construction of their own knowledge. Knowledge is constructed by the assimilation of information into existing **schema** (frameworks or outlines). As the child actively engages his environment, new schemas are built as understanding expands. A classic example of this progression in thinking is observed when a young child sees a zebra for the first time. Carla calls out, "horsie." She knows what a horse is but she has never seen a zebra. As she gains more experience with zebras, she begins to understand that they are different from horses. She forms a new category for large four-legged striped animals and calls this zebra. This process of **assimilation** (taking in information from the world) and **accommodation** (applying new information to aid ideas or schemas) continues as she is introduced to other animals.

According to the constructivist theory, development occurs through predictable stages. During the infancy stage, sensorimotor learning is of critical importance. Preschoolers in the preoperational stage are developing important symbolic representations in their play. Only later, in the formal operations stage, are children able to construct understanding by using abstract thinking.

Constructivists believe that learning is accomplished through exploring, experimenting, and manipulating objects or materials. This theory directly relates to the development of creative thinking and the necessity for active participation in the process. Using the constructivist theory as a basis for environmental

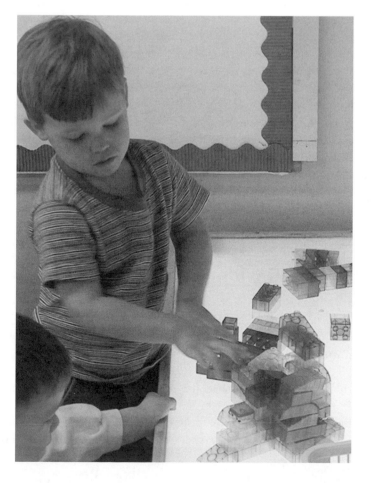

Building with plastic blocks on a light table provides a new way to view a construction. (Photo by Michael Talley)

design, the classroom should contain a variety of materials that can be explored and combined in many different ways. Active learning and social interactions are encouraged throughout the day. Individual interests of the child will be identified to provide opportunities for group work and long-term projects. The constructivist's curriculum is child-centered and based on the interests of the individuals that make up the group.

Social Constructivism

Vygotsky's **social constructivist theory** is built on the belief that learning is too complex to be studied in a vacuum. Instead, it must be studied in the social and historical context in which it occurs. He describes socially meaningful activity as the way we learn about ourselves as we interact with others. Vygotsky's **zone of proximal development** is a well-known concept. He believed that a gap exists between the child's level of actual development (what can be done independently) and his potential level of development (what can be accomplished with assistance). He further explained that this gap could be filled by the supportive collaboration of an adult or capable peer. This interpretation recognizes the importance of support, guidance, and interactions as children move toward their potential (Dixon-Krauss, 1996). Appropriate social interactions with both adults and peers can enrich and expand the creative possibilities for young children participating in the arts.

Collaboration is a tool used to assist children in working together on projects, sharing ideas, clarifying thinking, and mediating problems. In the search for information, the teacher poses questions, guides thinking, and challenges the children to think in new ways. For example, in a collaborative group, the students work together to determine how to combine pieces of fabric and make a classroom quilt. Laurie suggests gluing the pieces, Rhonda thinks tape might work, and William shares how his grandmother sews quilts together. He explains to the group how this is done and the tools that are used. They are very interested in the quilting frame that his grandmother uses and how many people work together to make beautiful hand-sewn quilts. William's knowledge about quilt-making has extended the understanding of the individuals in the group. Small cooperative groups work well in the early childhood classroom and support the development of independence.

Theory of Multiple Intelligences

In 1983, Howard Gardner published the first edition of *Frames of Mind: The Theory of Multiple Intelligences*. In this book, Gardner suggests there are at least seven different types of intelligence. More recently, he added an eighth—naturalistic—and is now working on a ninth, the existentialist intelligence (Hoerr, 2000). These different types of intelligence have added new dimensions that specifically relate to the creative arts and creative thinking. Gardner believed only two forms of intelligence were emphasized in most schools: verbal-linguistic and logical-mathematical. As a result, Gardner suggests that many of the other areas of intelligence have been undervalued and have the potential to be lost.

"What the child can do in cooperation today he can do alone tomorrow."

L. S. Vygotsky, 1962[2]

According to Gardner, the eight intelligences include the following.

1. **Verbal-Linguistic:** Related to words and language; producing language with sensitivity to the nuances, order, and rhythm of words.

2. **Logical-Mathematical:** Includes deductive or inductive reasoning; recognizing and manipulating abstract relationships.

3. **Musical:** Deals with the recognition of tonal patterns, environmental noise, and sensitivity to rhythm and beats; responsiveness to the emotional implications and elements of music.

4. **Visual-Spatial:** Relies on the sense of sight and the ability to visualize an object; creating visual-spatial representations of the world, and transferring them mentally or concretely.

5. **Bodily-Kinesthetic:** Includes physical movement and awareness and/or wisdom of the body; the body is used to solve problems, make things, and convey ideas and emotions.

6. **Interpersonal:** Deals with person-to-person relationships and communication: working effectively with others; understanding people; and recognizing their goals, motivations, and intentions.

7. **Intrapersonal:** Involves self-reflection and metacognition; understanding one's own emotions, goals, and intentions.

8. **Naturalistic:** Capacity to recognize flora and fauna, make distinctions in the natural world, and use this ability productively.

Gardner's theory of multiple intelligences identifies a variety of ways we learn and where we may excel. For example, a person with a high level of linguistic intelligence might become a poet, a dramatist, or a lawyer. Another person with exceptional kinesthetic intelligence may become a dancer or athlete. Gardner also recognized that artists might use several of these areas in combination. A dancer may use bodily-kinesthetic, musical, and spatial intelligence to perform effectively.

This theory provides support for a much larger role for the arts in the school curriculum. The different kinds of intelligence point to a variety of ways of knowing. Teachers should encourage students to use their individual strengths, which may be in music, movement, or drawing (Fowler, 1990). And teachers must provide various learning opportunities to meet the needs of their students' different learning styles. Teachers should try new ideas, approaches, and techniques so they move "out of the box" and create an environment that inspires problem-solving.

A classroom for young children working with this model will provide opportunities for the development of all areas of intelligence. Children can participate in visual-spatial, kinesthetic-movement, and music activities, as well as the more traditional areas of language, science, and math. Using this model to plan curriculum ensures that a variety of intelligences are used throughout the classroom and children's different ways of learning are supported through appropriate activities.

For example, when a project is developed by a group of children, they can choose how they will share the information they have collected. They may use a dramatic presentation, a mural, a dance performed to music, or a computer presentation. Providing options from different intelligences supports the varied ways children learn while building on their personal strengths. Gardner (Durie, 1997), in an interview, explained that if material is only taught in one way, only certain children will be reached. The more we can match children to congenial approaches to teaching and learning, the more likely these individuals will be to achieve educational success.

Brain Development

New brain-imaging technologies have enabled scientists to investigate how the brain develops and works. This fascinating area of research has stimulated new dialogue between neurologists, developmental biologists, psychologists, and educators. These neurological findings have increased interest in the amazing capabilities of young children. Articles in national publications and presentations at international conferences have focused on the significant learning that occurs during the early years of a child's life. This information has supported what early childhood educators have believed for many years: the early years are a critical time of development and experiences during this period impart lifelong learning. This knowledge about early brain development and the widespread interest in the early years can be used to support efforts to create quality programs for young children (Jensen, 1998).

When a child is born, the brain contains trillions of neurons. Connections between neurons and synapses are formed as we learn. Positive interactions with caring adults and meaningful experiences can stimulate a child's brain profoundly, causing synapses to grow and strengthening existing connections. The synapses that are used in a child's brain tend to become permanent fixtures. Brain cells that are not used or developed tend to be eliminated as the brain effectively "prunes" itself into an efficient, information-processing system (Healy, 1994).

If a child receives little stimulation during the early years, synapses will fail to develop and the brain will make fewer connections for learning. Brain research emphasizes that experiences, particularly during the first three years of life, are decisive for children to reach their full potential. Neurological plasticity, the brain's ability to adapt with experience, confirms that early childhood sets the stage for how children will continue to learn throughout life.

These neurological studies have increased our understanding of the "windows of opportunity" or **critical periods** in children's lives. Critical periods are sensitive times when the brain is primed for certain types of learning to take place. Language development, for example, begins in infancy, long before verbal language appears. Between ages three and 12, children are capable of developing an enormous vocabulary of 50,000 to 100,000 words. Some children in language-rich environments learn 50 words a day (Arcangelo, 2000). The window for beginning interest in musical sounds and composition is between ages three and 10. It has been found that few professional musicians begin their study after this important period of development. Knowing about this critical period of musical development emphasizes the need to include music in the lives of young children. Identifying windows of opportunity can assist teachers

> "If in early life, children have the opportunity to discover much about their world and to do so in a comfortable, exploring way . . . they can draw on it in later life."
>
> H. Gardner, 1993[3]

in developing an appropriate curriculum that capitalizes on these intense periods of learning.

Brain research does not suggest that children learn through drill or rote memorization. Instead, it supports the principles of developmentally appropriate practices that include meaningful experiences matching the child's level of development. The best learning for young children is active, hands-on, meaningful, integrated, and responsive. Active learning experiences, including the visual arts and music, can establish connections in the brain that will last a lifetime.

Holistic Development

Although many theories focus on one aspect of development, it is important to understand that children do not develop in unconnected parts. The different areas of development interact and allow the child to develop in a holistic way. In early childhood, there is a shared belief that young children should be provided opportunities to develop in all areas: physically, cognitively, and socially-emotionally. Creativity and the creative arts are essential components to the development of the whole child.

"Early experiences have a decisive impact on the architecture of the brain and on the nature and extent of adult capabilities."

M. McCain & F. Mustard, 1999[4]

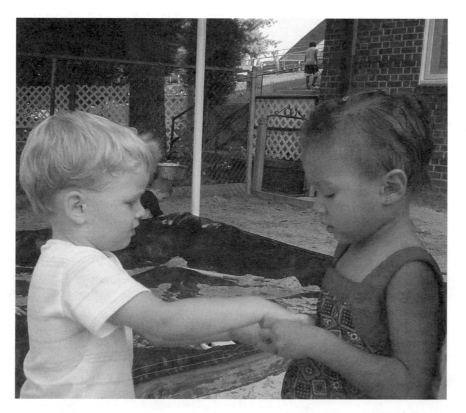

Young children interact socially, as they use both touch and words to express their ideas. (Photo by Michael Talley)

Relating Creativity to Programs for Young Children

Most definitions, theories, and models focus on the adult's ability to create. However, it is important to recognize the differences between a creative adult and a creative child. Adults have more experiences and their work styles are often rigid. Children have unique ways of thinking, exploring materials, and creatively playing with ideas. If one is trying to understand creativity as it occurs during the early years, it is important to study the development of young children. How do they grow and develop in the dimension of creativity? Are they naturally creative or does the environment nurture or delay this development?

Observing Creativity in Young Children

Creativity can be seen in many different forms during the early years. It can be observed when a toddler uses the handle of a push toy to get the teddy bear that he wants from behind the storage cabinet. It is observed when a preschooler designs a menu to add to the restaurant center. Creativity is observed when a kindergartner retells a favorite story with new elements and a surprise ending. These behaviors can be identified as creative. Although these actions are not new to the classroom, they are new for the individual child at that specific time.

For many years, the accepted view in early childhood education has been that the process is more important than the product. Teachers who observe children exploring and experimenting with materials support this conclusion. They see the creative process in action and the unique combinations that occur during each activity. Can young children who may not create a product be identified as creative? Yes! The observant and knowledgeable teacher can recognize creative acts as they occur, and support their value. The preschooler using colored yarn and white glue demonstrates creativity in an open-ended art activity as he experiments with color and shape. He is focused on the changes that occur when he glues more yarn to the art-board. Finally, the paper is a mass of glue and yarn. He demonstrated creativity while working on the art but the final product is unrecognizable. When working with young children, it is essential to understand that at different times and in particular activities, the process may be more important than trying to make a recognizable finished product.

Some children become interested in the product as they become more skilled in the use of varied materials and techniques. For instance, Mia, a first grade child, works on cutting small and intricate parts for her mask. She stands back and looks at her work. She is personally evaluating the product. Does it look the way she wants? Should she add another feature? For this child, the end product is important, but it is self-imposed and not demanded by the teacher. As in other areas of development, it is important to follow the lead of the child and assist him in the process as needed.

Barron (1988), a scholar of creativity, wrote about some variables that relate to creativity. The creative potential of young children can be seen when observing this process. Some of the attributes Barron discussed include taking risks, making connections and associations, and seeing things in new ways. If trained to see these indicators, teachers will begin to observe the creative process as it

> "As a human universal, creative behaviors abound in young children."
>
> **F. E. Williams, 1982[5]**

occurs. As a preschooler tries to find foil to add to his cardboard building, he is making new associations. When the kindergartner pours sand into his container of tempera paint, he is taking a risk. Will it work? How will it go on the paper? What will the teacher say? If the teacher understands the creative process, he will interpret this as creative experimentation and not mischievous behavior.

Young children are sensitive to internal and external stimuli, lack inhibition, and have the ability to become completely absorbed in an activity (Holden, 1987; Isenberg & Jalongo, 1997). These are characteristics that are often found in the highly creative individual. An example of sensitivity to stimuli can be seen when observing a toddler playing outside. He collects smooth stones, crunchy leaves, and prickly cones. These treasures are placed in a bag and examined again and again. His interest is maintained for an extended period of time because the collection is meaningful to him. The teacher is sensitive to the collecting toddler and allows him time to explore and select the natural items that are of interest to him.

It often is said that young children have a short attention span. Children's attention depends on their interest and absorption in the materials. If it is meaningful, they have a longer attention span. The child who truly is focused on something interesting has an amazing ability to stay with the project for a long period of time. During the early years, finding engaging and challenging things is

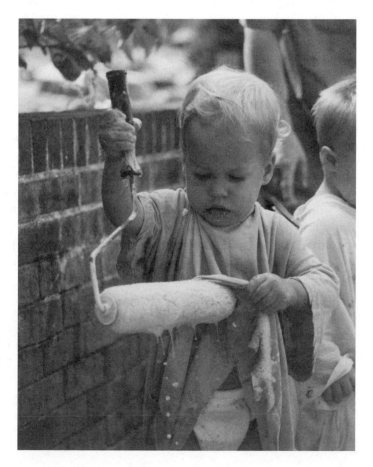

Painting with a roller requires concentration on the task. (Photo by Su Lorencen)

a substantial task for teachers, parents, and caregivers. In many cases, what is required is the ability to observe and follow the "real" interest of the child.

Imagination

In the study of creativity, one characteristic often identified as essential is an active **imagination**. Imagination is the ability to form rich and varied images or concepts of people, places, things, and situations when they are not present (Isenberg & Jalongo). The imaginations of young children are highly developed and frequently used in play and art. Imagination is at its peak during the early years. As children grow, they modify their behavior and become less willing to move out of traditional boundaries. In pretend play, the young child is able to create roles, settings, and events without concern for realism. A dog can be as big as a bear, a house can be a castle filled with jewels, and a special friend can be invisible. Young children seem to think with more creative freedom than older children. They alter reality to their own needs as they experiment with life through play (Piaget & Inhelder, 1969). This imaginative play helps children create a better understanding of their world.

Playfulness

Play often has been referred to as the "work" children do. Early childhood experts throughout the world recognize the importance of play. In 1991, the National Association for the Education of Young Children (NAEYC) issued a position paper concerning appropriate programs for children three to eight years of age. In this landmark document, they stated that one of the reasons play is so important is that it allows children to develop their imaginations and creativity (Bredekamp, 1993).

The relationship between play and creativity has been examined in hundreds of research studies. Kagan (1984) found that open-ended play provided more opportunities for creative behavior. Games with rules allow little flexibility and few opportunities for make-believe, fantasy, or symbolic play. In play, children are in a risk-free environment where there is no evaluation or fear of failure. Playing with objects is often a part of the experience, and is believed to be fundamental in the development of young children's thinking and imagination (Trostle & Yawkey, 1982).

Imagination comes alive as transformations evolve in play. Play allows children to invent many different ideas (divergent thinking) and ultimately decide which to use in a specific situation (convergent thinking).

Young Children's Creative Abilities

All children are creative during their early years of development. It is up to parents, teachers, and caregivers to support their creativity so that as they grow older, they can continue to be creative and self-actualized people.

Examples of creativity in young children include:
- inventing songs or using new words to familiar songs (music).
- painting different lines, shapes, and colors (art).

"The creative mind plays with the objects it loves."

C. Jung, 1921[6]

- experimenting with building different types of structures (blocks).
- using movement to express a feeling or thought (movement).
- taking on roles and acting out events (play).
- concentrating on a project for a long period of time.
- organizing or grouping items in their environment (math).
- using expressive language and creating new words (language).
- telling a story (drama).
- creating a dress-up outfit (art and play).

These behaviors are active, child-initiated, and displayed by most children at various times during the early years of development. Torrance (1969) believed that everyone is creative if given the opportunity.

It is impossible to identify all the characteristics of creative children and the many different combinations that exist. These observable behaviors help us recognize creativity in young children and appreciate their special abilities. However, these characteristics alone do not provide a total understanding of the complex workings that occur in the creative mind.

Individual Differences

Although creativity is part of the developmental process, children express creativity in individual ways. The process is influenced by the unique characteristics that emerge from each child. There is no profile that fits all creative children. Instead, each creative child possesses attributes that are combined in a special way. The environment in which the child lives interacts with individual abilities to produce even more variations (Tegano, Moran, & Sawyers, 1991). In this reciprocal relationship, the child influences his environment and, in turn, the environment affects the child.

A young child may be visually oriented and fascinated by shapes, patterns, and colors. If this child lives in a home where the father is a sculptor, the combination of their visually oriented traits and the opportunity to live in an artistic environment certainly will impact the child's visual arts development.

Early childhood is characterized as a highly creative period. It is perhaps the most creative phase in human development. All races and all people share this creative time (Cobb, 1977). Unfortunately, the creativity seen in preschoolers often is not maintained throughout life. Torrance (1962) reported a decline in creativity when children enter kindergarten. He also noted a significant slump between the third and fourth grade, and another between seventh and eighth grade. For many children, changes in the school environment can inhibit the growth of creative thinking instead of maintaining the momentum that was present in the early years. Torrance also observed that the two most powerful inhibitors to creativity during the early years seemed to be a premature attempt to eliminate fantasy and/or play, and the practice that allows children to learn only what is expected.

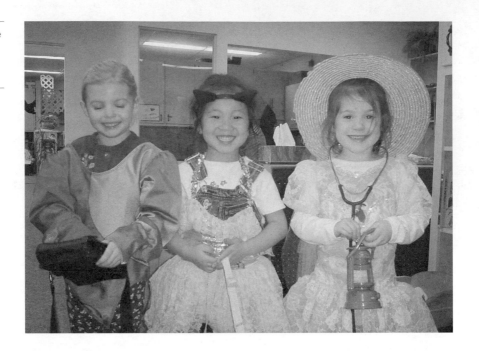

Environmental Conditions for Creativity

The environment consists of people, places, objects, and experiences. All of these elements can impact the development of young children. Children need real experiences as well as sources of inspiration to develop creatively. For example, the young child who has been to a home repair center with his parents can collect new ideas to use in the woodworking center. Or the child who has helped his dad prepare dinner will have more ideas for creating snacks. Children can use these real experiences to enrich their participation in the classroom.

An analogy that clarifies the relationship between the environment and creativity is a kaleidoscope (Parnes, 1967; Schirrmacher, 2002). The more colorful pieces that are included in the drum of a kaleidoscope, the greater the variety of possible shapes, colors, and patterns. In creativity, the more experiences a child has with people, places, or materials, the more possibilities will exist for use in creative activities. Young children's worlds should be filled with interesting experiences that build on their level of development. These should include many opportunities to experiment and combine a variety of materials and objects in different ways, and should allow them to make choices and work on projects across time.

The Importance of the Creative Arts

The creative arts have been an important part of many early childhood programs for a long time. In the early 1900s, Patty Hill Smith blended Froebel's methods and John Dewey's philosophy to create a curriculum that provided the foundation for kindergarten practice in the United States. One of her major contributions was the founding of the laboratory nursery school at Columbia University Teachers College, which became the model for training early childhood educators. Her second innovation was organizing the National Association for Nursery Education, which lead to the development of today's early childhood professional organizations. From that time until the present, the arts have been viewed as important to the development of children. Many globally recognized experts strongly support the inclusion of play and the creative arts in programs for young children.

Kieran Egan (1997) wrote about "The Arts as the Basis of Education." He challenges educators to "stimulate thinking" through the use of the creative arts. Lella Gandini, representative of the highly acclaimed Reggio Emilia schools in Italy, provides support for the integration of the arts into early childhood programs. The Reggio Emilia program demonstrates the importance of the arts and their effective integration throughout the early years. Italian children's in-depth projects, often lasting for more than a month, have served as an inspiration for early childhood programs around the world. These amazing projects demonstrate the unique capabilities of young children.

In 1990, the Association for Childhood Education International published a position paper written by Mary Renck Jalongo. This paper, endorsed by an international group of educators, focused on the rights of children to participate in the expressive arts that nurture the child's imagination as well as the intellect. A copy of this paper is included in Appendix A.

Across the nation, teachers are beginning to promote creative thinking. According to Amabile (1989), teachers who encourage creative thinking in children are helping them become lifelong problem-solvers. This will help society progress as they come up with new and better ways to solve problems.

A report by the J. Paul Getty Trust (Wolfensohn & Williams, 1993) concluded that the arts contribute to an overall culture of excellence in schools. They provide an effective way of connecting children to each other and understanding the creative people who came before them. The arts help to establish relationships across traditional disciplines and connect ideas.

Professionals recognize the importance of providing opportunities for young children to develop in all domains: socioemotional, psychomotor, and cognitive development. The creative arts, music, drama, movement, and the visual arts are essential in nurturing development in early childhood education (Fox & Diffily, 2000).

Several groups have developed standards for arts education. The Kennedy Center has created national standards for the arts, specifically for K–4. These competencies are described as "What every young American should know and be able to do in the arts." The K–4 standards for dance/movement, music, dramatic arts, and visual arts are included in Appendix B

At a time when there is a push for higher academic standards and more testing, it is important to recognize the importance of the arts. What is required for workers at all levels is that they be creative thinkers who can work well independently and with others. Schools can no longer train people for specific tasks. Instead, education must provide training for solving problems, skills, and strategies. No person can know all that is important. We must encourage the development of active learners who know how to work collaboratively, have the courage of their convictions, and are willing to try new things. The arts can help develop these abilities (Perrin, 1994).

"Teachers in Reggio Emilia believe that all children have the right to quality programs that promote aesthetic and creative development."

R. New, 1995[7]

Personal Development

The arts provide another way of learning about the world. They provide the opportunity to explore and examine art materials, to recognize the capabilities of the body in motion, and to enjoy the sounds of music. The arts allow us to discover new ways to feel good about ourselves in a rich and varied environment. The open-ended nature of the arts allows us to work at a level that is personally satisfying, and to find success and enjoyment in an important area of development.

What happens when a leaf is placed on a sticky board created with adhesive shelf paper? (Photo by Su Lorencen)

Cultural Diversity through the Arts

Play and the arts provide a way to communicate across cultures and regions. **Multicultural education** often includes race, values, parenting styles, food, and clothing. Music, drawing, dance, and drama provide an avenue for appreciating and understanding others. These various art forms provide a vehicle for young children to communicate in a nonverbal way. Creative experiences from various cultures provide a supportive environment for children less familiar with the classroom community. The arts can help children from different ethnic groups feel accepted by their peers as they play, dance, make music, or use puppets (Tubba, 1992). The arts help us understand how we are different as well as how we are the same.

Goldberg (2001) developed principles that focus on making connections between multicultural education and the arts. They relate to both the content and process of creativity, and can guide the many ways the arts influence learning for all children:

The following points illustrate some of the connections between multicultural education and the arts.

1. The arts expand the expressive opportunities and range of learning approaches to children.

2. The arts provide freedom of expression for second-language learners.

3. The arts are an avenue for building self-esteem.

4. The arts encourage collaboration and group harmony.

5. The arts empower students and teachers.

6. The arts develop a teacher's awareness of the different abilities of children.

7. The arts provide authentic cultural voices that support learning.

In addition, the arts provide opportunities for individual development and build a sense of community where all are respected. Because the arts are expressive, they bring new understanding to people and events being studied. They provide documentation for struggles, celebrations, and living together in our diverse and global world.

Summary

In a rapidly changing world, we must develop programs for young children that include the competencies they will need now and in the future. The experiences provided should nurture the child and include all domains important for total development. Each domain offers special features that contribute to the enrichment of the environment and the experiences of young children. The creative arts provide an avenue for learning and experiencing that is uniquely different. Their inclusion, during the early years of children's lives, establishes a rich foundation that adapts to change, provides joy, and inspires involvement. An appropriate, well-designed program will encourage each child to reach his potential in an environment that is interesting, challenging, and supportive of individual creativity.

Key Terms

creativity
cultural creativity
personal creativity
painting
display
creative process
preparation
incubation
illumination
verification
Creative Problem-Solving model
divergent thinking
convergent thinking
brainstorming
originality
fluency
flexibility
elaboration
psychoanalytic theory
behaviorist theories
psychologically safe environment

humanistic theory
self-actualized
constructivist theory
schemas
assimilation
accommodation
social constructivist theory
zone of proximal development
collaboration
verbal-linguistic intelligence
logical-mathematical intelligence
musical intelligence
visual-spatial intelligence
bodily-kinesthetic intelligence
interpersonal intelligence
intrapersonal intelligence
naturalistic intelligence
critical periods
holistic
imagination
multicultural education

Reflection

1. What is cultural creativity?

2. What is personal creativity?

3. Compare process and product as they relate to creativity.

4. Identify the steps that often are included in creative problem-solving.

5. What are the components of creativity as describe by E. Paul Torrance?

6. How do theories contribute to your understanding of the nature and importance of creativity?

7. Explain how the theory of multiple intelligences emphasizes the different ways children and adults learn.

8. Are young children creative? Describe how you support your belief.

9. What has caused the renewed interest in young children and their participation in the creative arts?

Thinking about the Creative Episode

1. What observation of Jonathan demonstrated his creativity?

2. Can you determine how this classroom environment nurtures Jonathan's development?

3. How did Jonathan's teacher respond to his individual needs?

Possibilities for Adult Learners

Activity: Theory to Practice

Goal: To determine the usefulness of theories as they relate to understanding creativity in young children.

Materials: Paper and pencil.

Procedure:

1. After reflecting on the many different theories discussed in this chapter, determine the one that provides the most insight for you.

2. Describe ways this theory could influence your teaching in an early childhood classroom.

3. Write a scenario that demonstrates this application of a theory.

Activity: Creative Child

Goal: To observe young children and recognize the creative behaviors they exhibit.

Materials: Paper and pencil.

Procedure:

1. Observe young children in a natural setting such as at home, in child care, or on a playground.

2. Record the behaviors that demonstrate creative abilities or problem-solving skills.

3. Share these observations in class.

Activity: *The Ducks That Could Not Swim* Story

Goal: To recognize that learned behavior could restrict thinking.

Materials: *The Ducks That Could Not Swim* (Appendix C).

Procedure:

1. Read or tell *The Ducks That Could Not Swim* to the class.

2. Pose questions such as:
   - Why did the ducks not swim in the pond?
   - How did they come to believe they could not swim?
   - Why were the ducks unable to change their behavior and swim?
   - Why is it difficult to think in new ways?

Open-ended Activities for Young Children

Pre-K through K

Activity: Box Possibilities

Goal: To develop flexible thinking using literature as a stimulus for the process.

Materials: The book *Christina Katerina and the Box* and three cardboard boxes.

Procedure:

1. During group time, discuss the cardboard boxes that you have brought. Include questions such as "What might have come in the box?" "How did the box get to your house?"

2. Read the book *Christina Katerina and the Box* aloud.

3. Reflect on how Christina used boxes in different ways.

4. How would you use a box? Brainstorm a list of ideas with the children.

5. Pose the question, "What could you create if you used two boxes together?"

6. Ask the children to sketch their ideas on paper.

7. Place boxes and various containers in the art center for the children to construct their ideas in three-dimensional form.

Activity:	Squiggly Lines
Goal:	To elaborate on a form created by another child while using art materials.
Materials:	Art paper, magic markers, crayons, chalk, watercolors, and scrap colored paper.

Procedure:

1. Give each child a piece of art paper.

2. Ask each child to draw a squiggly line on the paper with a dark marker.

3. Let the children exchange sheets of paper.

4. Suggest that each child incorporate the squiggly line on the paper into a drawing, or to create an object, place, or collection.

5. Provide time for the thinking and creating processes to occur.

6. Have the children share their creations with others.

7. A display can be designed for "Our Creations from Squiggles."

Notes

[1]Applewhite, A., Evans, W. R., III, & Frothingham, A. (Eds.). (1992). *And I quote.* New York: St. Martin's Press.

[2]Vygotsky, L. S. (1962). *Thought and language.* Cambridge, MA: M.I.T. Press.

[3]Gardner, H. (1993). *Creating minds: An anatomy of creativity seen through the lives of Freud, Einstein, Picasso, Stravinsky, Eliot, Graham, and Gandhi.* New York: Basic Books.

[4]McCain, M., & Mustard, F. (1999). *The early years report.* Ontario, Canada: Reference Group Report to the Minister Responsible for Children, 28.

[5]Williams, F. E. (1982). *Developing children's creativity at home and school. G/C/T (Gifted, Creative, and Talented), 24*(1), 2–6.

[6]Fitzhenry, R. I. (Ed.). (1993). *The Harper book of quotations* (3rd ed.). New York: Harper Collins Books.

[7]New, R. (1995). *Contributions from Reggio to issues of advocacy and social policy in the United States.* Presentation in Connection with The Hundred Languages Exhibit. Chicago, IL.

References

Amabile, T. M. (1989). *Growing up creative.* New York: Crown Publishers.

Arcangelo, D. (2000, November). How does the brain develop? A conversation with Steven Peterson. *Educational Leadership, 58*(3), 68–71.

Barron, F. (1988). Putting creativity to work. In R. J. Sternberg (Ed.), *The nature of creativity* (pp. 76–98). New York: Cambridge University Press.

Bredekamp, S. (1993). *Developmental appropriate practice in early childhood programs serving children from birth through eight.* Washington, DC: National Association for the Education of Young Children.

Cobb, E. (1977). *The ecology of imagination in childhood.* New York: Columbia University Press.

Dixon-Krauss, L. (1996). *Vygotsky in the classroom: Mediated literacy instruction and assessment.* White Plains, NY: Longman Publishers.

Durie, R. (Spring 1997). An interview with Howard Gardner. *Mindshift Connection.* Tuscon, AZ: Zephyr Press.

Egan, K. (1997). The arts as the basics of education. *Childhood Education, 73*(6), 341–345.

Fowler, C. (1990). Recognizing the role of artistic intelligences. *Music Educator's Journal, 77*(1), 24–27.

Fox, J. E., & Diffily, D. (2000). Integrating the visual arts—building young children's knowledge, skills, and confidence. *Dimensions of Early Childhood, 29*(1), 3–10.

Freud, S. (1964). *An outline of psychoanalysis: Standard edition of the works of Sigmund Freud.* London: Hogarth Press.

Gardner, H. (1983). *Frames of mind: The theory of multiple intelligences.* New York: Basic Books.

Goldberg, M. (2001). *Arts and learning: An integrated approach to teaching and learning in multicultural and multilingual settings* (2nd ed.). New York: Addison Wesley Longman.

Healy, J. M. (1994). *Your child's growing mind: A guide to learning and brain development from birth to adolescence.* New York: Doubleday.

Hendrick, J. (1986). *Total learning: Curriculum for the young child.* Columbus, OH: Merrill.

Hoerr, T. R. (2000). The naturalist intelligence. In A practical guide designed by the faculty of the New City School (Eds.), *Succeeding with multiple intelligences: Teaching through the personal intelligences.* Tucson, AZ: Zephyr Press.

Holden, C. (1987). Creativity and the troubled mind. *Psychology Today, 21*(4), 9–10.

Isenberg, J., & Jalongo, M. R. (1997). *Creative expression and play in early childhood.* Upper Saddle River, NJ: Merrill.

Jalongo, M. R. (1990). The child's right to the expressive arts: Nurturing the imagination as well as the intellect. *Childhood Education, 66,* 195–201.

Jensen, E. (1998). *Teaching with the brain in mind.* Alexandria, VA: Association for Supervision and Curriculum Development.

Kagan, J. (1984). *The nature of the child.* New York: Basic Books.

Maslow, A. (1970). *Motivation and personality.* New York: Harper & Row.

Osborn, A. F. (1963). *Applied imagination.* New York: Scribner.

Parnes, S. J. (1967). *Creative behavior guidebook.* New York: Charles Scribner's Sons.

Perkins, D. (1981). *The mind's best work.* Cambridge, MA: Harvard University Press.

Perrin, S. (1994). Education in the arts is an education for life. *Kappan, 75*(6), 452–453.

Piaget, J. (1960). *The child's conception of the world.* Totona, NJ: Littlefield, Adams.

Piaget, J., & Inhelder, B. (1969). *The psychology of the child.* New York: Basic Books.

Rogers, C. R. (1962). Toward a theory of creativity. In S. J. Parnes & H. F. Harding (Eds.), *A source book for creative thinking* (pp. 63–72). New York: Scribner.

Schilpp, P. (1949). *Albert Einstein: Philosopher scientist.* Evanston, IL: Library of Living Philosophers.

Schirrmacher, R. (2002). *Art and creative development in young children* (4th ed.). Clifton Park, NY: Delmar Learning.

Skinner, B. F. (1971). *Beyond freedom and dignity.* New York: Knopf.

Tegano, D. W., Moran, J. D., & Sawyers, J. K. (1991). *Creativity in early childhood classrooms.* Washington, DC: National Education Association.

Torrance, E. P. (1962). *Guiding creative talent.* Englewood Cliffs, NJ: Prentice-Hall.

Torrance, E. P. (1964). *Creativity: Progress and potential.* New York: McGraw Hill.

Torrance, E. P. (1969). *Creativity.* Belmont, CA: Fearon.

Torrance, E. P. (1969). *Dimensions in early learning: Creativity.* Sioux Falls, SD: Adaptation Press.

Torrance, E. P. (1992). Creativity. Cited in R. Hill, *Finding creativity for children.* Paper prepared for Leadership Accessing Symposium, Laffayette, IN.

Trostle, S. L., & Yawkey, T. D. (1982). Creative thinking and the education of young children: The fourth basic skill. *International Journal of Early Childhood, 14*(2), 67–71.

Tubba, J. (1992). *Cultural diversity and creativity in the classroom.* Flagstaff, AZ: World Organization for Early Childhood Education.

Wallas, G. (1926). *The art of thought.* New York: Harcourt, Brace & World.

Wolfensohn, J. D., & Williams, H. M. (1993). *The power of the arts to transform education.* Los Angeles: J. Paul Getty Trust.

Additional Reading

Berk, L., & Winsler, A. (1995). *Scaffolding children's learning: Vygotsky and early childhood education.* Washington, DC: National Association for the Education of Young Children.

Blythe, T., & Gardner, H. (1990). A school for all intelligences. *Educational Leadership, 47*(7), 33–37.

Campbell, L., Campbell, B., & Dickinson, D. C. (1996). *Teaching and learning through multiple intelligences.* Needham Heights, MA: Simon & Schuster Company.

Chenfeld, M. B. (1995). *Creative experiences for young children* (2nd ed.). Fort Worth, TX: Harcourt Brace Jovanovich.

Cohen, M. D., & Hoot, J. L. (1997). Educating through the arts: An introduction. *Childhood Education, 73*(6), 338–341.

Davis, G. A. (1992). *Creativity is forever.* Dubuque, IA: Kendall/Hunt Publishing Company.

Edwards, C. P., & Springate, K. (1995). The lion comes out of the stone: Helping young children achieve their creative potential. *Dimensions of Early Childhood, 23*(4), 24–29.

Edwards, L. C., & Nabors, M. L. (1993). The creative arts process: What it is and what it is not. *Young Children, 48*, 77–81.

Eisner, E. (1992). The misunderstood role of the arts in human development. *Phi Delta Kappan, 73*(8), 591–593.

Fowler, C. (1990). Recognizing the role of artistic intelligences. *Music Educator's Journal, 77*(1), 24–27.

Haiman, P. E. (1991). Developing a sense of wonder in young children. *Young Children, 46*(6), 52–53.

Hoffman, S., & Lamme, L. L. (1989). *The expressive arts: Learning from the inside out.* Wheaton, MD: Association for Childhood Education International.

Hughes, F. P. (1998). *Children, play, and development* (3rd ed.). Boston: Allyn & Bacon Inc.

Isaksen, S. G. (1992). *Nurturing creative talents: Lessons from industry about needed work-life skills.* Buffalo, NY: The Creative Solving Group.

Rankin, B. (1992). Inviting children's creativity: A story of Reggio Emilia, Italy. *Child Care Information Exchange, 85*, 30–35.

Torrance, E. P. (1987). Teaching for creativity. In S. G. Isaksen (Ed.), *Frontiers of creativity arts: Beyond the basics* (pp. 189–215). Buffalo, NY: Bearly Limited.

Children's Literature Connection

Gauch, P. L. (1971). *Christina Katerina and the box.* New York: Coward, McCann & Geoghegan, Inc.
Christina finds many uses for the large box that housed the new refrigerator. (Pre-K–2)

Hoban, T. (1988). *Look! Look! Look!* New York: Scholastic.
Photographs of familiar objects are viewed through a cutout hole, then in their entirety. Children can use problem-solving skills as they decide what the mystery object is. (Pre-K–1)

Pfanner, L. (1989). *Louise builds a house.* New York: Orchard.
Louise builds a marvelous fantasy house full of things she loves, then gives it to her sister. (Pre-K–1)

Pfanner, L. (1990). *Louise builds a boat.* New York: Orchard.
Louise imagines building her own boat with a wooden deck for games, a crow's nest for watching dolphins, and a figurehead to paint. (Pre-K–1)

Pinkwater, D. M. (1977). *The big orange splot.* New York: Scholastic, Inc.
When a splot of orange paint accidentally lands on his home, Mr. Plumbean is inspired to repaint his house and his neighbors can't believe their eyes. (K–3)

Shaw, C. G. (1947). *It looked like spilt milk.* New York: Scholastic.
A mystery book for young children presents a continuously changing white shape silhouetted against a blue background that challenges readers to guess what it is. (Pre-K–1)

Helpful Web Sites

The addresses and corresponding agencies below are taken from the Web sites. Due to the dynamic nature of the Internet, please remember that Web sites are subject to change at any time.

http://www.ericeece.org   Educational Resources Information Center (ERIC) Clearinghouse on Elementary and Early Childhood Education—The Educational Resources Information Center (ERIC) is a national information system designed to provide users with ready access to an extensive body of education-related literature.

http://www.acei.org/   The Association for Childhood Education International (ACEI)—Promotes and supports the optimal education and development of children in the global community, from birth through early adolescence, and influences the professional growth of educators and the efforts of others who are committed to the needs of children in a changing society.

http://www.artsedge.kennedy-center.org/   ARTSEDGE—Supports the place of arts education at the center of the curriculum through the creative and appropriate uses of technology.

http://www.kennedy-center.org/education/kcaaen   The Kennedy Center Alliance for Arts Education Network (KCAAEN)—Includes 46 state Alliance organizations operating in partnership with the Kennedy Center.

http://www.naeyc.org/   The National Association for the Education of Young Children (NAEYC)—Exists for the purpose of leading and consolidating the efforts of individuals and groups working to achieve healthy development and constructive education for all young children.

For additional resources involving creativity and the arts with young children, visit our Web site at **http://www.earlychilded.delmar.com**

Chapter 2

The Creative Teacher with Creative Children

This chapter examines the relationship between the creative teacher and the classroom that nurtures creativity in young children. Characteristics of creative teachers will be investigated along with the impact of these factors on environmental design. Included are examples of teachers who have taken "creative risk" and tried doing things in different ways. The results of their adventures and the effects on young children's thinking will be explored.

Creative Episode

Maria arrives at her kindergarten classroom early, long before the children. She is excited about the day and the plans she has made. She checks out the new greenhouse center that she set up on Friday. Potting soil is added to the area as well as some hand tools. Maria has been working on the center for some time. She asked the children's families to collect seeds, plant supplies, tools, and garden catalogs for the past month.

As the students begin to arrive, Maria focuses on individual children by inquiring about the plants that might be budding at their homes or in the city. She listens intently as the children share their personal stories. She relates that the dogwood trees at her home are beginning to open and that they are a beautiful shade of hot pink. She has brought some small limbs from the dogwood trees and they are displayed in a clay pot in the art area.

During circle time, Maria reads Planting a Rainbow *by Lois Ehlert (1988). They discuss the illustrations and the interesting plantings depicted in the book. The children are intrigued by the flowers that come from bulbs, something that Maria had not included in her original plans. She writes the names of the children who are interested in the bulbs on a sticky note. At the end of the day, Maria reflects on the activities and the children's participation. What things went well? What could be changed? Marie thinks about the children's interest in bulbs. How could she build on that curiosity? Perhaps she could bring in bulbs to add to the greenhouse center. The children could make drawings to predict what flowers would grow from each bulb. Maybe they could grow some bulbs in soil and others in water. What could they discover from this experiment? Tomorrow she will ask the children what they would like to know about bulbs and their flowers.*

Maria is a creative teacher with many ideas for her classroom but she also values the ideas of children. There is often a blending of her plans and the children's interests as the curriculum is constructed. Her flexible thinking allows her to let the activity develop as the day progresses and the study expands. Maria's excitement about learning with the children is contagious and her creativity inspires the children to think in new ways.

The world today represents the products of many creative people interacting with a changing environment. These changes are complex and challenge us in many different ways. Torrance (1992) stated that never before has there been such a need to create a climate that encourages the development of creative and inventive talent. Currently, many companies have responded to this growing need by offering **creativity training** to their employees. They believe that creative thinking is essential to being globally competitive and able to develop new technology.

Society needs people with creative problem-solving abilities and strategies to address the ever-increasing issues of society, education, and technology. Creative thinking can help adults achieve satisfying lives (Kerka, 1999). Our schools must lay the foundation to equip our children with the capability to deal with complex problems and solve them in creative ways. During the early years, children need opportunities to develop ingenuity and the capacity to creatively problem-solve. This can only occur if we have creative teachers working with young children during this critical period of development (Abdallah, 1996).

Early Childhood Teachers

Early childhood teachers are the most important element in making the classroom a wonderful learning place. The effective teacher learns about her children, shapes the curriculum, sets up the environment, and encourages the learning that she values. Most early childhood teachers are dedicated to nurturing the development of the **whole child**, which includes creativity and the creative arts. Central to the development of creativity is a teacher who realizes that creativity is not narrowly defined as an art or music program, but is much broader and can be nurtured in every area of learning. Teachers who understand the importance of creativity and the arts design their classroom so these areas are an essential part of the environment, and are integrated across the curriculum.

Creativity can occur as children use paper-towel rolls to build a castle or as they choose musical instruments to accompany a story they are telling. Creative thinking occurs when children write a story, determine a way to measure the growth of plants in the greenhouse, or find a new way to use an art medium.

The teacher poses questions to curious children as they examine natural materials. (Photo by Su Lorencen)

Interactions within the creative environment are a powerful way to nurture creativity in children (Mellou, 1996). Teachers that understand the benefits of promoting creativity, as well as the blocks that stifle creative development, can design a supportive environment.

Teachers are being asked to use more creative approaches to facilitate learning with this new generation of children. Many old methods of rote memory or direct instruction are no longer effective tools. There is a new emphasis on the importance of child-directed learning and the design of classroom environments. When creativity is studied and understood, the guiding principles can give teachers valuable tools that can be used to make their classrooms exciting learning places (Simplicio, 2000).

Teaching methods have changed and so has the relationship between teacher and pupil. Generally, approaches have moved from a predominantly teacher-directed or teacher-controlled practice to a teacher and pupil interactional system in which discovery learning is an integral part of the process. In the past, many teachers controlled the delivery, pacing, and content presented. There was little variation for individual needs or interest, and two concerns have led to significant changes in these practices.

1. Great numbers of children were not learning how to think; they were unable to generalize from the specifics they were taught.

2. The burst of information has expanded the need to know into many different directions; no one is sure what the basics are.

It is obvious that new methods are needed. The focus has now shifted to helping children use creative thinking skills to help them understand how to learn in a rapidly changing world (Torrance & Safter, 1986). Teachers cannot make children be creative. However, the teacher can provide a classroom that includes the ingredients that nurture children's unique abilities.

The Creative Teacher: Can Teachers Be Creative?

Creative teaching starts with the power of the teacher to be creative. Jeanrenaud and Bishop (1980) concluded that in order to promote creativity in others, we must be creative ourselves. Most early childhood teachers are creative, although they may not recognize this ability in themselves. Over the years, some teachers may have fallen into meeting expectations of conformity and compliance. As a result, they do not see themselves as creative people. But many teachers are very creative. For example, on a typical day, an early childhood teacher will choose appropriate books to read during group time, plan an interesting follow-up activity, add new items to spark center play, and decide what work will be included in a child's portfolio. All of these activities require creative thinking,

> "Children's creativity will be enhanced if teachers believe that children should be active learners with a sense of ownership and pride in their classroom."
>
> **T. M. Amabile, 1989[1]**

> "The creative individual can not only have a new idea but he can appreciate such an idea."
>
> **J. Haefele, 1962[2]**

The creative teacher enjoys playing with children.
(Photo by Su Lorencen)

38   Chapter 2

flexibility, and elaboration. In the field of early childhood, teachers have many opportunities to nourish their own creativity and use the arts to expand their possibilities. Early childhood teachers who may feel they are not creative, can recapture their "creative spirit" as they work with young children. They can observe the children's creative activities, notice how they experience the world, and celebrate their vast capabilities for investigating.

Learn to Be a Child Again

To become more creative awakens the child within you. You can discover how to let your playful spirit grow and blossom again. Young children represent and typify total "aliveness" and a joy of living. Think about young children when you are around them. Are they cheerful, alert, eager, and open? Are they energetic, sensitive, friendly, and inquisitive? Are they also playful, expressive, spontaneous, and loveable? These childlike qualities are magical and are essential elements for a creative life.

The Road to Creativity Guided by Young Children

How do these qualities match your attitudes about yourself and life?

Living in the moment. This is an incredible quality inherent in young children. They center on what they are doing and focus on the immediate situation. They have the ability to make the most of what they have at the current time. Permit yourself to experience the excitement of the moment and enjoy the everyday things you do.

Acceptance of the world. Children are incredibly accepting and have the ability to take things as they come. As adults, we face many challenges and often wish things were different. Sometimes things can be changed or improved, but other times it is important to accept the way they are and do the best you can in the situation.

Sensitivity to the world around you. Young children are excited and interested in the smallest items in their world: the leaf on the ground or the stone on the sidewalk. There are many wonderful things in your world. Are you enjoying them? Do you notice the colors in the sunset or the dew on the pampas grass? Take a moment to watch a young child examine and experience the dandelion on the playground.

Happiness, laughter, and smiles. Children are usually happy people. And many adults have positive attitudes, too. Children are sometimes silly, make jokes, and laugh. Some adults take themselves too seriously and have forgotten to see the humor around them. Many believe that one of the most important qualities of a healthy life is a sense of humor.

Playful attitude. Young children play with ideas and experiment with materials. Adults need to nurture their playfulness. Take time to experiment or play with possibilities. Fool around with clay, walk in the woods, dress up in fun clothes, or play a board game. Take a fun break and the creative ideas will flow.

Think you are creative. Roger VonOech, author of *A Whack on the Side of the Head*, is a well-known business consultant on creative thinking. In his work, VonOech (1983) discovered one trait that distinguished creative employees from others: creative people thought they were creative.

Prize individuality. Notice creative ideas and unique individuals. What is special about these actions and people? How can you appreciate these differences and learn from the experiences and interactions? What are your unique talents? And are you nurturing those interests?

Take a risk. Young children are afraid of very little. Most of them jump into new experiences with little concern about possible failure. Try something different and do something you have never done before. Taking these risks will stimulate your creative thinking, expand your interest, and allow you to venture into new areas.

Children's Books That Bring Out the Kid Inside

Reading children's books also can help us become more sensitive to their way of experiencing the world. The following selections can help in this process.

Anholt, C., & Anholt, L. (1991). *What I like.* G. P. Putnam's Sons.
Rhymed text and illustrations describe a child's likes and dislikes, and demonstrate each child's individuality.

Anholt, C., & Anholt, L. (1992). *Kids.* Cambridge, MA: Candlewick Press.
Illustrations and rhyming text present the traits, activities, and feelings of many different children.

Baker, J. (1991). *Window.* New York: Hudson.
A mother and baby look through a window at the beautiful wilderness and sky beyond their home. But as the baby grows into a boy, and then a man, the scene begins to change.

Borton, L. (1997). *Junk pile.* New York: Philomel Books.
Helping out in her father's auto junkyard has taught Jamie to fix the school bus and construct wonderful works of art with junk, but the other children's teasing still hurts until she learns how to fix a friendship as well.

Johnson, C. (1977). *Harold and the purple crayon.* New York: HarperCollins.
Come join Harold on an adventure with his purple crayon and see the many possibilities that exist.

Jonas, A. (1983). *Round trip.* New York: Scholastic.
Start at the beginning and read to the end. Then turn the book over and begin again!

Lester, A. (1990). *Imagine.* Boston: Houghton Mifflin Company.
This book invites the reader to imagine what it would be like to live in various locations such as a house, a jungle, and an icecap, and meet the animals that live there.

Small, D. (1985). *Imogene's antlers.* New York: Crown Publishers, Inc.
One Thursday, Imogene wakes up with a pair of antlers growing out of her head that cause a sensation wherever she goes.

Studies have found that children are more creative when working with creative teachers. Torrance (1965) found that kindergarten and primary school children made the most significant gains in creativity when they worked with creatively motivated teachers. The creative teacher who recognizes the importance of creative thinking can have a positive impact on the development of creativity in the classroom.

Tissue paper and glue provide a new way to combine materials to form a ball. (Photo by Michael Talley)

Characteristics of a Creative Teacher

The creative teacher understands children's development, and uses this knowledge to make decisions about activities and materials that will be included in the classroom. She observes children and knows when to ask divergent questions or add unique materials to a work area. The creative teacher is playful and experiments with new ideas, materials, and approaches. Interactions with children and their developing projects are unpredictable, and teachers are often in the mist of ambiguity. Creative teachers are comfortable with temporary confusion and enjoy anticipating how the project will evolve (Tegano, Groves, & Catron, 1999). She encourages divergent and messy activities because she understands their importance. She searches for **novel** toys and activities that elicit interest and questioning. She provides choices for herself and the children. She is supportive of the children's efforts and their unusual ideas. She asks questions that provide provocation and encourage thinking. The creative teacher finds ways to nurture this important ability, even in an environment that seems to stress teaching to a standardized test. She recognizes that competencies can be gained through creative activities and can produce children capable of solving difficult problems.

Many teachers in the **Reggio Emilia** school, reported to be the best early childhood program in the world, listen to, observe, and understand children. They serve as resources, and provide occasions of discovery and learning for the children in the Italian schools. Gandini (1992) explains that Reggio teachers are partners in the children's learning process. The Italian teachers enjoy discovering together with the children. The role of the teacher is both observer and learner who provides a wonderful model for the children to emulate.

The creative teacher is intrinsically motivated and interested in growing as a teacher. She is committed to attending conferences or seminars, reading a new

"The teacher, with the knowledge and attitudes about guiding the creative process, is the most important part of the environment."

R. S. Zener, 1995[3]

book on teaching, or taking additional classes. She knows professional development leads to making changes within the classroom. Creative teachers are constantly looking for and trying out new approaches and ideas that will help improve their classrooms and the children's learning. For example, Joseph attends a conference and chooses sessions especially related to art. He collects several new recipes for clay and learns about a simple drying rack that he can add to the art center.

In a study by McGreevy (1990), a group of high school students were asked to identify the most creative teacher they had ever had. When analyzing their choices, some interesting patterns emerged. These students believed teachers were the main source of recognition for their creative abilities and talents. Many students identified the creative classroom environment as comfortable and where ideas flowed. Students frequently mentioned that creative teachers were funny and had a sense of humor. Other qualities mentioned included an open and accepting mind, a willingness to share their personal side, spontaneity in the classroom, and an understanding and caring for individual students. They also mentioned that creative teachers managed to find unique ways to present material and students were given choices in implementing assignments. Many of these characteristics are the same ingredients good teachers incorporate into their classrooms today.

Good and creative teachers are seldom satisfied with the way things are. They understand that past accomplishments do not guarantee future success. Creative teachers are constantly seeking new ways to improve their abilities and eagerly explore different avenues that lead to greater insight.

Poole (1980) identified several important roles the teacher can play in fostering creativity in children. These roles include teacher attitudes, communication, classroom atmosphere, and the teacher's ability to design a creative classroom.

Teacher Attitudes

The teacher's attitude of trust is essential to developing creativity. She trusts that children can choose activities that will interest and engage them. The teacher believes that children can participate in these activities without a great deal of adult-imposed regulations. Her focus is on the children becoming competent decision-makers and allowing them to become fully engaged in what interests them (Kamii & DeVries, 1978). The children know they are trusted to choose an activity and work on it at their level.

This supportive attitude is demonstrated when the teacher follows a **teachable moment**. When children find an idea intriguing or look for expansions, she follows their lead. Support is not indiscriminate praise, but encouragement of the individual and her efforts (Shallcross, 1981). For example, when Jowanda brings an African flute into the classroom, all the children rush to examine the instrument. The observant teacher joins the group and poses questions about the flute. How is it played? Could Jowanda or a family member play the flute? What could the students use to make a flute? While this is happening, the teacher makes a mental note to bring in some books about African instruments to expand this budding interest of the children. She collects materials in the

> "Creativity is not a gift that few teachers possess and others envy. It is an ability that can be acquired and nurtured."
>
> **J. S. C. Simplicio, 2000[4]**

room that could be used to make a flute and adds them to the music center. The teacher recognizes that the children's interest in African musical instruments can be enjoyed and expanded into the study of music from another culture.

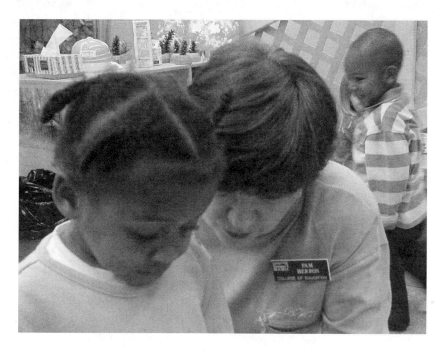

A teacher provides support during a challenging activity. (Photo by Michael Talley)

Communication

The creative teacher communicates to children that they can try new things and that unconventional work is valued. Young children may not have the vocabulary needed to describe their thinking when working creatively. However, children can be helped to put their ideas into words. If the teacher describes a building structure as "unique," she can explain that the cardboard cylinders added a special dimension to the top. Later, she will hear the children describing their work as "unique." They begin to understand that ideas can be original and that words can be used to express the special qualities.

A teacher encourages students to think and express themselves creatively. Her confidence in the child's ability to think in new directions will influence the child's estimation of her own creative abilities (Mellou, 1996). The climate of the creative classroom is positive, and supports collaboration between teacher and children and children and children. The teacher works to establish this sense of trust over a long period of time. Each successful experience and interaction builds the feeling of trust within children in the classroom as they grow in confidence.

Classroom Atmosphere

Children benefit from an **atmosphere** that is relaxed and based on respect. The classroom atmosphere communicates to children that it is all right to take a risk or make a mistake. In this place, no one puts down another person's ideas or unusual answers. The children are able to explain what it is they are trying to do without criticism or ridicule. It is essential for them to develop an internal sense of worth in order to feel secure, take risks, try new things, or venture into the unknown. Therefore, the atmosphere needs to provide opportunities for children to govern their own behaviors and make choices. In this setting, children will develop self-confidence and begin to take risks regarding creative problem-solving, and in other areas of the curriculum.

Because each child is unique, the classroom climate must reflect an atmosphere of acceptance for each person's individuality. Most young children are active and curious, but a very creative child may have a well-developed sense of humor that could be viewed by others as odd. In an atmosphere of acceptance, the child is appreciated without criticism and allowed to work in her own special way. The teacher sets the tone of respect, helps the child through difficult times, learns from these moments, and then goes on with life. The teacher's respect of all children demonstrates that each person is valued and treasured for her uniqueness in this diverse classroom community.

A responsive teacher listens and respects the ideas of a child. (Photo by Michael Talley)

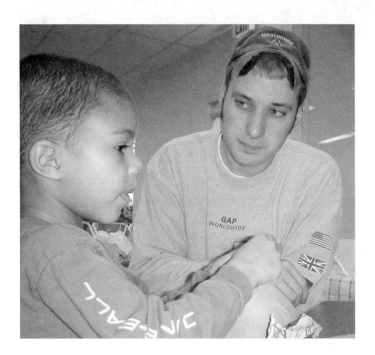

The Creative Environment

The early childhood **environment** plays an important role in enhancing or inhibiting creativity in children. Over a hundred years ago, nursery schools and kindergartens provided children with experiences that would develop perceptions, cognitive structures, and social interactions. Children were encouraged to experiment with the sand and water, to explore shapes with modeling clay, and to participate in play that allowed them to imagine. These experiences continue to be in evidence in appropriate early childhood classrooms today.

The school environment is important in the development of creativity in both children and adults. Environments that encourage creativity provide time and resources, develop expertise, give positive and constructive feedback, and encourage a spirit of play and experimentation. They provide children from diverse backgrounds with opportunities for group interaction, create a safe place for risk-taking, allow for choices, and encourage intrinsic motivation instead of controlling behavior (Kerka, 1999).

Communities and schools are a collection of personalities and educational styles. Teachers wishing to be creative should collaborate with others to gain new insights and identify new approaches to facilitate learning. Collaborative efforts between teachers, parents, and the community broaden possibilities, open a network for brainstorming, and provide stimulation for creativity. For example, a group of early childhood teachers have been studying their environment. They want to create a more homelike atmosphere in their center. In a group meeting, they discuss ways to improve the environment. They brainstorm possibilities and are careful to value each of the ideas contributed. Some ideas include uncluttering the rooms, adding plants, bringing in soft items, providing new light sources, adding curtains to the windows, and placing a couch in the parent area.

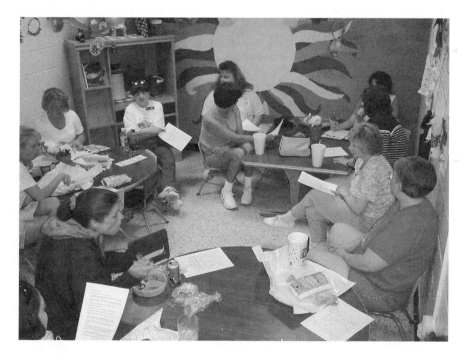

Teachers collaborate to generate more ideas and possibilities. (Photo by Michael Talley)

At the next group meeting, the teachers invite several parents to attend and share their goals for creating an inviting center. Parents provide additional suggestions that include area carpet pieces, wallpaper borders, beanbag chairs, and soft pillows. Two parents volunteer to begin collecting old pillows that can be reconditioned. At their next session, the teachers determine which items can be added quickly and those that may require more time. Together, they begin their plan of action to create a wonderful environment for children, teachers, and families.

In the study of creativity and collaboration, it is helpful to investigate how ideas are discouraged. It can happen to your ideas or you may squelch the ideas of others. In a nurturing environment, creative ideas are encouraged; but in some places, comments can make you hesitant to share your great idea.

The following are some ways to discourage creative ideas or new projects.
- It can't be done.
- We don't have the money.
- Let's form a committee to look into it.
- It's never been done before.
- It won't work.
- The administration would never allow that.
- I have a friend who tried it and it didn't work.
- Are you serious?
- Interesting . . .
- I have never seen anything like that before.
- What will the parents think?
- Where did that idea come from?
- Don't you think you should give that a little more consideration?
- What does everyone else think?
- We tried something like that once.
- It will take too much work.
- That is really weird.
- I am uncomfortable with that.
- Let's talk later.
- Bring in something to support your idea.
- Moving right along . . .
- Maybe we could do that next year.
- Let's get back to that.
- Hmmmmmmmmmm.
- Can you think of anything else?

Have any of these statements discouraged you from trying new things or suggesting possibilities? Have you ever used these phrases with others? Think of ways you can support new ideas and teachers who are being creative. For some reason, it seems easier for teachers to be supportive of children than other adults. In a community of learners where collaboration is valued, a supportive environment should be developed for both children and teachers.

Encouraging Creativity

To encourage creativity, teachers acknowledge the individual child's contribution to a particular idea or product, validate their unique and sometimes outrageous ideas, and let the child know it is all right to move beyond the common and expected. The following scenarios demonstrate how early childhood teachers can encourage creativity.

> A kindergarten child uses two materials in a different way. The teacher says, "Using that aluminum pie pan and the yarn was a very interesting way to make a puppet."

> A first grader insists there are 100 different toppings on the pizza she has made. Children begin to laugh and tease her. The teacher asks, "You have used many different toppings on your pizza. What are some of them?"

> A fourth grader wants more Popsicle sticks for her construction. She wants to build the tallest building in the world. The teacher responds, "You have a great idea and I will bring more Popsicle sticks for you to continue building tomorrow. Is there another building material you could use today?"

"Everyone is creative: we are born not only ready but anxious to act upon the creative proclivity within us."

M. Goldberg, 2000[5]

Making Mistakes

During the creative process, there are often mistakes, retries, and failures. Teachers experience this when a great activity doesn't work or the plaster of paris doesn't harden. They learn to accept the trials that occur during the creative process. As the following examples demonstrate, innovative teachers can help children understand that mistakes and accidents can happen, and sometimes these can be turned into an advantage.

> A kindergartner's box structure falls apart before the glue dries. The teacher sees the child's concern. She comments on the child's effort. "That is a very interesting **sculpture**. Is there some way you can support the structure until the glue dries?"

> A second grader is working on a poster to demonstrate what she had learned in her study of rocks. LaDonna tries to attach a large rock to the poster board and it falls off. After repeatedly trying to attach the rock, she angrily walks away from the project. The teacher recognizes her frustration and says, "I can see you are very upset. What are you trying to show by attaching the rock to the poster?" LaDonna replies, "I want them to see the different kinds of rocks I studied." The teacher encourages her to think of another way of displaying the rocks so the children can see

and also physically examine the rocks. LaDonna thinks for a moment and then concludes that she could put the rocks on a box in front of the poster. "Then the children could feel the rocks for themselves," she explains.

Respect for Differences

Within every classroom, there are a wide range of abilities and talents. Children's work can be less advanced, more advanced, or from a totally different perspective. These variations are recognized and respected in a sensitive environment, and are shown in the following examples.

A kindergartner who is making a book, fills the pages with uncontrolled scribbles. When other children see her book, they tell her "that's not the way you do it." The teacher explains, "people make books in different ways; some use words and some use pictures. The ideas and thinking are the most important parts of creating a book."

A third grader creates a **mobile** with unusual items such as feathers, pinecones, and dried flowers, and hangs them from a small limb. This mobile is very difficult to balance while allowing the parts to move with the airflow. The teacher recognizes that this child is building a very complex mobile, and provides the time and support for her to finish her work of art.

Children learn respect while observing their teacher interact appropriately with a child with special needs. (Photo by Michael Talley)

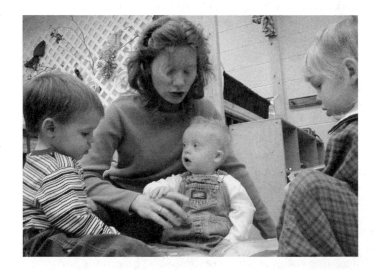

Cooperative and Interactive Thinking

Teachers understand they can learn from others and that working together can expand their own thinking. They model this when they share with children that a wonderful idea came from a helpful book or that another teacher suggested an activity. Children need to experience sharing ideas and learning from others.

During circle time, preschoolers share items brought from home. Cora shows a bridle. She tells the group she just learned to put the bridle in the horse's mouth. The teacher comments that she has learned something new from Cora's explanation because she has never tried to put a bridle in a horse's mouth. She asks if other children have ever had this experience.

In the third grade, children are talking about their recent trip to see the *Nutcracker Suite*. The teacher encourages Sarah to tell the children about her experience dancing in the local production of the *Nutcracker*. At the conclusion of the discussion, the teacher comments, "Sarah, we have learned so much from you about dancing in the *Nutcracker*."

Teaching for Creativity

Trostle and Yawkey (1982) identified seven specific ways teachers can encourage creative thinking. These relate to curricular activities, classroom lessons, and teacher actions.

1. **Facilitate creative thought in early childhood programs.** In the early years, the teacher should encourage children to use physical objects in their own way.

2. **Adult playfulness.** The teacher is playful and serves as a model of a creative person.

3. **Exploration.** The teacher provides sufficient time in the schedule for children to investigate and explore objects and materials.

4. **Oral cues.** The teacher talks to the children while they are involved in creativity activity, thereby extending their thinking.

5. **Verbal descriptions.** The teacher helps children express their creative ideas as vividly and clearly as possible.

6. **Modifying objects.** The teacher changes familiar objects into unfamiliar ones by changing their physical characteristics.

7. **Adding novel objects.** The teacher adds unusual materials to the children's role-playing activities in order to extend their play.

Strategies

There are a number of strategies for incorporating creative expression into the classroom. Strategies include problem-finding, problem-solving, project-based instruction, and reflective thinking.

Problem-finding and Problem-solving

Problem-finding refers to children identifying their own problems. They ask questions about the world and pursue what interests them. At least some of the time, children should have the opportunity to define their own issues, problems, and areas of inquiry. Teachers can initiate problem-finding by following the children's interests and posing provocative questions. The teacher becomes a resource and supports the child as she begins to solve her problem, and structures the day so there is sufficient time to work on solving problems.

This approach can be observed in the interactions of a teacher and a small group of children. The children have designed and planted a small garden on the playground. They are very concerned that birds are eating many of the seeds. The teacher poses the question, "How can we keep the birds out of our garden?" The children suggest several options including moving the garden, taking turns guarding the plants, and making a scarecrow. The teacher talks further with the children about their ideas and possibilities. They conclude that a scarecrow would work best. Logan and Jay explain that it cannot be an ordinary scarecrow; it must be enormous and make loud sounds when birds approach the garden.

The children work several days on the design of the scarecrow. When the plan is complete, they construct a large stuffed scarecrow and attach foil pie plates on the hat, chest, and back. The plan came from the identification of the problem and the ideas of the children. The teacher asked provocative questions, helped collect materials, and assisted in the construction of the enormous, noisy scarecrow.

Teachers who value creativity recognize that curriculum can emerge out of the interest and investigations of children. To plan in this way requires that teachers become researchers, and focus on listening and observing instead of telling and demonstrating (Carter, 1992).

Projects

Project-based instruction engages children in long-term initiatives. In sustained projects, children participate as inventors and researchers. Children find out how plants grow by planting a garden on the playground. Over a period of time, they observe, record, and draw conclusions about resources that the plants need. They take pictures of the garden at different points in time. They determine which plants grew best and which did not. Projects allow children to work together to maintain interest and develop a new depth of understanding. The interest in the garden project is sustained over a three-month period with intense focus at certain times during the process.

Reflective Thinking

Another strategy that supports creative development is reflective self-assessment. Assessment is often thought of as the teacher evaluating children. This teacher-oriented assessment makes the child dependent on the feedback of others and does not prepare her for independent learning. Reflective thinking encourages children to assess their own work and to think about what they have done. This self-evaluation encourages children personally to determine the merits of their work. Four questions can help children think about their work.

1. What does the work look like? The children describe or evaluate their work.

2. What was it like to do the work? The focus here is on the process by which the work was accomplished.

3. How can the work be improved? What can be done to revise the product, story, or painting? This requires critical and creative thinking.

4. How can you share what you have learned with others? This asks the child to determine if the work is ready to be shown or if she wants to share this time.

Reflective thinking can be encouraged informally as the teacher walks around the room and poses questions, or more formally when older children can record their responses to these questions on paper (Torff, 2000).

Fostering Creativity with Activities and Materials

Mayer (1989) describes three conditions for creative teaching.

1. The material must be meaningful to the children.

2. The children must actively engage in the learning process.

3. Evaluations of learning must include a measure of students' creativity.

Activities based on the interests of the children foster creativity. Young children can tell what they know about a topic, what they want to learn, how they want to explore the topic, and how they will share what they have learned. A nature item or new book brought to school by one child may cause other children to become interested and curious. Teachers who value and act on these interests give children a sense of ownership. Ownership leads to engagement that encourages creative behavior.

Including a variety of materials inspires experimentation on the light table. (Photo by Su Lorencen)

Open-ended Activities

Activities that foster creativity should be **open-ended**. Instead of giving a model or telling what the product should be, give children reasonable control over deciding what materials they want to use and how they will approach the product. In the process-oriented class, the thinking that occurs during the work is as important as the final product. Children need to have a wide variety of materials available, so they can select items that match what they are thinking or expand their existing ideas. Many possibilities and combinations allow children to think divergently. A number of studies have shown that children who are encouraged to use divergent thinking dramatically increase their ability to think creatively (Torrance, 1964; Chiatt, Shaw, & Sherwood, 1980).

Flexible Time

Children need time for uninterrupted work, investigation, and discussion. Flexible schedules and longer blocks of time allow children to see new concepts or make extensions. This allows them to work on a project or activity until they determine it is completed, instead of rushing to finish or even disband the work because there is not enough time. As the following scenario demonstrates, the gift of time encourages creative activity and more in-depth work.

> In the block center, several children are working on a structure to represent the new fire station that was built near their school. They have watched the construction, drawn pictures of the progress, taken photographs of the workers, and walked around the site. For several weeks, they have added parts to their own "work in progress." Just at the moment when center time is to be over, Jose has a great idea. The fire station needs a flying banner with a sign that says "Grand Opening." His teacher, who was moving around the room to encourage cleanup, sees Jose working frantically to make the sign and banner. She suggests that Will and Tara, who also have been working on the structure, help with the wonderful sign idea. They can come outside with the aide when they finish the banner. Together, the children create the sign and banner for the Grand Opening.

The Physical Environment

The physical environment of the classroom can have a tremendous impact on the creative actions of young children. Some early childhood classrooms are so filled with equipment, materials, and supplies that they overwhelm the children. A well-organized classroom groups materials together and displays them for children to make their own selection.

The classroom should be aesthetically pleasing with attractive elements included for the children to enjoy. Young children can appreciate a bouquet of spring flowers in a clay pot as well as a poster of a Monet painting. These additions to the classroom expose children to beautiful things, and provide opportunities to experience the color and texture of the flowers and the techniques used by the painter.

The physical arrangement of the space should include areas for both large and small group activities. A group meeting place encourages the sharing of ideas, learning from others, and building a sense of community. In this special area, stories are told, songs are sung, and projects are shared (Isbell & Exelby, 2001).

There should be places for small groups to work and play together. Learning centers or contained areas allow several children to interact frequently, shape their activity, and cooperatively carry the play to completion. Loud and active areas should be grouped together in a portion of the classroom so that quieter areas can function appropriately with a minimum of distractions. Included in the area is a space that provides privacy. In a busy classroom, young children need a place where they can escape to think or simply be alone. This private area can be created in a quiet corner with draped fabric, or in a large cardboard box with cutouts on the side and pillows inside.

A variety of spaces allow children to make choices and determine where they can work best on a specific day or on a special project. At another time, they may make different choices and participate in other activities (Isbell & Exelby).

Displays

There should be many examples of children's work throughout the room. These examples reflect the individual creations of the children who work in this

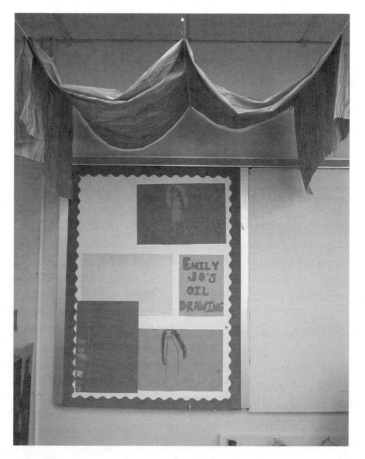

A visually attractive display of child's work demonstrates that it is valued in this classroom. (Photo by Michael Talley)

space. The work should be displayed in interesting ways and include a range of activities, not just art. Always ask the children if their work can be displayed and respect their decision. This will help them begin to evaluate work and determine the projects to share with others. Some children's work could be displayed on a large painted cardboard box that will add a three-dimensional look. Covering boards with textured fabric, contact paper, foil, or other different materials can vary the display effects. Children's work can be matted or framed to enhance the presentation of materials. Simple frames can be made from cardboard, poster board, or art board and covered with foil, satin, small pinecones, buttons, and other items. When children see their work framed, they feel proud and know that it is valued in their classroom.

Accessibility of Materials

Basic art and construction materials should be visible and easily accessible for children to use spontaneously, as well as with teacher-initiated activities. This allows children to choose the materials they want to use independently, without asking the teacher for help. This communicates to children that they are capable of selecting and using the materials they need. This independence allows children to go forward with an idea instead of waiting until they are able to get help from the teacher. Their great ideas may be lost during the wait.

Novel Materials

Novel items capture the interest of young children. The novelty of a toy is a primary reason for children to explore it. Novel items force a child to think in different ways and invent new possibilities that did not previously exist. Some novel items might include unusually shaped styrofoam scraps, industrial salvage, old postcards, hardware, maps, boxes, natural materials, recyclables, fabric, cork, buttons, old kitchen tools, antique/junk items, colored electrical wire, auto parts, wooden spools, building supplies, and discarded storage racks. Opportunities to work with novel materials can spark young children's creativity. Once exploration stops, there is a transition into play. In play, the emphasis changes from "What does this object do?" to "What can I do with this object?" (Frost & Klein, 1983).

> A kindergartner was intrigued by the pieces of PVC pipe that the teacher added to the block area. She explored the properties of the plastic material. Then she began to construct with blocks. She built a submarine from the blocks and added the pieces of pipe for the periscope. The pipe resulted in a new structure that she had not thought of creating before it was added.

> A first grader was very interested in the dulcimer her teacher brought in to play during group time. The experience with this new instrument inspired her to construct her own dulcimer from a cardboard box, complete with yarn strings.

Allow children to use materials in novel ways. Do not restrict them to using their resources in one prescribed way. This requires flexibility of thinking, an important component of creativity.

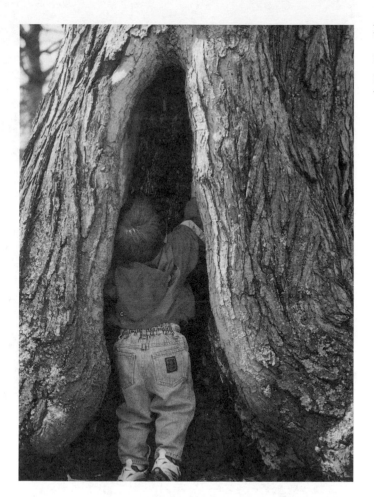

What does it look like inside a tree? (Photo by Su Lorencen)

Summary

There are many ways to encourage creativity in adults and children, but strategies alone are insufficient. A creative classroom environment requires a teacher with courage, a willingness to try new things, and an ability to do things in a different way. A teacher can use creativity each day as she plans an interesting lesson, creates a new learning center, or designs an aesthetically pleasing place. Two sets of creative faculties are interacting in the early childhood classroom: the teacher's and the children's. If the teacher values and develops her creativity, the children will notice. If a teacher is enthusiastic, innovative, and tries new things—even if some ideas fizzle—children thrive because this is an exciting learning environment. Children in the creative classroom will be more adventurous and try doing things for themselves. Both the teacher and children gain from these creative encounters in an environment that encourages their personal growth.

A creative teacher and child play with the idea of a "clay nose." (Photos by Su Lorencen)

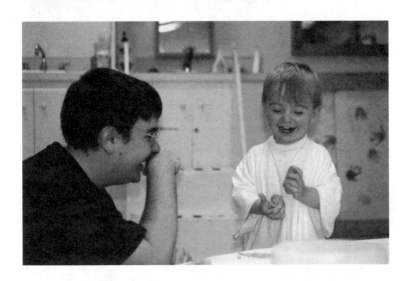

Key Terms

creativity training

whole child

novel

Reggio Emilia

teachable moment

atmosphere

environment

sculpture

mobile

self-assessment

open-ended

Reflection

1. Why is it important for a teacher of young children to be creative?

2. What are some of the characteristics of a creative teacher?

3. What is a value of collaboration for children and teachers?

4. Describe a classroom environment that nurtures creativity.

Thinking about the Creative Episode

1. What were some of the ways Maria demonstrated that she was a creative teacher?

2. In what ways did Maria value the ideas of the children?

3. How will Maria determine other additions and expansions to the green-house center?

Possibilities for Adult Learners

Activity: The Most Creative Teacher

Goal: To recognize the characteristics of creative teachers.

Materials: Paper and pencil.

Procedure:

1. Think about the most creative teacher you have worked with during your academic career. List the qualities this teacher possessed.

2. Share these remembrances in class with other students.

3. Make a list of the characteristics that are shared and determine those qualities that were identified most frequently in creative teachers.

Activity: Find Your Own Creativity

Goal: To recognize that each person is creative and demonstrates creativity in everyday activities.

Materials: Journal for recording creative moments, and pencil or pen.

Procedure:

1. During the past month, identify something that you have done that was personally creative.

2. Think about the personal and professional activities that have allowed you to be creative, playful, or thoughtful.

3. Write a paragraph about these creative moments.

Activity: Brainstorming with Others

Goal: To experience how collaboration with others can extend creative thinking.

Materials: Appendix D (Basic Rules for Brainstorming), everyday objects, chart paper for recording ideas, and markers.

Procedure:

1. Share the guidelines for brainstorming in Appendix D.

2. Divide the class into small groups of four to five people.

3. Present an everyday object and ask the groups to list all the ways it could be used. Remember the focus is on generating many ideas (fluency).

4. Give the groups five to eight minutes to produce a list of possibilities. When the groups seem to stall, encourage them to keep going and remind them that some of the best ideas come at the end of brainstorming sessions.

5. Share the number of ideas each group came up with, and ask them to identify the two or three most unusual ideas.

Activity: Recognizing the Beauty

Goal: To become more observant of beauty in the world around us.

Materials: Journal for recording creative moments, and pencil or pen.

Procedure:

1. On the way home from class, notice creative things you may not have seen before such as a sign with a creative slogan, a beautifully decorated door, a flower arrangement in a florist's window, or reflections of light on the wet pavement.

2. Make a conscious effort to notice and appreciate creative things in your environment.

Open-ended Activities for Young Children

Pre-K–K

Activity: New and Improved

Goal: To identify ways that a familiar item can be improved (flexible thinking).

Materials: Teddy bear, chart paper, and marker.

Procedure:

1. Bring an old teddy bear to group time.

2. Lead a discussion about the teddy bear and ways it may have been used.

3. Divide the class into small groups and ask the children to think of ways they can have more fun playing with the teddy bear.

4. Allow about three to six minutes, depending on the developmental level of the children and their experience with this type of activity.

5. Return to the group and ask them to share their ideas. Record their suggestions on the chart paper as they are given.

6. Comment on the uniqueness of the ideas and how they would improve the teddy bear.

Primary Grades

Activity: Putting It Together

Goal: Combine unrelated objects to develop flexibility of thinking.

Materials: A plastic bag for each small group containing three unrelated items. Examples of items to include in the plastic bags are pieces of yarn, paper clips, a small paper cup, a button, a piece of wire, a sheet of paper, a section of newspaper, masking tape, and a toothpick.

Procedure:

1. Divide the class into small groups.

2. Ask each group to use the three items in its bag to make something that would be useful.

3. Allow five to 10 minutes.

4. Combine the small groups and share the inventions that were created.

Extension: Return the participants to the small groups, and ask each to write an advertisement or create a sign to sell the new products.

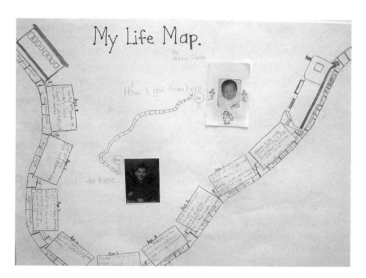

A creative activity visually demonstrates major events in a fourth grader's life.

Notes

[1]Amabile, T. M. (1989). *Growing up creative. Nurturing a lifetime of creativity*. New York: Crown Publishing.

[2]Haefele, J. (1962). *Management series: Creativity and innovation*. New York: Reinhold Publishing Corporation.

[3]Zener, R. S. (1995). Nurturing the creative personality. *The NAMTA Journal. 20*(1) 13–29.

[4]Simplicio, J. S. C. (2000). Teaching classroom educators how to be more effective and creative teachers. *Education, 120*(4), 675–701.

[5]Goldberg, M. R. (2000). *Arts and learning: An integrated approach to teaching and learning in multicultural and multilingual settings* (2nd ed.). New York: Longman Publishing Group.

References

Abdallah, A. (1996). Fostering creativity in student teachers. *Community Review, 14*(1), 52–58.

Carter, M. (1992). Training teachers for creative learning experiences. *Child Care Information Exchange*, 85, 38–40.

Chiatt, M. P., Shaw, J. M., & Sherwood, J. M. (1980). Effects of training on the divergent thinking abilities of kindergarten children. *Child Development, 51*, 1061–1064.

Ehlert, L. (1988). *Planting a rainbow*. San Diego, CA: Harcourt Brace Jovanovich.

Frost, J., & Klein, B. L. (1983). *Children's play and playgrounds*. Austin, TX: Playscapes International.

Gandini, L. (1992). *Creativity comes dressed in everyday clothes*. Child Care Information Exchange, 85, 26–29.

Isbell, R., & Exelby, B. (2001). *Learning environments that work with young children*. Beltsville, MD: Gryphon House.

Jeanrenaud, C., & Bishop, D. (1980). Roadblocks to creativity. In P. F. Wilkinson (Ed.), *In celebration of play: An integrated approach* (pp. 73–84). London: Croom Helm Ltd.

Kamii, C., & DeVries, R. (1978). *Physical knowledge in preschool education: Implications of Piaget's theory*. New York: Prentice Hall.

Kerka, S. (1999). *Creativity in adulthood*. Office of Educational Research and Improvement, Washington, DC. (ERIC Document Reproduction Service No. ED 429 186).

McGreevy, A. (1990). Tracking the creative teacher. *Momentum, 21*, 57–59.

Mayer, R. E. (1989). Cognitive view of creativity: Creative teaching for creative learning. *Contemporary Education Psychology, 14*, 203–211.

Mellou, E. (1996). Can creativity be nurtured in young children? *Early Child Development and Care, 119*, 119–130.

Poole, M. (1980). *Creativity across the curriculum*. Sydney, Australia: George Allen and Union.

Shallcross, D. J. (1981). *Teaching creative behavior*. Englewood Cliffs, NJ: Prentice Hall.

Simplicio, J. S. C. (2000). Teaching classroom educators how to be more effective and creative teachers. *Education, 120*(4), 675–701.

Tegano, D., Groves, M. M., & Catron, C. E. (1999). Early childhood teachers' playfulness and ambiguity tolerance: Essential elements of encouraging creative potential of children. *Journal of Early Childhood Teacher Education, 20*(3), 291–300.

Torff, B. (2000). Encouraging the creative voice of the child. *The NAMTA Journal, 25*(1), 10–14.

Torrance, E. P. (1964). Bringing creativity into play. *Education, 85*, 457–550.

Torrance, E. P. (1965). *Rewarding creative behavior*. Englewood Cliffs, NJ: Prentice Hall.

Torrance, E. P., & Safter, H. T. (1986). Are children becoming more creative? *The Journal of Creative Behavior, 20*(1), 2–13.

Torrance, E. P. (1992). A national climate for creativity and invention. *Gifted Child Today, 15*, 10–14.

Trostle, S. L., & Yawkey, T. D. (1982). Creative thinking and the education of young children: The fourth basic skill. *International Journal of Early Childhood, 14*(2), 67–71.

VonOech, R. (1983). *A whack on the side of the head: How to unlock your mind for innovation*. New York: Warner Books.

Additional Reading

Akande, A. (1997). Creativity: The caregivers' secret weapon. *Early Child Development and Care, 134*, 89–101.

Albert, R. S. (1996). Some reasons why childhood creativity often fails to make it past puberty into the real world. *New Directions for Child Development, 72*(1), 43–56.

Ashton-Warner, S. (1963). *Teacher*. New York: Simon & Schuster.

Byrnes, D. A., & Kiger, G. (1996). *Common bonds: Anti-bias teaching in a diverse society*. Olney, MD: Association for Childhood Education International.

Cecil, L. M., Gray, M. M., Thornburg, K. R., & Ispa, J. (1985). Curiosity-exploration-play-creativity: The early childhood mosaic. *Early Child Development and Care, 19*(1), 199–217.

Chenfield, M. (1991). Everything you need to know about being a creative teacher in four easy nudges. *Phi Delta Kappan, 73*(1), 332–334.

Colangelo, N., & Davis, G. A. (1991). *Handbook for gifted education*. Boston: Allyn and Bacon.

Craft, A. (1998). Educator perspectives on creativity: An English study. *Journal of Creative Behavior, 32*(4), 244–257.

Czikszentmihalyi, M. (1996). *Creativity*. New York: Basic Books.

Duckworth, E. (1996). *The having of good ideas and other essays on teaching and learning*. Olney, MD: Association for Childhood Education International.

Fisher, J. (1996). *Starting from the child*. Buckingham, PA: Open University Press.

Gandini, L. (1992). Creativity comes dressed in everyday clothes. *Child Care Information Exchange, 85*(1), 26–29.

Hoffman, S., & Lamme, L. L. (Eds.). (1989). *Learning from the inside out*. Olney, MD: Association for Childhood Education International.

Jalongo, M. R. (1999). How we respond to the artistry of children: Ten barriers to overcome. *Early Childhood Education Journal, 26*(4), 205–208.

John-Steiner, V. (1985). *Notebook of the mind: Exploration of thinking*. Albuquerque, NM: University of New Mexico Press.

Jones, C. F. (1991). *Mistakes that worked: 40 familiar inventions and how they came to be*. New York: Doubleday Books for Young Readers.

Keegan, R. T. (1996). Creativity from childhood to adulthood; A difference of degree not kind. *New Directions for Child Development, 72*(1), 57–66.

Powell, M. C. (1997). The arts and inner lives of teachers. *Phi Delta Kappan, 78*(6), 450–453.

Runco, M. A. (1996). Personal creativity: Definition and developmental issues. *New Directions for Child Development, 72*(1), 3–30.

Siegl, E. (1986). How to encourage creativity in teachers. *Roeper Review, 9*, 18–19.

Smith, M. K. (1996). Fostering creativity in the classroom. *Early Childhood Education Journal, 24*(2), 77–82.

Torff, B. (2000). Encouraging the creative voice of the child. *The NAMTA Journal, 25*(1), 195–214.

Children's Literature Connection

Allard, H. (1977). *Miss Nelson is missing!* Boston: Houghton Mifflin.
The kids in room 207 take advantage of their teacher's good nature until she disappears and they are faced with a vile substitute. (K–2)

Finchler, J. (1995). *Miss Malarkey doesn't live in room 10*. New York: Walker.
A first-grade boy is shocked, then pleased, when he discovers that his teacher has a life away from school. (Pre-K–2)

Glennon, K. (1990). *Miss Eva and the red balloon*. New York: Simon & Schuster Books for Young Readers.
Miss Eva, an old-fashioned school marm, leads a routine life until one of her students gives her a magic red balloon. (K–3)

Henkes, K. (1996). *Lily's purple plastic purse*. New York: Greenwillow Books.
Lilly loves everything about school, especially her teacher, but when he asks her to wait awhile before showing her new purse, she does something for which she is very sorry later. (Pre-K–1)

Houston, G. (1992). *My great-aunt Arizona*. New York: Harper Collins Publishers.
An Appalachian girl, Arizona Houston Hughes, grows up to become a teacher who influences generations of school children. (Pre-K–3)

Seuss, Dr., & Prelutsky, J. (1998). *Hooray for diffendoofer day!* New York: Knopf.
The students of Diffendoofer School celebrate their unusual teachers and curriculum, including Miss

Fribble who teaches laughing, Miss Bonkers who teaches frogs to dance, and Mr. Katz who builds robotic rats. (K–3)

Slate, J. (1998). *Miss Bindergarten celebrates the 100th day of kindergarten.* New York: Dutton Children's Books.
To celebrate one hundred days in Miss Bindergarten's kindergarten class, all of her students bring one hundred of something to school including a one hundred-year-old relative, one hundred candy hearts, and one hundred polka dots. (K–1)

Thaler, M. (2000). *The music teacher from the Black Lagoon.* New York: Scholastic.
A boy contemplates all the horrible stories he has heard about the music teacher, Miss LaNote, and the ordeals she forces her students to endure. (K–3)

Weiss, L. (1984). *My teacher sleeps in school.* New York: F. Warne.
Because Mrs. Marsh is always sleeping in her classroom before the students arrive and always stays after they leave, Mollie becomes convinced that her teacher has no home other than school. (K–2)

Helpful Web Sites

The addresses and corresponding agencies below are taken from the Web sites. Due to the dynamic nature of the Internet, please remember that Web sites are subject to change at any time.

http://www.ed.gov   The U. S. Department of Education

http://www.worldgifted.org   The World Council for Gifted and Talented Children (WCGTC)—Focuses world attention on gifted and talented children, and ensures the realization of their valuable potential to the benefit of humankind.

http://www.cef-cpsi.org/   The Creative Education Foundation—A not-for-profit organization committed to nurturing creativity, innovation, and leadership in order to help individuals and organizations maximize their creative potential.

http://www.creativeconnections.org/   Creative Connections—A non-profit international cultural exchange organization that sets up class-to-class exchanges between American schools and their counterparts in many countries.

http://www.hometown.aol.com/OMEPIntl   The World Organization for Early Childhood Education (OMEP - Organisation Mondiale pour l'Education Prescolaire)—An international, nongovernmental organization to benefit children under the age of eight throughout the world.

http://www.triangle.co.uk/ciec/   Contemporary Issues in Early Childhood—A new online, fully-refereed, international research journal.

http://www.users.sgi.net/~cokids/teacher.html   The Early Childhood Educators' and Family Web Corner—Lists teacher information pages on a multitude of subjects.

For additional resources involving creativity and the arts with young children, visit our Web site at **http://www.earlychilded.delmar.com**

Chapter 3

The Important Role of Play

This chapter examines the different types of **play** and their relationship to the development of young children. The importance of play is studied as it influences the cognitive, social, and physical development of young children. It includes ways to develop playfulness and design environments that encourage participation. During play, children construct and transform their world to be meaningful for them, and at their level of development.

Creative Episode

Niki, fourteen months old, is visiting in the home of her mother's friend. At first, her mother and Loretta play with Niki and encourage her to interact with them. As time passes, they begin to talk about adult subjects. Niki grows weary of all the talk and being ignored. She toddles around the room, obviously looking for something. She searches through a box of toys. She looks behind the furniture. Finally, Niki finds a small piece of fabric in the sewing area. She climbs up on the couch with the tiny piece of fabric in her hands. She closes her eyes, lovingly rubs the fabric, pretends to go to sleep, and snores, "Zzzzzz."

Niki has created a symbol for her "blankie" using the small scrap of soft fabric. She pretends to be asleep by closing her eyes and adds to the play by making a snoring sound. Niki is playing and using symbolic representation. This is the beginning of symbolic play that will become more visible during the preschool years when she begins to take on the roles of others and participate in cooperative play.

Historical Perspective

As early as the time of Plato (427–347 BC), play has been seen as a part of childhood. Rousseau (1712-1778) wrote that work and play are the same for the child: he knows no difference. In the 19th century, Froebel (1821) saw play as the vehicle for unfolding the inner good of the child. The play Froebel described focused on active engagement through motor play and concrete materials that were manipulated easily by young children. Play with these materials provided its own reward for the child. Froebel's play materials included soft wool balls, sets of small unit blocks, and parquetry (geometrically patterned tiles). The play Froebel suggested with these materials included structured activities with specific goals. He believed that play was the highest expression of human development in childhood; play alone is the free expression of what is in a child's soul (Froebel, 1887; Brosterman, 1997).

During the industrial revolution and colonial period, play was not as valued. It was viewed as a frivolous waste of time. The work of notable theorists and important research studies reestablished the importance of play during the next century. In recent years, play has become an area of serious empirical research and scientific recognition (Sutton-Smith, 1979; Elkind, 1987; Pelligrini, 1996). This expanding research base supports the contention that play is a developmentally important and purposeful behavior. Many early studies concluded that play follows a developmental sequence, serves as a reflection of social and cognitive development, and strengthens developing skills (Quinn & Rubin, 1984). Later, Russ (1996) concluded that fantasy play is important in childhood because it facilitates many of the cognitive and affective processes related to creativity.

Kindergarten boys using unique materials in their construction. (Photo by Michael Talley)

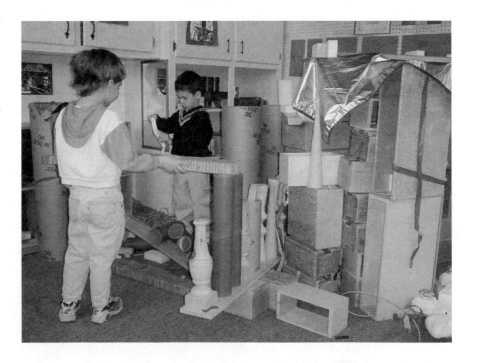

But even today, there remains some conflict over the value of play. This can be seen in the trend to push academic curriculum down to preschool levels, and to introduce structured sports and competition during the early years of children's development. Often, these additions eliminate the time and opportunity for young children to be involved in play. Should play be included in early childhood programs and what are the benefits of this inclusion?

Theories of Play

Play has a central role in many theories that relate to early childhood development (Erikson, 1950; Piaget, 1961; Montessori, 1964; Vygotsky, 1976). Each theorist describes the role of play by focusing on a particular element of the process and providing an interpretation.

Herbert Spencer (1896) developed one of the earliest theories of play. His **surplus energy theory** explained that children release their excess energy through play. Spencer also believed that children's play is an avenue for developing behaviors that are essential for adulthood. This view of play supports the need for physical activity and outdoor play in early childhood programs.

The **relaxation theory** of G. T. W. Patrick (1916) explained that play was a way to recover from fatigue or hard work. Patrick felt that recreational play was beneficial and restored energy. This theory relates to the practice in early childhood of rotating the daily schedule between active and quiet activities.

In the **practice theory**, developed by Karl Gross (1916), play was described as an intrinsic activity. Gross believed that play began naturally and continued to develop as a child matured. The young child exercised in playful ways. He believed that children need a period of play in childhood to practice the skills that will be needed in adult life. Gross further extended his theory by proposing that play is a preparation for life or a strategy for practicing life skills in a safe way. Today, this explanation of play can be observed when young children dress dolls or play in the salon center (Hughes, 1999). Play leads to the mastery of self and environment that is related to personality and intelligence (Frost & Kein, 1983).

Modern Theories

Theorists involved in the psychoanalytic movement focused on the emotional aspects of development. Freud (1963) believed the primary motivation for play was the **pleasure principle**. He explained that pleasure is achieved through wish fulfillment in play. Play provides a release from repressed emotion and thereby reduces anxiety in the child. This interpretation can be seen when Cassandra becomes a nurse and gives the doll a shot again and again. At first, the doll cries loudly. After several shots, the doll cries very little. When the last shot is given, Cassandra explains that the baby is "very brave." For Freud, this play is valued because it provides an avenue for release of emotional feelings, an opportunity to remold past experience, and practice for future experiences.

For Erikson, play has the role of cultural evolution and developmental progression in which the child adds new and more complex understandings of the world. Erikson identified three ways this play may occur:

1. **Autocasmic play:** Self, people, and things.

2. **Microsphere play:** Small objects and toys.

3. **Macrosphere play:** Shares play with others.

Through play, Erickson believed children develop cooperative relationships and gain mutual trust. He saw play as a vehicle that children use to find their identity and master the skills needed for everyday life. Solitary play is valued in this theory as a way for children to deal with emotions after difficult periods. In this process, the child plays alone. Play provides a vehicle to master anxiety and conflict.

A miniature train inspires a preschooler to "travel." (Photo by Michael Talley)

Constructivist Theory

For Piaget, a cognitive theorist, play was viewed from a cognitive perspective. Piaget devoted an entire book to the development of play entitled *Play Dreams and Imitation in Childhood*. He believed that play was a mode by which children learn to understand their experiences. During the process, children are engaged in cycles of assimilation and accommodation. During these cycles, modifications are made in the child's operating schema as he makes sense of the world. Play is considered an interaction among children and the physical environment. Their action on the environment is the primary force for adaptation (Gehlbach, 1991). Play is described as a vehicle for children to use in communication, expression, and reasoning. Piaget identified four types of play that change over time and have different focuses. Although these stages of play can be seen across childhood, there is often a concentration of a particular approach during specific stages of development.

Sensory-motor Play (Functional Play)

Sensory-motor play is the exploration of objects and materials in the child's environment. Very young children act on the materials, use their senses to examine them, and explore the properties of each item. For example, a group of bells are attached to elastic and hung on the baby's crib. First, the baby explores the bells through the senses: they are touched, mouthed, and visually examined. Later, the bells are intentionally hit with a foot, hand, head, or another toy. This action on the bells is repeated again and again. The baby laughs out loud. Now he is playing with the bells to produce an interesting sound and enjoy the activity. This enjoyment signifies that he has moved from exploration of the bells to play.

Hughes found that during infancy, the two most powerful predictors of intellectual development are parental involvement and availability of play material. Materials can be commercial toys or collected household items that the infant is able to explore and learn about. Infants and toddlers are very interested in materials and spend a great deal of time exploring them through their senses. Through manipulation and action, young children gain understanding of the objects that are in their environment.

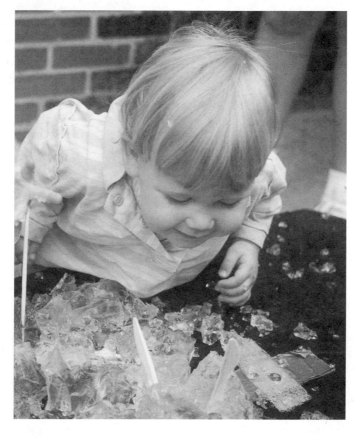

Ice is a new material for the toddler to explore. (Photo by Su Lorencen)

Preoperational Play

Preoperational play is dominated by the development of symbols. At first, the symbol must look like the object it represents such as a toy telephone that stands for a real one. Later, the symbol can look less like the object it represents. The child can substitute a block for a race car or a stick for a snake. At a higher level of symbolic representation, the children are able to pretend that the real object exists. For example, they drink from a cup that is invisible and eat food that is not there. During the preoperational period, children move into sociodramatic play where they take on roles and are involved in a sequence of events with other children. In housekeeping, for example, Carla and Jose check the refrigerator and find it empty. They decide to go to the grocery store (the block area) to get some food. They cooperatively prepare a dinner of tacos and refried beans, then eat the meal. The two children even wash the dishes at the end of dinner. Carla and Jose have taken on the roles of their parents. The play has been sustained, lasting over 20 minutes. They have talked together, compromised on the food for the dinner, and participated in a sequence of events. This sociodramatic play demonstrates many of the qualities of higher-level preoperational play.

The housekeeping center encourages sociodramatic play. (Photo by Michael Talley)

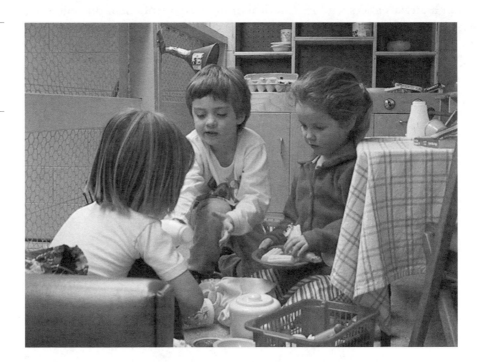

Construction Play

Piaget does not view **construction play** as a separate stage but rather as occurring across several stages. In this play, children build and construct using a variety of materials. The construction can be done individually or in social groups working together. Construction begins with the toddler simply stacking blocks and can progress to the third grader building a sailboat, complete with sail and rudder. Piaget believed that construction is uniquely positioned between play and intelligent work. This play can occur in a variety of settings with different materials including blocks, woodworking, sand, and clay.

Games with Rules

This type of play usually occurs when children have moved into the concrete stage of cognitive development at approximately seven to 10 years of age. At first, children construct their own rules that are strictly enforced: "You know the rule, the tallest goes first." If children do not abide by the rules, they are often banned from the play. Later, the rules become more standardized and associated with specific games: "You are out when you miss three times." These are the rules of the game and they are to be maintained during play. Piaget saw the role of play as being fundamental for intellectual functions. He viewed play as a strategy for children to transform the world and meet personal demands. As children move into higher levels of cognitive understanding, they begin to consider the rules imposed by others, and often associated with games and sports.

Piaget explained that children should be able to do their own experimenting and research in play. Teachers can guide or facilitate children's understanding by providing appropriate materials, but the child must construct and reinvent knowledge for himself.

> *"Every time we teach a child something, we keep him from inventing it for himself."*
>
> **J. Piaget, 1961[1]**

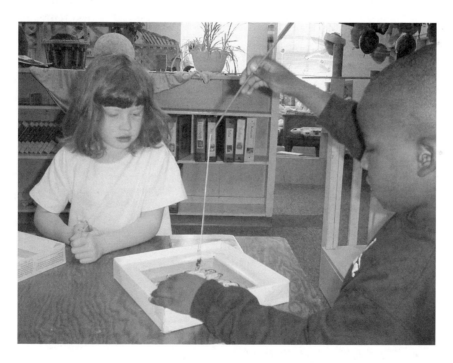

Primary grade children are beginning to play games with rules. (Photo by Michael Talley)

Social Constructivist Theory

In Vygotsky's theory (1978), social experiences shape children's way of thinking and interpreting the world. He believed that language has a crucial role in development because it is the primary avenue of communication and mental contact with others. Language serves as an indispensable tool for thought. According to Vygotsky, supportive guidance from adults can create a scaffold for children's learning, essential for moving children to higher levels of cognitive development.

Vygotsky's writings on play reveal several major themes. He emphasized representational play or make-believe play that develops during the preschool years, and later evolves into games with rules that dominate middle childhood. Vygotsky also believed that fantasy play was an important factor in development.

Vygotsky concluded that play has two features that make it unique and essential in a child's development. First, representational play creates an imaginary situation that permits the child to explore unrealized desires. Second, it contains rules for behavior that the children must follow to be successful in the play situation. In dramatic play, children learn to respond to external stimuli but in accordance with internal ideas. A child who is imagining himself to be a father with a baby, conforms to the rules of parental behavior that he has experienced. According to Vygotsky, pretend play helps children separate meaning from objects, which is vital preparation for the later development of abstract thought (Berk, 1994).

Brain Development

Research on the development of the brain indicates that experience and opportunities during play are essential to the development of neural pathways. These connections are a crucial feature of brain development during the early years of children's lives. Play provides the context for experiences and is vital to the development of learning. There is an unprecedented explosion of information about the importance of play for brain growth and child development (Frost, 1998). Lack of experience during this time will result in underdeveloped neural pathways. These important connections are formed as children explore their environment, play, and form positive relationships with adults and children (Kieff & Casberque, 2000).

Shore (1997) developed broad guidelines based on brain research that support the link between play and healthy brain development. These guidelines can assist adults working with young children.

Respond to the children's clues.

Play with children and follow their lead.

Move into play when children are interested; pull back when they have had enough.

Maintain an ongoing conversation about what they are doing.

Encourage play exploration.

Allow children to explore their relationships.

Arrange time for them to play with children their own age as well as other ages.

In both the psychoanalytic and constructivistic theories, the emphasis is on the self-directed nature of children's play. Play is viewed as self-developed when the child selects and participates in an activity. Both theories emphasize the need for children to control their own play if it is to achieve its purpose of supporting the development of cognition and positive mental health. Vygotsky added another important element needed in play: social interactions that occur between adults and peers.

Importance of Play

Play has been the focus of hundreds of research studies in early childhood. Findings from these studies have demonstrated the importance of play in children's development and has been acknowledged repeatedly as a primary vehicle for concept development and problem-solving. Play brings children into contact with multiple stimuli that support the development of categorization, generalization, and conceptual skills.

The importance of play has been emphasized by theorists and researchers that clearly documents the benefits. Many curriculum standards and professional guidelines emphasize the importance of play during early childhood. The NAEYC has taken a strong stand on appropriate practice for young children. In the guidelines for Developmentally Appropriate Practice, play emerges as a critical element in the appropriate early childhood environment. The NAEYC Position Statement (Bredekamp & Copple, 1997) stated:

9. Play is an important vehicle for children's social, emotional, and cognitive development, as well as a reflection of their development.

Understanding that children are active constructors of knowledge, and that development and learning are the result of interactive processes, early childhood teachers recognize that children's play is a highly supportive context for these developing processes (Piaget, 1952; Fein, 1981; Bergen, 1988; Smilansky & Shefatya, 1990; Fromberg, 1992; Berk & Winsler, 1995). Play gives children opportunities to understand the world, interact with others in social ways, express and control emotions, and develop their symbolic capabilities. Children's play gives adults insights into children's development and opportunities to support the development of new strategies. Vygotsky (1978) believed that play leads development, with written language growing out of oral language through the vehicle of symbolic representation abilities. Play provides a context for children to practice newly acquired skills and also to function on the edge of their developing capacities to take on new social roles, attempt novel or challenging tasks, and solve complex problems that they would not (or could not) do otherwise (Mallory & New, 1994b).

Research demonstrates the importance of sociodramatic play as a tool for learning curriculum content with three- through six-year-old children. When teachers provide a thematic organization for play; offer appropriate props, space, and time; and become involved in the play by extending and elaborating on children's ideas, children's language and literacy skills can be enhanced (Levy, Schaefer, & Phelps, 1986; Schrader, 1989, 1990; Morrow, 1990; Pramling, 1991; Levy, Wolfgang, & Koorland, 1992).

In addition to supporting cognitive development, play serves important functions in children's physical, emotional, and social development (Herron & Sutton-Smith, 1971). Children express and represent their ideas, thoughts, and feelings when engaged in symbolic play. During play a child can learn to deal with emotions, to interact with others, to resolve conflicts, and to gain a sense of competence—all in the safety that only play affords. Through play, children also can develop their imaginations and creativity. Therefore, child-initiated, teacher-supported play is an essential component of developmentally appropriate practice (Fein & Rivkin, 1986, p. 14).

Benefits of Play in the Curriculum

Children benefit in many ways from play. Researchers continue to document that learning occurs when children play (Berk, 1994; Isenberg & Jalongo, 1997; Isbell & Raines, 1994; Pellegrini & Boyd, 1993). Play provides children with opportunities for social development as they share materials, develop plans, negotiate differences, and cope with disappointments. Play helps build motor skills as children use eye-hand coordination, and engage in activities such as running, climbing, and throwing.

Play helps children's emotional development as they play out their fears and gain control of anxieties. Play is an integral strategy because it contributes to children's language, motor skills, and social, emotional, and intellectual development.

What Are the Qualities of Play?

It is important to be able to identify play and the special characteristics of this activity. There is no simple definition of play because the borders between play, exploration, and work are not always clearly defined. A number of typical play features (Nourot & Van Hoorn, 1991; Hughes, 1999) can help in the recognition.

"The most creative artist living today is the young child at play."

Author Unknown[2]

1. Play is intrinsically motivated. It is an end in itself. It is done for the sheer joy of doing it.

2. The child freely chooses it. In a study by King (1979), it was found that if the kindergarten teacher assigned a play activity to the pupils, they regarded it as work.

3. Play must be pleasurable. The child must enjoy the activity for it to be identified as play. The second grader who agrees to participate in T-ball because his parents insist fails to meet this requirement for play. He did not choose to do this and finds no pleasure in the activity.

4. Play may be nonliteral or symbolic. It involves an element of make-believe and allows the child to change reality. The child with a new brother at home is able to develop a play scenario where he continues to be the star.

5. Play actively engages the child. In play, the child participates in an activity that is personally meaningful. It is based on his experience and provides an avenue for following these interests at this point in time.

Playfulness

There is another way of thinking about children's play. This interpretation breaks away from old strategies of defining play by focusing on the child's behaviors or what the child does. This contemporary approach focuses on play as an internal predisposition to be playful.

Lieberman (1966) was one of the first to suggest the existence of the playfulness trait in young children. She identified components of **playfulness** as humorous, emotionally expressive, novelty-seeking, curious, open, and communicative. These factors were later supported by the work of Singer & Singer (1976).

Lieberman developed a questionnaire that was revised by Barnett (1990) to help teachers identify playfulness in children. They believe that playfulness is comprised of five dimensions.

Dimension	Questions
1. Physical Spontaneity	How often does the child engage in physical movement during play? Are his movements well-coordinated?
2. Social Spontaneity	Does the child show flexibility in his interactions in the group? Does the child play cooperatively?
3. Cognitive Spontaneity	Does the child use imagination in dramatic play? Is the child spontaneous during dramatic play?
4. Sense of Humor	How does the child show a sense of humor during play? Does the child enjoy joking or clowning around?
5. Manifest Joy	How often does the child show he enjoys the play activities? Does the child show enthusiasm during play?

These characteristics of playfulness provide another way of looking at the developing young child. They provide a way to assess play and the children who participate. Maintaining a playful attitude toward learning is an integral part of acquiring skills necessary to meet the challenges of the 21st century. Playfulness is an important part of learning to work with others, and attaining flexible thinking, persistence, and commitment (Boyer, 1997).

Playfulness and imagination are influenced by experience and training. This development progresses through phases, three of which occur during the early years of children's lives. The early childhood phases include the following.

1. **Sensory Exploration** (approximately birth to age five). This is a playful time when children are flexible and enthusiastically examining their environment. Playfulness can be enhanced in this phase by using the senses to explore objects and materials. An example of an appropriate toy is a large textured ball made of a variety of fabrics that produces a bell sound when moved. The very young infant feels the ball, sees the variation of fabrics, and hears the sound.

2. **Egocentric Speculation** (approximately two to seven years of age). Fantasy and the exaggeration of intuitive impressions dominate this phase; the possibility of "magical powers" exists. Enhance playfulness in this period by providing opportunities for dramatic play. Dress-up clothes including hats, men's and women's jackets, pocketbooks, wallets, shoes, boots, and scraps of fabric encourage dramatic play. Placing these items in a housekeeping center sets the stage for sociodramatic play.

3. **Personal Experimentation** (approximately six to ten years of age). During this period (the early school years), there is a trial-and-error approach to the world. Enhance playfulness during this period by experimenting with visual and auditory images. In the primary grades, learning centers can match the interest and/or areas of study. For example, set up a Mexican restaurant center when studying Mexico or a fitness center to encourage increased physical activity. These centers provide opportunity to play and experiment within the curriculum framework.

The development of playfulness provides children with opportunities to think, plan, and enjoy life and all the changes and challenges that will come their way (Boyer).

Social Play

Social play involves children's ability to interact with peers. Mildred Parten (1932) identified six types of play (listed below) that are developed during the early childhood years. These types of play begin with solitary play and progress to the more social level of cooperative play. Although originally viewed as developmental steps in social play, today these steps are viewed as descriptive of the different styles of play observed in children (Isenberg & Jalongo).

Types of Play

1. **Unoccupied Play**   The child is not engaged in play.

"Play is a natural function, and the learning it leads to is achieved by the well-accepted process of 'doing'. Actual learning comes from doing."

C. Cherry, 1976[3]

2.	**Onlooker Play**	Watches others in play but does not enter the activity. May ask questions or make suggestions, but does not enter the play.
3.	**Solitary Play**	Plays independently. Is not involved with other children. Pursues own activity without concern for what others are doing.
4.	**Parallel Play**	Plays beside or near other children. Plays independently with toys and is not influenced by the play of others.
5.	**Associative Play**	Plays with others in an informal way. Communicates about the common activity but there is no organization of the play.
6.	**Cooperative Play**	Involves complex play with others, sharing goals, and materials.

Knowledge of the types of social play provides the teacher with insight into the activity. It helps teachers appreciate play and the benefits play can provide for developing social skills. The teacher can understand that solitary play is very typical of the two-year-old, but is also important for the primary child who needs privacy and/or time to develop creative ideas. The teacher can offer support for cooperative play as children attempt to organize their play by determining roles, themes, or events. There is agreement that children can develop from playing alone as well as playing cooperatively with others (Parten, 1932; Iwanaga, 1973).

Play provides many opportunities for social interactions. (Photo by Michael Talley)

Sociodramatic Play

Sarah Smilansky's work (1968) provides insight into the development of **sociodramatic play**. She found that children around the world between the ages of two and eight engaged in different levels of social play. In dramatic play, the child takes on a role and pretends to be someone else. In this type of play, children imitate the person and often use props as they draw from personal experience. Dramatic play can begin as early as age two and develops at an accelerated rate from age four to six. It continues to develop in many children until the age of 10 or older.

Sociodramatic play is more narrowly defined. It involves at least two children who interact verbally and cooperate in their activity, adjusting their roles in response to others. This play is more sustained, lasts for longer periods of time, and involves a sequence of events. In both pretend play and sociodramatic play, the child's experiences and play environment affect their imitation. Children often use make-believe or imagination to create the play episode. This element allows children to play in ways that represent reality instead of making it an exact replica. Make-believe play relies heavily on oral language and interactions. Children often say, "Let's pretend that this is a bus," or, "I am going to be the daddy, okay?"

Smilansky identified six elements that exist in sociodramatic play.

1. The child takes on a role.

2. The child substitutes an item for a real object (toy or open-ended object).

3. Make-believe is used in the play.

4. The play is persistent and the focus is maintained for a reasonable period of time (10 minutes or more is suggested).

5. There is interaction between two or more children.

6. There is verbal interaction between members of the group.

Sociodramatic play focuses on roles and themes instead of on the materials that were emphasized in the sensory motor stage of development. Sociodramatic play stimulates emotional, social, and intellectual growth in children. In this type of play, children participate in problem-solving, developing social skills in meaningful activities, and using language to communicate with others. As children participate, they become more accomplished in sociodramatic play.

A number of studies (Lewis 1974; Smilansky & Feldman 1980; Smilansky, 1990) have found that there is a positive relationship between children involved in sociodramatic play and their ability to organize their thoughts through action and language. Smilansky concluded that role-playing was not the critical element for developing children's abilities. She believed it was make-believe (verbal and nonverbal) that was the most powerful element. Smilansky also believed appropriate adult interactions and a stimulating environment could support sociodramatic play.

Sociodramatic Play in the Early Childhood Classroom

Historically, the housekeeping center (Wendy's Corner or home living) was recognized as an important feature in the early childhood environment. Reasons for the inclusion of this area vary. Some believe the housekeeping area is a secure place where children can make the transition from home to school. Others feel that the home is where children have had many experiences and, therefore, provides numerous themes for their play. Whatever the reason, this center continues to be included in most preschool classrooms. Although its use with older children is sometimes questioned, it is interesting to note that in multi-age classrooms, many older children choose to play in the housekeeping center. They continue to want to be involved in play related to home and family.

Play Environment

The environment of play is very complex, and is composed of both physical and social elements. The physical environment—variety of materials, space available to play, and sufficient time—can affect the development of the child's play. The social environment can be affected by parenting styles, interaction with peers, and feelings of support. These physical and social elements interact with the child's level of development, experiential background, time, and protected space. To see young children absorbed in their play is a joy, but it can only happen when sufficient time and space is provided (Balke, 1997).

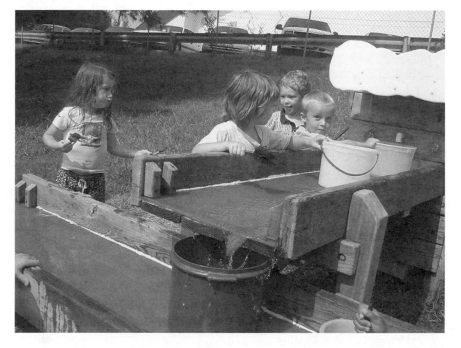

A water trough inspires creative play. (Photo by Michael Talley)

Time and Space for Play

When children play, they need space and time that will not be interrupted. Play is a flowing, creative process. Children require time to become engaged in and to carry out plans. An adult's most important contribution to children's play is ample time. A flexible schedule that includes large blocks of time allows children to remain in play activities that are interesting to them. This time frame provides a smooth transition from activity to activity, following the interest and focus of the children. It provides the time needed to become engaged in play and to be involved in more complex activities.

Rooms filled with desks and chairs provide little space for play. Areas that encourage active learning include places that are designed to communicate to children that active, pretend, and construction play is welcome. For example, the block area should be clearly defined with open storage that displays the variety of materials available for building. Low shelf units distinguish boundaries for the area and help children identify specific centers. Children understand that play and building are acceptable activities in the block area.

Play Materials

The selection and regular rotation of play materials is an important consideration for appropriate activity to occur. Materials should be chosen that match the age, developmental level, and interest of the children who will be using them. For example, toddlers need large vinyl covered blocks for building whereas kindergartners often prefer snap-together blocks that allow for more complex structures. Primary children may want to create the village they live in, complete with tiny homes, shops, and road signs. Play materials that relate to the culture and region in which the children live also can influence their involvement in a positive way.

In a crosscultural study of play, Feitelson (1972) found children's pretend play was richer and more complex when props and toys were provided that reflected the children's environment, and were specific to their culture and experience. In one Native American center, the level of dramatic play increased significantly when a Native American doll family was added to housekeeping. The new play items connected to the children's culture and their experiences. When selecting toys and materials, be sure to take into consideration the experiences of the children who make up the classroom.

Learning Centers (Play Centers)

Young children are active learners who benefit from an environment that responds to their special way of acquiring knowledge. An appropriate learning environment for young children provides a place where they are challenged to reach their potential while providing opportunities for successful experiences at their developmental levels. **Learning centers** provide a wonderful match for active young learners and a responsive environment.

In learning centers, young children can select the activity that interests them. They can work at their own pace and participate in activities that allow them to be successful. Here, children are motivated to work on the tasks that are important to them and where they are able to shape what is happening. The effective center is designed to relate to the children's environment and planned to encourage their involvement. In this "center world," children can try out many ideas and rearrange the events to fit their level of understanding. In this social setting, children have opportunities to work together, and get rapid feedback from their actions and language (Isbell, 1995).

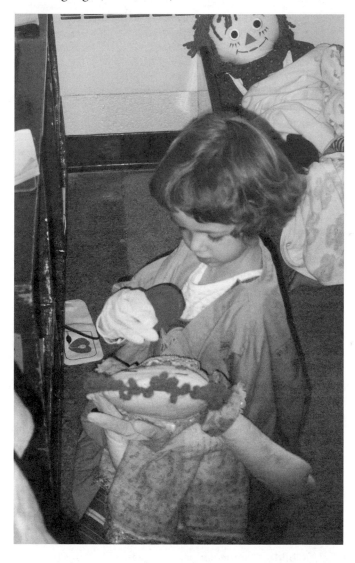

A health clinic center inspires play related to this theme. (Photo by Stacy Larsen)

There are many different types of learning centers that can provide opportunities for participating in sociodramatic play. Traditional centers include blocks, sand and/or water, housekeeping, library, and science and/or nature. Other centers are focused around specific themes and may take turns in the classroom for two to three weeks each. Such examples include grocery store, camping (indoors or outdoors), pet store, doctor's office, mall, and restaurant centers. These centers are equipped with props that support the development of themes and the related roles in play. The inclusion of unique centers into the classroom inspires new play and demonstrates that a creative environment can provide opportunities for change.

Ways to support play in centers include:
- allowing children to select the center where they play.
- providing sufficient time for children to move into roles and sequence.
- selecting equipment and props that are attractive and interesting.
- designing the areas so they are self-managing and do not require an adult in the area.
- changing the materials to stimulate new interests or expanded play opportunities.
- taking time to talk about center play after it is completed each day.

At the beginning of the year, it is helpful to introduce children to the traditional centers by visiting each and discussing the activities that can occur in these special areas. When a new center is set up in the classroom, have a "Grand Opening." During group time, talk about the area, some of the possibilities for play, and new props that are included. Children should choose the center that they would like to work in each day. This personal choice nurtures creative problem-solving and allows them to follow individual interests.

Blocks

One of the most appealing toys for young children is blocks because they are versatile and appropriate for many different age groups. The toddler can stack four small cubes on top of each other; the kindergartner can build a sophisticated parking garage; and the nine-year-old can create a mall including a variety of stores, an atrium, and a food court. Children of all ages enjoy playing with blocks because their open-ended quality allows countless possibilities for construction and transformation. Blocks provide many learning opportunities such as measurement, spatial relationships, and classification. Block centers also encourage language use as children talk about their building and ideas related to construction (Isbell & Raines, 1991). Children often progress in orderly steps as they use blocks in their play (Dodge, 1988).

1. Children carry blocks.

2. Children pile blocks and lay them on the floor.

3. Children connect blocks to create structures (enclosures, bridging).

4. Children make very elaborate constructions.

In the area of creativity, blocks can become anything the child wants. The diversity of blocks allows children to transform the materials in many different ways to follow their interest. Working with blocks encourages fluency and flexibility of ideas. Blocks can become a barnyard for horses, a bridge joining neighborhoods, or a landing strip for an airplane. These transformations and symbolizations encourage the child's creative and cognitive abilities.

There are many types of blocks available for young children including variations of size and material that can add challenges to the play. Different types of blocks include foam blocks, cardboard blocks, unit blocks, small cubes, bristle blocks, and hard plastic blocks that can be used outdoors. Wooden blocks can be made inexpensively from scraps of lumber and added to the area for little or no cost.

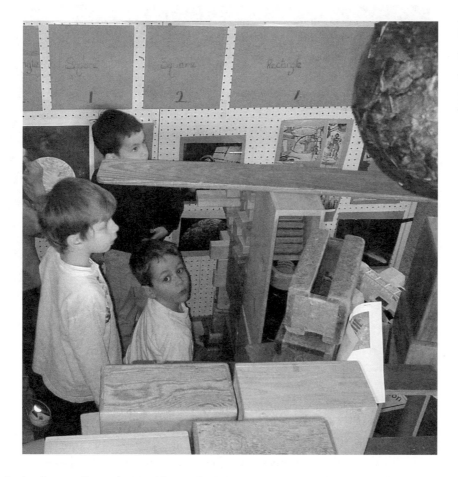

Cardboard cylinders and wooden boards provide variety in the block area. (Photo by Michael Talley)

Block play can be enhanced by including novel items in the space. Some interesting additions could include cardboard cylinders, a variety of sizes of boxes, pieces of styrofoam, tree branches, pieces of plastic pipe, rulers and yardsticks, Plexiglas pieces, carpet scraps, string and yarn, blankets, plastic animals, mini people, and duct tape. These items can be rotated into the block area on a regular basis so the area is changing, interesting, and challenging. Plastic containers can provide storage for small items and be visible for children to use in their play. These could include a collection of plastic farm animals, a collection of trucks, a multicultural family, and items that relate to a specific theme of study.

Water and Sand Play

Young children are drawn to natural materials such as sand, water, dirt, stones, and snow. These materials respond to children and give immediate feedback from their actions. This play can be at a water table, plastic tub, or in a puddle on the playground. Children explore the properties of a material to see how it pours, sifts, fills a cup, and spills on the floor. The young child's first experiences with these elements should be free and open for individual experimentation. Later, items can be added to sand or water for extensions of their thinking, new combinations, and unique possibilities.

Items to Enrich Play

Sand: Different size shovels, cups, spoons, buckets, plastic wheel toys, funnels, sifter, spoons, and ice cubes.

Water: Clear tubes, nested cups, clear bottles, funnel, plastic pump, small boats, plastic fish, spray bottles, medicine droppers, turkey baster, sponge, egg beater, tongs, and clear plastic tubing.

Have a broom or vacuum cleaner, dustpan, mop, bucket, and sponge near the area so children can be responsible for cleaning up when finished. Playing clean-up is a fun activity for most young children and involves them in the care of the area.

Extensions: Food coloring to change the color of the water or sand, soap to add bubbles and foam to the water play, and ice cubes with plastic items frozen inside.

Long-Term and Special Centers

Traditional centers such as blocks and housekeeping can remain set up in the classroom throughout the year, while others take turns in the area for a short period. Special theme centers add interest to the classroom and expand opportunities for learning (Tables 3–1 and 3–2). Since centers are open-ended, they allow children of varying abilities to work together successfully. In the music center, two children are playing tambourines to accompany a 1960s recording. Summer, a child with Down syndrome, is tapping the tambourine with her hand. Ronda, her friend, is creating a rhythm pattern by rotating her hand and elbow to create the sounds on the tambourine. Summer and Ronda are creating music together in the center. Each child is working at her level of development and being successful in a musical experience.

Long-term Centers	Special Centers
Blocks	Construction/Carpentry
Art	Fitness
Housekeeping/Home Living	Sensory Exploration
Library/Literacy	Drama/Puppets
Private Places	Pizza Parlor
Music/Movement	Beach
Nature/Discovery	Hair Salon

Table 3–1 Suggested Centers for Preschool and Kindergarten

Long-Term Centers	Special Centers
Library/Literacy Center	Carpentry
Fitness Center	Drama Center
Discovery Center (Science and Math)	Projects/Theme Centers
Writing/Communications	Literature Related Centers
Math/Manipulatives	Inventor's Laboratory
Blocks/Construction	Art Activities

Table 3–2 Suggested Centers for Primary Classrooms

The Teacher's Role in Play

There are many different ways for teachers to encourage play. The teacher can provide options that match the activity of the children, their level of development, and their need for intervention.

Teacher As Planner

The teacher plans the environment so children will participate in play. He is knowledgeable of the background and experiences that the children in this classroom bring with them. This information provides ideas for centers, materials, and themes that build on children's unique interests and provide extension to their learning. The teacher designs the classroom space so that quiet activities are not placed next to the music center or other noisy areas. In planning, the teacher determines which objects and materials will stimulate play: a hard hat in the block area, fancy hats and purses for housekeeping, or a collection of different size balls for outdoor play (Isbell & Exelby, 2001).

Teacher As Observer

Observing children in their play is one of the most important roles of the teacher. Being attentive to the activity of the children, the language they are using, and the happenings in their play can provide a teacher with much information. It can help determine the interests of the children, materials that are working, and when assistance is needed. The teacher can observe the children's social, motor, and cognitive skills during meaningful activities. Annotations of these observations can provide a record of the child's involvement in play, language development, and ability to work with others. This information is more meaningful than results obtained from more formal methods of evaluation. These observations document the skills children are able to use rather than those they can perform on a test.

A teacher is recording her observations of children involved in play. (Photo by Michael Talley)

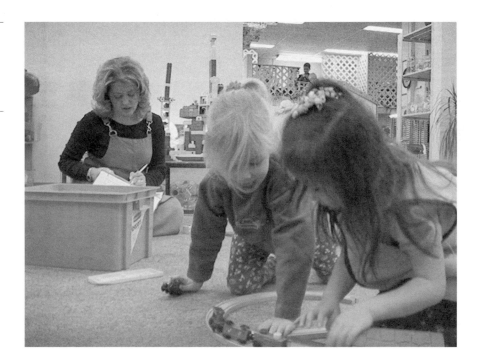

Teacher As Model

Sometimes, it is appropriate for a teacher to actively participate in the play and model a particular behavior. Some children seem to have difficulty moving into play. The teacher can assist the child in this process by assuming a minor role in the play. But the teacher should remove himself from the play once the activity is underway. Teachers must be careful not to take over play or insert personal interests in the activity. Follow the lead of the children and their focus.

Teacher As Mediator

When young children are playing, there will be conflicts and disagreements. Often, these disputes are left for the children to work out. Sometimes, however, there is concern and the teacher may need to intervene to support a peaceful solution. In this role, the teacher helps children in their problem-solving while maintaining a playful attitude. For example, in the greenhouse center, Louie and Sarah both want to be the clerk at the cash register who takes the money for the sales. Debate between the two children continues for a long period of time with no solution in sight. The teacher may enter the area and ask how they could work together to collect the money from the sales. "What are some of the different ways people may pay for the plants?" After some discussion, the children, guided by the teacher, decide that Louie will take the cash sales and Sarah will take the credit card purchases. They make a credit card machine from some wooden blocks and add some paper for the credit card receipts. Together, they run the sales collection for the greenhouse center.

Teacher As a Resource

A new role for the teacher is that of a resource person for the children's exploration. In order to nurture thinking and problem-solving, children need to learn how to find answers for themselves. The teacher can assist in their research by suggesting references, books, or friends they may ask. But the teacher should not provide immediate answers or take away a child's opportunity to learn how to find answers alone.

A first grader brings an abandoned bird's nest to be placed in the discovery center. Several children are interested in the nest and begin to question what kind of bird might have built it. The teacher suggests that they find a book in the classroom library that can help them find the answer. Or the teacher and the children might use the Internet to find information including pictures of different kinds of bird's nests. These examples demonstrate how teachers can be a resource for information instead of being the person with all the answers. Together, the teacher and children learn about birds and their nests.

Multicultural Considerations

Play is universal and has no national or cultural boundaries. It is central to the transmission of cultures and heritage of families. Play enables children to learn who they are and expand their view of the world. If appropriate materials are provided, children who have lived in the desert will bring this knowledge and experience into their play. A young child who lived in China will bring special interest and information into his play. Props from this culture will help Chinese children make connections in their play. It is important to help children explore their own cultural backgrounds and those of others by providing appropriate centers and play materials. Children from all cultures will benefit from having their experiences and understanding expanded through play.

Cultural and racial issues also can influence children's play. In today's world, teachers need to be sure that culturally diverse materials are available for children's play. Is diversity represented in the puppets, dolls, and dress-up clothing? Are there images of the major racial and ethnic groups seen in the classroom? Are there books in the play areas that include children of different races? Is there a balance of images of women and men doing jobs at home and jobs outside the home? For example, are there dress-up clothes for both men and women in the housekeeping center? Are elderly people from different backgrounds shown in recreational as well as work activities?

Sparks (1989) described the challenge for early childhood educators to increase the materials used in their classroom that show children and adults of many different colors, and persons of different ages engaged in nonstereotypical activities. An environment that includes many possibilities for exploring race and ethnicity, gender, and special needs provides the tools for practicing play.

Dramatic play should include:
- diversity of gender play. Rooms of the house other than the kitchen; male and female clothing; pictures of both males and females; and pictures and books that show a diversity of family composition.
- cultural diversity. Foods, cooking utensils, work tools, and items that reflect holiday celebrations from different cultures. Purchased or homemade dolls representing major ethnic groups, gender balance, and with different kinds of disabilities. Always begin with the diversity represented in your classroom and expand from there to other groups in the community.
- tools and equipment for people with special needs. Wheelchairs, walkers, braces, hearing aids, ramps, heavy glasses, books written in Braille, crutches, walking canes, magnifiers, and a respirator with mask.

Hardhats in the area inspire these girls to create a complex machine. (Photo by Michael Talley)

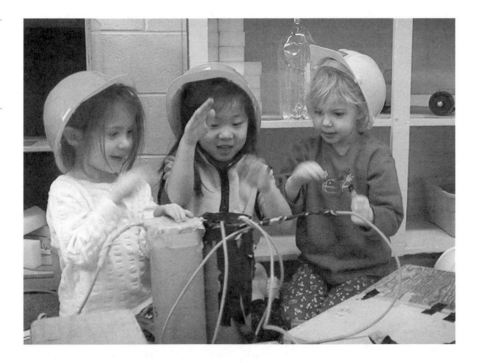

Children with Special Needs

Play provides a wonderful way for all children to interact. Because play is open-ended and self-selected, all children can feel successful in their participation and involvement. An inclusive environment encourages children to interact in play, communicate, and develop an appreciation for the strengths of a child who may look different or use an unusual piece of equipment.

A beautiful example of how this can occur was observed when Paulette, a four-year-old child who was deaf, was in an inclusive classroom. Paulette and Vera frequently played together during center time, and they became very good friends. Vera was indifferent to the fact that Paulette was deaf. When watching the girls play, it was difficult to identify any differences between them except that Paulette wore a sound amplifier around her neck. During the holidays, Vera received a doll as a gift. When she returned to school, her treasured doll had a small box strung around her neck. Vera said, "My doll is deaf, just like Paulette. Isn't she beautiful?"

Another example was observed in the housekeeping center. Three children were cooking dinner. One prepared the lasagna and another was making the salad. The child making the salad named the ingredients he was including such as lettuce, cheese, almonds, and tomatoes. Another child echoed the ingredients, "cheese and tomatoes." Although these children are at very different levels of language development, they interact and learn from the process. Each accepts the other's level of involvement and enjoys the participation.

Outdoor Play

There are many ways to extend play outdoors. Although there is a need for unstructured, active play, other possibilities also can be offered on the playground. Dramatic or sociodramatic play can be moved outdoors by providing the props and setting for this type of activity. A camping center or a farm can be created on the playground for the children to use as a theme in their play and dramatizations. A raised area with arena seating, made from logs or landscaping timbers, can become a stage for performances or dramatic productions. Moveable

Three children cooperate to use the tire swing. (Photo by Michael Talley)

parts encourage construction play that seems very different because it is done outdoors. Possible materials for construction include plastic milk crates, plastic blocks, wooden planks, pieces of plywood, plastic pipe with fittings, and cedar shingles. Riding toys, push-pull toys, and balls of varying sizes can encourage large motor activity and play.

A garden area can provide a place to plant, weed, and harvest a crop. Water and sand play also can move outdoors with an appropriate portable tub and the intriguing equipment that supports that play. It is helpful to view the playground and outdoor area as another place where play can occur.

Working with Parents

Play in a school setting differs from play at home. Helping parents understand the differences and how the two can complement each other can eliminate some concerns demonstrated in the phrase, "But they are just playing."

Play in the early childhood setting:
- provides a positive transition to the school environment.
- allows more opportunities for interaction with peers.
- makes available a wider variety of materials and equipment for play.
- enables adult-child interactions to facilitate and expand play.
- makes planning a central part of the play.
- provides more space for engaging in play and construction.

Home and school environments can foster different opportunities for children to learn social and cognitive skills. Play contributes to learning in both environments, and teachers can help parents understand and value the role of play in the early childhood environment (Brewer & Kieff, 1996).

Summary

Play has been discussed and studied for hundreds of years by philosophers, theorists, and researchers. The benefits have been recognized widely by researchers and teachers who have studied children engaged in play. They conclude that play encourages communication, cognition, social competencies, and creativity. The phrases "play is the child's work" and "children learn through play" have become widely used clichés. It is essential that early childhood educators be able to explain the benefits of play to parents and community. Although research and theories are helpful, the teacher must believe in the importance of play and be able to articulate the reasons for its inclusion in early childhood environments. The teacher must be able to prepare an environment that will nurture play, select materials appropriate for the classroom, and document the learning that occurs during the activity. Without the knowledge of "why," the "hows" cannot be put into practice or supported effectively. Play is an integral part of the early childhood tradition and it must be continued in the 21st century. Childhood play is timeless, powerful, and essential in a changing society.

Key Terms

play	sensory exploration
surplus energy theory	egocentric speculation
relaxation theory	personal experimentation
practice theory	social play
pleasure principle	unoccupied play
autocasmic play	onlooker play
microsphere play	solitary play
macrosphere play	parallel play
sensory-motor play	associative play
preoperational play	cooperative play
construction play	sociodramatic play
playfulness	learning centers

Reflection

1. Explain how the interest in play has changed over time.

2. How have different theorists interpreted the important influence of play on children's development?

3. What different types of play did Piaget identify in infants and young children?

4. How does language and interactions influence play in young children?

5. Identify the different types of social play.

6. What are some of the ways the environment can be designed to nurture children's play?

7. How would you support the inclusion of play in an early childhood program?

Thinking about the Creative Episode

1. How would you determine Niki's stage of cognitive development based on this creative episode?

2. What is the significance of the piece of fabric?

3. From this observation, what other play materials might be developmentally appropriate for Niki?

Possibilities for Adult Learners

Activity: Enriching Play

Goal: To evaluate a housekeeping center and determine how to improve the area.

Materials: These will vary, based on the needs of the specific center.

Procedure:

1. Visit an early childhood classroom that has a housekeeping center.

2. Evaluate the center as to its space, location, materials, and changing items.

3. Determine how the center could be improved.

4. Make a list of suggestions that can be shared in class.

Activity: Flexibility of Blocks

Goal: To record and analyze the language and interactions occurring in the block area.

Materials: Classroom with a well-equipped block area.

Procedure:

1. Visit a classroom that has a well-defined and equipped block area.

2. During block play, become an observer. Record or transcribe the children's play and language.

3. After leaving the area, review your notes, and refine your observations and language annotations.

4. Bring your written documentation to class.

5. Discuss the learning that is occurring in the block area with particular focus on interactions and language used by the players.

Activity:	Loose Parts Play
Goal:	To experience the play that can occur with a variety of loose parts.
Materials:	Cardboard boxes of different sizes and shapes, wooden blocks, hair rollers of varying sizes, pieces of plastic pipe, cardboard pieces, unusually shaped scraps of wood, milk cartons, plastic cups, twigs, and a camera (digital or instant preferred).

Procedure:

1. Divide the class into small groups of three to five people.

2. Give each group a box that includes a variety of materials.

3. Provide time for each group to construct something, using the materials in the box.

4. Take a picture of each construction and display the photos with the names of the players in the group.

5. Ask the students to describe the play activity.

Open-ended Activities for Young Children

Pre-K–K

Activity:	Multicultural Prop Box
Goal:	To provide materials that will extend the play of children by adding items from their culture or the culture of the community.
Materials:	These will vary, depending on the community in which the children live.

Procedure:

1. Review the backgrounds and experiences of the young children in the classroom.

2. Determine specific toys, props, materials, or books that relate to the cultures of those represented in the classroom or the community.

3. Add selected items to the housekeeping area, dramatic play area, or other centers.

4. Observe the children's play.

5. Talk with the children about the new props that have been added to the play areas.

Primary Grades

Activity:	Dramatic Center: Chinese Home (Developed by Bei Zhou)

Goals: It is useful to enrich the play opportunities of children as they learn to appreciate a culture (this center works well in a classroom where Chinese children and their families participate).

1. To promote understanding and appreciation for another culture.

2. To develop the children's language and vocabulary.

3. To expand knowledge of different foods and their preparation.

4. To experience music and art from another culture.

Vocabulary: Can be used during a discussion about the new center in the classroom.

- China
- traditional
- fans

- bamboo square pillows
- Chinese traditional painting
- calligraphy
- vase
- tea set
- Buddah
- steamed rice
- dumplings
- Jasmine tea

- chopsticks
- potted landscapes
- *zhao shang hao* (good morning) pronounced: sow chien how
- *ni hao* (hello) pronounced: knee how
- *xie xie* (thank you) pronounced: shay shay
- *qing* (please) pronounced: ching
- *yi* (one) pronounced: e
- *er* (two) pronounced: all
- *san* (three) pronunced: san
- *si* (four) pronounced; szz
- *wu* (five) pronounced: woo

Introduction to the Center

1. Read stories about people from China, their history, the Great Wall, panda bears, and the like.

2. Locate China on the globe and make a cutout map of the country.

3. Discuss and display pictures of China and its people.

4. Show filmstrips and videos of the land and culture.

5. Demonstrate chopsticks and add them to the center.

6. Discuss the vocabulary through experience and songs.

Teacher-collected Props

Plates, tea set, bamboo chair set, chopsticks, square bamboo pillow, Chinese vase, traditional Chinese painting or calligraphy for the wall of the center, tape player, recordings of traditional Chinese music, and paper cuttings for window decoration.

Literacy Extensions

1. Calendar showing Chinese characters and English symbols.

2. Writing activity with Chinese characters that children can imitate.

3. Experience chart that follows a visit to a Chinese restaurant.

4. A "thank you" note to the resource person or restaurant owner who visits the classroom.

5. Collection of books about China and its people to add to the center.

Connection to the Arts in the Chinese Center

1. Tissue paper for folding and making fans or flowers.

2. Music from the Chinese culture.

3. Fans that can be made from paper and used while dancing to Chinese music.

4. Moving to Chinese music.

Field Trips and Resource People

1. Visit a Chinese restaurant.

2. Invite a parent, friend, or someone who knows about China or has visited China to the classroom.

Resource Books about China

Feinstein, S., & Moore, J. (1989). *China in pictures.* Minneapolis, MN: Lerner Publications.
Describes the topography, history, society, economy, and government of China.

Flack, M. (1933). *The story about Ping.* New York: The Viking Press.
A little duck finds adventure on the Yangtze River when he is too late to board his master's houseboat one evening.

Haskins, J., & Hockerman, D. (1987). *Count your way through China.* Minneapolis, MN: Carolrhoda Books.
Presents the numbers one through 10 in Chinese, using each number to introduce concepts about China and Chinese culture.

Krach, M. S., & Zhang, H. (1997). *D is for Doufu: An alphabet book of Chinese culture.* Arcadia, CA: Shen's Books.
An alphabet book that explores the beauty and richness of the Chinese culture.

Lin, G. (1999). *The ugly vegetables.* Watertown, MA; Charlesbridge.
A little girl thinks her mother's garden is the ugliest in the neighborhood until she discovers that flowers might smell pretty but Chinese vegetable soup smells best of all. Includes a recipe.

Notes

[1]Piaget, J. (1961). *Play, dreams and imagination in childhood.* New York: Norton.
[2]Author unknown.
[3]Cherry, C. (1976). *Creative play for the developing child.* Belmont, CA: David S. Lake Publishers.

References

Balke, E. (1997). Play and the arts: The importance of the "unimportant." *Childhood Education, 73*(6), 355–361.
Barnett, L. A. (1990). Playfulness: Definition, design and measurement. *Play and Culture, 3*, 319–336.
Berk, L. E. (1994). Vygotsky's theory: The importance of make-believe play. *Young Children, 50*(1), 30–39.
Boyer, W. A. R. (1997). Playfulness enhancement through classroom intervention for the 21st century. *Childhood Education, 74*(2), 90–97.

Bredekamp, S., & Copple, C. (1997). *Developmentally appropriate practice in early childhood programs.* Washington, DC: National Association for the Education of Young Children.

Brewer, J. A., & Kieff, J. (1996). Fostering mutual respect for play at home and school. *Childhood Education, 73*(2), 92–97.

Brosterman, N. (1997). Child's play. *Art in America, 85*(4), 108–112.

Dodge, D. T. (1988). *The creative curriculum.* Washington, DC: Teaching Strategies.

Elkind, D. (1987). *Miseducation: Preschoolers at risk.* New York: Alfred A. Knopf.

Erikson, E. (1950). *Childhood and society.* New York: Norton.

Feitelson, D. (1972). Cross-cultural studies in representational play. In B. Tizard & D. Harvey (Eds.), *Biology of play* (pp. 6–14). Philadelphia, PA: Lippincott.

Freud, S. (1963). *A general introduction to psychoanalysis.* New York: Simon & Schuster Books.

Froebel, F. (1887). *The education of man.* New York: D. Appleton.

Frost, J. L., & Kein, B. L. (1983). *Children's play and playgrounds.* Austin, TX: Playscapes International.

Frost, J. L. (1998, June). *Neuroscience, play and child development.* Paper presented at the IPA/USA Triennial National Conference, Logmont, CO.

Gehlbach, R. D. (1991). Play, Piaget, and creativity: The promise of design. *Journal of Creative Behavior, 25*(2), 137–144.

Gross, K. (1916). *The play of man.* New York: D. Appleton.

Hughes, F. P. (1999). *Children, play, and development.* Boston: Allyn and Bacon.

Isbell, R., & Exelby, B. (2001). *Learning environments for young children that work.* Beltsville, MD: Gryphon House.

Isbell, R. T., & Raines, S. (1991). Young children's oral language productions in three types of play centers. *Journal of Research in Childhood Education, 5*(2), 140-146.

Isbell, R., & Raines, S. (1994). *Stories: Children's literature in early education.* Clifton Park, NY: Delmar Learning.

Isbell, R. (1995). *The complete learning center book.* Beltsville, MD: Gryphon House.

Isenberg, J. P., & Jalongo, M. R. (1997). *Creative expression and play in the early childhood.* Upper Saddle River, NJ: Merrill.

Iwanaga, M. (1973). Development of interpersonal play structure in three-, four-, and five-year-old children. *Journal of Research and Development in Education, 6*(3), 71–82.

Kieff, J., & Casberque, R. M. (2000). *Playful learning and teaching.* Needham Heights, MA: Allyn & Bacon.

King, N. (1979). Play: The kindergartner's perspective. *Elementary School Journal, 80*, 81–87.

Lewis, H. (1974). *The relationship between sociodramatic play and cognitive performance of five year old children.* Unpublished doctoral dissertation, Ohio State University.

Lieberman, J. N. (1966). Playfulness and divergent thinking: An investigation of their relationship at the kindergarten level. *Journal of Genetic Psychology, 107*, 219–224.

Montessori, M. (1964). *The advanced Montessori method.* Cambridge, MA: R. Bentley.

Nourot, P. M., & Van Hoorn, J. L. (1991). Symbolic play in preschool and primary settings. *Young Children, 46*(6), 40–50.

Parten, M. (1932). Social participation among preschool children. *Journal of Abnormal and Social Psychology, 27*(2), 143–269.

Patrick, G. T. W. (1916). *The psychology of relaxation.* New York: Houghton Mifflin.

Pellegrini, A. D., & Boyd, B. (1993). The role of play in early childhood development and education: Issues in definition and function. In B. Spodex (Ed.), *Handbook of research on education of young children* (pp. 105–121). New York: MacMillan Publishing Company.

Pellegrini, A. (1996). *Observing children in their natural worlds: A primer in observational methods.* Hillsdale, NJ: Lawrence Erlbaum Associates.

Piaget, J. (1961). *Play, dreams and imagination in childhood.* New York: Norton.

Quinn, J. M., & Rubin, K. H. (1984). The play of handicapped children. In T. Yawkey & A. Pellegrini (Eds.), *Child's play: Developmental and applied* (pp. 63–80). Hillsdale, NJ: Lawrence Erlbaum Associates.

Rousseau, J. J. (1911). *Emile, or on education.* London: Dent.

Russ, S. (1996). Development of creative process in children. *New Directions for Child Development, 72*, 31–42.

Shore, R. (1997). *Rethinking the brain: New insights into early development.* New York: Families and Work Institute.

Singer, J. L., & Singer, D. L. (1976). Imaginative play and pretending in early childhood. In A. Davids (Ed.), *Child personality and psychopathology* (pp. 142–169). New York: Wiley.

Smilansky, S. (1968). *The effects of sociodramatic play on disadvantaged preschool children.* New York: Wiley.

Smilansky, S. (1990). Sociodramatic play. Its relevance to behavior and achievement in school. In E. Klugman & S. Smilansky, (Eds.), *Children's play and learning* (pp 18–42). New York: Teachers College Press.

Smilansky, S., & Feldman, N. (1980). *Relationship between sociodramatic play in kindergarten and scholastic achievement in second grade.* Tel-Aviv: Tel-Aviv University, Department of Psychology.

Sparks, L. D. (1989). *Anti-bias curriculum: Tools for empowering young children.* Washington, DC: National Association for the Education of Young Children.

Spencer, H. (1896). *Principles of Psychology.* New York: D. Appleton.

Sutton-Smith, B. (Ed.). (1979). *Play and learning.* New York: Gardner Press.

Vygotsky, L. S. (1976). Play and its role in the mental development of the child. In A. J. Bruner, & T. S. Sylva (Eds.), *Play: Its role in development and evolution* (pp. 537–554). New York: Basic Books.

Vygotsky, L. S. (1978). The role of play in development. In M. Cole, V. John-Steiner, S. Scribner, & E. Souberman (Eds.), *Mind in society* (pp. 92–104). Cambridge, MA: Harvard University Press.

Additional Reading

Adcock, D., & Segal, M. (1983). *Play together grow together: A cooperative curriculum for teachers of young children.* White Plains, NY: The Mailman Family Press.

Casey, M. B., & Lippman, M. (1991). Learning to plan through play. *Young Children, 46*(4), 52–57.

Cecil, L. M., McPhail, G., Thornburg, K. R., & Ispa, J. (1985). Curiosity-exploration-play-creativity: The early childhood mosaic. *Early Child Development and Care, 19*, 199–217.

Chafel, J. A. (1991). The play of children: Developmental process and policy implications. *Child & Youth Care Forum, 20*(2), 115–133.

Chaille, C., & Solvern, S. B. (1996). Understanding through play. *Childhood Education, 75*(5), 274–277.

Drew, W. F. (1992). Let's play with our children! *Child Care Information Exchange, 85*, 36–40.

Eddowes, E. A. (1991). The benefits of solitary play. *Dimensions of Early Childhood, 21*(1), 31–34.

Fein, G. C. (1979). Echoes from the nursery: Piaget, Vygotsky, and the relationship between language and play. *New Directions for Child Development, 6*, 1–14.

Ferguson, C. (1999). Building literacy with child-constructed sociodramatic play centers. *Dimensions of Early Childhood, 27*(3), 23–29.

Goldhaber, J. (1994). If we call it science, then can we let children play? *Childhood Education, 71*(1), 24–28.

Jones, E., & Reynolds, G. (1992). *The play's the thing: The teacher's roles in children's play.* New York: Teachers College Press.

Klugman, E., & Smilansky, S. (Eds.). (1990). *Children's play and learning: Perspectives and policy implications.* New York: Teachers College Press.

Lewis, R. (1997). With a marble and a telescope: Searching for play. *Childhood Education, 73*(6), 346–350.

Miller, K. (1989). *The outside play and learning book: Activities for young children.* Mt. Rainer, MD: Gryphon House.

Morrison, G. S., & Rusher, A. S. (1999). Playing to learn. *Dimensions of Early Childhood, 27*(2), 3–8.

Nowak-Fabrykowski, K. (1994). Can symbolic play prepare children for their future? *Early Childhood Development and Care, 102*, 63–69.

Owocki, G. (1999). *Literacy through play.* Portsmouth, NH: Heinemann.

Smith, D. (1995). How play influences children's development at home and school. *The Journal of Physical Education, Recreation, and Dance, 66*(8), 19–24.

Wassermann, S. (1992). Serious play in the classroom: How messing around can win you the Nobel Prize. *Childhood Education, 68*(3), 133–139.

Children's Literature Connection

Blos, J. W. (1984). *Martin's hats.* New York: William Morrow and Company.
A variety of hats affords Martin many adventures. (Pre-K–K)

Moss, M. (1990). *Want to play?* Boston: Houghton Mifflin Company.
Two toddlers experience the frustrations of learning to share their toys. (Pre-K–K)

Rockwell, A., & Rockwell, H. (1981). *I play in my room.* Middletown, CT: Field Publications.
A young girl describes her activities and toys as she plays in her room. (Pre-K–K)

Russo, M. (1986). *The line up book.* New York: Greenwillow Books.
Sam lines up blocks, books, boots, cars, and other objects, all the way from his room to his mother in the kitchen. (Pre-K–K)

Siddals, M. M. (2000). *I'll play with you.* New York: Clarion Books.
A child asks the sun, wind, clouds, rain, stars, and moon to play. (Pre-K)

Thaler, M. (1974). *How far will a rubber band stretch?* New York: Parents' Magazine Press.
A little boy decides to find out how far a rubber band will stretch. (Pre-K–1)

Ziefert, H. (1988). *Chocolate mud cake.* New York: Harper and Row.
Molly and her little sister, Jenny, bake a make-believe cake out of mud, twigs, and berries when they spend an afternoon at their grandparents' house. (Pre-K–K)

Helpful Web Sites

The addresses and corresponding agencies below are taken from the Web sites. Due to the dynamic nature of the Internet, please remember that Web sites are subject to change at any time.

http://www.galstar.com/~davii/ImportanceofPlay.html   The Importance of Play in Early Childhood Education.

http://www.ncb.org.uk/cpc.htm   The Children's Play Council of the National Children's Bureau in Britain—Raises awareness of the importance of play in children's lives, and the need for all children to have access to better play opportunities and play services.

http://www.pta.org/programs/education/build2.htm   The National PTA's Building Blocks: Importance of Children's Play—A collection of information on child's play characteristics by age and how children are learning a variety of important skills through various types of play activities.

http://www.ipausa.org   The International Play Association (IPA)—Persons of all professions working for and with children.

 For additional resources involving creativity and the arts with young children, visit our Web site at http://www.earlychilded.delmar.com

Chapter 4

The Many Forms of Art

This chapter provides a foundation for understanding the artistic development of young children. Understanding the variety of materials available and the many creative possibilities that exist in the area of the visual arts will be the focus.

Creative Episode

Jessica goes to the art center and observes the activities that are going on in the area. She decides to work with "real" clay, the type potters use in art studios. She takes a plastic tray to the garbage pail containing a large amount of gray clay. She pulls, digs, and finally takes a plastic knife to chisel away a piece of clay the size she wants.

Jessica begins to experiment with the clay. She squeezes it with her hands, pounds it flat, and folds it into pieces. When the clay becomes dry to her touch, she goes to the sink and gets water in a small plastic bowl. She returns to the table where she adds a small amount of water to the stiff clay. She continues to experiment with the changes she creates: wet, smooth, and flexible. Next, she begins to punch holes in the clay with her fingers. She carefully adds water to each of the holes. She pulls the wet clay, full of holes, off the tray. She notices the difference in the depth of the holes and the amount of water they contain. She pounds the clay flat and punches more holes to determine their depth and the amount of water each can contain.

Now the clay becomes very wet and will not hold the shape of the holes. Jessica takes the tray and the wet clay to the container where it was stored. She returns the clay to the pail and carefully washes the tray. She goes to the table and wipes off the area where she worked.

Jessica is five-and-a-half years of age. She worked with clay for over 45 minutes. During this time, she worked independently and was focused intently on her work. She experimented with clay, learning about the properties of the substance. Jessica experienced art in a meaningful way.

Artistic Terms

Color: Primary and secondary hues created by light and pigments.

Composition: Arrangement of the design and space.

Form: Three-dimensional quality that includes height, width, and depth.

Line: A mark made by using a tool across a surface (can be vertical, horizontal, diagonal, or curved).

Pattern: The repeat of design, lines, or shapes in the artwork.

Perspective: Point of view created by techniques such as size and overlapping.

Shape: Configuration, contours, or outline.

Texture: The way an object feels or how the grain might feel when touched.

Art is Basic

Art is a basic component in early childhood education. This important area must be carefully designed during the early years to enhance children's artistic development and nurture an appreciation for beauty in their world. Art is rec-

Little hands can manipulate clay. (Photo by Michael Talley)

ognized as both a fundamental and distinctive way of knowing. Art is an important nonverbal language; a system of symbols that emerge from children's drawings. Appropriate early artistic experiences assist children in finding meaning about themselves and their world. Art enriches the lives of all children, not just a talented few. However, art should not be valued simply because of the benefits to learning. According to Fox and Diffily (2000), "Children's art has value in and of itself" (p. 5).

Theories Related to Art

There are several theories that provide insight into the artistic development of children. These theories provide understanding of how children grow artistically and identify factors that relate to this development. Although theories can assist in understanding complex phenomena, they also provide a framework for observation and reflection of the developing child.

Constructivist Theory of Art Development

The constructivist theory is drawn from the work of Jean Piaget and Lev Vygotsky. Although differences exist between these theorists, their writings have had a tremendous impact on the fields of early childhood and child psychology. This cognitive theory describes learning as a process that is influenced by children's level of thinking as they interact with the world around them. Children develop schema to organize their experiences while interacting with their environment. According to the constructivist theory, children develop through hierarchical stages and proceed in a predictable pattern. Children are recognized as powerful forces, influencing and shaping their own learning. In a constructivist environment, materials and activities are selected to encourage children's participation with little direction by the teacher. Children are encouraged to follow individual interests, make choices, and combine materials in their own way.

Vygotsky placed emphasis on the role of adults and peers in the scaffolding of children's learning experiences. He believed interactions in the zone of proximal development were helpful and assisted children in moving to higher levels of understanding. This social constructivist interpretation of the learning process could influence directly the teacher's involvement in the art program. In this environment, there is more opportunity for group and partner work. The teacher, as facilitator, poses questions, serves as a resource, and provides materials to assist the developing artist.

In the area of art, Lowenfeld and Brittain (1987) identified specific stages that occur during the artistic development of the child. These stages directly correspond to levels identified in the cognitive developmental theory. Producing art requires children to think of an experience, idea, or feeling, and construct symbols to represent or express what they know. Art is a highly symbolic activity; a form of cognitive expression (Seefeldt, 1995).

A Way of Expressing Feeling

The psychoanalytic theory describes art as a way for children to express deep feelings and emotions. Art is viewed as an emotional outlet that allows the child to release inner feelings. Proponents of this theory see children's art as an avenue for understanding their emotional workings. In times of crisis or emotional turmoil, children's drawings have been used to identify a child's true feelings about an event. Art therapists, who are highly trained professionals, use children's artwork to interpret feelings and suggest possible interventions.

Visual Perception

The **perceptual theory** is based on the assumption that children draw what they see. Supporters of this view assert that children see things in wholes as the brain structures images. Perceptual theorists believe that children can improve visual discrimination, if given appropriate opportunities. Using this theory as a base, perceptual theorists believe children can become better observers when guided to focus on specific features.

Left Brain-Right Brain

Recent studies on brain development have lead to discussions about the operation of the left and right hemispheres of the brain. It is believed that the **left hemisphere** specializes in logical operations whereas the **right hemisphere** is the visual-spatial portion of the brain. Creative thinking and producing require the child to move out of logical operations (left hemisphere) to experiment with new ways of thinking (right hemisphere). Some believe art activities can serve as a bridge for interactions between the two hemispheres. This also can be accomplished by integrating various aspects of the curriculum to include a variety of activities requiring the child to think in different ways. Integrated curriculum, that includes both content areas and the arts, is believed to provide activity for multiple portions of the brain.

Spatial Intelligence: Another Way of Knowing

Gardner (1983), in his theory of multiple intelligences, identified one of the areas as spatial intelligence. Individuals with spatial intelligence have the capacity to perceive the visual-spatial world accurately and use this knowledge when creating. Such individuals are often sensitive to color, line, shape, form, space, and the relationship between each. Gardner wrote that the right hemisphere is involved in both spatial tasks and the processing of information that relates to that area. Painters, sculptors, and architects demonstrate spatial intelligence in their work and products.

Gardner's writings have stimulated new interest in the arts and their importance in the development of children. The theory of multiple intelligences recognizes that children may be talented in specific areas and learn in different ways. For some children, art may be the way they learn best; for others, it may be a new way to experience the world. An environment that attempts to nurture all children recognizes the importance of these different dimensions of intelligence.

Use of Theories

Theories can provide new ways to understand the art of young children. However, it is important to remember that theories do not tell teachers how to develop an art education program for young children. Instead, they may help teachers learn how to recognize the factors that may be important in the artistic process. This theoretical knowledge can assist teachers, caregivers, and parents in creating art programs that are consistent with what we know about how children learn.

Stages of Artistic Development

Young children experience objects and materials in different ways as they progress through the levels of artistic development (Kellogg, 1969). A description of these stages can assist teachers as they work with young children and observe them in the area of art. Although there is a predictable pattern to their development, children move through the levels in different ways and at their own pace. These stages of development provide guidelines for planning for a specific group of young children. These experiences should include open-ended opportunities so individual variations can occur.

The developmental stages of particular interest to early childhood educators are the **scribble stage**, **basic form stage**, and the **pictorial stage**. It is important to remember that children at each stage of development can produce art. The scribble stage is the first step in the artistic developmental process. The toddlers' scribble art is just as important as the primary age child's drawings that may include a more complex picture. Positive support for the young child's beginning artistic efforts can provide a strong foundation for later development and enjoyment of artistic experiences. In the next section, the stages of artistic development will be discussed in further detail.

Scribble Stage (1–2 Years of Age)

Uncontrolled Scribble.   During the first two years of life, most young children are in the scribble stage of artistic development. Toddlers' first marks are uncontrolled, and made on paper, walls, or in sand. They use any tool that is available in their environment: crayons, markers, or sticks. They show little concern for the final product and instead are focused on making random marks. Since small motor development is not refined, motions in the scribble stage are large and often involve the entire body. They find that the materials they use are as interesting as the scribbles they produce. For example, toddlers are totally involved in sensory experiences as they feel, smell, and examine the physical properties of paint.

Controlled Scribble.   As toddlers move from the **uncontrolled scribble** stage to **controlled scribbles**, they begin to establish a connection between their actions and the marks produced on paper. They understand that they are creating an interesting scribble mark on the page. This awareness of cause and effect helps them move into using a more controlled scribble. Children begin to experiment with the different marks they can produce such as lines, zigzags, circles, and suns. This new ability—to control the scribble—is exciting to young children as they focus intently on their creations. Because their movements are still large, toddlers need large blank sheets of paper, and crayons or magic markers that do not restrict their motion.

> *"From the moment the child discovers what it looks like and feels like to put lines down on paper, he has found something he will never lose, he has found art."*
>
> **R. Kellogg, 1969[2]**

Uncontrolled scribble art—
age 2.1 years

Uncontrolled scribble art—
age 2.0 years

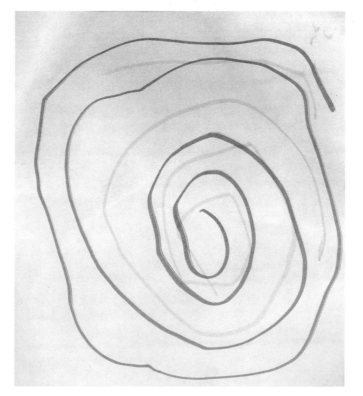

Controlled scribble art—
age 2.9 years.

Controlled scribble art—
age 3.4 years.

Basic Forms Stage (3–4 Years of Age)

In this stage, children's drawings begin to exhibit some form and organization. As preschoolers begin to develop better eye-hand coordination, they are able to make shapes and control their placement on the page. They begin to repeat patterns, often filling a page with similar forms. Although this usually occurs during the third and fourth year of a child's life, it can vary from child to child. Young children are very pleased with the shapes they produce and enjoy the process used to obtain these designs.

As young children gain more control of tools, they begin to produce basic forms and lines. It is important for them to have quality tools in this stage of development. Good tools support their growing artistic abilities and provide opportunities for successful experiences. Appropriate art tools for this stage include felt markers, crayons, colored chalk, paint brushes, and tempera paint.

Some of the first forms drawn by young children are ovals and circles. They also begin to make curved lines and arches. Later, more complex forms such as rectangles and squares are added to their creations. Although the forms appear to be simple and similar among young children, they represent more refined control of their hands and the materials they are using.

Basic forms—age 3.4
years.

Representational Art

Preschematic Stage (approximately 4–7 years of age). In the **preschematic stage** of development, children begin to use symbols in their work. However, these symbols may not clearly approximate the objects they represent. Their "first pictures" are seen in this stage as children draw a variety of forms and combine them into simple compositions. They move from the totally sensory experience to using symbols to represent their world. This symbolic representation establishes a new relationship between their artwork and the ideas they wish to express. Being able to think about something not present and find a way to represent it is a major cognitive accomplishment (Raines & Canady, 1990).

Often, the first symbol used in the pictorial stage is a person, composed of a round head and lines for legs. Young children also combine other basic symbols from previous drawings to represent important things in their environment. For example, a tree is composed of a circle and lines. A house is a triangle with two extra lines. As children attach meaning to their symbols, they frequently name the objects included in their pictures. They can name or label their drawings, using words to describe their symbolic representation. They continue to draw as they see things from their own perspective. This is demonstrated by the drawing of their family outside their home. The picture includes all of the family members, but the largest person in the drawing is the child.

Self-portrait—age 3.2 years.

Self-portrait—age 4.3 years.

Schematic Stage (approximately 7–9 years of age). After a great deal of experimentation with materials and tools, children move into the **schematic stage** of development. In this stage, children continue to develop symbols for their world, but the representations they use are more refined. Some children are concerned about the elements looking realistic. Their drawings are more individualized with the development of specific symbols to consistently represent objects in a

Schematic art—age 8.0 years.

unique way. Children are beginning to understand space relationships and experiment with the placement of objects on the page.

As children's drawing becomes more representational and detailed, more refined tools are needed. These tools provide the control children need to create features and details in their work. Thinner paint brushes, a wider ranges of colors, and rounded markers make creating the more detailed pictures more appropriate in the child's eye.

Beginning Realism (approximately 9–12 years of age). During the primary grades, children become concerned about **realism** in their art. Many children express the desire for their drawings to look real or like a photograph. Children are interested in size, proportion, placement, shape, color, and perspective. In the representational drawings of early elementary-aged children, the meaning of the figures becomes specific. The development of a unique picture is now replaced by the collective understanding of what is good and right in the drawing. Gardner (1980) stated that during this period, there is a loss of freedom, individuality, and creativity once apparent in the drawings of younger children.

Variations in Artistic Development

It is important to remember that although there are common characteristics during the periods of artistic development, there also are individual variations. Children in the same stage of development or even the same chronological age will vary significantly in the art they produce. For example, look at the work of three five-year-old children who are in kindergarten. Notice the differences in their work and their ability to produce a picture.

Variations in the artistic development of three five-year-old children.

"As we were walking, talking about nature, I asked a question and you threw up your hands and said I don't know, as a bird flew by."

Variations in the artistic development of three five-year-old children.

Principles of an Art Program for Young Children

In the early years of a child's education, certain principles should influence the development of the art program. These important beliefs provide the foundation for creating a developmentally appropriate art curriculum during the early childhood years. Each of these concepts will be identified and discussed to provide the framework for program development.

Provide Appropriate and Varied Experiences

It is the role of the teacher to provide a variety of materials and tools that challenge children to experiment and discover ways of expression in a visual form. Variation in activities, materials, and tools encourage children to experiment and learn about the artistic possibilities available in the classroom. Diverse materials allow children to think in divergent ways, and the possibilities for combinations and creations are increased. This experimentation should be encouraged and supported at all levels of development.

Process Versus Product

During the first five years of life, most children are more interested in the **process** of creation than in the **product**. At this time, the focus of art should be on participation and enjoyment of interesting art experiences. This means there may not be a product to display or take home. For example, a painting may go through many beautiful transformations as the child continues to add color, until the large paper is covered with a mass of brown paint. This is appropriate for the young child who has never worked with tempera paint or experimented with color. Children should not be bound to produce a picture to take home, a craft, or a gift. The creation process is far more important and essential at this stage of development than the product the child creates.

The creative process begins while exploring and playing with tools and materials. After many experiences, children move to the next step by focusing on a particular approach. Once an approach is chosen, children will use this method in the production stage. The fourth step is often stopping, evaluating, or re-working. It is difficult to pinpoint when one step ends and another begins in the visual arts. The very young child often spends more time in the exploratory step whereas the more experienced child may spend more time at the production level. Each step is intertwined and important for the developing child.

During later periods of artistic development, or for specific in-depth projects, children may want a product that meets their expectations. This may require that they revisit and rework their creations until they meet their expectations. It is important to note that it should be the child's desire to refine the product, not the teacher's. The observant teacher will recognize when the child wants to create a product that meets her expectations. When this need is recognized, a teacher should provide time and support for the child to continue the process.

Conformity or Originality

When children first use art materials, they often observe how others are using the items. For example, Ben may observe how Catherine is using the sponge to produce a print. He then tries the same sponge technique. This is an appropriate

> *"The key is access: access to a range of working spaces, access to materials, access to other kids and other adults; these in turn give students access to their own creative processes."*
>
> **R. S. Hubbard, 1996[3]**

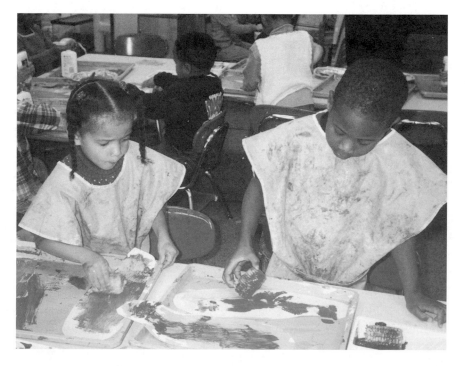

Painting with a new tool—a corncob. (Photo by Amy Carmichael)

The creation of a mural—
beginning. (Photo by Amy
Carmichael)

The creation of a mural—
continuation. (Photo by Amy
Carmichael)

way for a child to discover how a new tool is used or to expand on what she already knows. Accepting these shared experiences as effective ways of learning allows the teacher to see beyond what may look like sameness. Vygotsky helped us understand the value of children learning from each other and the benefits of these social interactions.

During the process of artistic development, it is important to encourage, value, and display original ideas. For example, unique ways of combining materials or making things in special ways helps children venture beyond the constraints of conformity. When this occurs, children will come to understand that thinking in divergent ways is valued and accepted in this environment.

Art Belongs to the Child

Art is a personal way of communicating and provides the child with a way to express unique ideas. A respect for the personal nature of the child's artwork means the teacher does not direct the process, but allows the child to proceed and experiment in the way she deems appropriate. The child is able to create and combine materials in ways that the teacher may have never imagined. During this process, the teacher may use questions to assist the child in thinking of new possibilities or techniques.

A Climate of Acceptance

An environment that nurtures artistic exploration is psychologically safe. It is a classroom where the teacher supports the children's creative efforts. Children know their ideas will be respected in this environment. The teacher models acceptance as she comments on the unique way that Marian is making wavy lines using the pastry brush. These small experiences help children understand that their work is special and will be valued.

Providing Role Models

When children see adults working creatively, they begin to understand that it is an important activity that grown-up people do. They observe that it gives the artist joy and satisfaction. They can see work in different stages of progress before the finished product is achieved.

Role models can be professional artists or individuals who have hobbies that relate to art. Visitors can bring their artwork into the classroom, or the children may go to a studio or museum to watch the artist work. The most influential role model is the classroom teacher. Through the teacher's efforts, even when she is not a professional artist, children learn that art activities are worth-while, pleasurable, and important (Dixon & Chalmers, 1990).

Art Education

In the field of **art education**, there are specific curriculum goals and standards that have been established by professional organizations. The National Art Education Association has identified these goals as creating, understanding, and appreciating. Art educators, who have specialized training related to the content of art, have provided new elements that should be examined to enrich the art program for young children.

In a National Art Education Association publication, Colbert and Taunton (1992) identified three major components of a quality, developmentally appropriate, art program for young children.

1. Young children need many opportunities to create art.

2. Young children need many opportunities to look at and talk about art.

3. Young children need to become aware of art in their everyday lives.

In the past, the primary focus of art in early childhood programs was creating. Although producing art remains a major component of the art curriculum during the early childhood years, the offerings are now being expanded to include experiences with great works of art. These experiences provide opportunities for children to develop personal preferences and share their opinion of art. Young children can recognize and appreciate artistic effort, and the work of the men, women, and children who create art. Although art historians are interested in artistic categories, styles, and movements, early childhood educators focus on expanding the concepts of art and developing an appreciation of artistic form.

Fourth graders' still life drawings using chalk. (Photo by Michael Talley)

It is challenging for teachers to design programs that include appreciation and creativity, follow the interests of the child, and are integrated across curriculum areas. Objectives for the integration of art might include the following.

1. Construct an understanding of art as a means of community.

2. Develop a view of themselves as artists who are capable of self-expression.

3. Discover the joy of art appreciation and creation through participation in self-selected art activities (Fox & Diffily, 2000).

The following lesson plan (Figure 4–1) demonstrates an art appreciation activity implemented among four-year-old children in a preschool classroom.

Goals

1. To introduce the idea of an artist as a profession.

2. To examine the concept of a gallery and studio.

3. To introduce the work of an artist.

4. To introduce the concept of art perceptions (we can see and feel something different when we look at a painting).

5. To discover that art is an expression of feelings.

6. To promote awareness of one's own feelings.

7. To integrate movement and/or music experiences with art.

8. To develop language skills.

9. To promote interest in reading, through the use of literature.

Objectives

1. Experience paintings by Georgia O'Keeffe.

2. Listen to stories and answer comprehension questions.

3. Express how she feels.

4. Participate in movement experiences to promote gross motor skills.

5. Describe, compare, and contrast paintings.

6. Express preference for paintings by selecting a favorite Georgia O'Keeffe painting.

7. Express thoughts and understandings about Georgia O'Keeffe's paintings.

Materials

1. Posters of Georgia O'Keeffe paintings.

2. One small O'Keeffe painting for each child (taken from old calendars).

Figure 4–1 Introductory art unit lesson plan for four- and five-year-olds. (Developed by Amy Carmichael)

Figure 4–1   Continued

3. *Today I Feel Silly* (1998) by Jamie Lee Curtis.

4. *The Perfect Spot* (1997) by Robert J. Blake.

5. Georgia O'Keeffe books.

Procedure

1. Ask if anyone has been to an art gallery. Explain that artists are professionals, and make their living by creating and selling art. The teacher will share her own love and appreciation for art.

2. Sing the song, "If You're Happy and You Know It." The teacher will explain that "happy" is a feeling. Then she will ask the children to name some other feelings.

3. The teacher will read *Today I Feel Silly*. Following the book reading, the teacher will ask the children how they feel, explaining that all feelings are okay.

4. The teacher will ask how we can let people know what we are feeling. She will explain that some artists let people know how they are feeling through their art.

5. The teacher will show three examples of paintings by Georgia O'Keeffe and briefly share background information about the painter's life.

6. The teacher will ask the children how they think the painter felt when she painted the different paintings.

7. The children will share which of the three paintings is their favorite.

8. The teacher will give each child a small print of an O'Keeffe painting. She will ask the children several high-order thinking questions such as, "Why do you think the artist chose this subject?" "Why did she use these colors?" "How does the painting make you feel?" "Are the subjects big or small?"

9. The teacher will ask each child to come to the front of the circle, hold up the picture, and say one thing about the painting. The teacher will invite children to express their ideas about the abstract paintings such as, "what do they think it is?" "Why?"

10. The teacher will read the book *The Perfect Spot*.

Closure

The teacher will explain that the children can paint watercolor paintings of fresh flowers during table activities. The teacher will ask the children if Georgia O'Keeffe painted flowers small or large, what kind of colors she used, and whether or not her paintings were happy or sad. The teacher will encourage the children to think about these things while they paint.

Figure 4–1   Continued

Did the learner:

- express how she felt?
- participate in movement and singing activities?
- answer comprehension questions following the stories?
- express perception of paintings?
- select a favorite painting?
- participate by sharing one thing about the print each child was asked about?

Georgia O'Keeffe Books for Children:

Turner, R. M. (1993). *Georgia O'Keeffe: Portraits of women artists for children.* New York: Little, Brown & Company.

Venezia, M. (1994). *Georgia O'Keeffe.* Danbury, CT: Grolier Publishing.

Winter, J. (1998). *My name is Georgia: A portrait.* New York: Harcourt.

Georgia O'Keeffe Books for Adults

Castro, J. G. (1995). *The art and life of Georgia O'Keeffe.* New York: Crown.

Lisle, L. (1997). *Portrait of an artist: A biography of Georgia O'Keeffe.* New York: Washington Square Press.

Aesthetics

Aesthetics is an area of art concerned with feelings and responses to color, form, and design. There is a basic need to make sense and appreciate the world in which we live (Schirrmacher, 2002) When children have opportunities to view and explore beautiful things in their classroom, they begin to appreciate their environment. Even the very young child can recognize the special features of her environment. She will notice a new item in the room, a vase of beautiful flowers, or textured paper on the wall. Children can appreciate the shape of objects, shades of light, color, pattern, and texture. Children's responses are unique and their aesthetic observations should be valued.

According to Schirrmacher, the classroom should be an aesthetically pleasing and sensory rich environment. For example, a light colored wall can serve as a background for beautifully displayed artwork, weavings, quilts, or photographs. A variety of textures should be used in the area including rough, smooth, shiny, and soft. Centers related to the arts are carefully constructed and designed to be aesthetically pleasing (Isbell & Exelby, 2001).

Primary children may enjoy visiting galleries and studying the techniques of specific artists (Johnson, 1997). They may want to explore different techniques and discover new possibilities for creating art. Learning about texture, color, balance, and contrast becomes real when discussing paintings viewed in an art gallery. Through guided discussion, children can develop a vocabulary about what is seen in a work of art, make comparisons, express personal responses, and make judgments about art (Cole & Schaefer, 1990).

A still life drawing inspired by the work of Georgia O'Keefe. (Photo by Amy Carmichael)

Creating Art

There are many different ways to create art, and a wide variety of materials and tools that can be used by young children. In an early childhood classroom, many options should be provided with appropriate choices for the individual child.

Sensory Experiences

Infants and toddlers, in the sensory stage of development, need experiences that support their way of learning. Older children also benefit from experiences that provide variations in sensory experiences. For example, toddlers can use colored shaving cream to create designs on tabletops. An older child would enjoy the same sensory experience extended by placing paper on the design, pressing, and producing a print of her creation.

Colored shaving cream provides a new way to create a masterpiece. (Photo by Su Lorencen)

Young children explore shells and leaves by touching, examining, and smelling. They progress to using these items in their creations and in varying combinations. Providing interesting items to be enjoyed and examined helps children become more focused on the beauty in the world around them. It helps children develop an awareness of the shades of colors, texture, shapes, and design. This sensitivity to the environment is helpful for children as they expand their experiences with art and develop representations for their thoughts.

Two-dimensional Art

Some of the earliest art experiences of young children are **two-dimensional** in nature. For example, toddlers often use large sheets of paper with big magic markers as they make uncontrolled scribbles on the page. A large crayon used on manila paper is a classic art activity in early childhood programs. But there are many additional possibilities for two-dimensional art activities to be included in the classroom.

Painting. Paint and a brush provide another way of creating forms or expressing ideas. Tempera paint, frequently used in early childhood programs, comes in a variety of hues and can be used in many different ways. It is less expensive in powder form although it is often bought as a liquid because of the convenience. Young children can control the use of tempera paint better when it has a slightly thick consistency. Children also can use watercolors by adding water to blocks of color and using smaller brushes. The lighter color produced by watercolors—with a more translucent quality—is an added way to explore the effects of painting.

Marking with Tools. Infants, as well as kindergartners, enjoy making marks. The primary medium used for creating these marks is crayons. Additional tools include markers, chalk, charcoal, colored pencils, and pastels. Young children prefer to work with tools that are easy to maneuver and produce strong colors. Older children will be interested in drawing, sketching, and shading. Pencil, charcoal, or pastels provide more possibilities for blending and shading, which the older child can appreciate.

Brushes come in many sizes and styles. They can be used to produce different types of strokes and size of lines. When a wide variety of brushes is available, children can select the tool that matches their preference for a specific activity. Sometimes young children repeat the same symbols or drawing using different types of brushes to experience the variations they produce. This experimentation encourages understanding of differences, contrast, and proportions.

Unique Tools. Including a variety of unusual tools to be used in art activities can stimulate fluency and flexibility of thinking in the classroom. A few of the many possibilities include sponges, feathers, paint rollers, pastry brushes, dried materials, stamps, and small mops. By adding these materials to the art center, children have the opportunity to experiment with new ways of painting. And using varied tools and materials will encourage children to think of additional items that can be used in their artwork. For example, a plastic squirt bottle of paint creates a unique line whereas a spray bottle makes a spatter design.

Surfaces for Art.   Most two-dimensional art is done on paper. There are a large variety of papers appropriate for paint, crayons, and markers. Newsprint, manila, and construction paper are most frequently used in early childhood programs. Other ideas for paper include wallpaper, shelf lining, computer paper, finger-paint paper, sandpaper, wax paper, textured fabric, recycled paper, and wallboard.

Other surfaces also can work well for artistic projects. Plexiglas provides a transparent surface that allows artwork to be enjoyed from both sides. Cardboard boxes and corrugated pieces of paper can provide unique textural backgrounds for paintings. Wood, foam pieces, and clear plastic also can stimulate additional ideas when they are used for drawing or painting projects.

Additional Two-dimensional Possibilities

There are many possibilities for two-dimensional art. Several examples include **rubbing**, printing, stenciling, spatter-painting, torn paper, cutting, pasting, and collage. The selection of specific experiences is determined by matching the developmental level of the children and considering their background of experience with art materials. A wonderful example for primary-age children is torn or cutout paper figures of a character from their favorite book. Encourage children to make figures with color paper, fabric, glue, and scissors. No pencils or markers are allowed. The children must visualize the needed shapes and cut or tear the paper accordingly. This challenges children to use their spatial intelligence.

Art with Computers

Today, it is possible to create art with the software currently available for computers. When selecting appropriate tools to use with art, it is important to use software that allows the child to design the art and control the creation of the pictures or illustrations. Children's creativity is limited when the software works like a workbook. This very restrictive approach is not effective in paper form or on a computer. There are, however, paint programs widely available for use on personal computers that work well with young children. Some of these are easy-to-use programs for freehand and shape drawing that allow the child to draw, create, erase, and add color to the pictures. These software programs match what we know about supporting the artistic development of young children.

Three-dimensional Art

Three-dimensional art refers to creations that have substance. They stand up instead of laying flat on the surface. This dimension will provide new ways of experiencing and creating art in an early childhood classroom. It can be used with both very young children and primary age children, although the level of their product will vary significantly.

For many years, play dough was widely used with young children in their homes and at school. The dough was commercially produced or made in the classroom. Each recipe produced varying textures and responsiveness. They ranged from a smooth consistency, made by cooking the mixture and using cream of tartar, to a rough texture made with a large amount of salt. Additional recipes and unusual combinations for dough are included in Appendix E.

Real Artist Clay

This type of clay is made from the earth, and often purchased in art stores or from a supply house. The clay is used by artists, and can be fired and painted, or glazed, and fired. It can be purchased in either powder or premixed form. This clay varies from gray to a reddish color, depending on the earth from which it was processed. Since the clay is water-based, it can be air-dried or fired in a kiln.

Young children are intrigued by the unique properties of real clay. It can be shaped, molded, and attached easily. Children can add water to the clay as they work with their hands to change its consistency and texture. Clay provides a new experience for many young children as they create sculptures and forms. If a child wants to return to refine the creation the next day, covering it with a wet cloth and plastic cover can keep the clay pliable. The clay can be stored in air-tight containers and reused for several months.

Tools for working with clay include:

pizza cutters	dowel rods	metal bearings
cookie cutters	wetting brushes	pieces of tile
plastic knives	meat tenderizers	string or twine
rolling pins	bottle caps	old scissors
melon ballers	baby forks	mallet shoe horns
pastry tubes	potato mashers	toothpicks
ice scrapers	buttons	pencils
ice cream scoops	screws or bolts	

Remember that tools are only added after children have had many opportunities to explore and manipulate clay with their hands. One or two new items are all that are needed to stimulate renewed interest in clay.

Clay sculpture of birds—age 4.5 years.

Recipes

The following recipes are examples of clay that can be used with young children. The textures of the clay are interesting and they can be stored well.

Best Play Dough Formula

Ingredients

2 c. flour	2 tbsp. oil
1 c. salt	2 tsp. cream of tarter
2 c. water	food coloring

Procedure

Stir ingredients over low heat until mixture has coagulated into a nice doughy ball. Allow time for the dough to cool thoroughly. Store in a plastic container with a tight-fitting lid. This play dough has a smooth texture and will last a long time when properly stored.

Creative Play Clay

Ingredients

1 c. baking soda	$2/3$ c. warm water
$1/2$ c. cornstarch	food coloring

Procedure

Mix baking soda and cornstarch in a saucepan. Add water and stir until smooth. Place over medium heat and bring to a boil. Stir mixture constantly until it looks like mashed potatoes. Remove saucepan from heat and pour clay onto a mixing board to cool. For color, knead food coloring into the cooled clay until well blended. This clay dries well and is perfect for painting on when dried. Makes about $1^1/_2$ cups and is easily doubled. Store in an airtight container.

Three-dimensional Constructions

Wood scraps and plywood pieces can be used to create three-dimensional projects. These materials can be glued, nailed, or clamped together to make substantial structures developed over a period of time. Large boxes can provide a base for projects and smaller boxes can be combined to create structures. Shoeboxes, gift boxes, pizza circles, or egg cartons are just a few of the possibilities that exist for making sculptures. Insulated, copper, or metal wire can be another material used to make three-dimensional representations. Wire is flexible and can be shaped into many forms or connected to other materials to create unique sculptures. Attaching the wire to a block of wood can provide a base for the creation and an attractive way to display the artwork. Foil sculptures, attached to a frame, can be pinched, folded, and crinkled to create an interesting three-dimensional shape.

Constructing with wood and glue. (Photo by Michael Talley)

Group Projects

Some art is created by an individual child while working on a specific item in her own way. But some of the most interesting art projects can be done by a group of children working together on group projects. These creations provide opportunities to plan, discuss, and create a work of art that is very different from those produced by individuals. During the early childhood years, children are learning to work together, to share materials, and discuss their work. Group work provides important and meaningful experiences as children create to-gether. These collaborative efforts provide opportunities for children of varying abilities to work together and create a masterpiece.

A **collage** is composed of different elements, and can be either two- or three-dimensional. For example, a group of young children can work together to make a collage of found nature items or favorite foods cut from magazines or advertisements. Another idea may consist of prints made by kitchen utensils. During this process, children can plan what utensils they will include, discuss where the prints will be located, and critique the elements that are needed to complete the picture.

Project work, a focused study on specific topics of children's interest, also can lead to a group art experience. For example, children who are working on a project related to their garden might draw how the area looks in the spring when the seeds have been planted. Later, they can draw pictures of the plants growing during the summer. The garden can be revisited in the fall when the harvest of vegetables is completed. The children's drawings can be displayed in sequence to demonstrate the changes that have occurred in the garden over time. Both artwork and photographs can provide documentation of group projects focused on the garden. The children's language, recorded during the project, can provide additional insight into the creative thinking and should be included on documentation panels.

Art Center

One of the traditional centers included in early childhood programs is the **art center**. This specific area of the classroom is designed to serve as the hub for artistic creations. In this space, art supplies and tools are stored to provide children with easy access while selecting materials. The environment is designed to support a variety of activities as children work together or individually.

Some important physical features of the art center are washable surfaces, a water source, and materials that are well-organized, visible, and accessible. Art activities can be messy. Children need to be able to work without concern for keeping the area clean during the creating process. Of course, one of the responsibilities of working in the art center is participating in cleaning up when the creative process is over.

Clothesline to hang pictures

Display of classroom weaving project

Artist of the month

Children's creations on display

Easel

Paper

Clay

Sink

Playdough

Trays

Art books

Cabinets

Junk box

Clay

Low open shelf

Project table

Wood scraps

Bench

Display artwork

Art center

Art supplies: paint, paper, brushes, glue, tape, books, markers, crayons, scissors, stapler, other tools

The art center should contain a wide range of materials and tools that support the budding artist while challenging them to try new approaches. These materials include basic art supplies such as a variety of paper, paint, tape, staplers, glue, scissors, and clay. Unique items should be rotated into the area as well. Textured wallpaper, pieces of sandpaper, or rough fabric, for example, could generate an interest in the effect of tempera paint on different surfaces. Natural materials can add a new dimension to the art area as children paint with pine branches or a pinecone. A box of collected "junk" materials should be available for the children when they need to find items to complete their ideas or projects. Fabric, decorative trims, pieces of foil, cardboard scraps, wire, wrapping paper, pom-poms, craft sticks, wood, and sandpaper inspire elaboration of ideas. The box also can include scraps left over from previous art projects. This reuse can help children learn to conserve materials in their environment.

The art area is used during center time when children choose to work on art activities. The art center also can be used throughout the day when children need a place to work or use art supplies. The additional use of this space expands the possibilities for children as they create illustrations for books or build something that relates to a project. Art and the art center provide many opportunities for integrated learning including science, math, social skills, and motor development. A web of some of the learning that can occur in this area is demonstrated visually in Figure 4–2 (Isbell, 1995, p. 58).

Theme Study

Recently, a concerted effort is being made to integrate the arts into the early childhood curriculum through **thematic units**. There are a number of different strategies for using themes in the classroom. In the past, early childhood teachers might have selected and implemented a unit on color that included color

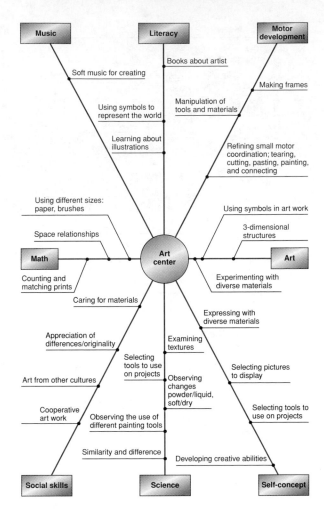

stories, color math, and color combining science. In this thematic unit, art is included to support the teaching of color. It might include placing the three primary colors of tempera paint in the art center, dying fabric with food coloring, or placing layers of colored sand in a bottle. In the emerging curriculum, a theme study or project may be developed from a child's interest. For example, several children are observed experimenting with materials that are rough and smooth. They are interested in the variation of textures they have found. The teacher's observation of the children's interest in rough and smooth can become the focus of a project or investigation of variations in texture.

Folk Art

Many people participate in some kind of **folk art** such as needlework, whittling, creating birdhouses, or making sculptures from recycled materials. Folk artists rarely have formal training, but have learned their craft from elders or peers in their family or the community. The aesthetics and techniques of their folk art are an expression of their individual creativity, as well as their cultural heritage.

Examples of folk artists include Sidney Slovack who uses fiber and seeds to weave symmetrical webs, Edith Hikaman who weaves Finnish rage rugs using a big wave pattern, and Jeremy Huddleston who creates bird carvings from cider wood. These folk artists create artwork that is both unique and individually special (March, 1990).

Most communities have folk artists that use different materials and techniques. These artists can provide young children with another way of viewing art. In the southern Appalachian area, quilters are an example of folk artists in the community. Quilters compose designs with complex patterns, color schemes, and intricate edges. Young children in this region would enjoy having a quilter visit their classroom and have the opportunity to sew fabric pieces together into a pattern. In addition, most quilts have wonderful stories that the quilters can share with children. Through this experience, they are able to see a folk artist at work and begin to identify art in the world around them.

A classroom quilt created by combining a piece of each child's favorite fabric. (Photo by Michael Talley)

The Reggio Emilia Approach

The Reggio Emilia schools in Northern Italy have received international recognition because of their excellent early childhood program. The environment in Reggio Emilia schools is different from many programs for young children. Here, children are seen as capable learners, able to think and create in ways never before thought possible. In these schools, children are focused intensely on long-term projects that follow their interest. Together, children and teachers question and learn about their world as they develop plans, create, and revisit their work, time and again. The Reggio Emilia approach views art as a language children use to think and express their ideas.

In Reggio, each school has an **atelierista**, or art specialist, who provides the catalyst for artistic expression. The atelierista works with the children and teachers as they create, experiment, and explore new avenues of expression. In each school, there is an **atelier**, or art studio. In addition, there is a smaller atelier attached to each classroom. These art areas contain an enormous array of natural materials, art supplies, and tools children can use while working on projects and creations. The materials in these spaces are beautifully displayed, sometimes grouped by color, texture, or function. Children's projects are displayed or stored for future work and refinement. The Reggio environment is visually attractive and intellectually challenging.

Learning from This Artistically Focused Program

Young children learn about aesthetics by living in an environment that includes beautiful items. How can we create classrooms that are more attractive and visually interesting? Begin by including natural materials that can be explored and enjoyed by young children such as a bouquet of spring flowers, a collection of interesting stones, or clear tubes of varying sizes that can add visual interest to the classroom space.

The next step is thinking about how children's work should be displayed. If their artwork is framed or arranged in an interesting pattern, it will be more impressive. The children have opportunities to appreciate the visual impact of the collage or group project when it is attractively displayed. It clearly demonstrates that artwork is valued. In addition, displaying children's art provides opportunities for children to revisit their work throughout the year.

Art materials and tools should be expanded to include many new possibilities that traditionally were not part of early childhood programs. Do not limit choices for young children; instead, think about unique materials that allow children to be creative. Three-dimensional materials can be added to provide opportunities for looking at things in a new way. Using sketching pads and charcoal pencils can provide a way of planning and thinking about what will be created by the children.

Begin to include long-term projects that can be reworked and revisited by the children. These in-depth experiences can replace the short time, one-shot, art activity that has dominated early childhood classrooms. Projects expand and continue explorations while allowing children to create, refine, and evaluate their work in ways not possible in a shorter time frame. By collaborating with their peers and teachers, young children will build confidence in their artistic abilities, and art will become an integrated component of the early childhood curriculum.

Children As Art Critics

Children should be encouraged to evaluate their own artwork and group projects. For example, a child can select a painting she wants to display from the three produced that week. This selection process allows the child to critique her paintings and offer an opportunity for aesthetic decisions. A gallery in the classroom or adjoining area can provide an opportunity for children to select the picture they would like to frame and exhibit. Photos of art work or group projects provide another way to document the progress. These photographs can serve to show the art history of the classroom and the artists that work there. As new art is completed, children can determine which works should be added to the growing display, and which items should be removed or placed in another area. Opportunities to evaluate, display, and document work can help children learn to value art and appreciate the work of others.

Display of the Children's Work

Children's artwork should be displayed so that all may appreciate the efforts of the child. Making a frame for a picture, choosing a textured background, or putting a clay sculpture on a wooden box can make the display more interesting. These special efforts demonstrate that the artwork of the children is valued in this classroom.

A grapevine "tree" holds paper flowers made by the children. (Photo by Michael Talley)

A corner cabinet attractively displays children's work. (Photo by Michael Talley)

Summary

Art is very important in the lives of young children. Many theories have attempted to explain what, why, and how children create. Although these theories explain the value of art in different ways, they conclude that art has a powerful influence on the cognitive, emotional, and physical development of young children. A developmental explanation uses stages to show how children move from scribbling to drawing in realistic ways. This observable progression can be seen in children around the world and in different cultures. Art in early childhood programs should provide opportunities for children to explore a variety of materials, choose techniques, and begin to see themselves as capable artists. The environment should provide opportunities for young children to experience the artistic elements of line, color, shape, form, pattern, and texture. Art helps children learn to appreciate and use these elements in their work. The early childhood teacher is both a facilitator and guide as she asks questions, poses problems, and provides resources and experiences needed by the children. In early childhood programs, the teacher is often the art specialist who needs to know about art and artists, and provide developmentally appropriate activities that match the child's level of development and personal interest.

Key Terms

color

composition

form

line

pattern

perspective

shape

texture

perceptual theory

left hemisphere

right hemisphere

scribble stage

basic form stage

pictorial stage

uncontrolled scribble

controlled scribbles

preschematic stage

schematic stage

realism

process

product

art education

aesthetics

two-dimensional

rubbing

three-dimensional

group projects

collage

art center

thematic units

folk art

atelierista

atelier

Reflection

1. Explain why many early childhood educators consider art "basic."

2. What theory or theories provide greater insight into the influence of art on the development of young children?

3. Describe the stages of children's artistic development. Give examples of children's artwork from each stage.

4. Art education has identified components of a quality art program. What are they, and how can they be included in the early childhood classroom?

5. Identify some of the different ways art can be created by young children.

6. What insights can be gained from the Reggio Emilia schools that have a strong artistic component?

Thinking about the Creative Episode

1. Describe the ways Jessica explores the properties of clay.

2. Why did Jessica work with clay for such a long period of time?

3. How was the environment designed to encourage Jessica's independence?

Possibilities for Adult Learners

Activity: Vase and Faces: Drawing on the Right Side of the Brain

Goal: This activity is designed to help the teacher shift from a left-hemisphere mode (logical operations) to the right hemisphere (visual-spatial operations). This activity is adapted from Betty Edwards' (1979) book, *Drawing on the Right Side of the Brain.*

Materials: Paper and pencil.

Procedure:

1. Draw a profile of a person's head on the left side of your paper, facing toward the center. If you are left-handed, draw the profile on the right side facing toward the center. Make your own version of the profile. It seems to help if this profile comes from your own memory and creation.

2. Next, draw horizontal lines at the top and bottom of your profile, forming the top and bottom of the vase.

3. Go back over your drawing of the first profile with a pencil. As the pencil moves over each feature, name them to yourself (forehead, nose, upper lip, lower lip, chin, and neck). Repeat this step at least once. This is a left hemisphere task: naming symbolic shapes.

4. Next, start at the top and draw the profile in reverse to complete the vase. The second profile should be a reversal of the first in order for the vase to be symmetrical. Watch for the faint signals from your brain as you begin

to shift modes of information processing. You may experience a moment of mental conflict while completing the second profile. You will find that you draw the second profile differently. Think about this and note how you solve the problem. This is a right-hemisphere mode drawing.

5. Now that you have completed the vase-faces drawing, think back on how you did it. The first profile was probably drawn rather rapidly and then, as you were instructed, redrawn, while verbalizing the names of the parts as you went back over the features. This is a left-hemisphere mode of processing: drawing symbolic shapes from memory and naming them. In drawing the second profile to complete the vase, you may have experienced some confusion or conflict. To continue the drawing, you had to use a different strategy or a different process. You probably lost the sense of drawing a profile and found yourself scanning back and forth in the space between the profiles, estimating angles, curves, inward-curving and outward-curving shapes, and lengths in relation to the opposite shapes that now became unnamed and unnamable. You made constant adjustments in the line you were drawing—checking where you were and where you were going—by scanning the space between the first profile and your copy in reverse. This is using the right hemisphere to draw.

Is it a vase or a face? (This drawing was inspired by an activity from Betty Edwards' 1979 book, *Drawing on the Right Side of the Brain*. (Courtesy of Stacy Larsen)

Activity:	Identifying Personal Creativity: Detective Work
Goal:	Many people are very powerful and creative people. A little sleuth work is in order to restore personal creativity. This exercise from *The Artist's Way: A Spiritual Path to Higher Creativity* by Julia Cameron (1992), will help you retrieve memories and misplaced fragments of your creative self.
Materials:	Paper and pencil.

Procedure: Complete the following phrases. You may feel strong emotions as you retrieve personal memories. Allow yourself to free-associate for a sentence with each phrase.

My favorite childhood toy was . . .

My favorite childhood game was . . .

The best movie I ever saw as a child was . . .

I don't do it much, but I enjoy . . .

If I could lighten up a little, I'd let myself . . .

If it were not too late, I'd . . .

My favorite musical instrument is . . .

The traits I admire in others are . . .

The amount of money I spend on treating myself to entertainment each month is . . .

Taking time out for myself is . . .

If I ever wrote a book, it would be about . . .

I am afraid that if I start dreaming . . .

I secretly enjoy reading . . .

My idea of a fun weekend would include . . .

If I'd had a perfect childhood, I'd have grown up to be . . .

If it didn't sound so crazy, I'd make or write . . .

My most cheer-me-up music is . . .

My favorite way to dress is . . .

Open-ended Activities for Young Children

Pre-K–K

Activity: Animal Paper Bags

Goal: In African cultures, animals occupy an important place in art and folklore. People who have lived in close contact with animals see them as models with special qualities. In Africa, the spider, bird, leopard, and chameleon are animals that provide sources of power, inspiration, and guidance. This activity will allow children to select an animal they admire and create a paper bag structure to represent the chosen animal.

Materials: Paper bags, scraps of fabric, newspaper, construction paper, glue, and scissors.

Procedure:

1. Ask the children to choose an animal they admire.

2. Provide materials for children to construct a sculpture using a paper bag as the base.

3. Stuff the paper bag with newspaper to provide structure and form.

4. Allow children to use materials to complete their animals.

Pre-K–K or Primary Grades

Activity: A Rubbing

Goal: To create a rubbing of items in the child's environment.

Materials: Art paper, crayons, and masking tape.

Procedure:

1. Select an item that will provide an interesting texture. Possibilities include, but are not limited to:

tree trunks	textured wall paper
shoe soles	keys
concrete	rug or carpet scraps
leaves	license plates
bricks	vents
rough stones	tombstones
tires	coins
flowers	embossed cards

2. Tape paper to or on top of the item.

3. Use crayons to rub the texture.

4. Evaluate the design, and determine if more rubbing is needed or if additional items should be rubbed.

Primary Grades

Activity: Box Painting

Goal: To create an abstract design with marbles and paint.

Materials: Cardboard box lids (should have a high rim), paper, tempera paint, marbles of different sizes, clear plastic cups, and spoons.

Procedure:

1. Select a lid that will be used for the painting.

2. Cut the paper to fit inside the lid.

3. Choose colors of paint and pour each into a plastic cup.

4. Using a spoon, put a marble into the selected color.

5. Place the marble on the paper inside the lid.

6. Roll the marble around on the paper.

7. Repeat the process with different colors and varied marbles.

8. Allow the abstract marble painting to dry in the lid before removing the creation.

Activity: Burlap Murals

Goal: Murals are an essential part of Mexican art. This activity allows children to construct a classroom mural while experimenting with a new media, burlap.

Materials: Burlap (a neutral color is preferable), tempera paint, and brushes.

Procedure:

1. Mural-making, a popular art activity in the elementary grades, can be even more exciting when burlap is used as the background. The heavy texture of the porous material absorbs the paint in a unique way.

2. Children should plan and discuss their mural as a group. This will help the mural become a composition instead of a sequence of unrelated pictures.

3. For variations, use other fabrics for painting or glue fabric to the burlap.

Junk List

wire

feathers

beads

buttons

costume Jewelry

broken Jewelry

tape (different sizes and colors)

string

ribbon

yarn

old keys

small machines that don't work (watches, clocks, and the like)

corks

golf Balls

bottle caps

leather remnants

plastic sock holders

shells

sponges

small seed pods

wood scraps

containers (white or transparent preferable)

baskets

cardboard pieces (all kinds and shapes, but without print)

paper (of different weights, textures, and colors)

nails

screws

small mirrors

wallpaper

wrapping Paper

lids

straws

material

lace

craft sticks

pom-poms

empty film canisters

Styrofoam

toothpicks

rubber bands

marker lids (from dried-out markers)

bows

spools

cotton balls

variety of glue (Elmer's, wood, paste)

salt (epsom salt and rock salt)

sponges

paint (finger, watercolor, acrylic, tempera, and fabric)

stapler (to be used with supervision)

paper clips

clay

play dough

matting board

frames

stamps and stamp pad

glitter

glitter glue

aluminum foil

crayons

markers

colored pencils

pastels

colored sand

brushes (a large variety of sizes)

droppers

baby oil

brads

chalk

scissors

felt

cellophane

pipe cleaners

A suggested caution: When working with children under three years of age, make sure that items selected as part of the junk list are not small enough to become a choking hazard.

Notes

[1]Koster, J. B. (1999). Clay for little fingers. *Young Children, 54*(2), 18–22.

[2]Kellogg, R. (1969). *Analyzing children's art.* Palo Alto, CA: Mayfield Publishing Company.

[3]Hubbard, R. S. (1996). *A workshop of the possible: Nurturing children's creative development.* York, ME: Stenhouse Publishing.

References

Blake, R. J. (1997). *The perfect spot.* New York: Putnam Publishing Group.

Cameron, J. (1992). *The artist's way: A spiritual path to higher creativity.* New York: Jeremy P. Tarcher/Putnam.

Colbert, C., & Taunton, M. (1992). *Developmentally appropriate practices for the visual art education of young children.* Reston, VA: National Art Education Association.

Cole, E., & Schaefer, C. (1990). Can young children be art critics? *Young Children, 45*(2), 33–38.

Curtis, J. L. (1998). *Today I feel silly and other moods that make my day.* New York: Harper Collins Publishers.

Dixon, G. T., & Chalmers, F. G. (1990). The expressive arts in education. *Childhood Education, 67*(1), 12–17.

Edwards, B. (1979). *Drawing on the right side of the brain: A course in enhancing creativity and artistic confidence.* Los Angeles: J. P. Tarcher, Inc.

Fox, J. E., & Diffily, D. (2000). Integrating the visual arts: Building your children's knowledge, skills and confidence. *Dimensions of Early Childhood, 29*(1), 3–10.

Gardner, H. (1983). *Frames of mind: The theory of multiple intelligence.* New York: Basic Books.

Gardner, H. (1980). Children's art: The age of creativity. *Psychology Today, 13*(12), 84–96.

Isbell, R. (1995). *The complete learning center book.* Beltsville, MD: Gryphon House.

Isbell, R., & Exelby, B. (2001). *Learning environments that work with young children.* Beltsville, MD: Gryphon House.

Johnson, M. (1997). Teaching children to value art and artist. *Phi Delta Kappan, 78*(6), 454–456.

Kellogg, R. (1969). *Analyzing children's art.* Palo Alto, CA: Mayfield Publishing Company.

Lowenfeld, V., & Brittain, W. L. (1987). *Creative and mental growth.* New York: MacMillan.

March, R. (1990). Close to home and close to heart: Exploring folk arts in education. *Spectrum, Journal of Wisconsin Art Education, 2*(1), 29–34.

Raines, S., & Canady, R. J. (1990). *The whole language kindergarten.* New York: Teachers College Press.

Schirrmacher, R. (2002). *Art and creative development in young children* (4th ed.). Clifton Park, NY: Delmar Learning.

Seefeldt, C. (1995). Art—a serious work. *Young Children, 50*(3), 39–45.

Additional Reading

Aylward, K., Hartley, S., Field, T., Greer, J., & Vega-Lahr, N. (1993). An art appreciation curriculum for preschool children. *Early Child Development and Care, 96*(1), 35–48.

Baker, D. W. (1991). The visual arts in early childhood education. In D. Elkind (Ed.), *Perspectives on early childhood education: Growing with young children toward the 21st century* (pp. 133–140). Washington, DC: National Education Association of the United States.

Bresler, L. (1998). "Child art," "fine art," and "art for children:" The shaping of school practice and implications for change. *Arts Education Policy Review, 100,* 3–10.

Brown, I. (1994). Comparing the best of both worlds: Cultures through art. *Art Education, 47*(1), 61–67.

Clemens, S. G. (1991). Art in the classroom: Making every day special. *Young Children, 46*(2), 4–11.

Colbert, C. (1997). Visual arts in developmentally appropriate integrated curriculum. In C. H. Hart, D. C. Burts, & R. Charlesworth (Eds.), *Integrated curriculum and developmentally appropriate practice: Birth to eight* (pp. 171–200). Albany, NY: State University of New York Press.

Czikszentmihalyi, M. (1996). *Creativity.* New York: Basic Books.

Dighe, J., Calomiris, Z., & Van Zutphen, C. (1998). Nurturing the language of art in children. *Young Children, 53*(1), 4–9.

Edwards, L. C., & Nabors, M. L. (1993). The creative arts process. *Young Children, 48*(3), 77–81.

Eisner, E. W. (1998). Does experience in the arts boost academic achievement? *Arts Education Policy Review, 100*(4), 32–39.

Feeney, S., & Moravcik, E. (1987). A thing of beauty: Aesthetic development in young children. *Young Children, 43*(6), 7-15.

Gardner, H. (1982). *Art, mind, and brain.* New York: Basic Books.

Hafeli, M. (1997). Connecting ideas through materials: Visual arts learning in the primary classroom. *Primary Voices K–6, 5*(2), 18–24.

Hamblen, K. A. (1997). Theories and research that support art instruction for instrumental outcomes. *Arts Education Policy Review, 98*(3), 27–33.

Hart, K. (1994). *I can paint!* Portsmouth, NH: Heinemann.

Heintz, J. R. (1991). Inspired by African art. *School Arts, 90*(6), 16–19.

Honigman, J. J., & Bhaunagri, N. P. (1998). Painting with scissors: Art education beyond production. *Childhood Education, 74*(4), 205–213.

Jalongo, M. (1995). Awakening a sense of artistry within young children. *Dimensions of Early Childhood, 23*(4), 8–14.

Schiller, M. (1995). An emergent art curriculum that fosters understanding. *Young Children, 50*(3), 33–38.

Sylwester, R. (1998). Art for the brain's sake. *Educational Leadership, 56*(3), 31–35.

Szyba, C. M. (1999). Why do some teachers resist offering appropriate, open-ended art activities for young children? *Young Children, 54*(1), 16–19.

Topal, C. W., & Gandini, L. (1999). *Beautiful stuff: Learning with found materials.* Worcester, MA: Davis Publications, Inc.

Torrance, E. P. (1962). *Guiding creative talent.* Englewood Cliffs, NJ: Prentice-Hall.

Warash, B. G., & Saab, J. F. (1999). Exploring the visual arts with young children. *Dimensions of Early Childhood, 27*(1), 11–15.

Wolf, A. D. (1990). Art postcards- another aspect of your aesthetics program? *Young Children, 45*(2), 39–43.

Wright, S. (1997). Learning how to learn: The arts as core in an emergent curriculum. *Childhood Education, 73*(60), 361–366.

Madeline inspired drawing

A drawing of Arthur

Children's Literature Connection

dePaola, T. (1988). *The legend of the Indian paintbrush.* New York: Scholastic, Inc.
Little Gopher, an Indian boy, learns to paint with the brilliance of the evening sky and becomes known as He-Who-Brought-the-Sunset-to-the-Earth. This is a story about the beautiful flower, the Indian Paintbrush. (Primary K–3)

dePaola, T. (1989). *The art lesson.* New York: G. P. Putnam's Sons.
Having learned to be creative by drawing pictures at home, young Tommy is dismayed when he goes to school and finds the art lesson there much more regimented. (Primary 1–3 and Teacher's Aide)

Gibbons, G. (1987). *The pottery place.* San Diego: Harcourt Brace Javanovich.
This book describes the history and process of pottery-making by following a potter through a day of work. (Pre-K–2)

Gibbons, G. (1998). *The art box.* New York: Holiday House.
Describes the many different kinds of tools and supplies that artists use to produce their work. (Pre-K–3)

Hurd, T. (1996). *Art dog.* New York: Harper Collins Publishers.
When the Mona Woofa is stolen from the Dogopolis Museum of Art, a mysterious character, who calls himself Art Dog, tracks down and captures the thieves. (Primary K–3)

Lionni, L. (1959). *Little blue and little yellow.* New York: Scholastic, Inc.
Little blue and little yellow are best friends. When they hug each other, something special happens! (Primary 1–3)

Lionni, L. (1991). *Matthew's dream.* New York: Scholastic, Inc.
Although his parents want him to become a doctor, after a trip to the art museum, Matthew dreams of becoming a painter. (Primary K–3)

McClintock, B. (1996). *The fantastic drawings of Danielle.* Boston: Houghton Mifflin Company.
Even though her photographer father urges her to try a more practical form of art, a young artist in turn-of-the-century Paris finds that her talent for drawing can be useful. (Primary 1–3)

McPhail, D. (1988). *Something special.* Boston: Little, Brown and Company.
Surrounded by parents and siblings with remarkable talents, Sam yearns to be good at something, and finds his own special talent when he discovers the pleasures of painting. (Pre-K–1)

Mallat, K. (1997). *The picture that mom drew.* New York: Walker and Company.
Introduces the seven basic elements of art by using colored pencils to add colors, lines, shapes, forms, shades, patterns, and textures—one at a time—to a piece of paper. (Primary K–3)

Markun, P. M. (1993). *The little painter of Sabana Grande.* New York: Bradbury Press.
Lacking paper, a young Panamanian artist paints the outside of his adobe home. (Primary K–3)

Moon, N. (1995). *Lucy's picture.* New York: Dial Books for Young Readers.
A young girl creates a special picture that her grandfather, who is blind, can "see" with his hands. (Pre-K and Primary K–3)

Rylant, C. (1988). *All I see.* New York: Orchard Books.
A child paints with an artist friend who sees and paints only whales. (Primary K–3)

Thomas, A. (1994). *Pearl paints.* New York: Henry Holt and Company.
When Pearl receives a set of watercolors for her birthday, all she wants to do is paint. As Pearl explores her new paints, the author highlights the painting styles of several well-known artists. (Primary K–3 and Teacher's Aide)

Walsh, E. S. (1989). *Mouse paint.* New York: Scholastic.
Three white mice discover the properties of color as they use paint to hide from a cat. (Pre-K–K)

Williams, K. L. (1998). *Painted dreams.* New York: Lothrop, Lee & Shepard Books.
Because her Haitian family is too poor to be able to buy paints for her, eight-year-old Ti Marie finds her own way to create pictures that make the heart sing. (Primary K–3)

Helpful Web Sites

The addresses and corresponding agencies below are taken from the Web sites. Due to the dynamic nature of the Internet, please remember that Web sites are subject to change at any time.

http://www.aep-arts.org   The Arts Education Partnership—A private, non-profit coalition of education, arts, business, philanthropic, and government organizations that demonstrates and promotes the essential role of arts education.

http://www.getty.edu   The J. Paul Getty Trust—An international cultural and philanthropic organization, educational in purpose and character, serving both general audiences and specialized professionals.

http://www.nassa-arts.org   The National Assembly of State Arts Agencies (NASAA)—The membership organization of the nation's state and jurisdictional arts agencies, whose mission is to advance and promote a meaningful role for the arts in the lives of individuals, families, and communities throughout the United States.

http://www.moma.org/   The Museum of Modern Art—An art collection containing more than 100,000 paintings, sculptures, drawings, prints, photographs, architectural models and drawings, and design objects.

http://www.arts.endow.gov   The National Endowment for the Arts—Serves the public good by nurturing the expression of human creativity, supporting the cultivation of community spirit, and fostering the recognition and appreciation of the excellence and diversity of our nation's artistic accomplishments.

http://americanart.si.edu/   Smithsonian American Art Museum

http://www.nga.gov/   The National Gallery of Art—Houses one of the finest collections in the world illustrating major achievements in painting, sculpture, and graphic arts from the Middle Ages to the present.

http://www.naea-reston.org/   National Art Education Association (NAEA)—A nonprofit, educational organization serving over 17,000 art educators from every level of instruction.

http://www.artresources.com   Internet Art Resources—Web site includes listings of art galleries, museums, artists, articles and book reviews, and an image catalog of over 5,000 constantly changing images.

For additional resources involving creativity and the arts with young children, visit our Web site at **http://www.earlychilded.delmar.com**

Chapter 5

Music: It Begins in Infancy

New studies on brain development indicate that music is an essential experience for young children. This chapter will explore the many ways music can be included in early childhood programs. Four aspects of music are included: listening to music, singing, making music, and moving to music.

Creative Episode

A tiny baby is lying in his crib. His arms and legs begin to move rapidly. He recognizes the voice of his father as he enters the room. The father sings his son's name in a simple rhythmic pattern: Ja-mal, Ja-mal. The baby's arms and legs move faster. He smiles in anticipation of an interaction with his father.

Jamal and his father are connecting through music. The sounds and interactions bring enjoyment to both the father and baby. This beginning musical experience will nurture Jamal's development by providing a secure base for future cognitive and emotional development. A positive beginning for Jamal's budding interest in musical sounds will help him learn about the world.

Today, there is great excitement about the use of music in the early years of children's lives. Almost weekly, there is an article or research study that identifies the positive benefits of listening to or playing music. Many authors have concluded that music can enhance the intellectual development of children, stimulate brain function, and produce gains in test scores (Rauscher, 1995).

Current media coverage has brought a surge of interest in music for young children to the public, administrators, and even governors.

Although media attention has created renewed interest in the field of music, it has always been an integral part of the lives of young children. Throughout history, singing, playing, and dancing have been important for children and adults across cultural and socioeconomic levels. Music provides opportunities for children and families to interact, develop understanding of their heritage, and enjoy shared experiences. Music has been a powerful thread that has woven many families and children together, and provided them with a special identity.

For many years, music has been considered an important component in early childhood programs. Music is valued because of its potential intellectual benefits and for the enjoyment that it provides to children. Nurturing music in early childhood should be considered essential because of the richness it brings to young children's lives (Feierabend, 1990). Music can draw diverse groups of children together, often reaching the most distant child. Songs move children smoothly from activity to activity during potentially difficult transition times. Musical recordings can quiet the active child for a period of relaxation. Music provides children with opportunities to actively participate during circle times. When music is an integral part of the early childhood classroom, it expands the learning experiences of children and broadens their world to include the creative arts. It has been suggested that an environment that includes music supports the development of the whole child (Blackburn, 1998).

Musical Terms

Dynamics: The volume of sounds; loud or soft.

Harmony: The blending of sounds. This may be produced by two sounds performed at the same time.

Melody: The tune of music. The pattern of sounds that make up the musical composition.

Pitch: The highs and lows of musical sound patterns.

Rhythm: The beat of music. This includes tempo and meter.

Timbre: The tone of sound; for example, the uniquely different qualities produced by a bong drum or steel drum.

Musical Development across the Early Childhood Years (Birth through Eight)

The development of most children follows a pattern that can provide helpful guidelines for planning an appropriate environment. Understanding the unique characteristics of young children during specific developmental periods can provide a framework for developing a responsive curriculum. An appropriate match can ensure that children are successful and challenged as they participate in meaningful musical activities. Although many similarities exist during each stage of development, there are individual variations as well. These individual differences may influence the pace, attitudes, and behaviors that make each child unique. In a developmentally appropriate classroom, group and individual needs must be considered in designing the music curriculum.

Intertwined with the developmental characteristics of children are specific abilities that impact musical development. An understanding of these developing musical skills ensures that expectations are congruent with children's capabilities. It is helpful to realize that adjustments must be made for the special needs and unique talents of the children within each classroom.

Infancy

During the first months of life, an infant is receptive to music. He responds to the sounds in his environment by moving his arms and legs, or turning his head toward the source. Later, more active listening occurs as he moves or makes sounds that seem to respond to the music.

Infants produce sounds that often have musical qualities. Their cooing and babbling have rhythm and pitch. The infant will find pleasure in his voice and can be heard playing with sounds, patterns, and pitches when alone in the crib. If a caregiver echoes the cooing and babbling sounds, an interaction may occur. The infant will learn from these exchanges that the sounds he makes are important. He discovers that repeating these sounds draws the caregiver's attention to him.

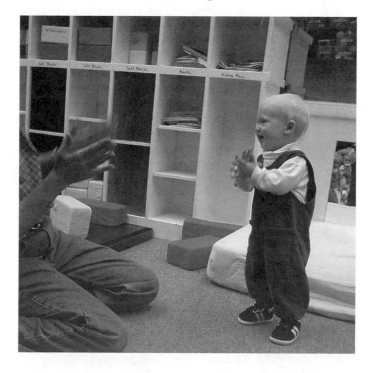

Infant clapping to the music. (Photo by Michael Talley)

As infants begin to gain some control of their bodies, they reach out to grasp, hold, and move toys. During these early months, they are particularly interested in toys that have musical sounds. For example, a mobile will be hit again and again to activate the bell sound. He will experiment with the different sounds that are produced when the mobile is hit with his foot, arm, or another toy. A wrist toy with sound is first randomly shaken. When the connection is made between the movement and the sound, the infant will increase his hand motion to produce additional musical sounds. He will begin to clap his hands along with music or hit a drum to produce a sound. These new skills bring him great joy, and are repeated again and again.

Toward the end of the first year, infants demonstrate their recognition of a song or **finger play** by moving or laughing in anticipation. Individual interest begins to surface as infants show a preference for specific songs, books, or finger plays. For example, the following finger play (Totline Publications, 1994) will have children anticipating the arrival of the bees and laughing with glee.

The Beehive (Traditional)

Here is the beehive. (Make a fist.)
Where are the bees? (Tilt head to one side.)
Hidden inside where nobody sees.
Here they come buzzing out of the hive. (Slowly begin to open fist.)
One, two, three, four, and five! (Raise fingers one at a time.)

With gestures or sounds, infants indicate when they want to hear the song or story again. When they tire of the activity, they conclude their involvement by simply turning away or crying in an irritated way. It is important to learn to read these infant messages, so adult interactions can follow their interest and pace.

A finger play is imitated by the toddler. (Photo by Michael Talley)

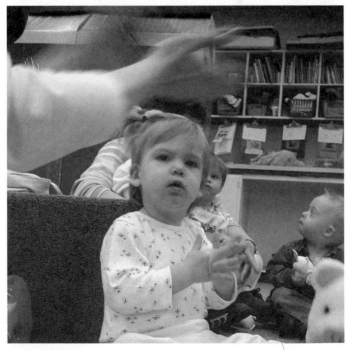

Toddlers

In this period of development, toddlers' first true words begin to appear. These words identify important people and meaningful objects in their world. Toddlers are interested in echoing words and phrases used by caregivers. This indicates their focus on these sounds and patterns. If a word is needed that is not in their vocabulary, toddlers will create a new label to identify the object. This practice clearly demonstrates the creative nature of the very young child. Toddlers are fascinated by the words and phrases that are repeated in songs, finger plays, and poems. They can be heard chanting unique sound patterns and interesting words to their caregiver, or to themselves throughout the day.

Toddlers are gaining more control of their bodies as they become mobile and move around their space. They are able to hold and manipulate objects to carefully examine materials. They experiment with hitting and tapping on a variety of objects to discover the sounds they can produce. They can play simple **percussion instruments** with a mallet or striker in a rhythmic pattern. Toddlers enjoy listening, and often dance to accompany the sounds.

Toddlers try to establish their autonomy and become more independent. This can be observed when the toddler chooses to join an activity or refuses to participate in another. During a song, the toddler may wander off to participate in another part of the room. Later, he may be heard singing a familiar phrase of the song from across the space. Toddlers can continue an activity or song long after the adult has stopped, indicating an enjoyment of the activity and the desire to continue. Their creativity is demonstrated as they develop new actions or sound effects to accompany familiar songs or finger plays.

Preschoolers

Three- and four-year-olds gain competencies in many different areas. Preschoolers' language becomes more refined and their communication is clearer. Songs and finger plays are of great interest to them as they repeat and sing familiar melodies. Preschoolers enjoy singing together as they begin to build their repertoire of songs. During this period, the group may sing around the melody while some children will sing in tune. Preschoolers use songs and music to accompany their activity throughout the day. They can be heard in the bathroom creating a song: "wash, wash, wash your hands—squirt, squirt, squirt the soap—wash, wash, wash it off." Preschoolers are using music to express themselves, and they are improvising and playing with musical sounds (Kenney, 1997).

Sensory and **small motor coordination** of preschoolers improves as they gain better control of their bodies. They can jump, walk, and clap to music. When an adult demonstrates and continues to play the pattern with them, preschoolers can keep a steady beat. Their movement to music becomes more consistent with the mood and rhythm of the recording. Some preschoolers will be comfortable participating in movement activities in a group whereas others will be self-conscious and only move when no one is watching.

Many opportunities to listen to and discriminate sounds should be provided in this developmental stage. Preschoolers can recognize melodies they have experienced previously. They can substitute new words for familiar songs. Preschoolers enjoy different types of music, varied instruments, and the sounds they produce. They can suggest different ways to accompany music with **rhythm instruments**. Some children are able to create simple songs and repeat the composition for others to enjoy.

Kindergartners

The kindergarten year is a time for refining abilities that were begun during the early years. Language skills are well-developed in many children. Kindergartners can express their ideas and make plans for future projects. They are able to work cooperatively, as they adjust their roles and use language in their play. Classroom learning centers, including a music center, provide expanded opportunities for them to make choices, use their language, and work in areas of interest. Kindergartners are growing in self-confidence as they understand their capabilities by successfully participating in classroom activities.

Literacy becomes increasingly important as kindergarten children become more interested in symbols, print, and writing. Visual symbols are recognized and can be used to direct participation in group activities. Books and tapes that include print are particularly interesting to children during this period. They can be observed "reading" these materials to themselves and others. Books that include sound effects capitalize on this interest and provide additional opportunities for experiences with music. Flip charts that contain the words of favorite songs are used in kindergarten classrooms for group singing and making another connection with print. These sing-alongs can provide a successful and enjoyable experience for children of varying levels of singing ability.

During this stage, children continue to investigate the use of tools and materials. They want to know how things work and how they can be combined in new ways. This interest can be nurtured through the use of musical instruments such as the **guitar**, **keyboard**, and **Autoharp**. Chording instruments provide a pleasant accompaniment for their developing singing voices. Their increased physical competencies and growing musical skills will allow kindergartners to produce more complex rhythm patterns with instruments. They also can begin to experiment with melody instruments.

A recorder and zither are used to make music. (Photo by Michael Talley)

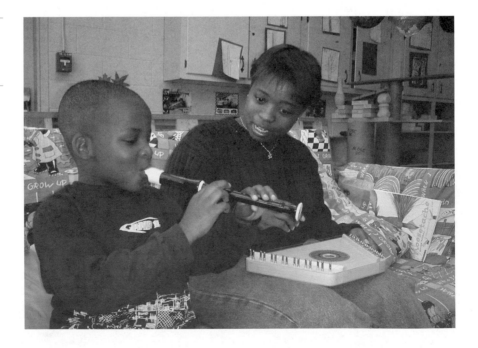

Primary Grades

Children in the primary grades are moving into a new educational environment where there are many challenges. In this new setting, the development of skills and abilities is often the focus. Primary children are emerging readers and writers. Their abilities in these areas vary significantly during the early years. Understanding and respecting their different levels of development is essential as children progress through this complex process. Some children will be able to read words of a song from a book or flip chart. They will be able to write new words for a song or develop a symbolic representation of a rhythm pattern on paper. But there also will be children who are trying to figure out how books and writing work. Providing varied opportunities for participation in musical activities will support literacy development, as well as enhancing different levels of interest in words, patterns, and print.

Primary children become more logical in their thinking although most are still bound to concrete experiences. They continue to need opportunities to explore, examine, and reflect. Meaningful experiences that integrate learning and the arts can provide new avenues for the development of thinking. Primary children are able to keep written records of their thoughts and gain additional understanding through reading. They can develop charts or graphs that indicate their musical preferences, participation, and interest. They can discuss how they feel about the music, the artist, or give an interpretation of the composition.

Children in the primary years continue to develop their **social competencies**. They are very concerned about rules and fairness. They enjoy singing games, playing instruments, and participating in musical groups. They can work well in large groups but most often prefer small ones. If interested in an area or project, they can work independently for long periods of time and return to refine the product at a later time.

For some children, the primary grades are the period when they begin music lessons in piano, dance, or instruments. During this time, a music teacher with a specialization in this area often handles the music program in the

> *"Music hath charms to soothe a savage breast, to soften rocks, or bend a knotted oak."*
>
> **W. Congreve[2]**

Kindergartners use PVC pipe, elbows, and joints to create musical instruments. (Photo by Michael Talley)

school. It is important to realize that music should be included in both the special setting and the regular classroom where children spend the major portion of their day. In the best situation, the classroom teacher and the music specialist collaborate to meet the needs and interests of specific children in the group. Together, they support projects and themes with music, instruments, and movement that can be used in both places.

Goals for Music in Early Childhood

The children will:

- enjoy participating in musical activities.
- express themselves using music, both vocally and instrumentally.
- experience a variety of types of music through listening, singing, playing music, and movement.
- understand and experience basic musical concepts appropriate for their level of development.

The Early Childhood Teacher

A teacher's interest in music is highly contagious. He does not have to be a great singer or musician to enjoy music with young children. The teacher must, however, understand the importance of including appropriate musical experiences in the early childhood classroom. He will plan opportunities for musical development while encouraging the spontaneous music that children produce each day. A vast number of music recordings and available instruments makes the integration of music possible for all early childhood teachers, even those who feel uncomfortable singing. It is important to note, however, that young children are not music critics concerned with pitch or tone. Young children enjoy a teacher who joyfully participates in making music with them.

Teachers can encourage the wonder and exploration that accompanies young children's interest in music. In the early years, it is important for the focus to be on divergent thinking that allows for many musical responses. The early childhood teacher, interested in creative development, may encourage the child to find different ways to play the xylophone instead of suggesting only one way.

Children can teach us how music develops when we listen and follow their interest. Young children are innately responsive to music when the environment is designed to nurture this interest. The teacher is not a performer: he is the facilitator who plans appropriate opportunities using elements of music. He plans for musical variety that exposes young children to many different kinds of music and diverse performers. Both the teacher and the children will benefit from a classroom filled with music.

Early childhood teachers should not strive for musical perfection or rehearse until the children's singing is totally accurate. Teachers understand that children's musical abilities develop at different rates, and vary from child to child. The teacher's goals for children during the early years should be to develop a love for music while joyfully participating in the process.

Playing musical instruments is a joyful experience. (Photo by Michael Talley)

Elements of Music

Music is composed of elements that include listening, singing, and making music with instruments and movement.

Musical Behaviors

Musical experiences should include learning about the basic components of music (melody, rhythm, timbre, and form) through musical behaviors (singing, listening, playing instruments, movement, and creating). These aspects are interrelated, and each influences the other while all are essential to the musical process. Some appropriate musical experiences can be planned, but many opportunities will be spontaneous and built on the observed interest of each child. Both planned and responsive musical experiences are important in an effective environment for young children.

Listening

The ability to hear is present in most infants at birth. During the first years of life, very young children begin to refine their ability to listen to sounds in their world. This focus on the sounds they hear, and their ability to respond to them, provide the basis for active listening that is important in musical development.

Listening is defined on several levels. **Auditory awareness** is simply attending to the sound and recognizing its presence. Recognizing the voice of his father or the siren of the fire truck are examples of the young child's auditory awareness.

Auditory discrimination is the ability to distinguish between sounds that are heard. Many early childhood educators recognize the importance of auditory discrimination because of its relationship to beginning reading. However, they often are unaware that auditory discrimination is essential to the development of musical ability. When the toddler can distinguish the opening of the refrigerator door from the opening of the house door, he demonstrates his ability to discriminate between two sounds. We know he can distinguish the difference when he calls out for "milk," when the refrigerator is opened.

Auditory sequencing is the ability to remember the order of sounds heard. This ability is demonstrated when a young child echoes a pattern on the rhythm sticks or repeats the verses of a song in order (Haines & Gerber, 2000). Auditory memory assists young children in many areas including reading, singing, and playing instruments.

Another level that has been identified is listening for **appreciation**. This refers to the listener enjoying the sounds of music that they hear. This directly relates to young children developing an appreciation for music and a preference for specific selections.

During the early years, young children need many opportunities to hear sounds and focus their attention on them. Listening and active participation in musical experiences are avenues that can enhance this ability. Infants demonstrate their need to combine listening and activity as they move their bodies in response to music. The continuation of this active listening is appropriate throughout the first eight years of children's lives.

Listening to Music

Focused listening helps young children attend to specific sounds or words that give direction. This listening is considered by many experts to be the basis for all musical learning (Bayless & Ramsey, 1986). Listening to a variety of music is important in the development of auditory abilities. Variety provides opportunity for children to determine the music they like and to make new connections with sounds they have never heard before. Young children enjoy hearing different kinds of music and examining new sounds. They also like to hear familiar music that connects with their background and previous experiences. Playing music from families of children in the classroom throughout the day can provide new opportunities for listening that will expand the offerings. It is important to include both familiar and new selections in planning musical listening experiences for young children.

Active listening opportunities can include singing games that give directions in the words. Music that consists of periods of moving and stopping encourages children to listen and respond. Records that have sound clues require children to listen closely and respond with clapping, movements, or repeated phrases. Playing instruments with specific passages of music requires focused attention to sound patterns. These are examples of the many opportunities to refine the listening abilities of young children.

Listening for enjoyment and appreciation is an important part of musical learning in early childhood. Experiencing a variety of music expands the opportunities for children to appreciate different types of music. Musical selections that can be used in early childhood classrooms include classical, jazz, folk, Native American, Cajun, African, marches, and polkas. Some popular music can be appropriate and connect to the children's current interests. Listening to these many variations encourages young children to enjoy a variety of music.

Music can produce strong emotional reactions or provide a calming effect. For this reason, soft and slow music often has been used to encourage children to relax during rest time. Listening to soothing music allows children to relax at their own pace and in their own way. Music also can excite children and encourage them to participate. Marching music can move children from place to place without demanding their attention. A variety in mood and tempo should be considered in planning listening experiences for young children.

Music can be performed in many different ways. Some possibilities include solo vocal, chorus, duet, orchestra, band, guitar, drums, piano, harp, or flute. Recordings of each of these are available and can be enjoyed by children. It is not necessary for these recordings to be specifically for children, but it should be a high-quality recording that will provide good listening possibilities for young listeners.

Listening to live performers is particularly motivating for young children. The performance should, however, be appropriate for the developmental level of the children. A high school band member playing the trumpet in the kindergarten classroom is very exciting for the children. Going to a choral rehearsal instead of attending a long performance will be enjoyed by young children and remembered fondly. Children will admire a parent who plays bluegrass on the guitar in an informal performance in the classroom. These live musical performances connect with children in a way not possible when using a recording or a CD.

Singing

The development of singing seems to follow a predictable pattern during the early years (Wolf, 1994). These steps provide insight to the parent or teacher who wants to encourage children to use their voices in song. The first step in the process is listening. Long before young children sing, they listen to songs. During this time, they are storing the melody, pattern, and rhythm for future use. These listening experiences provide the basis for singing and participating

> *"Music is the favorite passion of my soul."*
>
> **Thomas Jefferson**[3]

in musical activities during the early years. Songs can be recorded music or an adult singing to an infant. Although both can be beneficial, music sung by a caring adult can be especially effective. Toddlers who have been exposed to songs on a regular basis, will begin to tag on to familiar tunes. They will repeat "round and round" when hearing "The wheels on the bus" or clap their hands when they recognize the song. They will take the tune with them when participating in other activities. Toddlers may sing, "Wash, wash, wash your hands" as they play in the housekeeping sink or in water outside.

In the preschool years, children continue to listen and tag on, but most join along with the singing. During this period, singing in groups and learning new songs becomes very important. Children often have favorite songs that they want to sing again and again. Although it is important to expand their repertoire of songs, the familiar favorites should be sung on a regular basis. These comfortable singing experiences are filled with joy and provide opportunities for successful participation.

Singing independently usually appears during kindergarten. Many children are able to sing a song with some accuracy. The development of singing independently varies, as some children reach this independent stage earlier or later than others. Singing alone never should be pushed and only encouraged when the child indicates an interest.

In the primary grades, children can participate in broader singing experiences such as **duets**, small groups, or **rounds**. Songs of their heritage and personal favorites should remain the foundation for building new interests and abilities. These familiar songs can be varied, reworded, or accompanied in new ways while building from a secure musical base.

Singing together builds a sense of community in an early childhood classroom. (Photo by Michael Talley)

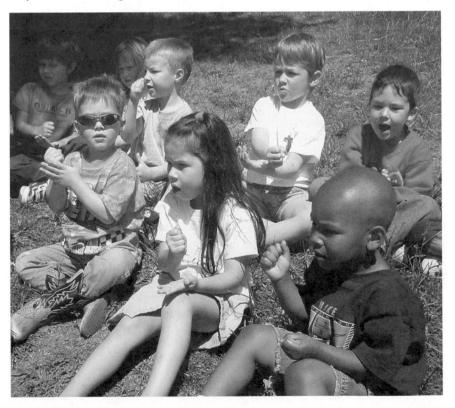

Selecting Songs for Singing

For many years, several categories of songs were used in early childhood programs. These continue to be widely used, although many new types of songs are being included as our understanding of cultures and the musical world is extended.

Nursery Rhyme Songs. The melodies of nursery rhyme songs are simple and easily remembered. Some children have heard these and others have been exposed to variations that have been used in the media or in modern books. Examples of these songs include London Bridge is Falling Down and Ba Ba Blacksheep. These songs are a part of the culture of childhood and should be included in early childhood programs. Songbooks that include collections of nursery rhyme songs are listed at the end of the chapter and several songs are included in Appendix F.

Lullabies. Lullabies are often soft and slow. They create a soothing mood that children enjoy and find calming. Some children have heard lullabies and use them to rock themselves or baby dolls to sleep. Well-known lullabies include Lullaby and Goodnight and All the Pretty Horses. There are many collections of lullabies that can provide songs appropriate to use in early childhood classrooms. Recordings of lullabies also can be used at rest time as children quietly sing along with the music or relax their bodies.

Teacher and baby move together as they rock during feeding time. (Photo by Michael Talley)

Folk and Traditional Songs. These catchy tunes are part of our heritage and have been sung by young children for hundreds of years. Some examples are Where Have You Gone, Billy Boy? and This Land is Your Land. Children enjoy singing their favorites over and over. Although the teacher may tire of singing these songs, the children find them comfortable and exciting. Young children often use the melodies as they create their first variations on a theme or accompany their activities with song. There are many traditional songs to choose from and the collection at the end of the chapter identifies some that will be helpful.

Chants. In the early years, children begin to **chant** phrases or directions. These **chants** are easy and very rhythmic in nature; they are often described as half-singing and half-talking. Since they are such a natural part of children's singing development, it is important to include them in the early childhood classroom. Some chants are spontaneously created by the child, and can be repeated by the teacher or shared in a group. Others come from stories and poetry they hear, and can be repeated in unison. Children use their voices to make the messages in chants come alive. Chants can be traditional singsong or developed to match the words in a poem. Young children enjoy experimenting with the rhythm and words of chants to find a way to respond to language (Buchoff, 1994).

A number of recording artists have used chants to draw children into participation with music. Ella Jenkins has many African chants that young children love and can quickly begin to repeat. The patterns are easy to learn and magnetic in quality. These chants can provide successful experiences for many beginning singers. Drums and rhythm instruments can be used very effectively with children singing chants.

Miss Mary Mack (Traditional)

Oh Mary Mack, Mack, Mack
All dressed in black, black, black
With silver buttons, buttons, buttons
All down her back, back, back
She asked her mother, mother, mother
For fifteen cents, cents, cents
To see the elephant, elephant, elephant
Jump the fence, fence, fence
He jumped so high, high, high
He reached the sky, sky, sky
And never came down, down, down
Till the fourth of July, ly, ly . . . (Bronner, 1988, p. 65)

Finger Plays and Action Songs. **Action songs** combine melody with movement. This is a wonderful combination for active young children. When a new song is introduced, many children only will participate in the movement that they can replicate easily. As they become more familiar with the song, they will sing and use the movement together. Action songs are great favorites for young children because of the repetition of the phrases and the combination of movements. Young children can extend these songs as they add new verses with appropriate actions. Creating extensions provides opportunities for children to develop their flexibility and originality.

Some rhymes are played as a game. Child number one speaks first, then child number two speaks those lines marked with a two, as shown in the following example (Johnson & Sayers, 1959).

> 1. I went up a pair of stairs.
> 2. Just like me.
> 1. I went up two pairs of stairs.
> 2. Just like me.
> 1. I went to the room.
> 2. Just like me.
> 1. I looked out the window.
> 2. Just like me.
> 1. And there I saw a monkey.
> 2. Just like me.

Additional rhymes and finger plays can be found in Appendix G.

Jump Rope Rhymes and Street Chants. Primary children are interested in street chants and jump rope rhymes because they invite them to interact orally and be active physically. These verses are part of the oral tradition that links rhyme, rhythm, and humor, and are meant to be shared aloud in a social setting.

Street chants originated in diverse cultures and provide a valuable contribution to what might be unique for one group or familiar to all society. *Street Rhymes Around the World* (Yolen, 1992) includes rhymes from different countries and are illustrated by artists from the areas represented. These chants help

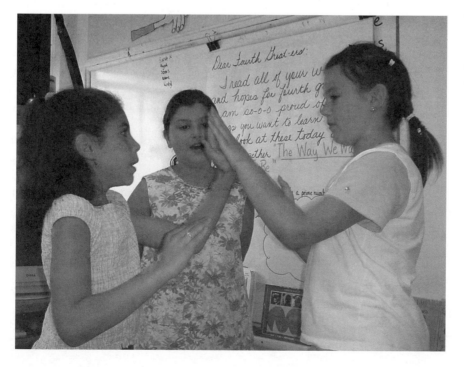

Fourth graders doing hand jives. (Photo by Michael Talley)

children recognize that rhymes can come from different parts of the world and be enjoyed internationally.

Many folk rhymes are sung or recited. They provide interesting sound patterns and humor that give children pleasure and a mechanism for all bouncing, handclapping, and rope-jumping (Buchoff, 1995).

Handclapping rhymes are popular with primary children. An example is the following (Bronner, 1988).

> Playmate, come out and play with me
> And bring your dollies three
> Climb up my apple tree
> Slide down my rain barrel
> Climb down my cellar door
> And we'll be jolly friends
> Forevermore. (p. 61)

Some sources for rhymes and chants include these publications.

Boardman, B., & Boardman, D. (1993). *Red hot peppers: The Skookum book of jump rope games, rhymes and fancy foot work*. Seattle, WA: Sasquatch.

Cole J. (1989). *Anna Banana: 101 jump rope rhymes*. New York: Morrow.

Cole, J., & Calmenson, S. (1990). *Miss Mary Mack and other children's street rhymes*. New York: Morrow.

Schwartz, A. (1992). *And the green grass grew all around*. New York: Harper Collins.

Withers, C. (1988). *A rocket in my pocket: The rhymes and chants of young Americans*. New York: Henry Holt.

Yolen, J. (1992). *Street rhymes around the world*. Honesdale, PA: Wordsong.

Playing Music

Music is an aural language that uses the basic elements of pitch, rhythm, timbre, and form. Countless combinations of these elements have given rise to a remarkable variety of music found throughout the world. Howard Gardner (1983) concludes that people who have frequent experience with music can use the elements in musical activities, including playing with instruments and composing. The foundation for this interest can be laid in the early childhood classroom by providing many opportunities for children to play and create with musical instruments.

Playing music can provide involvement with many different materials and instruments. For playing to be effective in developing discriminating taste, the musical materials should be of good quality. The sounds produced by the instrument or materials should be pleasant to the ear and easily manipulated by small hands. There are many possibilities for playing music in the early childhood classroom. The following suggestions are only a beginning list of the possibilities for the development of a music curriculum that includes making music and participating in the playing of instruments.

Instruments Played by the Children

Children can use their bodies to create rhythm or instruments to produce patterns of accompaniment.

Physical Accompaniments.   Children, using parts of their bodies, can produce many sounds and rhythms. Toddlers demonstrate this ability very early as they clap to the music they hear. The possibilities for producing these body sounds are almost limitless. Some of the most frequently used with young children are hand-clapping, tapping thighs, rubbing hands together, stomping feet, and tapping head. Older children will be able to snap fingers and clap hands with partners. Using these accompaniments with listening and singing provides another combination of sounds for developing young children.

Percussion Instruments.   One of the most popular instruments with young children is the drum. A drum should be easily accessible in every early childhood classroom so it can be used with songs and recordings during the day. Drums should be selected that produce a good sound, and can be played with either hand or mallet. Providing several sizes and types of drums will encourage children to experiment with the variations of sounds they produce. This encourages both auditory discrimination and creative problem-solving. Bongo drums (two drum heads) and larger African drums provide sounds that encourage different ways of playing and producing rhythm patterns. Children also use drums to experiment with loud and soft sounds. Using the hand to produce sounds helps establish an understanding of the relationship of force to volume. Making different kinds of mallets can encourage further experimentation with sounds. A sponge mallet will produce a very different sound from a mallet made of hard rubber. Young children discover these differences as they explore and manipulate the percussion instrument.

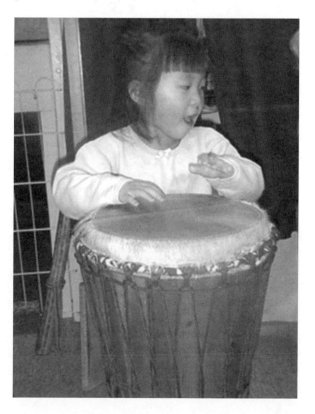

A musical instrument, the Ashiko African drum, makes a unique sound. (Photo by Susan Lachmann)

Rhythm Instruments.   Keeping the beat or creating a rhythm pattern is a very important ability to nurture during the early years. Beat competency reflects the ability to keep time with, or feel the pulse of, music (McDonald, 1979). For many years, rhythm instruments were the only musical instruments used in early childhood programs. Although they remain important, they are only one type of instrument that should be available in a classroom designed to enrich the arts.

Primary children using instruments to accompany recordings of classical music. (Photo by Michael Talley)

Some of the rhythm instruments that should be included in the classroom are:

- rhythm sticks (of varying length and thickness)
- triangle
- wood blocks
- maracas
- bells on sticks
- cymbals (use one side with a mallet)
- tambourine
- hand drums

a. Triangle, b. Maracas, c. Tambourine (Courtesy of Stacy Larsen)

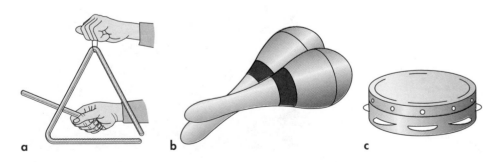

a   b   c

These rhythm instruments can be used by individual children or in small groups. They can accompany listening, singing, and movement activities. Remember that children will need to explore the sounds of these instruments before they are able to play at specific times or in certain patterns. Kindergarten and primary grade children will be able to use rhythm instruments in more complex ways, and develop charts with symbols for their playing.

Instruments Played by Teacher and Children

Some musical instruments can be played by the teacher to accompany songs or used to support the children's beginning efforts with specific instruments.

Alto recorder (Courtesy of Stacy Larsen)

Melody Instruments

Step Bells (xylophone). This set of bells contains metal bars on a frame that provide a C major octave. It has a stair-step design with the lowest tone on the bottom step and the highest tone on the top step. This allows children to connect the visual representation with the sound they hear. These bells are played with a mallet and produce a clear tone. Early experiences with the xylophone are simply exploring the sounds produced. Later in the development of musical skills, some children will be able to play simple patterns and melodies.

Resonator Bells. On a set of **resonator bells**, each bar is attached to an individual wooden sound box that provides a resonance to the sound. The bars can be separated and played individually, or specific notes can be grouped together to accompany a specific song. A set for an early childhood classroom should contain a scale from middle C to C in the octave above. The beautiful tone of the resonator bells makes them appropriate for inclusion in the early childhood classroom since young children are very sensitive to sound during this period.

Keyboard (piano or electronic). A piano or keyboard provides new opportunities to hear and play simple melodies. The children will enjoy teachers who can play simple melodies on the keyboard. Melody instruments help them establish the tune of a song. Children can experiment with the keyboard, recognize tonal effects, and improvise melodies.

Mandolin (Courtesy of Stacy Larsen)

Autoharp or Omni Chord (electronic). This simple chording instrument is an effective accompaniment for young children's voices. The teacher simply presses a button and strums. This activates the strings of a specific chord to accompany the song. These chords add richness to singing and opportunities for children to experience tones in harmony. Many songbooks include the chords the teacher can use with an Autoharp or guitar.

Guitar. The guitar can be used to accompany songs that young children enjoy singing in the early childhood classroom. Many of these songs are in the key of C or F, and require only three or four chords to support the children's singing. The guitar is a very popular instrument that children have seen many times. They are very interested in hearing and playing the guitar. When selecting a guitar for an early childhood classroom, be sure it produces a good sound and can be strummed by the children.

The guitar is an instrument that young children enjoy. (Photo by Michael Talley)

Moving to Music

Music and movement are interconnected for young children (Jalongo, 1996). The importance of movement in the early childhood years will be discussed extensively in Chapter 6.

Music Center

Every preschool and kindergarten should have a music center where children can explore sounds. The primary goal of an effective music center is to attract the children to the area and stimulate their music-making. A carefully designed center provides many opportunities for children to manipulate, compare, contrast, and create with a variety of musical materials. Some items that should be in the center on a regular basis are a good tape recorder with a variety of tapes, a collection of instruments, and songbooks. An interesting grouping of instruments for the center could include a drum, rhythm sticks, triangles, resonator, and step xylophone. These provide variations in sound to encourage rhythmic experimentation in the center. Other items should be rotated into the center to provide changes that will stimulate new exploration with sounds. A collection of African instruments encourages children to create new sound patterns and chants, chording instruments provide multiple sounds to examine, and melody instruments produce clear tones.

The center provides a music environment that is based on free-choice participation, allowing for exploration based on the needs, interest, and ability of the child. Here, children direct their own activity, decide how much time to spend in the area, and how they will use the materials (Achilles, 1992).

The teacher is responsible for setting up an effective music center and changing the materials in the area to maintain interest. But his most important role is to observe the children as they learn about music. This center provides

In the music center, the workings of a piano are mounted on the wall so children can experiment with the sounds the strings produce. (Photo by Michael Talley)

many opportunities for the teacher to observe children's interest, abilities, and expressive techniques The children can experiment with music, follow their interest, and work at their own pace. They are able to play with music without being tied to a specific song or group activity. This open-ended center provides a safe place for children to explore musical elements freely. Although the teacher can pose questions about the sound of the drum being played in the center, most frequently he is not involved in the musical play. The teacher is a model for the enjoyment of music during the day but it is the child who is creating the music for himself in the music center (Isbell, 1995; Kenney, 1995).

Creating Music

Music provides many opportunities to move beyond the repeating of a song to the creation of musical compositions. The early childhood teacher provides varied experiences that are the basis for the children's musical development. The teacher surrounds the children with music by weaving it throughout the day and across the curriculum (Hildebrandt, 1998). The songs of childhood, listening to the classics, playing instruments, and moving to music are the foundation for musical understanding and enjoyment in young children. These are essential components for all children to experience during the early years. Musical experiences that match the developmental characteristics of young children will provide pleasure and satisfaction. Early experiences in listening, singing, playing, and movement provide a secure foundation for creating music in their own individual way. From this base, established early, children will move on to creating new words for songs, expand verses, develop variations of melody, improvise with voice, and use instruments in new ways.

A stage in the music center encourages musical performances, singing, and dancing. (Photo by Michael Talley)

Summary

Music has long been valued in early childhood programs because it provides enjoyment, opportunities for participation, and relaxation for the weary child. Today, we are more aware of the potential for music to nurture not only the souls of children but also their intellects. Music has a magnetic quality that draws all children into the sounds, rhythms, and patterns it produces. Music provides opportunities to understand different cultures, appreciate musical preferences, and identify similarities and differences.

When music is an integral part of the early childhood program, it includes listening, singing, making music, and movement. It is interwoven throughout the day, and included in theme studies or projects. Young children enjoy participating in all aspects of music and are not concerned about obtaining perfection during the process. A classroom filled with music inspires young children to be musicians, singers, and composers while providing a positive experiential base for extending their budding musical interest.

Key Terms

dynamics	Autoharp
harmony	social competencies
melody	auditory awareness
pitch	auditory discrimination
rhythm	auditory sequencing
timbre	appreciation
finger play	active listening
percussion instruments	duets
small motor coordination	rounds
rhythm instruments	chant
guitar	action songs
keyboard	resonator bells

Reflection

1. Describe how musical abilities develop from infancy through the primary years.

2. What are some appropriate goals for music in early childhood?

3. How can an early childhood teacher demonstrate an interest in music?

4. What are the major elements of music that should be included in the early childhood classroom?

5. Identify the different types of songs and music that can be used with young children.

6. What instruments can young children play to accompany their singing or recordings?

Thinking about the Creative Episode

1. How can you determine that Jamal is attending to the musical chant?

2. Is this interaction important to Jamal and his father? Why?

3. In what musical ways can the father share his heritage with his son?

Possibilities for Adult Learners

Activity: Music Appreciation

Goal: To listen to different types of music and appreciate the preferences of others.

Materials: A CD player and recordings of at least three different kinds of music (jazz, marching bands, Native American, pop, classical, or bluegrass).

Procedure:

1. The teacher selects three recordings and plays them for the students without comment or critique.

2. Ask students to listen to all the recordings and select their favorite from these.

3. After listening, take a poll to learn each person's favorite selection and discuss their preference.

4. Discuss the different preferences and the reasons for the selection.

5. Can these selections be used with young children?

Activity: Expanding Your Repertoire

Goal: To discover some of the recordings that are on the market today specifically for use with young children.

Materials: A CD player or tape player, and a collection of some of the musical recordings used in early childhood programs.

Procedure:

1. Ask the students to identify recordings they have heard.

2. Play some recordings from musicians they have not heard to expand their repertoire.

3. Lead a discussion about using a variety of music with young children that includes popular favorites as well as other music.

Open-ended Activities for Young Children

Pre-K–K

Activity: On Stage

Goal: To encourage children to use their singing voice.

Materials: Microphone (this can be made from a paper tube with a round ball attached to the end), and tape player or recorder.

Procedure:

1. Add the microphone to the music center or drama area. Some children will immediately begin to song and perform. Others will watch the performance and add their own voice later.

2. The tape recorder will encourage the children to tape their recreations and listen to how the music sounds.

3. If they wish, the children can share their musical recordings with their classmates.

Pre-K or Primary

Activity: Making Instruments

Goal: To create musical instruments and use them to make music.

Materials: Pieces of wood dowel rods of varying thickness and lengths, sandpaper, several colors of latex paint, and brushes.

Procedure:

1. Children can select two pieces of dowel rods that they would like to use.

2. Have them sand the rough edges with sandpaper and paint in the colors they prefer.

3. After the paint dries, the children can use the rhythm sticks to accompany a musical recording or their singing.

Primary Grades

Activity: Our Musical Composition

Goal: Children will create their own musical composition.

Materials: Chart paper and markers.

Procedure:

1. Divide the class into small groups of two or three children.

2. Ask each group to create a musical phrase, and write the rhythm or notes on chart paper. (The phrase can be sung, clapped, or created in another way.)

3. Bring the children back together and let each group share their musical phrase.

4. Allow the entire class to determine the order in which the phrases will be used in the composition.

5. Place the chart papers in order of the composition. Group members can stand in front of their phrase.

6. Play the entire composition with each group performing its phrase.

7. Discuss the sounds, patterns, and sequence.

8. Allow the class to try the composition in a different order and evaluate again.

9. Keep the musical phrases and return to this project at a later point.

Music Resources

There are a number of different types of resources that can be used to enrich the music program for young children. Some of the most helpful are songbooks with collections of appropriate songs and books that follow a musical theme.

Songbooks

There are many collections of children's songs that are available to help the early childhood educator build his musical repertoire. Listed below are some sources for songs that young children will enjoy singing.

Glazer, T. (1980). *Do your ears hang low?: Fifty more musical fingerplays.* New York: Doubleday & Company, Inc.
This book resents words and music to 50 songs with directions for accompanying finger plays.

Guthrie, W., & Guthrie, M. (1992). *Woody's 20 grow big songs.* New York: HarperCollins Publishers.
This is a replication of an unpublished songbook, lost for over 40 years. It was written in the late 1940s by the legendary songwriter and folksinger, Woody Guthrie, and his wife, Marjorie Mazia, a modern dancer. Inspired by their own young daughter, the Guthries wrote these songs to perform and share with children.

Hudson, W., & Hudson, C. (1995). *How sweet the sound: African-American songs for children.* New York: Scholastic, Inc.
How Sweet the Sound gives readers a glimpse at the history of African Americans through their music. Key periods are spotlighted by a variety of songs from Africa, spirituals, work songs, gospels, jazz, blues, play songs, chants, soul, and popular music of our time. Includes music and bibliographic references.

Kidd, R. (1992). *On top of old smoky: A collection of songs and stories from Appalachia.* Nashville, TN: Ideals Children's Books.
A collection of eleven traditional songs and three folk tales from Appalachia, including The Frog He Went A'Courting, I Gave My Love a Cherry, and Jack and the Bean Tree.

Langstaff, N., & Langstaff, J. (1986). *Sally go round the moon.* Boston, MA: Nimrod Press.
These traditional songs form an extraordinary body of beautiful tunes—catchy, rhythmic, and fun—many of which contain a small child's first introduction to poetry and verse.

Manning, J. (1998). *My first songs.* New York: Harper Festival.
For toddlers who love to sing and dance, this collection contains ten favorite, easy-to-sing songs. (Infant-Toddler)

Orozco, J. (1994). *De colores and other Latin-Ameican folk songs for children.* New York: Dutton Children's
   Books.
This rich collection of children's music from the Spanish-speaking world represents the contributions of
many people from cultures in Europe, Africa, and the Americans who have handed down songs from one
generation to the next such as songs for special occasions and for every day, songs for learning, songs for
singing in a family or group, and songs just for fun.

Raffi. (1993). *Raffi: Children's favorites.* New York: Amsco Publications.
Over 50 songs written or adapted by Raffi for the delight of children everywhere. In easy-to-play, full-sound-
ing arrangements with complete lyrics and guitar chord boxes.

Raffi. (1996). *Raffi's top 10 songs to read.* New York: Crown Publishers, Inc.
Includes lyrics, music, illustrations and a suggested activity for each of the ten children's songs. (Pre-K–2)

Musical Instruments

Several books include directions for making musical instruments and others
have a theme that relates to the playing of an instrument. Both of these resources can provide another way to create music and appreciate the process.

Doney, M. (1995). *Musical instruments.* New York: Franklin Watts.
Provides step-by-step instructions for making a variety of musical instruments from around the world including Mexican rhythm sticks, Ethiopian bells, and a paper prayer drum from India. (Primary)

Hausherr, R. (1992). *What instrument is this?* New York: Scholastic, Inc.
Identifies an array of popular musical instruments, and discusses how they are made, how they sound, and
the styles of music for which they are best suited. (Primary K–3)

Martin, B., Jr. (1994). *The maestro plays.* New York: Henry Holt and Company.
A colorful book that shows the maestro playing a variety of musical instruments. (Pre-K–K)

Moss, L. (1995). *Zin! Zin! Zin! A violin.* New York: Simon & Schuster Books for Young Readers.
Ten instruments take their parts, one by one, in a musical performance. (Pre-K–K)

Oates, E. H. (1995). *Making music: Six instruments you can create.* New York: Harper Collins.
Includes instructions for making a variety of simple musical instruments from ordinary household items.
(Pre-K–3)

Schaff, P. (1980). *A violin close up.* New York: Four Winds Press.
A close-up look at the violin: naming and illustrating its parts, and describing how it makes music. (Pre-K–1)

VanKampen, V., & Eugen, I. C. (1989). *Orchestranimals.* New York: Scholastic Inc.
A band of animal musicians introduces the symphony orchestra. (Pre-K–1)

Selected Musical Recordings

Collections of Various Artists:

Smithsonian Folkways Children's Music Collection: This collection of 26 songs, play-party games, and poems
   was selected from over 200 outstanding recordings of music performed for and by young children.
Collection. (1998). *Smithsonian folkways children's music collection* [sound recording]. Washington, DC:
Smithsonian Folkways Recordings.

A Fish That's a Song: Songs and Stories for Children: Nineteen culturally diverse songs by legendary perform-
   ers to delight young children.
Collection. (1993). *A fish that's a song: Songs and stories for children* [sound recording]. Washington, DC:
Smithsonian Folkways Recordings.

Ella Jenkins:

You'll Sing a Song and I'll Sing a Song: This lively recording invites children to sing, play rhythm instruments, whistle, hum, clap, and chant.
Jenkins, E. (1992). *You'll sing a song and I'll sing a song* [sound recording]. Washington, DC: Smithsonian Folkways Recordings.

Multicultural Children's Songs: Ella introduces young children to the chants, songs, and rhythms of a variety of cultures, with this collection of 23 songs.
Jenkins, E. (1995). *Multicultural children's songs* [sound recording]. Washington, DC: Smithsonian Folkways Recordings.

African American Folk Rhythms: This compilation of songs celebrates the musical heritage of African Americans.
Jenkins, E. (1998). *African American folk rhythms* [sound recording]. Washington, DC: Smithsonian Folkways Recordings.

Songs and Rhythms from Near and Far: Ella and her friends take listeners on a journey to many lands. They treat us to songs and dances and a variety of musical instruments and textures.
Jenkins, E. (1997). *Songs and rhythms from near and far* [sound recording]. Washington, DC: Smithsonian Folkways Recordings.

Greg & Steve:

We All Live Together: Greg Scelsa and Steve Millang present music that will invite young children to participate.
Scelsa, G., & Millang, S. (1995). *We all live together* [sound recording]. Huntington Beach, CA: Young Heart Music.

Kids in Motion: Songs for Creative Movement: Fifteen spirited songs that invite children to get up and move to the music.
Scelsa, G., & Millang, S. (1995). *Kids in motion: songs for creative movement* [sound recording]. Huntington Beach, CA: Young Heart Music.

Pete Seeger:

Birds, Beasts, Bugs, and Fishes (Little and Big): These songs create an irresistible collection of songs to sing along with, draw pictures about, play hand games to, and be enjoyed and learned by the entire family.
Seeger, P. (1998). *Birds, beasts, bugs, and fishes (little and big)* [sound recording]. Washington, DC: Smithsonian Folkways Recordings.

American Folk, Game, and Activity Songs for Children: A compilation of two previously released albums, this collection includes 22 classic folk and activity songs for children of all ages.
Seeger, P. (2000). *American folk, game, and activity songs for children* [sound recording]. Washington, DC: Smithsonian Folkways Recordings.

Raffi:

Singable Songs for the Very Young: Raffi fascinates children and encourages self-respect and appreciation for diversity.
Raffi. (1996). *Singable songs for the very young* [sound recording]. Cambridge, MA: Rounder Records Corp.

Rise and Shine: Cheerful songs let kids get into the act with fun-to-do sound effects and simple body movements.
Raffi. (1996). *Rise and shine* [sound recording]. Cambridge, MA: Rounder Records Corp.

Thomas Moore:

I am Special Just Because I'm Me: This recording combines active music exploration, while emphasizing positive self-images and demonstrating vital early childhood concepts.
Moore, T. (1986). *I am special just because I'm me* [sound recording]. Charlotte, NC: Thomas Moore Records.

Singing, Moving and Learning: Thomas and the children sing about the bus driver, the doctor, the opera singer, and waiter. This recording also includes a rock'n'roll version of *Itsy Bitsy Spider* and reinforces geometric shapes with *Moving Hands*.
Moore, T. (1989). *Singing, moving and learning* [sound recording]. Charlotte, NC: Thomas Moore Records.

Songs Children Love to Sing: Including many of the traditional songs that are sung with young children. Instrumentals of all songs are included on this recording.

Moore, T. (2000). *Songs children love to sing* [sound recording]. Charlotte, NC: Thomas Moore Records.

Woody Guthrie:

Nursery Days: Woody Guthrie combines delicious-sounding words from down to earth imagery and flavors it all with humor.

Guthrie, W. (1992). *Nursery days* [sound recording]. Washington, DC: Smithsonian Folkways Recordings.

Notes

[1]Andress, B. (1980). *Music experiences in early childhood.* New York: Holt, Rinehart & Winston.

[2]Fitzhenry, R. I. (Ed.) (1993). *The Harper book of quotations* (3rd ed.). New York: Harper Collins Books.

[3]May, B. (1970). *Jefferson himself: The personal narration of a many-sided American.* Charlottesville, VA: University Press of Virginia.

References

Achilles, E. (1992). Current perspectives on young children's thinking. In B. Andress (Ed.), *Readings in early childhood education* (pp. 67–74). Reston, VA: Music Educators' National Conference.

Bayless, K., & Ramsey, M. (1986). *Music, a way of life for the young child.* Columbus, OH: Merrill.

Blackburn, L. (1998). *Whole music: A whole language approach to teaching music.* Portsmouth, NH: Heinemann.

Bronner, S. J. (Ed.). (1988). *American children's folklore.* Little Rock, AR: August House Publishers.

Buchoff, R. (1994). Joyful voices: Facilitating language growth through rhythmic response to chants. *Young Children, 49*(4), 26–30.

Buchoff, R. (1995, Spring). Jump rope rhymes in the classroom? *Childhood Education, 71*(3), 149.

Feierabend, J. (1990). Music in early childhood. *Design for Arts in Education, 91*(6), 15–20.

Gardner, H. (1983). *Frames of mind: The theory of multiple intelligences.* New York: Basic Books.

Haines, J. E., & Gerber, L. L. (1999). *Leading young children to music.* Upper Saddle River, NJ: Prentice Hall.

Hildebrandt, C. (1998). Creativity in music and early childhood. *Young Children, 53*(6), 68–74.

Isbell, R. (1995). *The complete learning centers book.* Beltsville, MD: Gryphon House.

Jalongo, M. R. (1996). Using recorded music with young children: A guide for non-musicians. *Young Children, 51*(5), 6–14.

Johnson, E. S., & Sayers, F. C. (1959). *Anthology of children's literature.* Boston: Houghton Mifflin Co.

Kenney, S. (1995). The voice within. *Teaching Music, 2*(5), 36–37.

Kenney, S. (1997). Music in developmentally appropriate integrated curriculum. In C. H. Hart, D. C. Burts, & R. Charlesworth (Eds.), *Integrated curriculum and developmentally appropriate practice: Birth to eight* (pp. 103–144). Albany, NY: State University of New York Press.

McDonald, D. (1979). *Music in our lives: The early years.* Washington, DC: National Association for the Education of Young Children.

Rauscher, F. (1995). Does music make you smarter? *PTA Today, 20*(5), 8–9.

Totline Publications. (Eds.). (1994). *1001 rhymes & fingerplays for working with young children.* Torrance, CA: Totline Publications.

Wolf, J. (1994). Let's sing it again: Creating music with young children. *Young Children, 47*(2), 56–61.

Yolen, J. (1992). *Street rhymes around the world.* Honesdale, PA: Wordsong.

Additional Reading

Achilles, E. (1999). Creating music environments in early childhood programs. *Young Children, 54*(1), 21–26.

Andress, B. L., & Walker, L. M. (Eds.). (1992). *Readings in early childhood music education.* Reston, VA: National Association for Music Education.

Beaton, P. (1995). The importance of music in the early childhood language curriculum. *International Schools Journal, 15*(1), 28–38.

Campbell, L., Campbell, B., & Dickinson, D. (1996). *Teaching and learning through multiple intelligences.* Needlam Heights, MA: Allyn & Bacon.

Gharavi, G. J. (1993). Music skills for preschool teachers: Needs and solutions. *Arts Education Policy Review, 94*(3), 27–30.

Lang, S. S. (1999). Music: Good for not only the soul, but the brain. *Human Ecology Forum, 27*(2), 24.

Merrion, M., & Rubin, J. E. (1996). *Creative approaches to elementary curriculum.* Portsmouth, NH: Heinemann.

Nantais, K. M., & Schellenberg, E. G. (1999). The Mozart effect: An artifact of preference. *Psychological Science, 10*(4), 370–374.

Nichols, B. L., & Honig, A. S. (1997). Music teaches children about themselves and others. *Early Childhood Education Journal, 24*(4), 213–217.

Peery, J. G. (1993). Music in early childhood education. In B. Spodex (Ed.), *Handbook of research on the education of young children* (pp. 207–223). New York: Macmillan Publishing Company.

Silberg, J. (1998). *The I can't sing book: For grown-ups who can't carry a tune in a paper bag but want to do music with young children.* Beltsville, MD: Gryphon House.

Snyder, S. (1996). Early childhood music lessons from "Mr. Holland's Opus." *Early Childhood Education Journal, 24*(2), 103–105.

Tarnowski, S. M. (1999). Musical play and young children. *Music Educators Journal, 86*(1), 26–29.

Webster, P. R., & Richardson, C. (1993). Asking children to think about music. *Arts Education Policy Review, 94*(3), 7–11.

Children's Literature Connection

Degan, B. (1983). *Jamberry.* New York: Harper & Row.
A little boy, walking in the forest, meets a big lovable bear that takes him on a delicious berry-picking adventure in the magical world of Berryland. (Pre-K–1)

Greenfield, E. (1991). *I make music.* New York: Black Butterfly Children's Books.
A young girl experiences music with the help of her mother and father. (Infant)

Harter, D. (1997). *Walking through the jungle.* New York: Mulberry.
A young explorer discovers the different animals and terrains of the world before arriving home, safe and sound, for supper. (Pre-K–1)

Hurd, T. (1984). *Mama don't allow.* New York: Harper Collins.
Miles and the Swamp Band have the time of their lives playing at the Alligator ball until they discover the menu includes Swamp Band Soup. (Primary K–2)

Johnston, T. (1991). *Grandpa's song.* New York: Dial Books for Young Readers.
When a young girl's beloved, exuberant, grandfather becomes forgetful, she helps him by singing their favorite song. (Primary K–3)

Kraus, R. (1990). *Musical Max.* New York: Simon & Schuster Books for Young Readers.
The peace and quiet following Max's decision to put his instruments away drives the neighbors just as crazy as his constant practicing. (Primary K–3)

Krementz, J. (1991). *A very young musician.* New York: Simon & Schuster Books for Young Readers.
Text and photographs feature a boy who is learning to play the trumpet. (Primary 1–3)

Kuskin, K. (1986). *The philharmonic gets dressed.* New York: Harper Collins.
The 105 members of the orchestra are shown showering, dressing, traveling, and setting themselves up on stage for an evening's concert. (Primary 1–3)

McDermott, G. (1997). *Musicians of the sun.* New York: Simon & Schuster.
In this retelling of an Aztec myth, Lord of the Night sends Wind to free four musicians that the Sun is holding prisoner, so they can bring joy to the world. (Primary 1–3)

Rowe, J., & Perham, M. (1993). *Making sounds.* Chicago: Children's Press.
The book describes different sounds, how they are made, and how they travel. (Primary 1–3)

Sage, J. (1991). *The little band.* New York: Margaret K. McElderry Books.
A little band marches through town, delighting everyone with its beautiful music. (Pre–K)

Schuch, S. (1999). *A symphony of whales.* San Diego: Harcourt Brace & Company.
Young Glashka's dream of the singing of whales, accompanied by a special kind of music, leads to the rescue of thousands of whales stranded in a freezing Siberian bay. This book is based on a true story. (Primary K–3)

Weatherford, C. B. (2000). *The sound that jazz makes.* New York: Walker & Company.
An illustrated history of the origins and influences of jazz from Africa to contemporary America. (Primary K–3)

Williams, V. (1983). *Something special for me.* New York: Greenwillow Books.
Rosa has difficulty choosing a special birthday present to buy with the coins her mother and grandmother have saved, until she hears a man playing music on an accordion. (Primary K–2)

Williams, V. (1984). *Music, music for everyone.* New York: Mulberry.
Rosa plays her accordion with her friends in the Oak Street Band and earns money to help her mother with expenses while her grandmother is sick. (Primary K–3)

Helpful Web Sites

The addresses and corresponding agencies below are taken from the Web sites. Due to the dynamic nature of the Internet, please remember that Web sites are subject to change at any time.

http://www.mtna.org/index1.htm   Music Teachers National Association (MTNA)—A nonprofit organization of independent and collegiate music teachers committed to furthering the art of music through programs that encourage and support teaching, performance, composition, and scholarly research.

http://www.menc.org/   National Association for Music Education—Advances music education by encouraging the study and making of music by all.

http://musiceducator.org/index.html   Music Educator—An online community for music educators worldwide.

http://www.isme.nl/index.shtml   The International Society for Music Education—Stimulates music eduction as an integral part of general education.

For additional resources involving creativity and the arts with young children, visit our Web site at **http://www.earlychilded.delmar.com**

Chapter 6

Creative Movement: More Than the Hokey Pokey

During the first eight years of development, children are gaining control of their bodies. A major goal for early childhood teachers is to enhance **motor development** through creative experiences. Using **creative movement** allows young children to respond to open-ended activities in unique ways. Designing movement experiences with creativity in mind provides an opportunity for all young children to experience success, and build confidence in their physical and expressive capabilities.

Creative Episode

*C*onnor was a joy to watch as a four-year-old. He enjoyed racing through his grandmother's house, making sputtering sounds like a race car or playing hide and seek with his grandfather. When Bethany, his seven-year-old sister, asked her aunt to hold the limbo stick, it was evident from Connor's expression that he did not know how to do the limbo. With her aunt holding a long broom handle level to the floor, Bethany tried bending backward low enough to get under. Connor simply jumped over the top until Bethany explained the dance. Then Mary Kate, the two-year-old, joined in and crawled under the broom instead of bending under like her sister. This activity persisted for over thirty minutes, with each child making variations on the theme of getting under or over the limbo broom. Eventually, they each adopted the others' methods. Bethany and Kate tried jumping over the *broom like their brother. Connor and Bethany crawled under, in Mary Kate's style. Finally, all three children tried bending backward low enough to get under the broom. The only people who were tired at the end of the thirty minutes were the adults holding the limbo broom.*

Movement Terms

Nonlocomotion. Stationary actions that include stretching, bending, swaying, and shaking.

Locomotor. This is movement through space that includes walking, marching, jumping, and skipping.

Energy. The force that is used to show intentions. This can include smooth or sharp, and sudden or sustained.

Personal Space. The personal or shared area that is used by the body during movement. This includes the levels of high and low, and directions such as forward, backward, up, and down.

Time. Time includes rhythm, speed, emphasis, and duration of the movement.

Kinesthetics. The use of the body to learn about physical capabilities, develop body awareness, and gain understanding of the world.

"Creative rhythmic movement is the individual's interpretation of thoughts and feelings expressed through the use of the body."

G. Andrews, 1954[1]

Movement is fun for children. When they play on their own, invent new games, and want to liven up what is happening, they move. The physical development demonstrated by two-year-old Mary Kate, four-year-old Connor, and seven-year-old Bethany is appropriate for their age and stage of development. They move like healthy active children. Play experiences provide evidence of children's neuromuscular development, movement skills, cognitive interpretations, communications, and personal-social abilities. Their development was further enhanced by the lively impromptu play at grandmother's house, designed by the seven-year-old to entertain herself and joined by the other children in her family.

Movement for movement's sake is significant because children who learn to use their bodies well and move with confidence, feel more self-assured, enjoy themselves, and develop a physical awareness that enhances their ability to explore on their own. The child's innate desire to move is appreciated by educators who provide unstructured time for movement, and who incorporate movement, and activity into the daily schedule.

Sometimes, early childhood educators and physical educators stress different movement approaches. Early childhood educators tend to focus on creative movement as a part of play and the curriculum. Physical educators stress learning to move in structured and prescribed ways. Today's educators combine the two. Certainly, early childhood educators value play and the child's own interpretation of movement, as in Connor's racing through the house, revving-up his engine while starting and stopping like a race car driver. Learning to play limbo prompted a different type of motoric movement and control that was a response to a structured activity learned in a physical education class. The early childhood classroom teacher will incorporate both, while providing a significant amount of open-ended activities that allow the individual child to interpret movement and to express her own individuality.

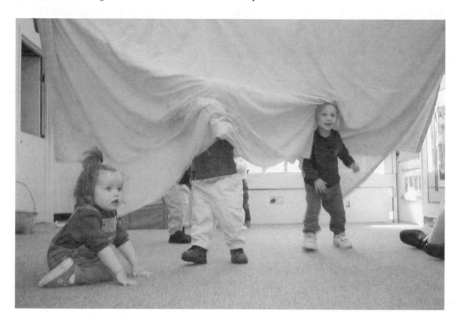

Theory

Rudolph Laban's perspective on young children and movement provides a theory that both early childhood educators and physical education teachers can embrace. Laban (1963) recommends that children develop **body awareness**, **space awareness**, effort, and relationships. Present-day authors rely on Laban's work and apply it to the modern day curriculum. Hoffman, Young, and Klesius (1981) expand creative movement activities and curricular suggestions for programs with young children.

Bodily-Kinesthetic Intelligence

Howard Gardner's (1983) theories of multiple intelligences describe bodily-kinesthetic intelligence as the ability to unite the body and mind in physical performance. Beginning with control of automatic and voluntary movements, kinesthetic intelligence progresses to using the body in highly differentiated and skilled ways. All talented performances require an acute sense of timing and the transformation of intention into action. Highly developed kinesthetic intelligence is discerned easily when observing actors, athletes, or dancers. It also is evident in inventors, jewelers, mechanics, and others who work skillfully with their hands or objects. According to Campbell, Campbell, and Dickinson (1996), "bodily-kinesthetic intelligence is the foundation of human knowing, since it is through our sensory-motor experiences that we experience life" (p. 67). Drama, dance, and musical expression involve active problem-solving that challenges children to use their physical learning system (Given, 2000).

Logical-Mathematical Intelligence

Piaget (1962) theorized that children learn about space, geometry, and physics through their explorations and interactions with objects. In Gardner's (1973, 1983) theory of multiple intelligences, he postulates that logical-mathematical intelligence allows the learner to discern patterns, chains of reasoning, and relationships.

Constructivist Theory

Piaget (1963) and Vygotsky (1962) are associated with constructivism, a theory of learning that has implications for movement education. Through the processes of assimilation and accommodation, learners construct concepts. When assimilating information, they add to their information by sampling information, and confirming or rejecting it based on their predictions. Their predictions are supported by concepts formed by past experiences and stages of development. When accommodating new information that does not fit their present concepts, learners must construct or reconstruct their concepts based on information that is strong enough to cause a reformation of the concept. New information is assimilated into existing schemas and new constructs must be formed to accommodate this new information (Raines, 1995).

Assimilation and accommodation are associated with the Piagetian theory of learning. Vygotsky (1962) emphasized the importance of learning from others in the zone of proximal development. Through the assistance or mediation of more advanced learners, the child can operate on the next level of development or zone of proximal development. The child's own self-talk, adult-child interactions, and the influence of culture and expectations on learning also are a part of the Vygotskian theory of learning (Raines).

> *"Knowledge is tied to actions. It is through children's exploration and discovery among their actions that the first structures of the mind are formed."*
>
> **J. Piaget, 1973[2]**

Principles of Physical Development

Very young infants move in random ways. These movements become more coordinated and purposeful as they develop into toddlers. As they repeat actions and interact with adults, they gain greater control. Young children enjoy practicing their growing collection of movements and skills. As they learn to use their bodies, there are several interactive components at work: **sensory development** (seeing, hearing, touching, tasting, and smelling) and motor development (large and small muscles). Sensory experiences provide a foundation for the curriculum of young children. Through the senses, young children learn about the world and explore the properties of objects around them. It is valuable for young children to gather information through their senses and to have opportunities to develop these abilities during the early years.

Motor development, the ability to use and control the body, is often broken down into two distinct categories: **gross motor skills** (large muscles like those in the arms, legs, and trunk) and **fine motor skills** (small muscles like those in the hands and fingers). Many educators have consolidated motor skills and sensory skills into a single phrase that they term **sensorimotor development.**

Maxim (1997) summarizes a number of developmental principles that can assist early childhood educators in understanding the progression of motor development.

Directional Growth

It is expected that physical growth progresses from the head down to the toes (**cephalocaudal**), and from the center of the body outward (**proximodistal**). The muscles closest to the head are the first the child is able to control. For example, an infant will be able to lift her head first, and later, be able to raise her body from the floor and crawl. First, the infant will use her shoulder muscles to swat at an object. During the first year, she will be able to pick up a tiny piece of fuzz with her fingers, using a pincer grip.

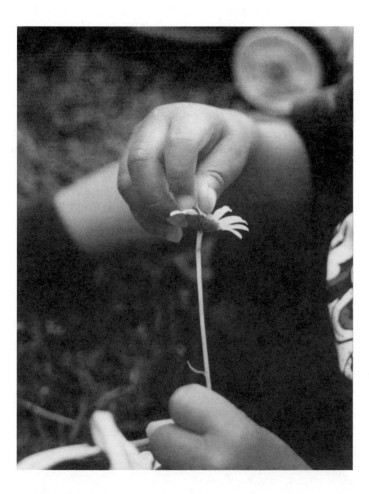

Child using a pincer grip to explore a daisy. (Photo by Su Lorencen)

General to Specific

Physical development progresses from large muscle to small muscle control. The random movements of the infant progress to the specific movements of drawing and cutting observed in preschool. During this differentiation, the child gains control over specific parts of the body and refines their use.

Individual Variations

Growth rates vary from child to child, and each child has her own timetable. In the area of motor development, these individual differences are very observable. There is, however, an orderly sequence of development. Most children crawl before they walk or run. Both heredity and the environment can influence this development as the child gains coordination and control of her body through use and experimentation.

Stages of Development

Developmental specialists describe movement in terms of **locomotion skills** such as walking, running, jumping, hopping, galloping, and skipping. **Manipulative abilities** are reaching, grasping, releasing, throwing, catching, and striking. **Dynamic balance** is maintaining equilibrium while moving. **Static balance** means staying balanced when still. **Axial movements** involve twisting, turning, and extending the body (Gallahue, 1993).

Each of these motor skills has milestones for the observer to determine if the child is in the range of normalcy. While there are overlapping stages of development, the child is expected to refine her movements along a continuum, gaining more control with age and experience. Developmental movement authors have described ranges of locomotion skills in months, years, and levels of refinement.

A teacher is helping a girl successfully walk on the balance beam. (Photo by Michael Talley)

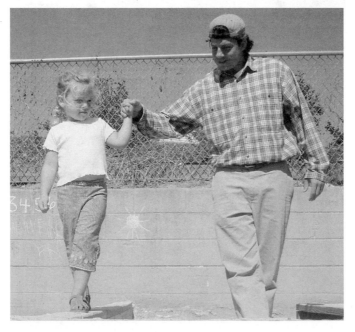

Developmental movement is evaluated in general terms:

walking (13 to 25 months)

running (18 months to 5 years)

jumping (18 months to 6 years)

hopping (3 to 6 years)

galloping (4 to 6 years)

skipping (4 to 6 years) (Gallahue, 1989; Hoffman et al., 1981)

Manipulative abilities include:

reaching, grasping, and releasing (2–4 months to 14–18 months

throwing (2–3 years to 6 years)

catching (2 to 6 years)

kicking (18 months to 6 years)

striking (2–3 years to 6-7 years)

Movement patterns include:

dynamic balance (3 to 7 years)

static balance (10 months to 6 years)

axial movements (2 months to 6 years)

An important point for the early childhood educator to remember is that children move through these stages of locomotion, manipulative, and balance movements by biological timing, experiences, and environment. Developmentally, children are biologically expected to start walking by their first birthday; however, some will walk at nine months and some at 15 months, and still be considered in the range of normalcy. Children can balance on a low balance beam or walking board by the time they are three whereas others may not be proficient until they are four, but still should be considered in the range of normalcy. Young children can strike a ball at the age of three if it is stationary, but many will not develop proficiency until they are five (both children would be considered in the range of normal development). Developmental milestones provide information used to identify children who do not seem to be progressing at the expected rate. Additional evaluation by specialists such as physical and occupational therapists, may identify issues of development that need to be addressed during the early years.

Planning for Movement Activities

Movement programs for young children should be conducted in a noncompetitive environment, with an emphasis on the child receiving individual satisfaction and enjoying the company of others instead of competing with them. Contemporary specialists in children's physical education agree that body management activities, locomotion and nonlocomotion tasks, manipulation opportunities with equipment, and fundamental motor skills should be in the framework of a curriculum for young children (Carson, 1994).

To help educators plan effectively for movement activities, Hoffman et al. refined six developmental themes that reflect Laban's earlier work.

1. **Becoming aware.** Learning about and establishing basic movement capabilities.

2. **Becoming independent.** Increasing self-reliance and confidence in moving.

3. **Accepting and expressing feelings and ideas.** Communicating through movement.

4. **Accepting responsibilities and working cooperatively.** Sharing the movement environment, and respecting and interacting productively with others.

5. **Improving quality of response.** Refining and elaborating movement capabilities for a purpose.

6. **Drawing relationships.** Comprehending the significance of movement in one's lifestyle.

Rae Pica (1995) described three methods of including movement in early childhood programs. These different approaches provide options for early childhood educators as they plan experiences that encourage motor development and creative movement.

Direct Approach

Some motor activities are best taught through direct instruction. Through demonstration, modeling, and imitation, young children can learn about moving their bodies in specific ways. For example, doing a forward roll can be demonstrated and imitated by young children who have never participated in this activity.

Teacher and toddler clap responsively. (Photo by Michael Talley)

Guided Discovery

This child-centered approach allows experimentation and inventiveness as the teacher guides children through the process. Questions can be posed as the children discover ways to use their bodies to complete an activity. The child is guided to move like a turtle, slowly and carefully. Or she is asked the question, "How does a rabbit move?"

Exploration

A divergent problem-solving approach should be used as frequently as possible. This approach matches how young children learn and allows them to determine ideas for themselves. When children are given open-ended possibilities, they can produce a variety of responses. This allows the child to develop creative thinking as well as different movements. For example, if children are asked to move two parts of their bodies at the same time, numerous combinations are possible. If this approach is combined with the opportunity to move to the tempo of music, even more experimentation is encouraged.

Becoming Aware of Bodies in Space and Movement

In the next few pages, several developmental themes will be discussed with recommended accompanying, open-ended movement activities. The first stage is becoming aware of one's own body: the space that it occupies and capability of movement. For example, a two-year-old might look in the mirror as a parent or caregiver sings, "Head, shoulders, knees, and toes." The child will move in response to the song. Then, if the child points to a body part, the adult simply incorporates that into the song: "head, chin, tummy, and shin."

A four-year-old developing body awareness might travel through an obstacle course, with the teacher asking the children to crawl under the table, jump over the blocks, go around the chair, and hide under the blanket. Then, a child can take a turn giving directions to others, using the directional words that help children develop awareness of what they are asking their bodies to do. After the children have experience with obstacle courses, they can design their own with the teacher following their suggestions.

Seven-year-olds can enjoy more sophisticated movements such as curling up like a sleeping caterpillar, stretching arms out like the wings of a bird awakening in the morning, diving like a pelican, or yawning like a waking parent. Then, the children can think of other movements they want to describe and others can follow their lead. A variation on this theme would be to have the children pantomime or demonstrate a movement, and let others guess what they are doing.

"The truest expression of a people is in its dance and its music."

A. de Mille, 1952[3]

Music and Movement

Young children can experience music and movement together. Their innate responses and rhythmic motions feel appropriate to them. The infant, lying on her back, responds to fast music by quickly kicking her feet. Later, she is soothed and relaxes when music with slow wind instruments plays in the background. Toddlers often bounce up and down in response to lively music. Preschoolers play simple rhythm instruments and march in response to the beats they create, especially responding to the tempo. Kindergartners, who have more muscle control, enjoy twirling around, and interpreting the sounds of music ranging from classical to jazz, or Latin to rock and roll. Primary children enjoy dance movements, interpreting the feelings of a piece of music, or responding with exaggerated frantic movements when they hear maracas and kettledrums. They may use light floating movements with music that is played by flutes and recorders.

Preschoolers move to the music. (Photo by Michael Talley)

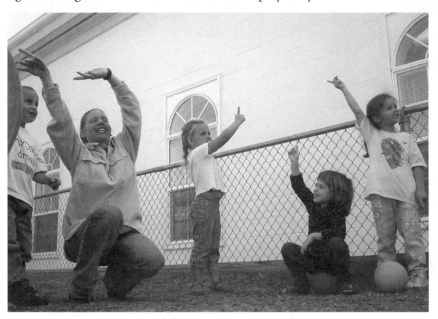

Children with special needs benefit from movement opportunities. For example, Erica is five years old and has spastic cerebral palsy. She uses a wheelchair for mobility. When some children are moving to music, Erica is partnered with Adam who is very sensitive to her needs. He holds Erica's hands, and helps her move her arms in rhythm to the music. The teacher comments that each child is moving in different ways. Erica's unique way of moving is appreciated by the teacher and the other children.

According to Pica (1999), "When a child tiptoes to soft music, stamps her feet to loud music, moves in slow motion to Bach's *Air on the G String* then rapidly to Rimsky-Korsakov's *Flight of the Bumblebee*, sways to a $^3/_4$ meter and skips to a piece in $^6/_8$ time, she is experiencing music on many levels. Not only is she listening, but also she is using her body, mind, and spirit to express and create. Because she is using a multimodal approach, what she learns will make a lasting impression" (p. 113).

Dance

Excellent early childhood teachers engage children in movement in response to music, and incorporate music and movement throughout the curriculum. Another professional who uses music and movement is the dance teacher.

Numerous dance classes and dance academies are available for young children. Dance teachers may employ the more creative and free flowing activities that early childhood teachers promote. However, they may suggest that imitation and learning choreographed movements can help children become aware of their bodies and learn to control their movements.

The issues of what constitutes quality dance education for young children have been debated for decades. The concept of "creative dance as guided exploration" has many similarities to our descriptions of appropriate movement for young children. Blythe Hinitz (1980) reviewed the literature for dance in early childhood education. Hinitz states, "Creative dance is the guided exploration of movement concepts, designed to increase the child's awareness and understanding of his own range of movement and that of others. It is offered as a pre-dance, pre-sport movement experience, one in which the child is the center, and creative involvement and challenge are part of each experience" (p. 1).

For many dance instructors, meeting the parents' expectations of choreographed dance movements, complete with costumes, forces more of an emphasis on performance than early childhood educators would advocate. Yet the concept of imitation is valued by early childhood educators as a form of learning, provided there is room for the child to use what has been learned through imitation and creatively design movements for herself. Some dancers argue that through imitation, they become aware of their bodies and their movements, then they use the movements in their own expressions. The aesthetics of dance are rooted in movements that express feelings, emotions, and actions. Certainly, the great ballets are stories and interpretations of events with highly choreographed movements. However, highly trained adults perform these ballets. The freedom of interpretive dance is more in tune with the life of the young child.

Mary Ann Lee (1993) suggested that children use interpretive dance with *The Tale of Peter Rabbit* by Beatrix Potter (1976). Lee uses an approach of "springboards of activity" rather than choreographed movement. Each child is able to interpret the movements throughout the story in her own way. For example, in the beginning of the story, when the little bunnies are waking up, the children can pretend to wake. Then pretend to get dressed. The springboard for the movement is what is implied in the story. They simply act it out with movement in their own way. Later in the story, when Peter is squeezing under the gate of Mr. McGregor's garden, the children use the idea as a springboard to interpret the movement as they lie on their tummies and wiggle under the imaginary gate. The instructor does not tell them what to do; she allows for individual interpretation. This approach allows children to move in their own way using the motor skills they currently have available. They experience the joy of using the body instead of developing feelings of inadequacy that might occur if they were unable to perform a choreographed pattern.

> "*Nothing is more revealing than movement.*"
>
> **M. Graham, 1935**[4]

Centers and Curriculum Activities That Incorporate Movement

Another way to integrate music into the early childhood classroom is through the use of music centers. These centers are designed and equipped to encourage active involvement in the music process.

Music and Movement Center

Create a music and/or movement center in the classroom. Plan to store materials for both individual and small group activities. Tape and CD players, rhythm instruments, hoops, scarves, ribbons, and crepe paper streamers are a few of the necessities. Perhaps the most important ingredient for the music and movement center is space. While the space for music and movement as a small group selected activity is confined, there are times that the entire classroom, activity room, or outdoor area becomes the space for music and movement activities. For example, a large space is need for movement with a parachute. This activity requires cooperative action as they move the fabric high and low, or smooth and fast.

In the previous chapter, you learned the importance of music as a form of expression. The following reiterates the relationship of music and movement. Children naturally respond to music by moving. An interesting movement experience is to darken the room, play slow classical music, and let the children hold flashlights in their hands as they move around the room. The movement of the light responds to the actions of the child and the music provides a catalyst for the activity.

Responding to rhythm takes practice for some children whereas others seem to grasp it quickly. Help youngsters hear the rhythms by echoing the patterns or counting for emphasis. Using drums, which allow the teacher to emphasize the rhythm pattern, often helps movement in response to the rhythm. Always provide opportunities for the children to make up their own rhythms and let others imitate them. This encourages creative responses. Linking Jennifer's rhythm to Jeff's rhythm is a way to expand the rhythm and repeated pattern.

For many cultures, frozen statues is a popular childhood game. Add music to the game and let the children move as they please to the music. When the music ends, the children must stop and "freeze" in place. Using partners to move together and then freeze can extend the game and the enjoyment. Copeland's Grand Canyon Suite includes the composition Rodeo. This music provides a great deal of variation of tempo that encourages children to move slowly in certain sections and to explode into vigorous movement in other parts of the piece. Asking children to freeze when the music is stopped provides another opportunity to respond to the music.

Dance: Planned and Improvised

Both planned and improvised dances have a place in the early childhood experience. However, improvisation is the better choice for the young child. Ways to increase the enjoyment of dance can include some old-time favorites of early childhood teachers or dances from the children's cultures.

Mirror activities are fun for children. One child can move in a certain way, a right hand on her head, while the other child faces her and places a left hand (mirror image) on her head. By adding more complicated and more exaggerated movements, the children mirror each other. They can take turns creating the images for their partners to mirror. Very young children enjoy mirroring in a real mirror to observe their movement.

Folktales are easily remembered stories from many cultures. Interpretations of folktales are excellent movement devices for storytelling and movement experiences. Start with short tales the children know well such as *Goldilocks and the Three Bears* or *Henny Penny*. At first, the children can play all of the parts and simply move in ways that interpret what the teacher is telling or reading. Later, several children in the class can play parts of the story. For example, three children might be Goldilocks, three children the Papa Bear, and so on. Longer and more complicated tales can be introduced as the children become comfortable in their movements.

Movement As Interpretation of Knowledge

Movement activities also can be used to interpret knowledge from the curriculum. For example, the water evaporation cycle may begin by becoming a vapor from a lake, moving to a cloud, and returning to earth as a raindrop. This cycle can be interpreted through movement. Similarly, the butterfly's life span of egg, larvae, caterpillar, butterfly, can be demonstrated in movement. Movement to weather such as storm clouds gathering to a great thunderstorm crashing, can be interpreted by children moving in response to music, the teacher's direction, or flashing lights on and off to simulate the lightning. Learning experiences through movement provide another way of understanding a concept or process, and match some children's style of knowing.

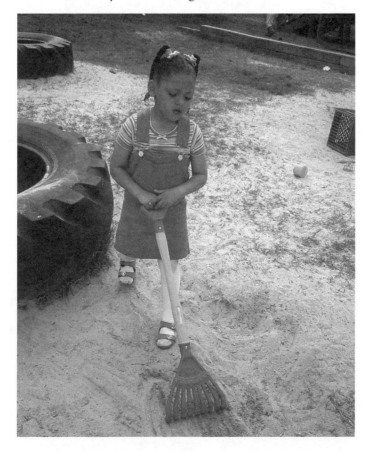

Preschooler raking in the sand. (Photo by Michael Talley)

Outdoor Play

Most outdoor play involves movement. Young children tend to move with great ease in an outdoor environment and use their large muscles. Playground equipment can be arranged to encourage movement practice. For example, a low balance beam with boards securely nailed and raised off the ground a few inches, is an excellent balance practice. Walking railroad ties embedded in the ground or a white line painted on the tricycle track also can be walked for balance.

Tricycles, three-wheelers, and other wheeled toys are great fun for children as they engage in dramatic, imaginative play. Setting up an obstacle course for the wheel toys can benefit the young child learning to follow directions. Safety courses that teach children to obey the safety signals and yield to pedestrians crossing also are helpful for the wheel toy riders.

Various sizes of balls, hoops, beanbags, and lengths of rope are excellent items to add to the playground. Children often will invent their own games and ways of moving. Bouncing, rolling, and catching balls is excellent for eye-hand coordination. A variety of sizes and textures encourage different skill levels.

Moving fabric with a partner. (Photo by Michael Talley)

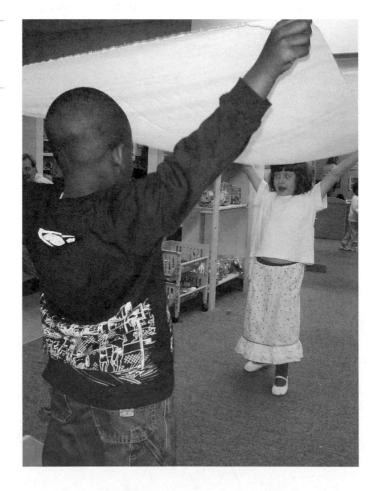

Summary

Early childhood educators stress the need for young children to have opportunities to develop in all domains including cognitive, social-emotional, and physical. Although this view often is expressed in the area of physical development, it is neglected frequently or left to chance occurrences during outdoor play. Recent educational studies, including Gardner's work with kinesthetic intelligence and the study of different learning styles combined with the recognition of today's inactive child, have lead to new interest in the inclusion of motor activities in early childhood programs.

Movement activities—directed, guided, and creative—provide unique opportunities for young children. These motoric experiences help children gain control of their bodies and discover their physical capabilities as they move through space. They also provide another way for children to make connections that unite the mind and body in kinesthetic intelligence.

Creative movement combines the benefits of motor activities and divergent thinking. It provides children the opportunity to respond in personal ways, learn in different styles, and explore the use of their bodies. As young children discover their growing abilities in the use of their bodies and creative thinking, they build their self-esteem and generate a positive view of themselves.

Music inspires children to activate their bodies, respond to rhythm, and experiment with body movements. The combination of music and movement provides another avenue for adding motoric experiences into the early childhood program that is dedicated to the development of the whole child, which certainly includes movement.

Key Terms

motor development

creative movement

nonlocomotion

locomotor

energy

personal space

time

kinesthetics

body awareness

space awareness

sensory development

gross motor skills

fine motor skills

sensorimotor development

cephalocaudal

proximodistal

locomotion skills

manipulative abilities

dynamic balance

static balance

axial movements

Reflection

1. In the past, early childhood educators and physical educators did not always agree on movement instruction. Today, however, their views are more alike. Discuss the two perspectives.

2. Describe a good movement activity for a two-year-old, a four-year-old, and a seven-year-old.

3. Imagine yourself as an early childhood educator who enjoys movement activities, and is committed to involving children in creative movement and learning to move effectively. Describe three movement activities that are open-ended and promote creative responses while helping children increase their motor proficiency.

4. Body awareness activities begin in infancy and continue through a child's development. Select an age that interests you and design an activity that encourages body awareness.

5. Discuss the pros and cons of dance education for preschoolers. Define dance education, as you know it, and the ways it may differ from the discussion in this book.

Thinking about the Creative Episode

1. What typical activities did Conner, the four-year-old, demonstrate?

2. In this episode, children of different levels were participating in the limbo. What were the benefits of this multi-age collaboration?

3. Explain how each child moved in a way that matched her level of motor development.

Possibilities for Adult Learners

Activity: A Trip Down Memory Lane

Goal: For students to remember favorite activities of their childhood.

Materials: Paper, and chart board or dry-erase board.

Procedure:

1. Ask each student to take a sheet of paper and write, on a separate line, five of their favorite activities when they were children, before they started school. For example, the list may include playing hide and seek, coloring, racing my big brother, playing in the sandbox in our backyard, or building a pretend fort or house with blankets and chairs.

2. Ask each student to write down five of the favorite activities to do when not in school but during the primary grades. Examples may include riding my bicycle, jumping rope, learning cheers, playing with dolls, or playing ball.

3. On the board, categorize the activities. Ask your students to share their favorite activities and categorize them by gross motor, fine motor, independent, or small group. For example, riding a three-wheeler is gross motor whereas drawing is fine motor. Jumping rope is usually independent, while one is learning, but it can become a small group activity in the primary grades as children learn to jump to chants and rhymes.

4. Continue the exercise and decide what other major area of development was involved in each activity. For example, playing hide and seek is social development because it involves playing by the rules, and is mathematical because children learn to count by waiting until the counter reaches ten, twenty, or one hundred.

Activity: Personal Space

Goal: To discover ways to help children and adults understand the concept of personal space.

Materials: Sheets of newspaper, hula-hoop, or long pieces of rope.

Procedure:

1. Explain the concept of personal space as it relates to movement activities.

2. Ask each student to place the newspaper, hula-hoop, or rope on the floor.

3. Have them stand inside the hoop or rope formed into a circle.

4. Ask the students to move inside the boundaries as many different ways as they can. Suggest that the hoop or paper provides them with concrete identification of their space.

5. Make suggestions for movements such as bending, stretching, shaking, or moving specific parts of their bodies; and vary the use of space (high, low).

6. After the activity is concluded, discuss the different ways they moved and how the materials help them understand personal space.

Open-ended Activities for Young Children

Pre-K–K

Activity: Let's Move

Goal: To identify the movement required using an object.

Materials: A collection of items from home or the classroom (for example, a broom, clothes brush, eggbeater, towel, or dust cloth).

Procedure:

1. Let the children choose one item and ask them to show how to move when using this object. For example, a broom is used for sweeping, an eggbeater is used for beating eggs, and a towel is used to dry things.

2. Let the children invent a new way to use the object. Ride the broom like a horse; turn the eggbeater up on end and pretend it is a space ship while rotating the beaters with the blast; or swing the towel overhead like a helicopter.

3. Invite the children to collect other objects and think of ways they can use them to move in a new direction or pretend to be something else.

Activity: Scarves and Music

Goal: To experience using a material that responds to movement.

Materials: A colorful collection of scarves of varying sizes.

Procedure:

1. Let the children who are interested select a scarf.

2. Ask the children to experiment with the scarves: see how they float, swerve, and respond to fast movements.

3. Play different types of music such as classical, rock, jazz, or hip-hop, and let the children move however they feel, using their scarves to interpret the music.

4. Other materials could be used such as crepe paper streamers, pieces of fabric, or netting.

Group cooperation allows all children to stand from a sitting position. (Photo by Michael Talley)

Pre-K–K or Primary Grades

Activity: Obstacle Course

Goal: To use the body effectively while moving through obstacles.

Materials: Large cardboard boxes, tubes, blanket or sheet, chairs, sturdy table, blocks, and directional arrows or written signs and symbols.

Procedure for Pre-K–K:

1. Set up a simple obstacle course using a box, chairs covered with a sheet, table, and other items.

2. Place footprints or directional arrows that show children how to move through the obstacle course.

3. The children can rearrange the materials and directions, repeating the movement through the course.

Procedure for Primary Grades:

1. Construct a more complex obstacle course and include signs with written directions. These could include over, under, around, stop, and so forth.

2. Music could be added to encourage movement that matches the tempo of the recordings.

Extension: A course can be set up outdoors using different materials such as barrels, spools, collapsible tunnels, tumbling mats, and landscape timbers.

Primary Grades

Activity: Copy Cat

Goal: To develop body awareness by imitating the movements of others.

Materials: Can be done with a musical recording.

Procedure:

1. Form a circle of children.

2. One person in the group starts to move and the others imitate the movement. The same motion is repeated around the entire circle.

3. The next person in the group creates a different movement that is repeated around the circle.

4. Questions can guide the children to try various movements such as "How do feet move when walking on hot sand?" "How would you catch a gigantic snowball?" "What two parts of your body can move at the same time?"

Kindergarten

Activity: Personal Space Game

Goal: To develop understanding of the term personal space.

Materials: Hula-hoops, carpet squares, or newspapers.

Procedure:

1. Explain the concept of personal space before beginning the movement activities.

2. Give each child a hula-hoop, carpet square, or newspaper.

3. Ask each child to place the object on the floor and stand inside her personal space.

4. Ask the children to move as many different ways as they can while remaining in their personal space. The hula-hoop, carpet square, or newspaper will give them a concrete way to identify the boundaries of this space.

5. Make suggestions for movements such as moving a specific part of the body or the use of space (high or low).

6. After the activity is concluded, discuss the different ways the children moved while staying in their personal space. Later, the same activity can be repeated without the physical boundaries of the hula-hoop, carpet square, or newspaper.

Notes

[1]Andrews, G. (1954). *Creative rhythmic movement for children.* Englewood Cliffs: Prentice-Hall, Inc.

[2]John-Steiner, V. (1985). *Notebooks of the mind: Explorations of thinking.* Albuquerque, NM: University of New Mexico Press.

[3]Partnow, E. (2001). *The quotable woman, the first 5,000 years.* New York: Checkmark Books.

[4]*Ibid.*

References

Campbell, L., Campbell, B., & Dickinson, D. (1996). *Teaching and learning through multiple intelligences.* Needlam Heights, MA: Allyn & Bacon.

Carson, L. M. (1994). Preschool physical education: Expanding the role of teacher preparation. *Journal of Physical Education, Recreation & Dance, 65*(6), 50–53.

Gallahue, D. L. (1989). *Motor development: Infants, children, adolescents.* New York: Benchmark Press.

Gallahue, D. L. (1993). Motor development and movement acquisition in early childhood education. In B. Spodex (Ed.), *Handbook of research on education of young children* (pp. 24–41). New York: Macmillan Publishing Company.

Gardner, H. (1973). *The arts and human development.* New York: John Wiley and Sons

Gardner, H. (1983). *Frames of mind: The theory of multiple intelligences.* New York: Basic Books.

Given, B. K. (2000). Theaters of the mind. *Educational Leadership, 58*(3), 72–75.

Hinitz, B. F. (1980, November). *History of dance in early childhood education.* Paper presented at the Annual Meeting of the National Association for the Education of Young Children, San Francisco, CA.

Hoffman, H. A., Young, J., & Klesius, S. E. (1981). *Meaningful movement for children: A developmental theme approach to physical education.* Dubuque, IA: Kendall/Hunt.

Laban, R. (1963). *Modern Educational Dance.* London: MacDonald and Evans.

Lee, M. (1993). Learning through the arts. *The Journal of Physical Education, Recreation & Dance, 64*(5), 42–47.

Maxim, C. W. (1997). *Sensory motor skills in the very young: Guiding children from infancy through the early years.* Upper Saddle River, NJ: Merrill.

Piaget, J. (1962). (1962). *Play, dreams, and imitation in childhood.* New York: Norton.

Piaget, J. (1963). *The psychology of intelligence.* Totowa, NJ: Littlefield, Adams.

Pica, R. (1995). *Experiences in movement: With music activities and theory.* Clifton Park, NY: Delmar Learning.

Pica, R. (1999). *Moving and learning across the curriculum.* Clifton Park, NY: Delmar Learning.

Potter, B. (1976). *The tale of Peter Rabbit.* New York: Frederick Warne and Company.

Raines, S. C. (1995). *Whole language across the curriculum: Grades 1, 2, 3.* New York: Teachers College Press.

Vygotsky, L. V. (1962). *Thought and language.* Cambridge, MA: M. I. T. Press.

Additional Reading

Achilles, E. R. (1996). Musical awareness through creative movement. *General Music Today, 9*(3), 5–8.

Andrews, A. G. (1996). Developing spatial sense: A moving experience! *Teaching Children Mathematics, 2*(5), 290–294.

Bagheri, H. (1990). Dance as a multicultural education for young children. In W. J. Stinson (Ed.), *Moving and learning for the young child* (pp. 189–199). Reston, VA: American Alliance for the Health, Physical Education, Recreation, and Dance.

Bond, K., & Deans, J. (1997). Eagles, reptiles and beyond: A co-creative journey in dance. *Childhood Education, 73*(6), 366–372.

Bucek, L. E. (1992). Constructing a child-centered dance curriculum. *Journal of Physical Education, Recreation & Dance, 63*(9), 39–42.

Clements, R. L., & Oosten, M. (1995). Creating and implementing preschool movement narratives. *Journal of Physical Education, Recreation & Dance, 66*(3), 24–30.

Diem. L. (1991). *The important early years: Intelligence through movement experience.* Reston, VA: American Alliance for Health, Physical Education, Recreation and Dance.

Downey, V. W. (1995). Expressing ideas through gesture, time, and space. *Journal of Physical Education, Recreation & Dance, 66*(9), 18–22.

Dyer, S. M., & Schiller, W. (1993). Not wilting flowers again! Problem finding and problem solving in movement and performance. *Early Child Development and Care, 90*(1), 47–54.

Eastman, W. (1997). Active living: Physical activities for infants, toddlers and preschoolers. *Early Childhood Education Journal, 24*(3), 161–164.

Friedlander, J. L. (1992). Creating dances and dance instruction: An integrated-arts approach. *Journal of Physical Education, Recreation & Dance, 63*(9), 49–54.

Gillbert, A. G. (1992). A conceptual approach to studio dance, preK-12. *Journal of Physical Education, Recreation & Dance, 63*(9), 43–49.

Griss, S. (1994). Creative movement: A language for learning. *Educational Leadership, 51*(5), 78–81.

Ignico, A. (1994). Early childhood physical education: Providing the foundation. *Journal of Physical Education & Dance, 69*(9), 33–38.

Koff, S. R. (2000). Toward a definition of dance education. *Childhood Education, 77*(1), 27–31.

Marxen, C. E. (1995). Push, pull, toss, tilt, swing: Physics for young children. *Childhood Education, 71*(4), 212–217.

Rodger, L. (1996). Adding movement throughout the day. *Young Children, 51*(3), 4–6.

Sanders, S. (1998). Challenging movement experiences for young children. *Dimensions of Early Childhood, 26*(1), 9–17.

Schoon, S. (1998). Using dance experience and drama in the classroom. *Childhood Education, 74*(2), 78–83.

Schwartz, P. (1993). Creativity and dance: Implications for pedagogy and policy. *Arts Education Policy Review, 95*(1), 8–16.

Stevens, D. A. (1994). Movement concepts: Stimulating cognitive development in elementary students. *Journal of Physical Education, Recreation & Dance, 65*(8), 16–24.

Stinson, S. W. (1990). Dance education in early childhood. *Design for Arts Education, 91*(6), 34–41.

Swaim, S. (1997). Dancing a story: Myth and movement for children. *Early Childhood Education Journal, 25*(2), 127–131.

Weikart, P. (1987). *Key experiences in movement for children ages 3 to 5: Round the circle.* Ypsilanti, MI: High Scope Press.

Werner, P., Sweeting, T., Woods, A., & Jones, L. (1992). Developmentally appropriate dance for children. *Journal of Physical Education, Recreation & Dance, 63*(6), 40–45.

Werner, P. (1994). Whole physical education. *Journal of Physical Education, Recreation & Dance, 65*(6), 40–44.

Children's Literature Connection

Ackerman, K. (1988). *Song and dance man.* New York: Alfred A. Knopf.
Grandpa demonstrates some of the songs, dances, and jokes he performed when he was a vaudeville entertainer for his visiting grandchildren. (Primary K–3)

Carle, E. (1997). *From head to toe.* New York: Harper Collins.
Twelve animals invite children to imitate them as they stomp, wriggle, thump, and clap across the pages. (Pre-K)

Cauley, L. B. (1992). *Clap your hands.* New York: G. P. Putnam's Sons.
Rhyming text instructs the listener to find something yellow, roar like a lion, give a kiss, tell a secret, spin a circle, and perform other playful activities. (Pre-K)

Harter, D. (1997). *Walking through the jungle.* New York: Orchard Books.
A young explorer discovers different animals and terrains of the world before arriving home, safe and sound, for supper. This is a wonderful chant-like story. (Pre-K)

Hoff, S. (1994). *Duncan the dancing duck.* New York: Scholastic.
All Duncan wants to do is dance. He becomes so famous that he gets a big show-business award. (Pre-K–K)

Hoffman, M. (1993). *Amazing Grace.* New York: Scholastic.
Although a classmate says that she cannot play Peter Pan in the school play because she is an African American, Grace discovers that she can do anything she sets her mind to do with the encouragement of her grandmother. (Primary K–3)

Holabird, K. (1983). *Angelina ballerina.* New York: Clarksin N. Potter.
A pretty mouse wants to become a ballerina more than anything in the world. (Pre-K–1)

Martin, B., & Archambault, J. (1985). *Here are my hands.* New York: Henry Holt and Company.
The owner of a human body celebrates it by pointing out various parts and mentioning their function, from "hands for catching and throwing" to the "skin that bundles me in." (Primary K–3)

Marzallo, J. (1990). *Pretend you're a cat.* New York: Trumpet Club.
Rhyming verses ask the reader to purr like a cat, scratch like a dog, leap like a squirrel, and bark like a seal. (Pre-K–K)

Helpful Web Sites

The addresses and corresponding agencies below are taken from the Web sites. Due to the dynamic nature of the Internet, please remember that Web sites are subject to change at any time.

http://www.deadance.com   Dance Educators of America (DEA)—A dance professionals' organization dedicated to improving the quality and teaching abilities of its member teachers, to enhance their education of students, and to further the professional and ethical standards in the performing and stage arts, and dance in all its forms.

http://www.movingandlearning.com   Moving and Learning—A Web site created by a movement education specialist, and a musician and composer.

http://www.pecentral.org   PE Central—Assists teachers, parents, and others who work with youngsters to guide them in becoming physically active and healthy for a lifetime.

http://www.pelinks4u.org   PELinks4U—The online journal has information about adapted physical education (PE), coaching, elementary PE, interdisciplinary PE, and health, fitness, and nutrition.

For additional resources involving creativity and the arts with young children, visit our Web site at **http://www.earlychilded.delmar.com**

Chapter 7

Creative Drama in the Early Childhood Classroom

Creative drama is an appropriate avenue for young children to express and improvise their ideas. Several types of creative drama will be examined in this chapter including pantomime, group drama, literature enactment, sociodramatic play, and conflict resolution. In each area of the dramatic arts, children create their own action, dialogue, sound effects, and props. The focus is not on performance but on the nurturing of children's ability to express their ideas in a supportive environment.

Creative Episode

A group of young children listen intently to a folktale entitled The Turnip. *At the end of the telling, the teacher revisits the story with them. They discuss how the seed was planted, how it was cared for, and how they harvested the enormous turnip. Next, the teacher asks what characters would be needed to act out the story. He records the information on chart paper. The children select which part they would like to play in the dramatized story. Mary Ann is very anxious to play the important part of the little girl. Jessie wants to be the father who helped pull up the large turnip. Cassandra wants to be the tiny bird that helped the others pull the turnip out of the ground.*

The children enthusiastically acted out the story and added their own creative version of the dialogue. They repeated the common line from the story, *"They pulled, and pulled, and pulled, but the turnip would not come up."* When the little bird, played by Cassandra, flew in and added her pull, the imaginary turnip popped out of the ground. All the children cheered and said, *"We did it, we did it, the turnip is free."* After a brief pause for reflection, they added, *"Let's do it again!"*

In this episode, young children were active and creative as they reenacted the folktale about the turnip. Children were able to choose the part they wanted to play, allowing them to work at a level where they felt comfortable and successful. The young actors worked cooperatively and appropriately adjusted their lines in response to the other players. At the end of the dramatization, they asked to *"Do it again."* They obviously enjoyed the experience and wanted to repeat the dramatization.

Kindergartner using her imagination as she experiments with props. (Photo by Michael Talley)

Creative drama is a powerful learning medium, emerging from the spontaneous play of children. It utilizes the art of theater to build and enhance participants' artistic sensitivity and develop dramatic imagination. Creative drama allows participants to imagine and reflect on experiences, real or imagined. The dramatic process is practical, immediate, and engages both the emotions and the intellect. Children are asked to step out of real situations and project themselves into imagined ones and roles. Individual and group drama experiences enhance the participant's ability to communicate ideas, images, and feelings through action (Pinciotti, 1993).

Drama Terms

Characters. The people who carry out the story and action. Often, the characters use dialogue as they communicate with each other.

Cooperative work. The ability to work with a group and adjust personal ideas during the process.

Focus. Concentrating on the drama and staying involved in the process.

Plot. The sequence of events in the drama that creates the meaning; setting the place where the action occurs.

Use of body. The coordination of the body in drama to communicate with the use of gestures, facial expressions, and movement.

Verbal expression. Speaking clearly and effectively using volume, tone, pitch, and pauses. It includes the ability to improvise dialogue.

Drama Matches How Young Children Learn

According to the theories of cognitive learning, most child development theorists and researchers agree that young children learn through play and experiences within their environment. Piaget (1963) explained that gesture and mime are language in motion. They are the real social language of children. Drama provides a connection between language and movement, bridging the spoken word and the real thing.

Drama begins with the concept of meaningful communication, and provides many opportunities for social interaction and feedback. These interactions offer the support Vygotsky (1978) deemed necessary for the internalization of new knowledge. For example, Talley is pretending to be the troll who lives under the bridge that scares the three Billy Goats Gruff. While practicing the role, a classmate reminds him, "The troll is scary, but not too, too, scary." As a result of this interaction, Talley uses a low voice and big gestures, but he tries not to make the sounds "too scary."

Multi-Sensory Learning

Drama is well-suited to the way young children learn because it is **multi-sensory**. The dramatic arts involve three of Gardner's (1983) multiple intelligences: bodily-kinesthetic, spatial, and linguistic. In drama, action and visual elements support verbal language, creating multiple connections in the brain. During the enactment of the turnip, the little girl determined where the seed was planted (spatial intelligence) and how hard she would pull (bodily-kinesthetic intelligence). She used her language (linguistic intelligence) to ask for help when unable to get the turnip out of the ground. This drama required that she use three types of intelligences, which made connections between different parts of her brain and integrated thinking.

Social-emotional Development

Social skills can be developed in drama. Working together, children and adults determine the conclusion, overcome difficulties, and solve problems that arise

"I hear and I forget. I see and I remember. I do and I understand."

Chinese Proverb[2]

in the story to be dramatized. During the dramatic process, they interact and cooperate in an active partnership. Children also experience working with peers as they negotiate plans and implement the drama. In these interactions, children begin to understand how to work together while having an impact on their creation. These collaborative efforts are effective in fostering a community of learners where there is mutual respect for diverse ideas and approaches.

Flowers added to an area inspire a wedding. (Photo by Amy Carmichael)

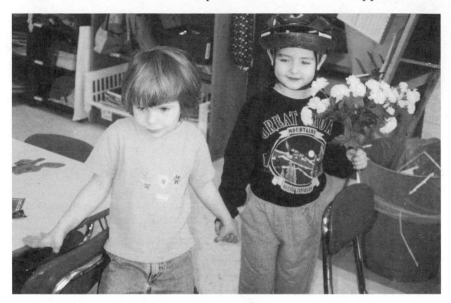

Background of Creative Drama for Young Children

With respect to young children, the field of drama has impacted policy decisions where commitments can be seen at two levels. On the preschool level, there has been increased interest in the importance of drama. This has been developed through the reexamination of play and physical activity as essential for social and cognitive growth during the early years. In addition, developmentally appropriate models have used dramatic play to integrate learning into the curriculum. At the primary school level, new regulations for states have embraced the arts as an essential component of the curriculum. They have included drama as equal to other forms of art. For the first time, the language of dramatic learning is being incorporated into early childhood programs.

Stages of Drama Development

The artistic and developmental roots of creative drama are seen as a learning continuum that extends from the beginning of spontaneous imaginative play in the very young child, to the creative activity and production of a theater performance. Creative drama provides the medium that elaborates and extends young children's dramatic play. It develops into an understanding and respect for the process, and later the product, of theater. Early experiences begin with imitation and expand into new areas. The child is able to make a connection between imagination and action. Although both creative drama and imaginative play utilize many of the same dramatic learning strategies, creative drama is a more structured and complex learning activity. Both involve communication, movement, gesture, and dialogue about imagined objects, events, or characters.

Imaginative play requires unstructured time, a place for things to happen, and props to support the activity. It is the process that is most meaningful. In creative drama, there is a leader who encourages and stimulates dramatic learning. This person sets the goals, introduces the experiences, and assists in dramatic production. The group may work together to create the **story line**, events, and conclusion.

Children become aware of drama's purpose and power as they are better able to transform self, objects, and place to create a shared reality. This ability to transform begins early as the toddler uses a toy telephone to represent the real thing. As ability progresses, the preschooler may use a block to represent a bulldozer. In later childhood, a child places an imaginary crown on the king's head, demonstrating that he has an internal symbol for the object.

Creative drama activities allow children to experiment, rehearse, and recreate actions and words in a social setting. As children get older, they develop an understanding of setting, mood, conflict, plot, time, relationships, and theater. They begin to explore the roles of actor, writer, director, designer, and audience member. These expanded abilities provide an avenue for complex discussion of story and roles.

Creative drama is not **junior theater**. Creative drama is not performed for a paying audience and does not include endless rehearsals. The emphasis is on the educational and artistic benefits for the participants, not on the quality of the final production.

Benefits of Creative Drama

Creative drama activities require children to recall personal, sensory-rich experiences and select dramatic actions to express these images. In *The House of Make-Believe*, Dorothy and Jerome Singer (1990) discuss the benefits of imagery and imagination. As children grow older, drama becomes the extension of their imaginary play. The connections between imagination and action, begun as a young child, become more flexible and fluent with experience.

Language Development

Oral language is used and expanded in drama. During this critical period of language learning, young children need many opportunities to talk, expand their vocabulary, and listen to the words of others. Research indicates that children who attend programs with a creative dramatics component, have advanced language and are able to communicate their ideas verbally. In a summary of research studies investigating the relationship between drama and oral language, 21 studies showed significant improvement in oral language or reading skills (Vitz, 1983). Similar results were found in both kindergarten and primary children.

Oral language is an essential element in cognitive development during the first eight years of life, and provides the basis for literacy development including reading and writing. Drama is an effective tool for positively impacting the oral language development of young children.

Group Cooperation

One of the strengths of creative drama is the opportunity for small group work. In drama, children interact and communicate to create a community of ideas, images, and actions. As they adjust their action in response to the group, children gain skills in negotiating and collaborating. Through improvisational activities, young children begin to adjust to the responses of the group. They develop the ability to reflect and think on their feet. Working in a group continually requires the child to participate in cognitive, social, and emotional exchanges. Drama facilitates social development because it requires interaction, negotiation, and cooperation. Emotional development is also enhanced, as children are encouraged to express and explore their feelings.

Process or Product

Most drama professionals believe that young children should participate in drama that is process-oriented without a focus on the product. Young children learn by participating in the drama without unnecessary demands that relate to an effective performance (Brown, 1990). Informal drama allows children to respond extemporaneously and to adapt to the situation in a flexible way. The focus is on learning with participation throughout the creative process.

Children enjoy creating props for their dramatic play. (Photo by Michael Talley)

Empowering Children

In modern society, older and more powerful human beings govern young children's lives. Yet learning to control one's life is a crucial developmental task. It is important for early childhood educators to provide safe and appropriate ways for the child to explore his independence. Drama provides an excellent vehicle for children to make choices or decisions, and solve problems. The teacher-learner partnership in drama provides a forum for cooperative undertaking where children are able to negotiate and work with others toward a satisfying goal (Warren, 1993).

The long-term benefits of creative drama include:
- independent thinking.
- problem-solving.
- collaboration skills.
- empathy for others.
- putting creative ideas into action.
- development of imagination.
- expanding oral language.
- developing moral and spiritual values.
- understanding of self.
- learning to make decisions and choices.

Types of Drama for Young Children

There are a large variety of appropriate drama activities to use with young children. Their developmental level and background experiences, as well as their interests and needs, should be considered when determining what drama experiences are appropriate for a specific group of children. The range of possibilities provides options for early childhood educators designing a program to nurture the arts that includes drama.

Dramatic Play and Sociodramatic Play

Sociodramatic play is the imaginative play that occurs during the early years of a child's life. During this play, children explore familiar experiences as they take on roles, develop sequence, and use language in the activity. Dramatic play helps young children move from egocentric thinking to becoming more capable of adapting and adjusting to others (Smilansky, 1990). It allows them to practice roles and experiences as they try to understand how the world works.

Suggestions for the Classroom

Play in learning centers provides an appropriate environment to encourage sociodramatic play. Open-ended centers such as blocks and housekeeping allow children to choose their roles and construct an understanding of the world during their play. In the pretend roles, they are able to communicate in meaningful ways and develop social skills. Thematic centers establish the setting and direct the play that occurs in the area. For example, a greenhouse center will encourage roles and activities that focus on growing plants, arranging a display, and selling the flowers.

It is helpful to plan centers by establishing learning objectives, selecting props, making a plan for the space, and evaluating the effectiveness of the center. Observations of the learning centers and the activities of the children using the areas allow the teacher to add props as needed, make adjustments, and close the center when interest is dwindling. An example of a creative center for the classroom is found in Figure 7–1. Figure 7–2 illustrates the web of integrated learning in the flea market/garage sale center.

Figure 7–1 A Creative Center for the Classroom: Flea Market–Garage Sale (Isbell, 1995)

Learning Objectives of the Center

1. To collect and produce items that can be sold to others.
2. To experience the buying and selling of products.
3. To expand language by communicating with others.
4. To learn that some items can be recycled instead of thrown away.

Vocabulary Enrichment

Some new words that might be included in the flea market are:

- display
- products
- recycle
- treasure
- useful
- mark down
- sale
- purchase
- cost
- change
- receipt
- haggle
- money
- booths
- barter
- free
- names of specific items that will be sold

Teacher-collected Props

1. Several low tables, sheets of fabric, or canopies to cover some displays.
2. Items for selling such as old clothing, small appliances, car accessories, used books, old children's toys, and kitchen tools. The choices are unlimited.
3. Money box with play money and receipts.
4. Labels, markers, and plastic bags (in which to put purchases).

Child-made Props

1. Advertisements for the sale.
2. Items that could be sold such as original paintings, clay sculptures, plants they have started (spider plants, piggyback plants, and ferns), and flower bouquets they have made.
3. Refreshments that could be sold such as popcorn, cookies, lemonade, hot chocolate, fruit, or trail mix.

Adding a Spark

When interest in the center is fading, have a sale. Mark down all the items in the center and sell out. Children can create new price tags, regroup items, or change displays to encourage selling.

Evaluation of the Flea Market Center

1. Are children making items to sell in the flea market center?

2. Are children talking about reusing items, creating products, and setting up appealing displays?

3. Are children using "money," as they buy and sell in the market?

4. Is creativity enhanced as they think about new products and displays?

5. Are children working cooperatively to set up and maintain the flea market?

Figure 7–1 Continued

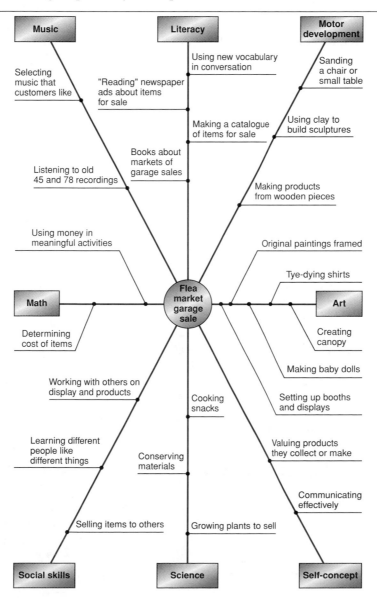

Figure 7–2 Web of integrated learning in the flea market/garage sale center. From Isbell R. (1995). *The complete Learning center book.* Beltsville, MD: Gryphon House.

When a center is designed appropriately, children are able to play for an extended period of time. The teacher is free to observe and record what is happening in the area. These observations provide the teacher an opportunity to determine the effectiveness of the center and document skills the children use when involved in meaningful activities. These annotations provide a tool for assessing the development of young children who are using the center.

Pantomime

Pantomime is the use of movement and gestures to express ideas or feelings. Communication is obtained through action, not words (Salisbury, 1986). Pantomime can be an effective beginning drama experience for young children because it does not require language or dialogue. Therefore, pantomime can provide both a safe and successful initial experience with drama. It is easier for young children to begin pantomiming familiar activities such as walking in snow or sand. More advanced pantomimes ask the child to express a mood or feeling. For example, a child could walk as though he had just found out that his best friend could not come home with him. Later, children can begin to work with characterizations: the funny shoe salesman, the clumsy pizza maker, or the fisherman who can't catch a fish.

With each positive experience in drama, children build their confidence. They become more willing to take risks, try out roles, and make suggestions for improvement. Pantomime shapes perception and stimulates imagination as children remember actions, objects, and feelings.

Suggestions for the Classroom

Pantomime
Preschool to kindergarten:
- eating an ice cream cone
- walking a big dog
- mopping the floor
- getting dressed
- climbing on a play structure
- playing with a baby
- pretending to be a snowman on a hot day

Primary grades:
- eating different foods such as spaghetti, sour pickle, hot cereal, pizza, or a gigantic taco
- visiting the grocery store, discount store, hair salon, shoe store, shopping mall, post office, restaurant, or other local spot
- a sequence of events such as playing soccer, ballet class, eating lunch, and a baseball game
- visiting an aquarium, museum, or other field trip

Creative Dramatics and Playmaking

Children can participate in drama by improvising dialogue and action. For young children, the goal is the personal development of the players instead of a professional performance. Creative drama is often guided by the teacher or leader, but seldom includes any scenery or costumes.

Geraldine Siks, a leading authority on children's drama, believes that young children (up to the age of eleven) should participate only in informal drama. Children should have many opportunities to create their own dialogue before they move into reciting memorized lines. According to Siks and Dunnington (1967), in creative dramatics, the child is an active participant who shapes the happenings. This is an important step in the development of dramatic ability. With each playing of the story, it becomes more organized and detailed, yet it remains extemporaneous and is not designed for the audience (McCaslin, 1990).

Story Dramatization

Story dramatization involves creating an improvised play based on a story or piece of literature. A leader guides the development and possibilities that can occur during the creative process. The children act out the play using improvised dialogue and action. There are many different ways literature can inspire drama such as providing content for puppet shows, sequence for pantomime, and characters for shadow plays. Several stories to dramatize with young children are included in Appendix H.

> *"The unique thing about creative dramatics is that it is always improvised. It is never fixed by being written and memorized, but is different at each playing."*
>
> **W. Ward, 1952**[3]

Suggestions for the Classroom

Read *The Little Red Hen* to a group of preschoolers. Discuss the story line and characters with the children. Dramatize the story. After the drama, talk with the children about their thoughts and feelings during the process.

Child-created Plays

Plays created by children can be the culmination of a study or project. The plays are developed over a period of time, and the children design and make simple scenery and costumes. Lines, or dialogue, are not memorized. The children know the story line and plot because they created the play. Older children actually may write a play and then perform it, using a script.

For example, within a primary classroom, children have been studying medieval times. From their research came a play that was written by several children to perform for other members of the class. It was an inspiring experience, and other members of the class wanted to present the play again and again. Each time, the original cast assisted the other children in their production. This play provided the children with an avenue to put their research into action and enriched their understanding of the medieval period of history.

Puppetry

Storytelling and **puppetry** are ancient forms of oral expression that developed historically in similar ways. The oral story was passed down from generation to generation. These stories were a binding link for families and cultures. The puppeteer often augmented the storytelling by providing visualization and surprise elements to the story presentation. The design and use of puppets has been influenced greatly by the culture and society of the puppeteer. A diverse cultural influence can be seen in ornate Chinese shadow puppets and in the pure geometric form of African rod puppets. From these historical roots of oral language and cultural transmission, a new view of puppets has emerged.

Puppets encourage children to develop dialogue and dramatizations. (Photo by Mary Myron)

Currently, a new variety of puppets are appearing that are personally expressive and appeal to wider audiences. These changes have moved puppets from being used exclusively for entertainment to tools that can be used in education, therapy, and communication. Jim Henson's Sesame Street Muppets have had a powerful influence on this transformation. His popular use of large, expressive Muppets has led to an increased interest in puppets and the role they can play in education (Raines & Isbell, 1994).

Young children are drawn to puppets. This magnetic quality can provide a powerful experience in drama for young children. A puppet becomes a tool for children to use in expressing ideas and personal views. Some shy children may become quite verbal when the puppet does the talking. Young children believe the puppet is real whereas primary children pretend that the puppet is alive. Both age groups enjoy listening to a wonderful story presented by the teacher/puppeteer or use puppets to tell the story themselves.

Rolled paper tubes

Some simple puppets

Posterboard figure

Hamburger box puppet

Finger puppets

Old glove

Holes for fingers

Paper cup

Slit

Hollow rubber ball

Small cream box

Paper bag puppets

Sock puppet

Suggestions for the Classroom

Provide a collection of puppets in the dramatic area. Select animals that could be used in the enactment of a number of stories. For example, a group of farm animal puppets can be used in many different stories and experiences. These will provide the stimulus for a puppet show.

Storytelling

Stories told orally, without the use of written text, provide children with opportunities to visualize characters and events. The storyteller uses words, gestures, and sometimes props to convey the meaning of the story. Storytellers often use folktales that have a long history of being shared orally and continue to be effective with today's children. The teller selects and adapts the story to match the developmental level of the children in the audience. The teller creatively weaves his story and captures the imagination of the children as they enjoy both the teller and the story.

Toddlers and preschoolers particularly enjoy stories that have:
- predictable patterns that include repetitive phrases.
- characters that are understandable.
- a setting they can visualize.
- a moral that gives meaning to the story.
- sounds or gestures that accompany the telling.

It is important to select appropriate stories for each age group. Examples of stories appropriate for preschool and primary children can be found in *Tell it Again* (1999) by Raines and Isbell, and *Tell it Again 2* (2000) by Isbell and Raines. Stories for telling preschoolers include Three Billy goats Gruff (1999), Teeny Tiny (1999), The Little Red Hen (2000), and Johnny Cake (1999). Primary children enjoy stories that are more complex in nature. The stories should be selected to match the specific group of children and their interests. Examples of stories to tell primary children include The Four Musicians(1999), The Story of the Ugly Duckling (1999), The Lost Mitten With Tiny, Shiny Beads (1999), The Boy Who Cried Wolf (2000), and some of *Aesop's Fables*. Less familiar stories as well as personal stories, can add spice to storytelling experiences.

Children who have experience listening to stories begin to tell their own stories. Their first tellings often will be very close to the stories they have heard. Later, they will change characters and elements of the story as they tell it again. When they have gained confidence in their storytelling ability, they will begin to create original stories. These will include elements of story understanding such as a beginning, "Once upon a time;" and an ending, "That's the end of my story;" and a narrative, "The donkey said hee-haw, hee-haw all the way home." These demonstrate a "sense of story" described by Applebee (1978) in his studies of young children. Stories that are told by the teacher or a visiting teller can serve as a stimulus for creative drama. Hearing stories told aloud allow children to internalize the images and characters that will assist them as they begin to dramatize a story.

Suggestions for the Classroom

Prepare for telling Rudyard Kipling's story about the curious elephant's child who can't stop asking questions. The story provides the answer to "How the elephant got a long trunk." Provide a tape recorder for children to tell their own version of the elephant's child or to create another "how" story.

Children's Theater

In the **children's theater** type of drama, a play is written by a playwright and presented by actors in front of an audience. Actors can be adults and/or children who are selected for the parts through audition. Lines are memorized, action is directed, and scenery and costumes are used. This is a formal presentation with the primary purpose of providing entertainment. This formal type of drama is inappropriate for young children because there is a strong focus on practice and performance. Informal drama is more effective where young children develop their abilities in relaxed drama experiences.

Readers' Theater

Readers' theater is a relatively new concept in the creative arts. It is particularly appropriate for older children who are able to read fluently. Readers' theater is a way of enjoying good literature through an oral presentation using a written script. There are many different ways to implement a readers' theater, ranging from sitting in a chair to including movement that coincides with the text. Stories also can be partially narrative with readers assuming the roles of specific characters during the presentation. Readers' theater does not require an audience beyond the members of the classroom. Some of the values of this technique are obtained through the selection process, the oral interpretation of the literature, and the practice in reading aloud. A readers' theater lesson plan is presented in Figure 7–3.

Goals

1. Students will work in small groups to create and perform a mystery Readers' Theater production.

2. Students will practice social and personal skills while working with a group of peers.

3. Students will engage in a meaningful literacy activity.

Objectives

The students will be able to:

- interact easily with peers when working cooperatively.
- use discussion and compromise to resolve conflicts.
- make independent choices of materials, activities, and work.
- sustain attention to work over a long period of time.
- follow directions that involve a multistep sequence of actions.
- understand and interpret a story.
- read text fluently, independently, and for varied purposes.
- personally assess their involvement with the use of a rubric.

Materials

The following materials will be needed to conduct this project:
- Readers' Theater Checklist
- Readers' Theater Rubric
- Director's Job List
- Six copies of three plays
- Folders (for the children to store their checklists, rubrics, and scripts)
- Highlighters, pencils, paper, copy machine, tape recorder, audiotape, and video recorder

Introduction

The teacher will enlarge a copy of the Reader's Theater Checklist and tape it to the Plan of Action board. Step one of the day's Plan of Action will ask students to read the checklist to become familiar with the steps of this project. During Morning Meeting, the students will discuss the following question: "How can

Figure 7–3

Implementation of Readers' Theater Lesson Plan: Primary Grades (Developed by Stacy Larsen and implemented in a third grade classroom)

Figure 7–3   Continued

we be responsible while working on our Readers' Theater performance?" The students' responses will be recorded on the board.

Readers' Theater Checklist

Name: _____

You will be working with your group to perform a Readers' Theater mystery production. This is not a play, but more like listening to an old-time radio show. Use this checklist to complete the daily activity requirements. Check off the requirements as you complete each one.

Monday

———— Watch *The Ice Cream Caper*

Tuesday

———— Review the grading rubric and checklist

———— Break up into your assigned group and read the play

———— Pick someone to be the Director

———— Assign roles and complete the following questions:

My play is: _____

My role is: _____

The director is: _____

Wednesday

———— Highlight your lines

———— The Director will begin the first reading of the play with everyone reading his or her lines

———— Pick a prop (one prop per person)

Thursday

———— Run through the play with everyone reading their lines and using/wearing a prop

———— Write the program and give it to the teacher to copy (The program should include the title of the play, the Director's name, a list of characters and the actors' names, and an illustration)

Friday

———— Perform your Readers' Theater for the third grade

Readers' Theater Checklist (Courtesy of Stacy Larsen)

Procedure

1. During project time, the teacher will begin the discussion by handing out a rubric for the readers' theater. The rubric will be discussed, and the teacher will role-play instances of specific behavior and ask the students what evaluation they would receive if they did these things. For example, if I really got upset and decided I didn't want to play a specific role, and stopped practicing and listening to the director, what evaluation would I receive?

2. After the rubric is discussed, the teacher will hand out the Readers' Theater Checklist. This checklist will be used by students to complete daily requirements as they work toward performing their show. The teacher will discuss each step listed on the checklist and highlight the requirements for today (review the rubric and checklist, break into groups, individually read the play, assign a director and roles, and complete three questions).

3. The next step is to break students into three groups (teacher can assign groups or let the students decide who should be in each group). Each group will meet in a designated area of the classroom. The students will follow the order of requirements found on the checklist. The teacher will

Figure 7–3   Continued

Readers' Theater Rubric

Name: _____

3
———— Worked well with the group
———— Didn't goof off during practice
———— Presented best effort during performance
———— Completed all items in the checklist book
———— Used self-control
———— Listened to the director
———— Did not misuse props

2
———— Used most of the practice time
———— Performed with so-so effort
———— Completed most of the checklist book
———— Participated in the performance
———— Didn't misuse his or her prop
———— Usually worked will with the group
———— Listened to the director

1
———— Did not work well with the group
———— Goofed off during practice and rehearsal
———— Completed less than half of the checklist book
———— Did not listen to the director
———— Had trouble using self-control
———— Misused props
———— Poor effort during performance

Readers' Theater Rubric. (Courtesy of Stacy Larsen)

Figure 7–3   Continued

The Director's Job

❑ Help everyone pick a role

❑ Help everyone read their lines correctly

❑ Help people pick a prop

❑ Do the final check of the program and make sure it is given to the teacher to make copies

❑ Hand out the programs

❑ Introduce the play and actors

❑ Help everyone in the group work well together

Remember, you can always ask the teacher for help if you need it.

GOOD LUCK!

The Director's Job (Courtesty of Stacy Larsen)

walk around to facilitate discussion and model appropriate group behavior. When roles have been assigned, the director will make a list to turn in to the teacher. This list will be enlarged and displayed on the project board. This activity time will be followed by a question and answer session.

4. This project will take one to two weeks to complete, and the teacher will facilitate the students' work during daily project time. The activity will wrap up with a performance by each group that the teacher will audiotape and videotape. The teacher will make duplicate copies available to the students and their families. Each group has the additional option to present its mystery readers' theater performance to other classrooms in the school.

5. Following the performances, students will review their rubric and evaluate their work throughout the project. The teacher will have a conference with each student individually to assess their work together.

Figure 7–3   Continued

1. How did each student interact within his or her group?

2. Did the students use discussion and compromise to resolve problems in the group?

3. Were students able to make independent choices for props, roles, and work?

4. How well did students sustain attention to their work throughout the week?

5. Were students able to follow multistep directions when completing the checklist? Did most students complete the checklist appropriately?

6. How well did students interpret their mystery story? Did they convey the meaning appropriately in the performance?

7. How did the students feel about their performances? Did they enjoy the project?

Extension

Provide students the opportunity to write and produce their own mystery story.

Dealing with Classroom Issues

Sometimes, drama provides an avenue for dealing with class issues. The situation is set, roles selected, and the action occurs spontaneously. This **group process** or playing out of problems allows children to resolve issues and observe the effects of their behavior on others. Children are able to see the situation from another perspective and respond in appropriate ways. For example, the teacher observes Roberta having a difficult time getting into block play. A group of boys seems to be controlling the people who can play in the area. During group time, the teacher leads a discussion about block play. As a class, they brainstorm the different kinds of structures that can be built in the block center. Then the teacher presents a problem: a child wants to play with blocks but is having trouble getting into the area. How can the children playing in this area help this new child join in block play? One of the boys in the block group is given the role of the new child trying to play with blocks. They act out the situation and discover ways to invite the new child into their play. After the dramatization, the children's solutions are discussed and extended. Practicing appropriate responses provides new options for the children and helps them become more aware of the importance of involving everyone in block play.

Planning Drama

As with most learning experiences, careful planning by the teacher is essential. But at the same time, the experience must be designed so it allows input from the children. The early childhood educator who is planning drama experiences needs to decide the objectives for the activity, the stimulus for the drama (story, experience, and the like), the focus or problems to be presented, and ideas for possible roles in the drama.

The details of the story line and the actions of the characters in the drama will be left for the children to decide as the drama progresses. Planning for the drama occurs spontaneously, as the activity progresses in response to the children's ideas and suggestions. It is important for the children to see their own ideas included and functioning effectively. An appropriate drama experience is one where the children's ideas are respected and the teacher provides guidance. The teacher must be able to ask questions that will help draw on the children's knowledge and extend their understanding in new ways. Bruner and Haste (1988) and Vygotsky (1986) use the term scaffolding to describe the teacher's important role of extending and developing children's knowledge of the world. This approach works effectively in the dramatic arts as the teacher uses the story and the children's dialogue to extend their playmaking.

It often is necessary for the beginning teacher to work closely with a plan. With more experience in drama, the teacher will be able to move to a more skeletal plan that allows the children to have more say in determining their part. The most child-centered drama begins with children's interests and takes direction from the ideas they offer (Brown & Pleydell, 1999). The following is an example of a plan to implement drama in the classroom.

Reading a story to children can be followed by a dramatization. (Photo by Michael Talley)

1. *Introduction*
   Before beginning any creative dramatics activity involving imagination, the class must be prepared. The children need to understand what they are going to do and how the activity works. It may involve reading a story, imagining a place, or revisiting personal experiences. The purpose is to engage the attention of the children and help them relate their own experiences to the idea, story, or poem that will be used in the drama.

This preparation period helps young children understand the boundaries and feel more comfortable with the activity.

2. *Presentation of the Story or Situation*
   A story can be told or read. Telling the story allows the children to imagine the happenings in their head without binding them to the illustrations in the book. The reader, or teller, uses his voice to make the story interesting and to emphasize specific parts. Young children should be invited to join in when phrases are repeated throughout the story.

3. *Plan of Action*
   After listening to the story, the teacher and children make a plan of action to act out the story. First, talk about the story or situation with the children; then, review the sequence of events. Let the children volunteer for parts in the drama. Some children will want to have the starring role whereas others are ready to be the tree. It is important for children to decide which part to play; only they can determine their comfort level. As children gain more experience in drama and when their involvement is valued, they will increase their level of participation.

4. *The Teacher's Role*
   Teachers have at least three roles to choose from during drama experiences. One is the side coach, where the teacher gives suggestions from the sideline without stopping the action. A second possibility is to participate in the drama to help the children keep the action going. Sometimes it is helpful for the teacher to have a role with authority so questions can be asked and action encouraged. With more experienced children, the teacher may assume a minor role that does not shape the drama. The third opinion is often the best: to be a member of the appreciative audience.

5. *Dramatization*
   Try to keep the playful spirit of the drama. Allow children to follow their intuitions and create responsive dialogue. Remember to be interested in the process being enjoyable and supportive of the children's efforts.

6. *Closing and Evaluation*
   Evaluation is an important part of the dramatic process. The children will want to talk about their experience and reflect on the performance. The teacher may ask questions related to the objectives and evaluation of the activity. This often is a forgotten step in creative dramatics, but it is very important. Bringing closure to the activity helps children return to reality and brings them back home.

7. *Plan and Replay*
   Repeat the process of planning, acting, and evaluating. Another part of the story could be used or the same story can be repeated with different children playing the roles. The replay allows different children to have parts or change the dialogue to revisit the story.

Children As an Audience

Creative dramatics often is performed in small working groups. The children who are not performing become the audience. After one presentation, these groups may exchange places, where the original actors become the audience and the audience becomes the players. In drama activities, children develop listening skills on two levels. The first level consists of basic listening skills that are required in order for the dramatization to continue, such as listening for clues. The second level involves the evaluative listening skills that develop when children serve as audience members, such as considering how the action is progressing and what they could do differently (McMaster, 1998).

Young children enjoy learning about the role of the audience and their participation in this part of the dramatic production. Children begin to understand that the audience will need to see and hear what is happening in the drama. They learn to listen and watch carefully during the play. Being an audience member is important to the drama because the audience laughs at the appropriate time, cheers for the hero, and shows their appreciation by clapping at the end of the show.

Conventions of the Theater

Before attending a live theater event, it is helpful for children to understand some of the experiences that are part of this event. Before a performance begins, the lights in the lobby may blink. This tells the audience to take their seats because the performance is about to begin. The performance begins when the lights are dimmed. The curtain closing indicates the act or performance is over. After the performance is over, actors come back on stage to bow while the audience applauds. This is a "curtain call." Young children who have never been to a play or musical production will not understand these signals. It is helpful to talk about the special ways audiences communicate before attending a production. Kindergarten and primary children will enjoy including these conventions in their dramatic play.

Appreciating Theater

Children can enjoy attending plays, puppet shows, or other performances if the selection is appropriate for their level of development. Productions should be chosen that would be enjoyable for young children to attend. This should not be a stressful experience that requires active children to be quiet and still for a long period of time. Also important in the selection process is the location of the performance. If it requires a one-hour ride on the bus before a two-hour performance, it is probably inappropriate for preschoolers. It would be much more appropriate to attend the rehearsal of a play that is being performed at a closer location.

One of the best ways for young children to enjoy a production is to attend a **rehearsal**. In this less formal setting, young children can be active and curious without distracting the actors or audience. Often, there may be a time when the children can talk with the actors or go on the stage to see the scenery. Primary children may be able to cope with longer programs, but they also need the opportunity to take breaks. Remember that attending a performance is designed to encourage children's interest and nurture an appreciation of drama. It should not be so demanding that it would turn young children off to attending future performances.

Attending live performances also can provide inspiration for reenactment of the play when children return to the classroom. After attending a performance of *Pinnocio*, a marionette could be added to the library area. The performance and the addition of this puppet can provide the stimulus for recreating the story. The observant teacher will be able to determine the children's comprehension of the production by observing their language and play.

Grouping for Drama

Another consideration, when planning drama, is how children will be grouped for the experience. Should the children work individually, in pairs, in small groups, or in one large group? Pairs and small groups provide more opportunity for children to use language, and provide further opportunities for more complex dialogue. When using a large group, there is more waiting, less sharing, and a smaller audience. These aspects, as well as the drama and form, will be used to determine the grouping for specific activities. As in all areas of art and creativity, it is important to provide variety. Grouping is one of the components that can provide further variation.

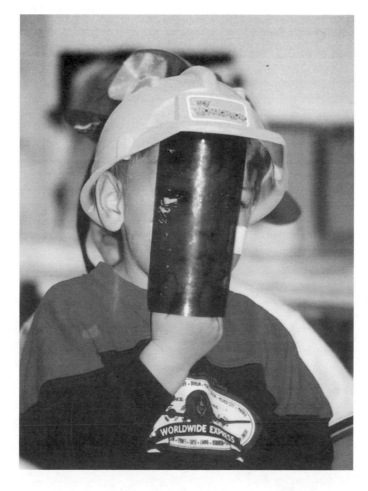

Appropriate props can encourage role-playing in a center. (Photo by Su Lorencen)

Summary

The foundation for the theater arts is built with young children through the use of creative drama. Dramatizations can be developed from improvised stories based on literature, personal experiences, or children's imaginations. All children can be involved in drama as they experience success, learn to listen, contribute ideas, collaborate with others, and support their classmates' creative endeavors. At times, children may want to share their drama with others outside the classroom, but the entertainment of an audience is not the goal. Rather, the goal is the personal growth of individual children as they actively participate in shaping the creative drama.

It is important that dramatic learning does not stop at the housekeeping center or the block area. Creative drama is indeed a unique art that is appropriate for use with young children in an early childhood classroom. It has the potential for communicating to young children in their own language, the language of make-believe. The physical, visual, and verbal elements of drama make it a multi-sensory learning experience that is very powerful with young learners (Brown, 1990).

Key Terms

creative drama	junior theater
characters	oral language
cooperative work	pantomime
focus	story dramatization
plot	storytelling
use of body	puppetry
verbal expression	children's theater
multi-sensory	readers' theater
social skills	group process
story line	rehearsal

Reflection

1. How does creative drama match the developmental level and learning styles of young children?

2. Discuss the similarities and differences of sociodramatic play and creative dramatics.

3. What are some of the benefits of using drama with Pre-K–K and primary children?

4. Identify and describe some types of drama that are appropriate to use in early childhood classrooms.

5. What are the steps in planning an interesting dramatic experience for a group of young children?

6. What stories or literature would you use to inspire children to participate in drama and re-enactment?

Thinking about the Creative Episode

1. How was the story used to encourage the development of a drama?

2. Why is it important for children to select the part they will play?

3. In the production, some lines are repeated, as in the book, while the characters create others. Why is this important?

4. What were the benefits of the story dramatization for the children?

Possibilities for Adult Learners

Activity: Mirror Images

Goal: This activity allows learners to experience drama through a pantomime activity.

Materials: None needed.

Procedure:

1. Pair the students so two people are working together.

2. In the pantomime experience, one person faces the other with hands touching. One person is the mime and the other is the mirror reflecting the action. Allow a few minutes for them to experiment with the leading and following experience.

3. Next, ask the mime to use facial expressions that communicate feelings of happiness, upset, anger, and mischief. Give time between each direction to let the mirror image respond.

4. Now, have the pair reverse roles. This time, ask the mime to communicate without words: very hungry, feeling ill, being upset, and acting silly.

5. Talk about the process and how each person felt in the different roles. Ask them to brainstorm other emotions, actions, or experiences that could be used in this activity.

Activity: Fractured Stories

Goal: This activity will demonstrate the use of connecting drama and literature.

Materials: None needed.

Procedure:

1. Divide the class into small groups of five to six students.

2. Ask each group to select a familiar children's story that they can dramatize.

3. After they have determined the story they will use, give them about 10 minutes to choose the roles, the events, and the way they will change the story. If they wish, they can rehearse some parts, but the focus is on the roles and story line. Remind the groups that they can recreate the story in their own way.

4. Each group will share its story and experience, extemporaneously creating the dialogue.

Open-ended Activities for Young Children

Pre-K–K

Activity:	Mask-making
Goal:	To encourage the development of language and role-playing though the use of masks.
Materials:	Paper plates, yarn, pieces of fabric, metallic paper, hole punch, pipe cleaners, colored paper, and other collected items.
Caution:	Masks may frighten some young children and some cultures may find them offensive.

Procedure:

1. Masks can be an extension of creative drama. The mask can be simple, elaborate, or grotesque, but it is not realistic. A paper plate can serve as a base for a simple mask.

2. Children can experiment with materials to create a three-dimensional quality and make each mask unique. Holes for eyes, mouth, and nose can be cut in the appropriate places, with the teacher's assistance, if needed.

3. The children play out a drama while their faces remain hidden behind the created mask. The children can dramatize a story they have heard or create one that uses masked characters.

Primary Grades

Activity:	Making and Using Shadow Puppets
Goal:	To create a puppet than can be used in a different way: shadow play.
Materials:	Sheet, lamp, cardboard, art board, poster paper, scissors, masking and duck tape, dowel rods, and rulers.

Procedure:

1. Flat puppets or rod puppets can be created and used in shadow shows by primary children. Placing a lamp behind a sheet enables the child to make shadows on the sheet.

2. When flat puppets are moved between the light and the sheet, they create silhouettes. These puppets can be cut out of light-weight cardboard or art board, and glued to tongue depressors or sticks.

3. Each child can create a unique puppet of his own design, or a group of children can decide on a play and make specific characters for the drama.

4. Some children may want to create moveable parts for the puppets, by using brads in the connecting joints. When attached to a long stick, these puppets can be moved to make body motions.

5. Music and dialogue can be added to the shadow show to create additional interest.

Extension: In Asian theater, where shadow plays originated, puppets were made of wood or hide and decorated with elaborate openwork patterns.

Resources for Masks and Puppets

Doney, M. (1995). *Masks.* New York: Franklin Watts.

Fleming, C. S. (1983). *Puppets put learning center stage.* Learning, 11(9), 94–98.

Hunt, T. (1984). *Pocketful of puppets: Never pick a python for a pet and other animal poems.* Austin, TX: Nancy Renfro Studios.

Lynch-Watson, J. (1980). *The shadow puppet book.* New York: Sterling Publishing Co., Inc.

Renfro, N., & Armstrong, B. (1979). *Make amazing puppets.* New York: The Learning Works.

Puppet Junk Box

cardboard tubes and boxes	pencils
paper plates	tape
paper bags (various sizes)	paint
cups (various sizes)	stapler
yarn	dowels
string	craft sticks
lace	rubber bands
ribbon	paper clips
wallpaper scraps	egg cartons
plastic bottles	buttons
lids	pom-poms
scraps of cloth	corks
felt	envelopes
cardboard	socks
tinfoil	sewing machine
paper	pipe cleaners
markers	old jewelry
glue	cotton balls
scissors	tape recorder
crayons	blank tapes
cartons	flashlights (for lighting)

Some simple puppet stages

Blanket over chair

Bush or hedge

Box

Felt story apron

Window

Behind table

Hinged plywood

Blanket across doorway

Shoe box for finger puppets

Refrigerator box

Turn upside down for marionettes

Box top

Puppet Stages

windows

a table turned on its side

a card table or piece of cloth across a doorway

a broomstick and blanket between two chairs

a table top

a big box with a hole in it

PVC pipe

behind a sofa

Notes

[1]Siks, G. B. (1983). *Drama with children* (2nd ed.). New York: Harper & Row Publishers.
[2]Fitzhenry, R. I. (Ed.) (1993). *The Harper book of quotations* (3rd ed.). New York: Harper Collins Books.
[3]Ward, W. (1952). *Stories to dramatize.* Anchorage, KY: Children's Theatre Press.
[4]Mayesky, M. (1998). *Creative activities for young children* (6th ed.). Clifton Park, NY: Delmar Learning.

References

Applebee, A. (1978). *The child's concept of story.* Chicago: The University of Chicago Press.

Brown, V. (1990). Drama as an integral part of the early childhood curriculum. *Design for Arts in Education, 91*(6), 26–33.

Brown, V., & Pleydell, S. (1999). *The dramatic difference: Drama in the preschool and kindergarten classroom.* Portsmouth, NH: Heinemann.

Bruner, J. S., & Haste, H. (Eds.). (1998). *Making sense: The child's construction of the world.* New York: Routledge.

Gardner, H. (1983). *Frames of mind: The theory of multiple intelligences.* New York: Basic Books.

Isbell, R. (1995). *The complete learning center book.* Beltsville, MD: Gryphon House.

Isbell, R. T., & Raines, S. C. (2000). *Tell it again 2: Easy-to-tell stories with activities for young children.* Beltsville, MD: Gryphon House.

McCaslin, N. (1990). *Creative drama in the classroom* (5th ed.). New York: Longman.

McMaster, J. C. (1998). Doing literature: Using drama to build literacy. *The Reading Teacher, 51*(7), 574–584.

Piaget, J. (1963). *The origins of intelligence in children.* New York: Norton.

Pinciotti, P. (1993). Creative drama a nd young children: The dramatic learning connection. *Arts Education Policy Review, 94*(6), 24–29.

Raines, S., & Isbell, R. (1994). *Stories: Children's literature in early education.* Clifton Park, NY: Delmar Learning.

Raines, S. C., & Isbell, R. T. (1999). *Tell it again: Easy-to-tell stories with activities for young children.* Beltsville, MD: Gryphon House.

Salisbury, B. T. (1986). *Theatre arts in the elementary classroom: Kindergarten through grade three.* New Orleans, LA: Anchorage Press, Inc.

Siks, G. B., & Dunnington, H. B. (Eds.). (1967). *Children's theatre and creative dramatics.* Seattle, WA: University of Washington Press.

Singer, D. G., & Singer, J. L. (1990). *The house of make-believe.* Cambridge, MA: Harvard University Press.

Smilansky, S. (1990). Sociodramatic play: Its relevance to behavior and achievement in school. In E. Klugman & S. Smilansky (Eds.), *Children's play and learning* (pp. 18–42). New York: Teachers College Press.

Vitz, K. (1983). A review of empirical research in drama and language. *Children's Theatre Review, 32*(4), 17–25.

Vygotsky, L. S. (1986). *Thought and language.* Cambridge, MA: M.I.T. Press.

Vygotsky, L. S. (1978). The role of play in development. In M. Cole, V. John-Steiner, S. Scribner, & E Souberman (Eds.), *Mind in society* (pp. 92–104). Cambridge, MA: Harvard University Press.

Warren, K. (1993). Empowering children through drama. *Early Child Development and Care, 90*(1), 83–97.

Additional Reading

Boutte, G. S., VanScoy, I., & Hendley, S. (1996). Multicultural and nonsexist prop boxes. *Young Children, 52*(1), 34–39.

Einarsdottir, J. (1996). Dramatic play and print. *Childhood Education, 73*(1), 352–358.

Howell, J., & Corbey-Schullen, L. (1997). Out of the housekeeping corner and onto the stage: Extending dramatic play. *Young Children, 52*(6), 82–88.

Isbell, R. T., & Raines, S. C. (2000). *Tell it again 2: Easy-to-tell stories with activities for young children.* Beltsville, MD: Gryphon House.

Johnson, A. P. (1998). How to use creative dramatics in the classroom. *Childhood Education, 75*(1), 2–5.

Kelner, L. B. (1993). *The creative classroom: A guide for using creative drama in the classroom, K–6.* Portsmouth, NH: Heinemann.

Maguire, J. (1985). *Creative storytelling: Choosing, inventing and sharing tales for children.* Cambridge, MA: Yellow Moon Press.

Martinez, M., Rosner, N. L., & Strecker, S. (1999). "I never thought I could be a star:" A readers' theater ticket of fluency. *The Reading Teacher, 52*(4), 326–334.

Mellou, E. (1994). A theoretical perspective on the relationship between dramatic play and creativity. *Early Childhood Development and Care, 100*(1), 77–92.

Merrefield, G. E. (1997). Three billy goats and Gardner. *Educational Leadership, 55*(1), 58–61.

Naumer, K. (1999). The magic drum: Making drama emergent. *Stage of the Art, 11*(1), 14–21.

Pigott, I. (1990). Drama in the classroom. *The Gifted Child Today, 13*(1), 2–5.

Siks, G. B. (1977). *Drama with children.* New York: Harper & Row.

Straub, C., & Straub, M. (1984). *Mime: Basics for beginners.* Boston, MA: Plays, Inc.

Wagner, B. J. (1979). Using drama to create an environment for language development. *Language Arts, 56*(3), 268–274.

Warash, B. G., & Workman, M. (1993). All life's a stage: Children dictate and reenact personal experiences. *Dimensions of Early Childhood, 21*(4), 9–12.

Williamson, P. A. (1993). Encouraging social competence and story comprehension through fantasy play. *Dimensions of Early Childhood, 21*(4), 17–20.

Children's Literature Connection

Bond, F. (1983). *The Halloween performance.* New York: Scholastic, Inc.
Tonight is the Halloween play and Roger's part is coming up! He's the Halloween pumpkin. Follow along as the class prepares and performs a successful play. (Pre-K–K)

Brandenberg, F. (1984). *Aunt Nina's visit.* New York: Greenwillow Press.
Aunt Nina's six kittens disrupt a puppet show given by her nieces and nephews. (Pre-K–K)

Brown, M. (1985). *Hand rhymes.* New York: E. P. Dutton.
A collection of nursery rhymes with diagrams for accompanying finger plays. (Pre-K–1)

Cohen, M. (1985). *Starring first grade.* New York: Greenwillow Books.
Even though he doesn't like his part in the first grade play, Jim saves the performance when one of the key players get stage fright. (Pre-K–1)

Ehrlich, F. (1992). *A class play with Ms. Vanilla.* New York: Viking.
When Ms. Vanilla's class puts on a play of Little Red Riding Hood, the wolf is played by Ms. Vanilla. (Pre-K–K)

Harley, B. (1996). *Sarah's story.* Berkeley, CA: Tricycle Press.
Sarah cannot think of a story to tell in class for her homework assignment, but on her way to school, she gets help from some unexpected sources. (Primary)

Krementz, J. (1991). *A very young actress.* New York: Alfred A. Knopf.
A ten-year-old girl who starred in a workshop production of Annie 2 describes her experiences on- and offstage, from audition through rehearsals to opening night. (Primary)

Loxton, H. (1989). *Theater.* Austin, TX: Steck-Vaughn.
An overview of theater as an art form with emphasis on the English-speaking theater. Includes information on the history of the theater, acting methods, staging, putting on a play, and theater careers. (Primary)

Mason, J. (1994). *Now hiring: Theater.* New York: Crestwood House.
A good reference book full of information and descriptions of jobs available in the theater. (Primary)

Ormerod, J. (1996). *Ms. MacDonald has a class.* New York: Clarion Books.
After visiting the farm, the children in Ms. MacDonald's class learn to move and look and sound very differ-ent while preparing to present the performance of a lifetime. (Pre-K–1)

Tryon, L. (1992). *Albert's play.* New York: Atheneum.
Albert helps the children of Pleasant Valley School stage a play. (Pre-K–1)

Helpful Web Sites

The addresses and corresponding agencies below are taken from the Web sites. Due to the dynamic nature of the Internet, please remember that Web sites are subject to change at any time.

http://www.etassoc.org   The Educational Theatre Association—Provides a broad range of professional services and support to theatre educators and their students.

http://www.aate.com/   The American Alliance for Theatre and Education—Promotes standards of excellence in theatre and theatre education.

http://www.sagecraft.com/puppetry/   The Puppetry Home Page—A free re-source for the puppetry community dedicated to helping people connect with the world of puppetry.

http://www.itdc.sbcss.k12.ca.us/curriculum/puppetry.html   The World of Puppets—An exploration of world cultures through their puppetry.

http://www.creativedrama.com/   Drama links

http://www3.sk.sympatico.ca/erachi/   The Drama Teacher's Resource Room—This site strive to make it easier for teachers to encourage creative and challenging experiences for students in drama classrooms.

For additional resources involving creativity and the arts with young children, visit our Web site at http://www.earlychilded.delmar.com

Chapter **8**

Creativity across the Curriculum and throughout the Classroom

Creativity can be nurtured in all areas of the early childhood curriculum and classroom. Opportunities for creativity are enhanced by giving children choices, allowing them to follow their interests, stimulating new ways of thinking, and encouraging creative expression. Creativity will be discussed as we examine ways the curriculum can be organized through **themes**, units, and projects.

Creative Episode

Darren, a seven-year-old, was the photographer for a class project that was to clean a small creek near school. At first, he pointed and clicked posed pictures. Then, as the work began, he watched one of the mothers taking pictures of the refuse the children were collecting in their garbage bags including an old tire and soft drink containers. Inquisitive, Darren asked about her camera and what she was photographing. The woman explained that she was making some pictures to show the kinds of trash and litter that found its way into streams. She showed Darren what the picture would look like by having him look through her viewfinder. For some shots, she crouched low in the weeds. For others, she stretched out, propping up on her elbows and holding the camera steady to take a picture of tossed candy wrappers.

Darren imitated a few of the mother's postures and tried her shots, but soon he returned to taking pictures of his classmates. However, after his exchange with the adult photographer, he asked the children to hold up the trash they were collecting. He tried different views from the ground, through the weeds, and even propped up on his elbows to get a shot of a child's feet and the soda can near his classmate's muddy shoes.

Was this a creative episode? Yes. It was indeed creative for a child to learn from someone else, interpret what he was shown, and adapt it in his own manner. The pictures accomplished what Darren wanted: to show his friends cleaning up the creek. He experimented with different ways to capture images that demonstrated flexible thinking. In addition, he photographed the types of litter found so that when the photos were displayed in the classroom, the children could discuss and speculate about how the trash might have gotten there.

Introduction

Collecting trash from the creek near the school was part of a larger environmental education unit in this second grade classroom. One might wonder if a science project, focusing on the need to keep our environment clean, also could provide opportunities for creative expression. As the creative episode demonstrates, it certainly does. Included are examples that illustrate the children's creative representations of what they learned while studying about the environment.

In this school-wide project, each classroom bulletin board displayed children's posters illustrating slogans about cleaning up the environment. Some slogans included, "Don't be a trashy person," with a collage-person made from pieces of trash collected at the site. "Fill up your stomach; don't fill up the field" was depicted with fast-food wrappers. "Toss it in" was shown with wire mesh stapled to poster board to represent a wastebasket where gum wrappers and bits of paper were tossed in.

At the front door of the school, representatives from each of the classrooms created another large exhibit. The representatives painted a huge blue stream onto a white sheet, and hung it from a rod to illustrate the South Elkhorn Creek. They stacked old tires at the bottom of the painted creek. A sign read, "I'm the creek, and I'm tired of tires." The exhibit was at the front door where those who passed were told to take their old tires to the recycling center. The center's address was given in bold print.

Children's representation of new knowledge was interpreted in their poster displays and the message exhibited at the front door. The significance of their learning was clear from the children's posters, Darren's photos, and a whole array of activities that touched each content area of the curriculum. The curriculum unit was evident at different times throughout the day, used different children's interests, and provided opportunities for them to choose their own ways of expression.

Definitions of Curriculum Development

The "Cleaning Up Our Creek" unit is an example of a science project that integrates all areas of the curriculum. There are many ways to organize curriculum depending on personal perspectives of child development, knowledge of various disciplines, and curriculum content. Ways of organizing units of study are numerous. However, their perspectives on child growth and development influence teachers by knowledge in various disciplines and by the content of the curriculum. Each influence casts shadows on the early childhood practitioners' views. Yet the basic questions are, "What is to be learned?" and "How, when, and why?" (Bredekamp & Rosegrant, 1995). Theorists, from as early as Rousseau in the 1700s, Pestalozzi and Froebel in the 1800s, and Dewey in the early 1900s, have influenced the answers to these questions on curriculum development (Ornstein & Hunkins, 1988; Raines & Canady, 1990).

Recently, the term **Developmentally Appropriate Practice (DAP)**, as referred to by the **National Association for the Education of Young Children (NAEYC)**, has influenced the current thinking of early childhood educators. In discussions of developmentally appropriate practices, some educators talk about them as if they were the curriculum. Instead, developmentally appropriate practices refer to the way the teacher carries out the curriculum, the organization of the learning environment, the materials, and the children's interactions with each other and the teacher. According to Bredekamp & Rosegrant (1992), "Curriculum is an organized framework that delineates the content that children are to learn, the processes through which children achieve the identified curricular goals, what teachers do to help children achieve these goals, and the context in which teaching and learning occur. The early childhood profession defines curriculum in its broadest sense, encompassing prevailing theories, approaches, and models" (p. 10).

According to the Association for Childhood Education International (ACEI), the thematic unit, "embraces the teaching of all content areas, presented as integrated experiences that develop and extend concepts, strengthen skills, and provide a solid foundation for learning in language, literacy, math, science, health, art and music" (Moyer, Egertson, & Isenberg, 1987, p. 23). Jarolimek and Foster (1989) define curriculum as a "coordinated series of learning activities planned around a broad topic that will involve the whole class in a comprehensive study" (p. 54).

The questions of the quality of the experiences—breadth versus depth of the curriculum—and the element of time cause us to examine our curriculum plans. In many discussions on the definition of early childhood curriculum, questions are raised about the nature of the experiences planned as part of a quality curriculum. When considering the quality of the experience, quality can be judged by whether the experience leads to "meaning-making" by children (Raines, 1997). Given that the teacher and the children plan the curriculum around a topic or theme that fits into larger curriculum units and disciplines, the need for concept development is based on the quality of the experience that promotes children making sense of their experiences. How one makes sense of the experiences is explained by learning theory where constructing concepts is the creative endeavor of the mind. How the learner represents what he or she has learned is an opportunity for creative expression.

Issues of time and breadth versus depth are serious in early childhood classrooms. The most common complaint of teachers is that they do not have time to devote to all the topics they want to cover, which infers with a breadth approach (Jalongo & Isenberg, 2000). The depth viewpoint is not how many different topics or themes are covered but what children gain from an in-depth study of a topic, including the learning processes, information-gathering strategies, and the quality and meaningfulness of the experiences. Both the breadth and depth questions are exacerbated by the issue of time.

Planning for a Creative and Integrated Curriculum

The way a teacher organizes the curriculum allows children to express what they have learned, gain competence at representing what they have learned, and use their own creativity. Themes, units, and the **project approach** provide ways of organizing the curriculum to promote creative thinking and expressions.

Early childhood educators value child-centered, experience-centered, and knowledge-centered approaches to curriculum planning. Themes, units, and project approaches to curriculum planning provide possibilities for the integration of information, learning processes, and creative expression. Many preschool and kindergarten teachers organize units around themes from social studies or science. Topics chosen often include families, friends, neighborhoods, transportation, simple machines, environments, plant life, wild animals, and pets. Projects may include "learning about pets and caring for pets," "a study of families and my family history," and "cleaning up our creek."

A project on the environment begins with concrete experiences such as examining a pinecone. (Photo by Su Lorencen)

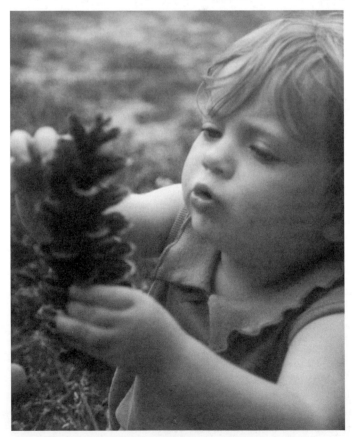

Beliefs about How Children Learn

Themes, units, and projects provide the mechanism for organizing activities that often are referred to as integrated learning. This way of designing curriculum is based on the beliefs that early childhood educators have about how children learn.

Young children learn best when exploring what interests them.

Being able to make choices motivates children.

Young children learn best as active participants in firsthand experiences.

When firsthand experiences are not available, connections must be made between the known and the unknown.

Active, expressive, engaged learning fosters a child's social, emotional, cognitive, language, and physical development.

The curriculum operates through learning environments inside the classroom, the outside physical setting, and interactions between the teacher and child. The curriculum also operates through a plan that the teacher has about opportunities to learn, including concepts and skills, the child can retain long after the unit, theme, or project is finished. Children may recall what they experienced whereas the teacher recalls what was learned, and how the children changed in their creative expressions, behaviors, skills, and interpretations of what was learned.

A major influence in curriculum design and implementation is derived from the laboratory schools of the John Dewey era. The curricula were planned around **human impulses** (Dewey, 1902; Raines & Canady, 1990). Smith, Stanley, and Shores (1957) simplified Dewey's impulses to include:

- socializing
- constructing
- inquiring
- questioning
- experimenting
- expressing or creating artistically

Dewey's human impulse view of curriculum planning has a place in this century because over time, we have come to recognize that Dewey's descriptions are accurate. The desire to socialize, inquire, question, experiment, and express and create artistically are the processes and learning styles that also are expressed in many of Gardner's (1993) descriptions of multiple intelligences.

Well-developed themes, units, and projects meet the needs of Dewey's human impulses. For example, teachers provide opportunities for children to socialize because of the belief that children need to learn how to get along with each other. Children also learn from social engagements with each other and with adults in their environment. Early childhood educators believe that when children construct representations of what they have learned to express their gained knowledge, they also gain experience in construction and are motivated by being able to choose what they will construct.

A project on gardening includes growing and caring for plants. (Photo by Su Lorencen)

Children are inquisitive, curious, learners who enjoy inquiry and want to know more. Children's questions should be taken seriously and used as points for directing classroom inquiry, whether individually or collectively. Experimentation leads to discoveries and simple experiments that often are the foundation of more complex constructs of knowledge. Support of children's individual and collective expressions occurs by promoting creative and artistic choices. Creative expression helps children learn at deeper levels, provides enjoyment, and leads to problem-solving. Allowing children to be inventive and use their own ingenuity shows respect for them as children and as individuals.

Curriculum planners may question whether child-centered, experience-centered, and knowledge-centered methods of planning can coexist. Certainly, teachers and program models follow along a continuum. Some programs for young children base the entire day on children's choices. In other settings, the daily focus follows a theme, broadening the children's experiences with weekly field trips and firsthand involvement. There are programs that are fact-, skill-, and knowledge-driven with drills, lists of information to be learned, and demonstration of abilities. Curriculum planners who consider themselves purists and following the interest of children, are at the extreme when looking

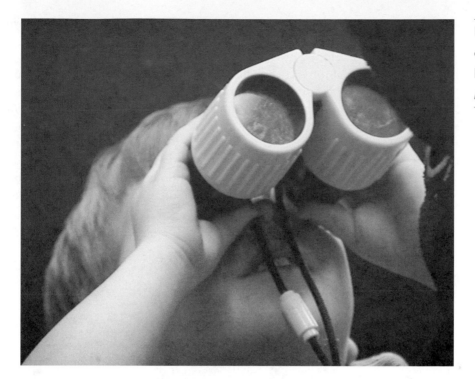

along a curriculum continuum. However, many early childhood educators propose a balance of child-centered choices with teacher-directed activities. For example, teachers may offer periods of time with choices or time set aside to observe the skills acquired. Teachers may balance inside play in a controlled environment with outside time in a more active mode. Directed lessons are balanced with choices of activities to express what has been learned, as well as opportunities to express oneself artistically for the sake of the art and for the enjoyment of play and self-expression.

Developmentally Appropriate Practices

Early childhood educators often use the term developmentally appropriate practices to govern the choices teachers make to plan and carry out the curriculum. Developmental appropriateness refers to what is known about human growth and development for the age of the child, and the stage of individual development. According to Bredekamp & Copple (1997), "two dimensions, age appropriateness and individual appropriateness are cornerstones of the teacher's thinking when planning the curriculum" (p. 2).

Developmental appropriateness refers to the universal, predictable sequences of growth and change, and the individual appropriateness of each child's timing of growth, individual personality, learning styles, and family background. What is developmentally appropriate for three-year-olds may not be challenging enough for most seven-year-olds. What is appropriate for some may not be appropriate for all because of who they are as individuals. For example, insisting the shy, hesitant, child perform alone in front of others is not developmentally appropriate although she might enjoy moving to music with a group of children.

Children's development is also shaped by the social context in which they live. There is a need for early childhood educators to understand the influence of the social-cultural context on learning, and to respect children's different ways of expressing their ideas, feelings, and achievements (Bredekamp & Copple).

Taking into account our beliefs about how children learn, developmentally appropriate practices, and social and cultural context, early childhood educators are left with the question of what they should include in the curriculum, and how to organize their time, space, and resources to maximize children's opportunities to learn.

How does paint work when used on a tree limb? A three-year-old paints a limb outside. (Photo by Su Lorencen)

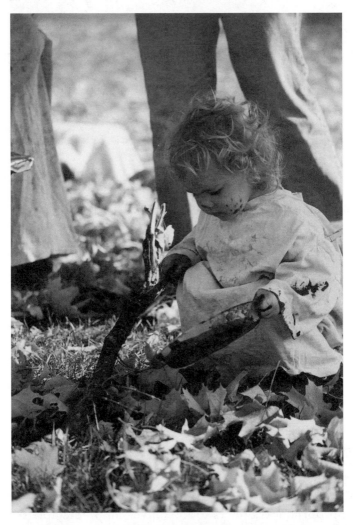

Deciding the "What": the Topic of the Theme, Unit, or Project

Choosing appropriate themes or topics for study is based on the teacher's view of the child as a learner. Some themes are chosen from social studies or science, and are used to support art, music, literature, mathematics, play, and learning centers as a way to distribute opportunities to learn throughout the curriculum and classroom. The social studies curriculum typically places the child at the center and units relate to those topics that have a degree of immediacy to the child's social environment. For example, families, friends, neighborhoods, community workers, feelings, and celebrations are viewed from the child's perspective. The "lived social studies curriculum" of the classroom is how the child learns to get along with others and be a productive member of the group while retaining her own identity.

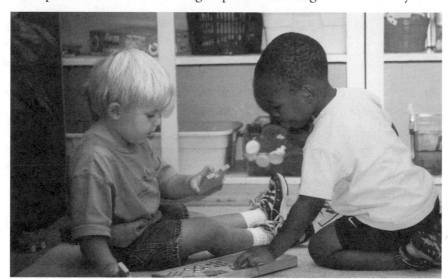

Children learning to work together through group projects. (Photo by Michael Talley)

Themes, topics, and units of the science curriculum are based on children's interests and the physical environment in which they live. The child's ability to experience the theme immediately drives the early childhood curriculum choices. Appropriate science themes might include food sources, nature, health, caring for pets, birds, and animals native to the region.

The immediate curriculum experience does not mean that teachers cannot expose children to other cultures, physical environments, or literature from another time and place. It does mean that the teacher begins with the children's own experiences, and builds connections and comparisons between what the children already know and what they are attempting to understand. Relating the unknown to the known builds a bridge to understanding from the experienced to the inexperienced. However, enough connections must be present for the child to build and retain new concepts. Several examples of creative units are listed in Appendix I and Appendix J.

The Project Approach

In their book *Engaging Children's Minds: The Project Approach*, Lilian G. Katz and Sylvia C. Chard (2000) use many of the same descriptors discussed in this chapter. Katz and Chard state, "In some countries, project work is referred to as theme or topic work. Others refer to a project as a unit. Some teachers combine project work with a learning-center approach" (p. xii). A project is an in-depth study of a particular topic that one or more children undertake that emerges from the child's interest. Often, thematic teaching in the United States refers to

> **"Project work relies on intrinsic motivation. It capitalizes on the child's own interest in the work . . . and a much wider range of possible activities."**
>
> **L. Katz & S. Chard, 2000[2]**

Building a space ship is part of a project focusing on space. (Photo by Michael Talley)

> **"Well developed projects engage children's minds and become adventures that teacher and children embark on together."**
>
> **J. H. Helm and L. G. Katz, 2000[3]**

the entire class of children studying a topic or children working in smaller groups. For example, in a unit on pets, different children may choose to learn individually about their own pets whereas the whole class will be involved in the group activities related to pets. A project idea might evolve from an individual, a group, or the whole class. Projects involve the children in planning and require their sustained interest in the topic.

Katz and Chard also describe projects on going shopping, including setting up a classroom shop or market. This approach is much like the one described by Isbell (1995) in the Grocery Store Center. Many primary children study the weather as part of the recommended science curriculum. Katz's and Chard's description of weather projects includes temperature studies, wind, shade and shadow, rain, animals, climate, and sayings and myths.

The project approach begins with the children's emerging interest and may last for several weeks to months. Through planning, the teacher and children discuss what already is known about a topic and decide how to learn more. Then, while the project is ongoing, the teacher expands the learning with visitors to the classroom, special investigations, or connecting to other areas of the children's interests. Finally, the children reflect on what they have learned, and make representations and engage in play related to the topic. For example, children might make a book or build a car after making careful observations, sketches, measurements, and taking photographs. The newly built car can be used for dramatic play to extend the learning until the children's interest wanes.

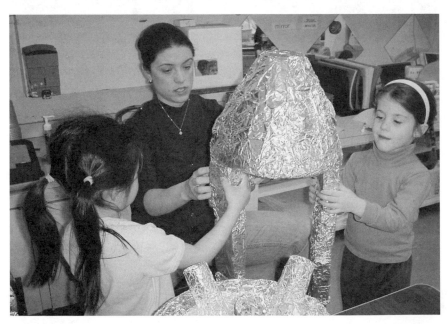

Emerging Curriculum and the Reggio Emilia Approach

The term **emerging curriculum** is used to differentiate between structured, preplanned lessons, and those that emerge from the child's interests and exploration of a topic. Susan Wright (1997) described the Reggio Emilia preschools to illustrate how children may choose their topics and become engaged in them through a variety of activities that continue over days, weeks, or sometimes months. Ideas emerge from the children's desire to know rather than from special objectives for the lessons or experiences predetermined by the teacher. Instead, the teachers create a learning environment, rich with materials for construction, artistic expression, and general exploration. Then, when a topic of study is selected, teachers and children plan together, collect additional materials, and work on ways to learn about the topic. Parents can be included by informing them of the topics children are exploring and requesting their input of possibilities for expanding the study. The curriculum emerges without the designation ahead of time of what will be learned and what will be achieved (Rinaldi, 1993).

Some of the ingenuity of the Reggio Emilia approach and the emergent curriculum is that the teachers listen to the children, follow their curiosity, and find ways to support exploration. For example, in a discussion of the emerging curriculum, Rinaldi described teachers who discussed summer vacations with their children and observed that the children frequently mentioned "the crowd." From the children's interest in and perceptions of being in a crowd, a rich study emerged. The children observed crowds, drew themselves and others in crowds, dramatized their feelings in crowds, photographed crowds, counted people, and researched what drew crowds. The project emerged from the teachers' careful observation of the children while listening to their ideas.

In the Reggio Emilia approach, young children become immersed in learning. Instead of moving children through a schedule, preschoolers spend great expanses of time focused on a project. The teacher or facilitator helps with vocabulary, possibilities for representing what is learned, and provides materials that support research in order to nurture learning, language, and the arts.

> "We think of a school for young children as an integrated living organism, as a place of shared lives and relationships among many adults and very many children."
>
> **L. Malaguzzi, 1993[4]**

Providing a variety of materials for art projects is essential. (Photo by Michael Talley)

Rinaldi described a long jump project where the children generated 22 different activities from looking at pictures of Olympic long jumpers. The children set up rules for a long jump contest, designed discreet measurements during the contest, and planned the ceremony for winners. In Reggio Emilia classrooms, children express, represent, and extend what they are learning. Teachers are highly observant and spend a great deal of time documenting what they see. They provide provocation for the children's learning by adding materials to the learning environment. In the Reggio classroom, the curriculum comes from the children and leads to in-depth study. The work of the children is focused and intense. Their language (including drawing, sculptures, and dramatic productions) often demonstrates their learning.

Clay is used to represent children's ideas. (Photo by Michael Talley)

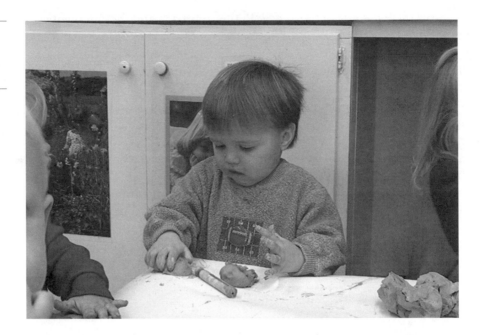

High/Scope Approach

The **High/Scope** approach to curriculum planning, formerly known as the cognitive curriculum and the cognitive-oriented curriculum, provides a framework for teachers to organize around the content of creative representation, language and literacy, initiative and social relations, movement, music, classification, serration, number, space, and time. Lessons or interactions are staged in the "plan-do-review" format, for teachers to assist children in organizing their thoughts. Key experiences are identified, and serve as a guide for planning and evaluation. They are embedded in activities that can be extended with language and nonverbal representation. Active learning, choices, and child-initiated and adult-initiated sequences are recommended (Hohmann & Weikart 1995).

The structure is derived from the planning of the space, the requirements of the curriculum, and the ways of organizing the children's thinking and responses (Bredekamp, 1996). The teacher's role is to instigate problem-solving by providing a variety of materials and activities, asking children to plan what they are going to do, and asking questions and making suggestions that stimulate children's thinking.

While the High/Scope curriculum is more structured than the project approach and the Reggio Emilia approach, there is room for children's choices, following their interests, and creative responses to what is being learned.

Time and Scheduling for the Integration of Curricular Themes

The thematic unit is most apparent during circle or group time with book selections in the classroom library, in the choice of special projects and activities, and in the addition of special centers. Major ideas or theme concepts are revisited several times during the day when children are scheduled for circle time, library and read-aloud, special projects and activities, and special centers.

Thematic units include:

- circle or group time
- classroom library
- special projects and activities
- centers

Young children need blocks of time to work at their own pace, to experience activities, use materials, and engage with other learners. This schedule design employs less teacher-directed time and greater child-choice time. Jalongo and Isenberg propose a kindergarten schedule that meets the requirements of larger blocks of time for child-choice activities related to a theme, and

A complex block structure that was developed over several days. (Photo by Michael Talley)

interactions with the teacher in a whole class setting or small groups. Tables 8–1 and 8–2, adapted from Raines (1995), contain schedules taken from a kindergarten and a primary classroom. Each reflects a respect for the young child's need for time and choice of activities. Variations on these schedules are appropriate, but teachers must protect the need for larger blocks of time that promote child-choice and in-depth work.

Table 8–1 Kindergarten Schedule

Time	Activity
8:50	Arrival, greeting, group time
9:25	Centers and work time
10:45	Whole-group sharing and debriefing
11:00	Gross motor activity (indoors or out)
11:30	Lunch
12:00	Whole-group story and discussion
12:30	Integrated language arts, science, or mathematics
2:30	Group share, story, and music
3:00	Preparation for home

Reprinted by permission of the publisher from Raines, S. C. (1995). *Whole language across the curriculum: Grades 1, 2, 3.* New York: Teachers College Press, p. 37. ©1995 by Teachers College Columbia University. All rights reserved.

Table 8–2 First Grade Schedule

Time	Activity
8:30	Signing in: Choice of reading or games
9:00	Class meeting at area rug - presentation of major concept in the unit of study
9:30	Reading and writing centers or workshop - snacks on their own
10:45	Outside play or gym
11:15	Teacher reads aloud book associated with theme - washing up for lunch
11:30	Lunch
12:00	Review of morning activities, highlighting children's writing, and discussion of theme
12:30	Mathematics and science
1:15	Social studies, science units, or projects
2:00	Art, music, or library media specialists
2:30	Clean-up, prepare for departure, and highlights of the day
3:00	Dismissal

Reprinted by permission of the publisher from Raines, S. C. (1995). *Whole language across the curriculum: Grades 1, 2, 3.* New York: Teachers College Press, p. 37. ©1995 by Teachers College Columbia University. All rights reserved.

Steps in Planning the Thematic Unit Project

After teachers have selected a topic for the thematic unit, several organizing devices help with planning. Teachers need to consider major concepts they want to promote throughout the study such as activities, materials, use of space, and time. Themes can be project-, question-, problem-, or issue-driven such as cleaning up our creek. They can be topic-driven such as families or neighborhoods, or literature-based such as tall tales or poetry.

Step one in planning any thematic unit or project is to decide on the theme. The teacher selects the thematic unit and the project develops from children's interest. The second step is to list the major concepts associated with this theme and the supporting ideas, which the teacher will highlight throughout the study. For proponents of integrating literature throughout the curriculum, the third step is to select between five and ten books that capture the major concepts of the theme. The fourth step is to brainstorm as many activities as possible that will support the development of these concepts. And the fifth step is to select the activities and make plans on a daily basis. In the following section, each step will be discussed in greater detail.

Step One.   The first step in planning a thematic unit is selecting a topic. Once the topic is determined, list the major concepts and supporting ideas. Begin your web design by drawing a circle with the topic inside (Figure 8-1).

Unit Theme-"Families"

FAMILIES

Figure 8–1   Unit Theme—"Families." (Courtesy of Delmar Learning)

Step Two.   Decide on the major concepts to be gained from this unit of study and the supporting ideas. For example, see the concept web in Figure 8–2 for the unit on families. Two of the major concepts are listed below.

1.   There are many definitions of family.
   • Not all families are alike.
   • Families have different members.

- There are adopted families and foster families.
- Family names are used to identify families.

2. We learn value from our families.
- Right and wrong.
- Working together and cooperating helps our family members get more done.
- Respect for others is learned in families.

Other major concepts that the teacher hopes the children will build and retain long after the study is complete relate to the distinctiveness of home, family celebrations, relationships within families, and who our relatives are. For the purpose of the web, these concepts have been shortened to single words: definition, values, feelings, home, celebrations, relationships, and relatives.

Figure 8–2 Concept web. (From Raines, S. C., & Isbell, R. T. (1994). *Stories: Children's literature in early childhood* (p. 348). Clifton Park, NY: Delmar Learning.)

Concept Web

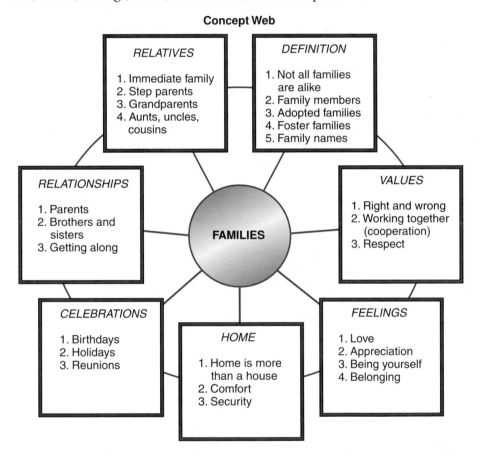

Step Three.   Select feature books that have the same theme and concepts are shown in Figure 8–3. For example, Norma Simon's (1976) *All Kinds of Families* is an excellent book to illustrate the major concept that there are many different definitions of a family. Ann Morris' (1990) *Loving* provides beautiful photographs of families in loving embraces, and with loving expressions on their faces or in their actions. Russell Hoban's (1964) *A Baby Sister for Frances* is one of a large number of books that tackles the situation of a new child joining the family.

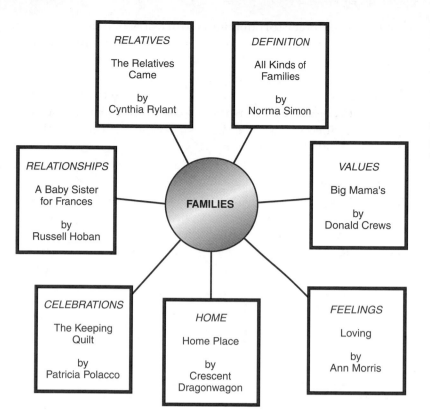

Figure 8–3 Concept web with books. (From Raines, S. C., & Isbell, R. T. (1994). *Stories: Children's literature in early childhood* (p. 348). Clifton Park, NY: Delmar Learning.)

Step Four. Brainstorm ideas for different areas of the classroom. Preschool, kindergarten, and child care teachers may choose to think of different centers in the classroom, as illustrated in the eight-cell planning sheet (Figure 8–4.) Some primary teachers may choose to use a tool that reflects their classroom areas or subject areas.

Group Time/Story Time	Library/Literature/ Writing Center
Art/Displays	Music/Movement
Creative Dramatics/ Housekeeping	Blocks (Small & Large) and Math/Manipulatives
Science/Nature	Sand/Water/Carpentry/ Special Projects/Events

Figure 8–4 Eight-cell Planning Sheet. (Courtesy of Shirley Raines)

Step Five. Use brainstorming ideas to select activities and place them on the web with the major concepts and featured book selections. Deciding which activities to select will vary with materials, investment of time, and interests of the children. These theme-supporting activities are ones available to children but they are not required of every child. Open-ended activities of the art, music, sociodramatic, blocks, and construction centers will remain available to children. Special activities, indicated as story s-t-r-e-t-c-h-e-r-s, are selected to support the concept development associated with the theme topic. The relationship to focus books helps reinforce the concepts around which the unit is built.

From the story s-t-r-e-t-c-h-e-r web (Figure 8–5), it is clear that there are numerous opportunities for creative responses. Some examples include drawing my family who lives with me, dramatizing special family moments, storytelling on a front porch, writing "thank-you" notes on cards of one's own design, singing lullabies, and devising ways to show the geography of a car trip to visit relatives.

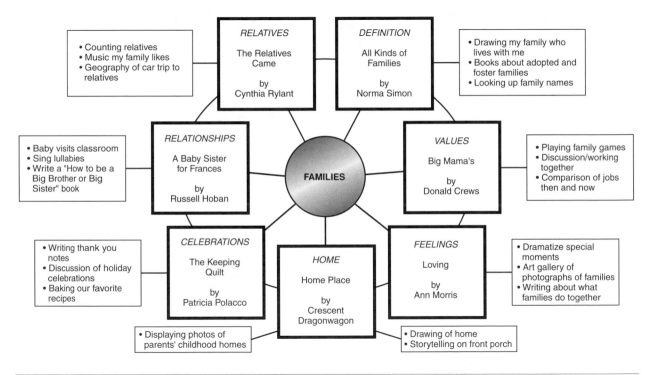

Figure 8–5 Story S-T-R-E-T-C-H-E-R Web for family unit. (From Raines, S. C., & Isbell, R. T. (1994). *Stories: Children's literature in early childhood* (p. 348). Clifton Park, NY: Delmar Learning).

Integrated Curriculum and the Subject Area Disciplines

Many primary teachers say they enjoy thematic teaching, but are compelled to teach more discreet lessons to be sure their students are learning to read well, write well, compute, think scientifically, and know the basics of geography and historical facts. Concerns over learning the basics of a discipline or **subject area** are valid issues. In fact, the skills and basics of subject areas such as reading, writing, and mathematics are often emphasized more than the fundamentals of social studies, science, and the arts.

In thematic teaching, the unit of study often concerns social studies or science. The expression of what one has learned is frequently represented artistically. Teachers wonder if reading, writing, and mathematics instruction will suffer when using thematic approaches to the curriculum. Certainly, if the teacher does not plan for adequate instruction, practice of skills, and application of the fundamentals of a discipline, the basics will suffer. However, the advantage of the thematic teaching approach is that it gives the child some interesting ways to apply what she is learning as a reader, writer, and mathematician. The skills are used in meaningful activity and relate to a topic of interest instead of being presented in isolation.

Below are some applications of the fundamentals, basics, or skills usually associated with pre-k, kindergarten, and the primary grades. Using the example of the "Families Thematic Unit" (Figures 8–1, 8–2, 8–3, and 8–5), the teacher can apply reading, writing, and mathematics instruction while thinking about families. For example, from the scheduled read-aloud, circle, or group time, the teacher can present a reading lesson. When the teacher reads Norma Simon's book, *All Kinds of Families*, the lesson likely will begin with a discussion of what the word "families" means. The teacher may ask young children to identify the letters that make up this word and note the children in the classroom who have names starting with the various letters of the word. In addition, the teacher might write a sentence or two that the children dictate about families. For example, on a chart tablet, the teacher may print:

"Aaron said, 'My *family* is my mother, father, grandmother, and baby sister.'"

"Michael said, 'My *family* is daddy, Aunt Susan, and my big brother.'"

"Leah said, 'My *family* is my mother and my brother.'"

"Simone said, 'I have two *families*. I live with a foster *family* and my other *family* is my mother and my little brother.'"

"Norma Simon, the author, wrote, 'There are all kinds of *families*.'"

From the emphasis on the word family and families, a reading lesson is constructed and the concept of a family is developed. After the circle, group time, or read-aloud time in the schedule, children are free to choose activities. There also may be some required activities. The teacher may ask that the children complete one of the tabletop activities before progressing on to selecting a center. At the tabletop activities, children may be asked to draw, paint, use colored chalk or markers, or use clay to create an image of their family, and to label their artistic rendering with the word family or families.

During mathematics instruction time, the children can count the number of family members in their family and the teacher can emphasize for younger children the numeral that represents the number of family members. For older children, after reading the book *All Kinds of Families*, the children can identify the number of different types of families from the book, then graph the number of different family members represented in the class. Addition and subtraction can be illustrated with story problems of Michael's family visiting Leah's family to determine the number of parents, children, babies, and so forth. Having a school event and preparing for those who will attend can represent the problem of larger numbers.

Social studies are taught throughout the unit because of the nature of the families theme while teaching the fundamentals of geography by stretching the content of Cynthia Rylant's (1985) *The Relatives Came*. In the story, the relatives travel from Virginia. The teacher can illustrate where they might be going by helping the children locate Virginia on a map, and discussing how people talk about where they are going such as "down to Grandmother's in Atlanta," "over to my cousin's in Roanoke," or "up from Virginia" to any place north of Virginia. Younger children may focus on the concept of where they live whereas older children can construct comparisons of where they live versus where their relatives live. The concept focuses on relatives as part of a study of families so an application can be made in the social studies and geography contexts.

Cleaning Up Our Creek

In the thematic unit on "Cleaning Up Our Creek," opportunities were replete for using the basics of reading, writing, and mathematics. For example, after visiting the South Elkhorn Creek, the children read the book *Come Back, Salmon* by Molly Cone (1991). The children wrote a class letter asking the local Sierra Club for additional environmental materials. Reading the brochures provided a wonderful opportunity for the teacher to illustrate that reading is for different purposes, a basic understanding in reading instruction.

While focusing on the main concept of our responsibility to take care of the physical environment, children browsed the Sierra Club materials for facts about the cost of littering and stream pollution. Their writing portfolios included accounts of what was learned at different times throughout the study. In mathematics, children weighed the amount of refuse they collected, measured the distance between various points on the South Elkorn Creek and the Kentucky River on a geological survey map, and calculated the cost of their class effort to clean up the creek if they had been paid $5 an hour.

As the creek unit demonstrates, learning the basic and practicing skills can be done in a thematic unit. The significance of unit thematic curricular organization is that skills are applied to interesting subjects and the need to know the skills is meaningful. Thematic unit teaching does not preclude the need for some students to have additional practice, one-on-one instruction with the teacher, and dedicated time to focus on skills. The difference is that the teacher, in the thematically organized unit of instruction, will make certain that children are applying skills in interesting ways that help them internalize and retain what has been practiced, in isolation from the content.

Initiating Activities, K-W-L Charts, and Culminating Activities

Many teachers and curriculum planners begin units with **initiating activities** that focus the children's attention on the topic to be studied. K-W-L charts are useful for keeping track of the inquiries that drive the child's investigations and as a way to document what has been learned. Culminating activities are designed for reflecting on what has been learned, consolidating understanding, and affirming one's role in learning.

The initiating activity might be as simple as reading the book *All Kinds of Families* or as exciting as asking parents to bring a new baby to class. The objective of the initiating activity is to focus children's attention on the topic, stimulate questions, and include children in the planning. Exhibits of family photographs may start a family unit that culminates in a special photography day for families to come to the school and have their pictures made.

The initiating activity for the "Cleaning Up Our Creek" unit was a walk to the creek from school. Children observed the creek and the debris, then made guesses about the source of the pollution. They also discussed their concerns for the fish, wildlife, and plants affected by the pollution, and their need for a fresh water supply.

To help teachers and children keep track of what they are learning during a unit of study, teachers can use K-W-L charts. K stands for what is known. W is what we want to know. And L indicates what has been learned. Some teachers construct K-W-L charts to begin the questioning and inquiry that motivates children to find answers. Some use the charts on a daily basis whereas others construct the charts at intervals to investigate the children's understanding.

Figure 8–6 is an example of a K-W-L chart developed by a multi-aged primary classroom during their study of "Cleaning Up Our Creek."

K-W-L Chart for Cleaning Up Our Creek	
K	**What we know about our creek**
	It is the closest creek to our school.
	There are other creeks with names similar to our creek.
	It is not straight; it twist and turns.
	It is at different levels, at different times of the year.
	Heavy rains cause it to flood in places.
W	**What we want to know about our creek**
	Where does our creek end?
	How does the trash get into the creek?
	What animals live on the banks?
	Are there any fish, frogs, or turtles living in the creek?
	Who owns the creek?
L	**What we have learned about our creek**
	Our creek flows into the Kentucky River, which flows into the Mississippi River, which flows to the Gulf of Mexico.
	Trash gets into the creek because people throw it into the creek or the water picks up trash on the banks, when it floods over into parks, roads, and fields.
	We could hear the creek and the animals and insects, when we stood very still and listened.
	There are many animals that live in the creek or along the banks.
	Some people, who live near the creek, have seen animals such as raccoons, opossums, muskrats, beavers, squirrels, and chipmunks.
	Ducks, crows, cranes, kingfishers, cardinals, blue jays, finches, hummingbirds, buzzards, and geese have been seen floating on, bathing in, and flying around the creek.
	Frogs, toads, and turtles live in the creek or on the banks.
	Thousands of insects, mosquitoes, gnats, spiders, and butterflies have been seen and heard near the creek.
	Minnows and small catfish have been seen in the creek. We don't know the names of the fish.

Figure 8–6 K-W-L Chart for Cleaning Up Our Creek.

The last statement in the K-W-L chart is an important one. Often, the chart will be revised and dated to list new questions so that every few days, a new chart is constructed. As the children learn more, the new K is based on the L from the previous days, and new questions become the new W, or what we want to know. The children's notation that they did not know the names of the fish in their creek became one of the points for the new W. The **culminating activity** was planned to be a clean-up day at the creek. However, after the actual clean-up day, the children wanted to "do something," and their public awareness campaign for the entire school and community began. It resulted in slogans, bulletin boards of artwork and photographs, a large display at the entrance to the school, newspaper accounts of the children's clean-up efforts, and a broadcast on the school's closed-circuit television station.

Creative Expression in the K-W-L Chart on "Cleaning Up Our Creek"

In addition to the creative expressions of the slogans, bulletin boards, and large displays, there were numerous other opportunities for the children to be creative. A wood duck with a beautiful green head floating in the creek inspired several paintings. The twists and turns of the creek were modeled in the sand and water table, with packed mud added to simulate the banks. The litter patrol made up a song to accompany their walk along the banks of the creek. And an audiotape of a gurgling creek inspired a story about children camping out but not being able to sleep because of the unfamiliar night noises.

Summary

Creative expression is possible throughout the early childhood curriculum and classroom. The curriculum can be planned to meet children's developmental needs, individual needs, and to provide avenues for human impulses to be expressed such as the need for self- and artistic expression. Some of the curriculum approaches that can be used include thematic units using learning centers, the project approach, emerging curriculum, and the High/Scope plan with structured interactions.

Classroom organization of learning centers, scheduling, and steps in planning themes also impacts the implementation of the curriculum. The thematic unit based on families provided an example of supporting children's learning through children's literature. Ways of organizing the curriculum by thinking of the various disciplines or subject areas is another way of organizing the thematic presentation of units. Initiating and culminating activities, and K-W-L charts illustrate another way for drawing attention to a topic, the children's learning, and the synthesis of information in a culminating activity.

The emerging curriculum provides the opportunity for children and teachers to follow their interests and actively participate in meaningful activities. The individual children and the teacher shape the framework for this approach as they plan and select unique ways of finding answers and learning. The project approach provides the opportunity for more in-depth learning, to move in different directions, and have more diverse ways of documenting what is learned. These approaches match what is known about how young children learn and give options for the teacher's role in this process.

Key Terms

theme

Developmentally Appropriate Practice (DAP)

National Association for the Education of Young Children (NAEYC)

project approach

human impulses

emerging curriculum

High/Scope

subject area

initiating activities

culminating activity

Reflection

1. Review Dewey's list of human impulses and think about an excellent classroom you have observed. Make a list of each of the human impulses and recall how the teacher provided for each need.

2. Explain the use of projects in an early childhood classroom. What are some of the strengths of this approach? Are there weaknesses?

3. Read more about the Reggio Emilia approach. Do you think this format promotes creativity? Explain why or why not.

4. Creativity and self-expression in this chapter are associated with what the children learn. How can you ensure that children's art products will all look different while they participate in many of the same activities?

Thinking about the Creative Episode

1. What was Darren interested in photographing?

2. How were photographs used to document a class project?

3. How did Darren's photography change after he observed and talked to the adult photographer?

Possibilities for Adult Learners

Activity: Unit Planning the Systematic Way

Goal: To develop a unit using a systematic plan.

Materials: Textbook with the directions for planning a unit.

Procedure:

1. Divide into small groups, teachers who are planning to work in Pre-K–K or with primary children.

2. Select a thematic unit that you might teach.

3. Use the steps outlined in the chapter to create curriculum planning webs by brainstorming and using the eight-cell planning tool.

Activity: To Teach Thematically or Not to Teach Thematically: That is the Question

Goal: To observe the use of thematic units in an early childhood classroom.

Materials: Notebook, and pen or pencil.

Procedure:

1. Visit a preschool, kindergarten, child care, or primary classroom.

2. Write down the schedule for the day.

3. Note times when thematic teaching is incorporated into the schedule, and if it is not, times when it could be incorporated.

4. Share your observations in class discussion.

Open-ended Activities for Young Children

Pre-K–K

Activity: A New Baby in the Family

Goal: To use information about a baby in play.

Materials: Baby clothes, bottles, diaper bag, baby toys, audiotape of lullabies.

Procedure:

1. After the new baby's visit to the classroom, collect baby items.

2. Place the items in the housekeeping corner.

3. Observe the new play that occurs as children explore the roles of having a new baby in the family.

Kindergarten

Activity: Building Homes for Families

Goal: To construct homes representing places where families might live.

Materials: Poster board, paste board, paint, small blocks, pieces of wood, glue, twigs, small stones, and other such items.

Procedure:

1. Read the book *My Great Grandpa* by Martin Waddell (1990).

2. Provide construction materials for the children to make houses.

3. Observe what kind of houses the children make.

4. Display their creations to be appreciated by all.

5. Some children may decide to make houses like Great Grandpa described; others simply may construct something associated with houses and neighborhoods.

Primary Grades

Activity: What I Have Learned

Goal: To identify ways to share what children have learned.

Materials: Chart paper and other display materials.

Procedure:

1. How can children let others know what they have learned?

2. In a class discussion of the theme, note all the different concepts the class has learned.

3. Let the children decide how they might show others what they have learned, through paintings, drawings, drama, photos, block displays, and the like.

Notes

[1]Fitzhenry, R. I. (Ed.). (1993). *The Harper book of quotations* (3rd ed.). New York: Harper Collins Books.

[2]Katz, L. G., & Chard, S. C. (2000). *Engaging children's minds: The project approach.* Norwood, NJ: Ablex.

[3]Helm, J. H., & Katz, L. G. (2000). *Young investigators: The project approach in the early years.* New York: Teachers College Press.

[4]Malaguzzi, L. (1993). History, ideas, and basic philosophy. In C. Edwards, L. Gandini, and G. Forman (Eds.), *The hundred languages of children: The Reggio Emilia approach to early childhood education* (pp. 41–89). Norwood, NJ: Ablex.

References

Bredekamp, S. (1996). 25 years of educating young children: The High/Scope approach to preschool education. *Young Children, 51*(4), 57–61.

Bredekamp, S., & Copple, C. (1997). *Developmentally appropriate practice in early childhood programs.* Washington, DC: National Association for the Education of Young Children.

Bredekamp, S., & Rosegrant, T. (Eds.). (1992). *Reaching potentials: Appropriate curriculum and assessment for young children—Volume 1.* Washington, DC: National Association for the Education of Young Children.

Bredekamp, S., & Rosegrant, T. (Eds.). (1995). *Reaching potentials: Appropriate curriculum and assessment for young children—Volume 2.* Washington, DC: National Association for the Education of Young Children.

Cone, M. (1994). *Come back, salmon: How a group of dedicated kids adopted Pigeon Creek and brought it back to life.* San Francisco: Sierra Club Books for Children.

Dewey, J. (1902). *The child and curriculum.* Chicago, IL: University of Chicago Press.

Gardner, H. (1983). *Frames of mind: The theory of multiple intelligences.* New York: Basic Books.

Hoban, R. (1964). *A baby sister for Frances.* New York: Harper & Row.

Hohmann, M., & Weikart, D. P. (1995). *Educating young children: Active learning practices for preschool and child care programs.* Ypsilanti, MI: High Scope Press.

Isbell, R. (1995). *The complete learning center book.* Beltsville, MD: Gryphon House.

Jalongo, M. R., & Isenberg, J. P. (2000). *Exploring your role: A practitioner's introduction to early childhood education.* Upper Saddle River, NJ: Merrill.

Jarolimek, J., & Foster, C. D. (1989). *Teaching and learning in the elementary school.* New York: Macmillan.

Katz, L. G. & Chard, S. C. (2000). *Engaging children's minds: The project approach.* Norwood, NJ: Ablex.

Morris, A. (1990). *Loving.* New York: Mulberry.

Moyer, J., Egertson, H., & Isenberg, J. (1987). The child-centered kindergarten. *Childhood Education, 63*(4), 235–242.

Ornstein, A. C., & Hunkins, F. P. (1988). *Curriculum: Foundations, principles, and issues.* Englewood Cliffs, NJ: Prentice Hall.

Raines, S. C. (1995). *Whole language across the curriculum: Grades 1, 2, 3.* New York: Teachers College Press.

Raines, S. C. (1997). Developmental appropriateness: Curriculum revisited and challenged. In J. P. Isenberg & M. R. Jalongo (Eds.), *Major trends and issues in early childhood education* (pp. 75–89). New York: Teachers College Press.

Raines, S. C., & Canady, R. J. (1989). *Story s-t-r-e-t-c-h-e-r-s: Activities to expand children's favorite books.* Mt. Rainier, MD: Gryphon House.

Raines, S. C., & Canady, R. J. (1990). *The whole language kindergarten.* New York: Teachers College Press.

Raines, S. C., & Canady, R. J. (1991). *More story s-t-r-e-t-c-h-e-r-s: More activities to expand children's favorite books.* Mt. Rainier, MD: Gryphon House.

Raines, S. C., & Canady, R. J. (1992). *Story s-t-r-e-t-c-h-e-r-s for the primary grades: Activities to expand children's favorite books.* Mt. Rainier, MD: Gryphon House.

Rinaldi, C. (1993). The emergent curriculum and social constructivism. In C. Edwards, L. Gandini, & G. Forman (Eds.), *The hundred languages of children: The Reggio Emilia approach to early childhood education* (pp. 101–111). Norwood, NJ: Ablex.

Rylant, C. (1985). *The relatives came.* New York: Bradbury Press.

Simon, N. (1976). *All kinds of families.* Niles, IL: Albert Whitman.

Smith, B. O., Stanley, W. O., & Shores, J. H. (1957). *Fundamentals of curriculum development.* New York: John Wiley.

Waddell, M. (1990). *My great grandpa.* New York: G. P. Putnam.

Wright, S. (1997). Learning how to learn: The arts as core in an emergent curriculum. *Childhood Education, 73*(6), 361–365.

Additional Reading

Allen, D. D., & Piersma, M. L. (1995). *Developing thematic units: Process & product.* Clifton Park, NY: Delmar Learning.

Altwerger, B., & Flores, B. (1994). Theme cycles: Creating communities of learners. *Primary Voices K–6, 2*(1), 2–6.

Bayman, A. G. (1995). An example of a small project for kindergartners that includes some 3Rs learning. *Young Children, 50*(6), 27–31.

Cadwell, L. (1997). *Bringing Reggio Emilia home: An innovative approach to early childhood education.* New York: Teachers College Press.

Chard, S. C. (1994). *The project approach: A practical guide, I and II.* New York: Scholastic.

Cornett, C. E. (1999). *The arts as meaning makers.* Upper Saddle River, NJ: Prentice Hall.

Dodge, D. T., & Colker, L. (1992). *Creative curriculum for early childhood.* Washington, DC: Teaching Strategies.

Edwards, C. P. (1993). Inviting children into project work. *Dimensions of Early Childhood, 22*(1), 9–12, 40.

Edwards, C., Gandini, L., & Forman, G. (Eds.). (1998). *The hundred languages of children: The Reggio Emilia approach-advanced reflections* (2nd ed.). Stamford, CT: Ablex.

Elgas, P. M., & Peltier, M. B. (1998). Jimmy's journey: Building a sense of community and self-worth through small-group work. *Young Children, 53*(2), 55–59.

Elliot, M. J. (1998). Great moments of learning in project work. *Young Children, 53*(2), 55–59.

Freeman, C. C., & Sokoloff, H. J. (1996). Children learning to make a better world: Exploring themes. *Childhood Education, 73*(1), 17–22.

Gandini, L. (1993). Fundamentals of the Reggio Emilia approach to early childhood education. *Young Children, 49*, 4–8.

Giffard, S. (1997). Theme studies and the arts. *Primary Voices K–6, 5*(2), 2–5.

Goldberg, M. R. (2000). *Arts and learning: An integrated approach to teaching and learning in multicultural and multilingual setting* (2nd ed.). New York: Longman Publishing Group.

Goldhaber, J. (1998). Oh, Miss Jones! Where did you get that beautiful butterfly? *Young Children, 53*(2), 60–63.

Hartman, J. A., & Eckerty, C. (1995). Projects in the early years. *Childhood Education, 71*(3), 141–147.

Helm, J. H., & Katz, L. G. (2001). *Young investigators: The project approach in the early years.* Washington, DC: National Association for the Education of Young Children.

Hendricks, J. (Ed.). (1997). *First step toward teaching the Reggio way.* Upper Saddle River, NJ: Prentice Hall.

Hohmann, M., Babet, B., & Weikart, P. (1979). *Young children in action.* Ypsilanti, MI: The High/Scope Press.

Jones, E., & Nimmo, J. (1994). *Emergent curriculum.* Washington, DC: National Association for the Education of Young Children.

Leekeenan, D., & Edwards, C. P. (1992). Using the project approach with toddlers. *Young Children, 47*(4), 31–36.

Marcon, R. A. (1992). Differential effects of three preschool models on inner-city 4-year-olds. *Early Childhood Research Quarterly, 7*(4), 517–530.

Rankin, B. (1992). Inviting children's creativity: A story of Reggio Emilia, Italy. *Child Care Information Exchange, 85*, 30–35.

Sloane, M. W. (1999). All kinds of projects for your classroom. *Young Children, 54*(4), 17–20.

Trepanier-Street, M. (1993). What's so new about the project approach? *Childhood Education, 70*(1), 25–28.

Workman, S., & Anziano, M. C. (1994). Curriculum webs: Weaving connections from children to teachers. *Young Children, 49*(1), 4–9.

Children's Literature Connection

Family Thematic Unit

Brown, M. (1987). *Arthur's baby.* New York: Joy Street Books.
Arthur isn't sure he is happy about the new baby in the family, but when his sister asks him for help in handling the baby, Arthur feels much better. (Pre-K–3)

Crews, D. (1991). *Big mamma's.* New York: Greenwillow Books.
Banished to the hallway for disrupting the class on the day of a favorite author's visit, best friends Chris and Jeremy write the most outlandish apologies they can think of. (Pre-K–3)

Dragonwagon, C. (1990). *Homeplace.* New York: Macmillan.
While hiking, a family comes on the site of an old house and finds some clues about the people that once lived there. (Pre-K–3)

Henkes, K. (1991). *Julius, the baby of the world.* New York: Greenwillow Books.
Lilly is convinced that the arrival of her new baby brother is the worst thing that has happened in their house until Cousin Garland comes to visit. (Pre-K–3)

Hines, A. G. (1986). *Daddy makes the best spaghetti.* New York: Clarion.
Not only does Corey's father make the best spaghetti, but also dresses up like Bathman and acts like a barking dog. (Pre-K–K)

Hoban, R. (1964). *A baby sister for Frances.* New York: Harper & Row.
When things change around the house after her baby sister is born, Frances decides to run away; but not too far. (K–3)

Morris, A. (1990). *Loving.* New York: Mulberry.
This book offers a look at families throughout the world and how they show love. (Pre-K–K)

Polacco, P. (1988). *The keeping quilt.* New York: Simon and Schuster.
A homemade quilt ties together the lives of four generations of an immigrant Jewish family, and remains a symbol of their enduring faith and love. (K–3)

Rylant, C. (1985). *The relatives came.* New York: Bradbury Press.
The relatives come to visit from Virginia and everyone has a wonderful time. (Pre-K–3)

Shelby, A. (1995). *Homeplace.* New York: Orchard Books.
A grandmother and grandchild trace their family history. (Pre-K–K)

Simon, N. (1976). *All kinds of families.* Niles, IL: Albert Whitman.
This picture book is an essay on family love and communities. (Pre-K–3)

Waddell, M. (1990). *My great grandpa.* New York: G. P. Putnam.
Spending a memorable Sunday with her great-grandfather and her other grandparents, eight-year-old Deborah realizes that with good health, the elderly can live a rich and varied life. (K–3)

"Cleaning Up Our Creek" Unit

Bang, M. (1996). *Chattanooga sludge.* New York: Harcourt Brace & Company.
John Todd attempts to clean the toxic waters of Chattanooga Creek with a Living Machine. (K–3)

Berger, M. (1992). *Look out for turtles!* New York: HarperCollins.
Describes the remarkable turtle which can live almost anywhere, eat almost anything, ranges in size from tiny to gigantic, and lives longer than any other animal. (K–3)

Cone, M. (1994). *Come back, salmon: How a group of dedicated kids adopted Pigeon Creek and brought it back to life.* San Francisco: Sierra Club Books for Children.
An inspiring story of young scientists in action in Everette, Washington. These children worked with their teacher to clean up Pigeon Creek and reclaim it as a salmon spawning ground. (K–3)

George, W. T. (1989). *Box Turtle at Long Pond.* New York: Greenwillow Books.
On a busy day at Long Pond, Box Turtle searches for food, basks in the sun, and escapes a raccoon. (Pre-K–K)

Guilberson, B. (1992). *Spoonbill swamp.* New York: Henry Holt.
In a tropical swamp, a spoonbill and an alligator care for their young throughout the day. (Pre-K–K)

Lewin, T. (1992). *When the rivers go home.* New York: Macmillan.
An introduction to an exotic endangered habitat—the Pantanal—a vast swamp in central Brazil. (Pre-K–3)

Reiser, L. (1993). *Tomorrow on Rocky Pond.* New York: Greenwillow Books.
Vacationing in the country, a child anticipates tomorrow's activities of fishing and hiking. (Pre-K–K)

Say, A. (1989). *The lost lake.* Boston: Houghton Mifflin.
A young boy and his father become closer friends during a camping trip in the mountains. (Pre-K–K)

Helpful Web Sites

The addresses and corresponding agencies below are taken from the Web sites. Due to the dynamic nature of the Internet, please remember that Web sites are subject to change at any time.

http://educate.si.edu   The Smithsonian Center for Education and Museum Studies—Interprets the collective knowledge of the Smithsonian and serves as a gateway to its educational resources.

http://www.rcs.re.it/unita/notter/esped/erchild.htm   Information about Reggio Children

http://www.stanford.edu/dept/bingschool/itp/   The Innovative Teacher Project—Dialogue between the educators in Reggio Emilia and the United States.

http://www.mpi.wayne.edu/teacher.htm   The Merrill-Palmer Institute—Offers development programs for early childhood educators interested in exploring how the principles of Reggio Emilia can enrich their classrooms.

http://www.creativecurriculum.net/   The Creative Curriculum from Teaching Strategies—A nationally validated curriculum that helps teachers create effective learning environments in their preschool classrooms by focusing on the indoor and outdoor spaces where learning takes place.

http://www.highscope.org/   High/Scope® Foundation—Promotes the learning and development of children worldwide from infancy through adolescence, and supports and trains educators and parents as they help children learn.

http://www.pta.org/   National PTA—A not-for-profit association of parents, educators, students, and other citizens active in their schools and communities.

http://users.sgi.net/~cokids/highscope.htm   Links to information on the Internet about the High/Scope Foundation and its curriculum.

For additional resources involving creativity and the arts with young children, visit our Web site at **http://www.earlychilded.delmar.com**

Chapter 9

The Expressive Arts in the Early Childhood Classroom and Curriculum

This chapter provides the rationale for the arts as part of the curriculum, how the creative arts can be interwoven into the curriculum, and glimpses into classrooms. Examples from centers, themes, and emerging curriculum projects will be presented. The chapter also explores the child's creative expression and enjoyment of art, music, movement and dance, drama, and storytelling in many forms.

Creative Episode

Inspired by dandelions blooming on the school lawn in April, several four- and five-year-olds picked the yellow flowers for their teacher. A white pottery coffee cup holding a bunch of dandelions was perched on top of a low bookcase in full view of the painting easel. Other dandelions lay wilting on top of the bookcase. Another bunch was placed in a styrofoam cup on the science table, accompanied by a chart that in large print asked, "Is it a flower or is it a weed? What do you think?" Two columns were drawn on the chart: one was labeled weed and the other flower. Green markers were provided for children to mark weed and yellow markers for those who chose flower.

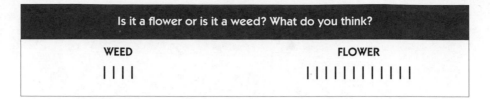

Is it a flower or is it a weed? What do you think?	
WEED	**FLOWER**
I I I I	I I I I I I I I I I I I

Without the teacher's prescription but with the teacher's inspiration, dandelions were painted the most. Many of the painters concentrated on painting yellow, white, and green, although there were many other colors in the paint tray of the easel. Several struggled with how to show the white cup on the nearly white paper. Most of the children painted huge renditions of the dandelions. Some of the older children in the group drew themselves picking the dandelions, then painted their pictures. One child made green lines and yellow splotches near the bottom of his paper to illustrate the wilting dandelions, but most of the children concentrated on the cup of flowers. The chart was true to their language; most believed that the dandelion was a flower.

What does the creative episode tell us about the teacher, the children, and the organization of the classroom? Why did the teacher capitalize on the occasion of the dandelion gifts? The teacher in this pre-K classroom provided time in the schedule and materials, and he planned for connections between the expressive arts and the curriculum. Although not a formal curricular topic, dandelions emerged as an interest when they surfaced on the lawn near the outside play area. The teacher could have accepted the bouquet of flowers as a gift from the children, but instead capitalized on the occasion and incorporated the dandelions into the classroom activities.

Definitions and Rights of the Child for the Expressive Arts

In the Association for Childhood Education International's (ACEI) position statement, "The Child's Right to the Expressive Arts: Nurturing the Imagination as Well as the Intellect," Jalongo (1990) writes, "The expressive arts— music, art, drama, dance, writing—are important because they are the means of communicating our creative productivity and imaginative thinking." The entire position statement can be found in Appendix A.

Children are constructors of language and of other representations of what they know, feel, and desire to express (Raines & Canady, 1990). The expressive arts give children multiple means of communication as they create with materials, and as they examine the representations and creations of others. In 1902, John Dewey proposed that the early childhood curriculum should be driven by "the human impulses to socialize, to construct, to inquire, to question, to experiment, and to express or to create artistically" (Smith, Stanley, & Shores, 1957, p. 265). The human impulse to express oneself and create artistically is a time-honored tradition, worthy of continuing in the early childhood classrooms of today.

ACEI's position paper on "The Child's Right to the Expressive Arts"
(Jalongo) gives educators a statement of seven rights that can guide classroom
practice.

1. **Every child has a right to opportunities for imaginative expression.**
   Time, materials, and artistic instruction must be provided for all
   children, not just those dubbed as gifted and talented.

2. **Educating the child's imagination is education for the future.**
   We are told by futurists that tomorrow's children will need to be
   creative, flexible, imaginative, risk-takers, able to work with multiple
   images, see issues from different perspectives, and enjoy change. The
   expressive arts can enhance each of these characteristics.

3. **The educated imagination is the key to equity and intercultural
   understanding.**
   Creativity and the expressive arts lead us to explorations of our
   own self-expression and an appreciation of how others express
   themselves. From children's self-perspectives, they use their
   imaginations to identify with others, to interpret others' expressions,
   to see new cultural interpretations, and to build connections
   (Hansen, 1986; Hoffman & Lamme, 1989; Jalongo, 1990).

4. **Children's creative productivity is qualitatively different from adults'.**
   Children grow in their ability to control media. While there are

similarities among children in their productions in artistic expression, their originality and imagination should be appreciated instead of expecting that the renderings, music, and other productions should be like little adults.

5. Creative expression should permeate the entire curriculum.

   Children's play, drawing, painting, sculpting, building, storytelling, movement, and music are available to children long before they can express themselves in the standards of reading and writing. Opportunities to express one's self and to understand others' expressions is central to the early childhood curriculum, and transcends the curricular areas.

6. Imagination is the key to artistry in teaching and excellence in our schools.

   Dull and uninspired curriculum can come alive when children and teachers use their imaginations to express what they are learning. According to Kieran Egan (1997), the arts and creative expression are not alternatives to education, but rather a basic to all educational activity.

7. We must refashion our schools for creative expression.

   Given our ambitions for education to provide opportunities for children to grow as thinkers, reflective decision-makers, risk-takers, and expressive human beings, our schools must change their view of the arts and creative expression as extras, and see them as basic to our human needs and desires.

Orientation to the Arts Curriculum

Bresler (1993) researched teachers' orientations to incorporating art experiences into daily classroom practices. They described three orientations to the arts curriculum:

1. the **little-intervention** orientation

2. the **product-oriented** orientation

3. the **guided-exploration** orientation

A brief review of the three orientations provides insight into appropriate integration of the arts. The little-intervention orientation is most often associated with the belief that if one provides the materials for artistic expression, time in the schedule, and the expectation that children will engage with the materials, then the children will express themselves creatively. This view most often is associated with the visual arts and is prevalent in early childhood classrooms.

Many primary classrooms are product-oriented, meaning children are expected to produce a product whether in the visual or performing arts. In fact, this view is often associated with music and drama productions.

In the guided-exploration orientation view, children are taught about art forms and aesthetic qualities found in the specialists' classroom or the classrooms of teachers with an interest in the arts. This view is also consistent with the Getty Center for Education in the Arts position paper, "Beyond Creating: The Place for

Art in America's Schools" (1985). The visual arts guided-exploration orientation teaches children about line, form, shapes, balance, and color. Similarly, the language of music, theater, and literature are used to describe the artistic and creative expression of others, whether children's works or those of famous artists.

Teachers in the little-intervention orientation emphasize creativity, the child's exploration of materials, self-expression, and independence. Authors Stake, Bresler, and Mabry (1991) criticize early childhood classrooms for the lack of an aesthetic environment, little knowledge of the arts, and concern that children may miss meaningful learning when the substance of the arts is available mostly through raw materials. In this environment, children may miss opportunities to expand their understanding of the arts. However, children's products in the little-intervention classroom are highly individualized, which meets the goals in early childhood classrooms.

Product-orientation often results in uniformity, little self-expression or independence, and rather simplistic expectations. Copied materials for coloring result in rows of art products that look the same, much like craft patterns. In music and drama, children are expected to perform exactly as the material was written, with little creativity or self-expression. The children's products are mostly the same as craft productions.

The guided-exploration orientation classrooms included a diversity of materials similar to the little-intervention orientation, but the teacher guided the children's explorations of the art forms, the associated symbols, and the development of concepts, skills, and knowledge of the arts. In the guided-exploration orientation, the children's products were more individualized, but there were more products associated with the study of the arts and art forms, as well as opportunities for self-expression.

In early childhood classrooms, there are opportunities to use several of these approaches, alone or in combinations. The children in the classroom, their level of development, and the activities influence the selection and level of guidance. When a material or activity is first introduced, there is an essential period of exploration. This is how the young child learns about the material's properties. Later, or in a more advanced level of work or activity, a child may request help or guidance from either the teacher or his peers. The teacher must

Project work often includes group discussion and planning. (Photo by Michael Talley)

observe and respond appropriately to encourage the child and his growing abilities in the arts.

Developmentally Appropriate Practices and the Process Versus Product Issue

Early childhood educators are guided by long-held practices, recommendations from experts and professional associations, and their own experiences. Generally, emphasis is placed on the process versus the product, given that the young child has much to experience and learn (Dixon & Chalmers, 1990). An early childhood teacher who makes play dough available to children may expect, at the end of clean-up time, that all of the dough will be returned to the tubs, with no remaining product. As many teachers of preschoolers have noted, the children may paint a picture, then get caught-up in the process of painting and completely cover the sheet of paper on the easel with one color of paint. During the process, the child created a painting but chose to paint over it. The process was more important than the product. Children often have difficulty finding their paintings at the end of the day when they are dry enough to take home. It was the process of painting that was important. As children progress in their experiences with various art media, they begin making products they want to keep.

The position reflected in the Developmentally Appropriate Practices documents from the National Association for the Education of Young Children, is that "Children have daily opportunities for aesthetic expression and appreciation through art and music. A variety of art media are available for creative expression, such as easel and finger painting and clay" (Bredekamp & Copple, 1987, p. 52). Moyer, Egertson, and Isenberg (1987) describe the child-centered kindergarten as "emphasizing the process of learning, rather than focusing on finished products" (p. 236). According to the ACEI position, the child-centered kindergarten is noted for "allowing children to make choices and decisions within the limits of the materials provided, resulting in increased independence, attention, joy in learning, and feelings of success necessary for growth and development" (Jalongo, p. 239).

Experts Versus Classroom Teachers

Clearly, early childhood teachers can profit from collaborating with specialists in art, music, movement, and drama. Yet to truly integrate the arts throughout the curriculum, the classroom teacher must organize the time, materials, and instruction. Obviously, early childhood educators will not have the same depth of knowledge as an arts educator. However, a basic understanding of the field and an appreciation for the arts should be part of the early childhood teacher's training and background of experiences. Likewise, a depth of knowledge in child growth and development is an asset to the arts educator.

In primary schools, where music and art teachers are more widespread, teachers may not attend each other's classes. If one is fortunate enough to have a music, art, dance, or movement teacher, he should attend the class with the children and provide opportunities during the week for children to use what they have learned from the arts educator. Collaborate to have the specialist support current projects and themes in the classroom. Use music, art, or drama activities occurring in special classes to enrich classroom experiences. The interweaving of the activities of the specialist and teacher helps children learn that the arts are for all people, not just a special few.

Artist-in-Residence Programs

Another source of expertise is the **Artist-in-Residence** program. Practicing artists, often supported by school districts or community arts councils, agree to spend some of their time with children where they demonstrate their art, facilitate lessons, and help children learn about their profession. Few artist-in-residence programs have been adapted to very young children, yet children enjoy live performances and can learn the language of art, new concepts, and discover what skills are needed. Older children who have developed some proficiency in their art form, and adults who are hobby artists, also are excellent resources to provide expertise or performances in the early childhood classroom. A violinist may play music for the children, then let the children pluck the violin strings, try the bow, and feel the vibrations. A potter may throw a pot, then teach the children a simple coiling and shaping method. Opportunities to observe, interact, and appreciate an artist's work enrich children's learning and inspire their artistic abilities.

Atelier and the Atelierista in Reggio Emilia Programs

Reggio Emilia programs have prompted educators in the United States to reflect on the importance of the arts. Teachers have examined extensive murals and sculptures created by young children in Reggio Emilia, and noted their highly individualized responses and connection to the project being studied. Educators recognize that young children are far more capable in the arts than previously believed. The Hundred Languages of Children refers to the different modes of expression that lead children to a greater symbolic representation than experts thought them capable of reaching. The success of Reggio Emilia is credited to the teachers' beliefs in the capabilities of children, keen observation skills, and their methods for working with the atelierista.

According to Edwards, Gandini, and Forman (1993), the atelier is a workshop, or studio, furnished with a variety of resource materials, used by all the children and adults in a school." The atelierista is a "teacher trained in art education, in charge of the atelier, who supports teachers in curriculum development and documentation" (p. 313). The atelier is a special arts space, replete with materials and tools. Children and teachers move freely between the space and their classrooms. Instead of having a designated time to interact, the atelierista engages children in whatever topic or project they are currently investigating. The atelierista and teachers work together to support children as they create. An addition, the atelierista works to document the children's creative process. One example, given by Malaguzzi (1993), was of children using images such as turning a poppy into a spot, a light, a bird in flight, a lighted ghost, and a handful of red petals within a field of green and yellow wheat. The exploration of the arts, art forms, and study of the problems of artistic expression are supported by the atelierista and the atelier.

Loris Malaguzzi founded and directed the Reggio Emilia municipal early childhood programs (Edwards, Gandini, & Forman). Malaguzzi lists nine beliefs that guide the program:

1. Creativity should not be considered a separate mental faculty but a characteristic of our way of thinking, knowing, and making choices.

2. Creativity seems to emerge from multiple experiences, coupled with a well-supported development of personal resources, including a sense of freedom to venture beyond the known.

3. Creativity seems to express itself through cognitive, affective and imaginative processes. These come together and support the skills for predicting and arriving at unexpected solutions.

4. The most favorable situation for creativity seems to be inter-personal exchange, with negotiation of conflicts and comparisons of ideas and actions being the decisive elements.

5. Creativity seems to find its power when adults are less tied to prescriptive teaching methods, but instead become observers and interpreters of problematic situations.

6. Creativity seems to be favored or disfavored according to the expectations of teachers, schools, families, and communities as well as society at large, according to the ways children perceive those expectations.

7. Creativity becomes visible when adults try to be more attentive to the cognitive processes of children than to the results they achieve in various fields of doing and understanding.

8. The more teachers are convinced that intellectual and expressive activities have both multiplying and unifying possibilities; the more creativity favors friendly exchanges with imagination and fantasy.

9. Creativity requires that the school of knowing finds connections with the school of expressing, opening the doors (that is our slogan) to the hundred languages of children (pp. 70–71).

The factors of time, space, adult interactions with children, and the extensiveness of the children's investigations differ from other models of early childhood education and the usual practice in the United States. Like Vygotsky and Piaget, Malaguzzi is a constructivist who is concerned about children constructing meaning. Interactions of the cognitive and affective are intertwined. Like Vygotsky, Malaguzzi points out, "how thought and language operate together to form ideas and to make a plan of action, then for executing, controlling, describing, and discussing that action" (p. 79). In Reggio Emilia classrooms, the teacher's role is to assist the child in constructing his own learning using rich problem-solving situations.

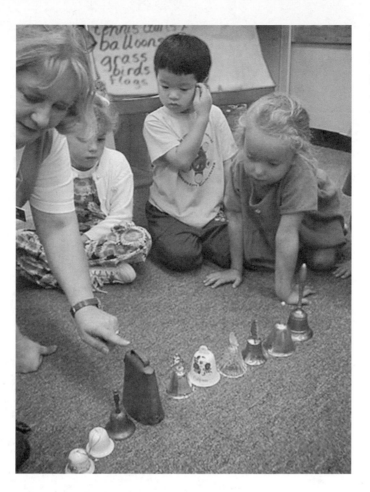

Exploring a variety of bells by seeing and hearing them. (Photo by Michael Talley)

Creating a Classroom for the Expressive Arts

Early childhood teachers design experiences for children in the expressive arts that provide:

- a plan based on the characteristics of young children as artists.
- an understanding of the artistic process.
- a positive atmosphere for experimentation.
- time, materials, and background skills.
- knowledge of the basic elements of the various art forms.
- enthusiastic involvement in the arts by the children and the teacher.
  (Raines & Canady, 1990, p. 157)

The artistic process in early childhood classrooms involves problem-solving in which children select a medium of expression, manipulate materials, explore the possibilities of the medium, and create representations of their thoughts or feelings (Raines & Canady, 1990). The expressive arts occur best in a supportive learning environment where children are free to express themselves without an expected adult-like product. The teacher's positive attitude toward the arts and the aesthetic environment are an acknowledgment of the child's right to the expressive arts.

Centers, Themes, Projects, and Stories

Organizational vehicles for early childhood classrooms have been described throughout this book. For this discussion, descriptions of centers, themes, projects, and stories that support the expressive arts will be provided. These glimpses into the classroom are mere snapshots of a much richer context and include essential elements of the creative arts.

In early childhood classrooms, teachers often organize space and materials into learning centers. Art, music, blocks, construction, and drama areas are places where materials provide ready access for children to play, create, use as accessories, or construct representations of what they are learning. Adding centers and/or appropriate materials supports themes, projects, and stories that are part of the curriculum and program. An open-ended quality allows children of varying levels of development to successfully participate in creating, collaborating, and participating in the arts.

Taking an order for a pizza in the restaurant center. (Photo by Mary Myron)

Integrating the Arts into a Study of Spring

In a preschool classroom, teachers look at how to integrate art, music, and story or children's literature into a unit on spring. The teacher has a variety of activities planned including planting flowers in a window box, sprouting bean seeds, and observing trees in the atrium. One of the teacher's favorite books about spring is based on a folk song, *The Green Grass Grows All Around: A Traditional Folk Song* adapted by Hilde Hoffman (1968). This is the story of a little boy's city back yard, and what happens in the spring when he plants a tree in the ground. The reoccurring refrain is, "And the green grass grows all around, all around, and the green grass grows all around." The story begins with a hole in the ground, and ends with a back yard celebration of the boy's tree and a mother bird living there. Bright yellow and green illustrations include gleeful children of different ethnic backgrounds as they frolic, sing, and play (Raines & Canady, 1989).

The music center has rhythm instruments and a tape recorder stored on low shelves. It is near the group or circle time area rug. After reading the book, the teacher provides the children with the words to the song. The children decide which musical instruments will represent different parts of the song. When that word is read in the book or sung in the song, the child holding the instrument plays it. After some discussion about the sounds of the instruments, they decide that the bongo drum will signify the hole and shakers the roots. The tambourine will symbolize the tree and the long rhythm sticks the branch. The twig is represented by a clang of the cymbals and the sand blocks are the bird's nest. The bird is characterized by a run on the xylophone with the mallet and a tinkle of the triangle represents the feather.

As the teacher rereads the story, children play their instruments whenever they hear the word it represents. Since the refrain repeats the previous words, the children learn to listen closely and everyone sings, "And the green grass grows all around, all around, and the green grass grows all around." The teacher then asks them what they could do to help remember the words. First, there is a hole in the ground, then roots in the hole, then a tree on the roots, then a limb on the tree, then a branch on the limb, then a twig on the branch, then a nest on the twig, then birds in the nest, then eggs in the nest, and ends with a feather on the bird. The children decide to draw pictures to help them remember the words. They understand that everyone's tree will be different as will the nest, eggs, bird, and even the feather. The children have fun creating their versions of the song, and combining art and music.

Using instruments to represent characters in a story. (Photo by Mary Myron)

The value of story as a means to connect the arts to the children's lived and vicarious experiences is written about eloquently by Kieran Egan (1997) in *The Arts as the Basic of Education*. In children's sociodramatic play, stories are enacted: some real, some imagined. After the children become comfortable with art materials and have explored possibilities, they begin to paint pictures and tell the teacher stories about an event depicted in their pictures. When children play with puppets, they recall and perform stories associated with that puppet, or they make up their own stories. Storytelling is another basis for drama productions, dance, opera, and theater. It is the story that helps organize children's thoughts because they include beginnings, endings, characters, and narratives. The story told allows children to change, enhance, and develop their creative thinking in the oral tradition. These drama techniques interweave the arts into programs for young children.

The Expressive Arts in a Study of "Life in the Sea: Real and Imagined"

Thematic units provide opportunities to integrate the arts into curricular studies whereas children learn about the arts at the same time. A glimpse inside the classroom of a primary teacher in California whose unit is "Life in the Sea: Real and Imagined" provides some examples of the integration of art, music and movement, and storytelling (Raines & Canady, 1992).

The teacher reads five different focus books dealing with the unit topic. *Ibis: A True Whale Story*, written and illustrated by John Himmelman (1990), is one of the focus books. Ibis and Blizzard are two whales that become so accustomed to the whale-watching boats that Ibis becomes entangled in a net. Blizzard pushes Ibis's body to the surface where whale-watchers find a way to rescue her.

After reading *Ibis: A True Whale Story*, the teacher and children decide on an art project that follows the book. They examine the ways that John Himmelman illustrated his book with below the water, partially submerged, and above water scenes. Learning to see from different perspectives is an artistic concept. While the teacher merely calls attention to the illustrator's work, a wide selection of art materials for painting, drawing, and collage are made available to the children. Several children decide to team together and show the story of Ibis and Blizzard in three different scenes on a large poster board. They negotiate with each other about who will do what and finally decide to use water colors for the background, cut out the whales from poster board, and construct the hulls of the boats by painting forms they cut from a Styrofoam tray.

The drama of the story is compelling and some children decide to write a short version to dramatize. Later, they share their script with the other children in front of the large posters. Two children decide to write a song about Ibis and Blizzard to introduce the drama to the class. The song is adapted to the tune of Row, Row, Row Your Boat, and several children add movements to reinforce the words and rhythm.

In the reference materials at the end of *Ibis: A True Whale Story*, Himmelman refers the reader to the Center for Coastal Studies in Provincetown, Massachusetts. The children brainstorm some questions they would like to ask whale-rescuers and write them a letter. When the center sends the class materials, they

> "Row, row, row your boat,
> Out to see our whale,
> Attach a float, attach a float,
> Pull her on home.
> Cut, cut, cut the net
> Out our dear Ibis.
> Swim, swim, swim away
> Goodbye, Goodbye,
> Goodbye, free Ibis"
> (Raines & Canady, 1992, p. 144–145).

thank the people in Massachusetts by returning snapshots of the children's posters and a tape of the children singing their Ibis rescue song.

After a visit to an aquarium, a center is added to the classroom, complete with a fish tank, fish, underwater equipment, and a museum library with books about ocean life. In this area, children are able to play with ideas, investigate materials, and replay the visit.

Integrating the visual arts with the curriculum study of life in the ocean enriches the study. However, an arts educator might ask if there are other lessons that could have been included in the art activities. Some suggestions might include adding a display of maritime art to the classroom, mixing paints for different shades of blue, using lines to suggest the presence of a boat on the surface, or creating shadows of whales under the sea. The children are inventive with their selection of materials, but using a vocabulary of color terminology to describe the physical properties of water could have been added to the lesson with artistic terms such as hue, value, and intensity. The pattern of waves is illustrated in the children's painting by a rhythm of lines with strong and weak accents. Even the repetition of the wave patterns can be emphasized in the children's work and in descriptions of what is on the posters. Line, shape, contour, texture, and color are evident in the illustrator's work and in the children's renderings. To enrich the experience, the teacher can talk about what can be seen in Himmelman's illustrations and how the child artists have used similar design elements in their work.

Artist-in-Residence Inspires Multiple Creative Activities

An Artist-in-Residence, a local storyteller, visited a kindergarten classroom. The storyteller told the folktale of *The Lost Mitten With Tiny, Shiny Beads* (Raines & Isbell, 1999), an adaptation of an old Ukrainian folktale (the entire story can be found in Appendix H.) The storyteller wore a highly decorated vest, trimmed with embroidery, tiny buttons, and ribbons. He said it was a vest from the Ukraine, and invited the children to create their own vests using a paper bag. The steps in the process included forming each vest by cutting out a neck hole and two arm holes on the sides, then cutting down the center of one side of the bag to make it open like a vest. The children glued buttons, ribbons, fabric, fringe, yarn, cotton, decorative trim, and braid on the vest. Although some were very ornate and others were simple designs, each was unique.

Children's literature is an essential component of the early childhood curriculum. (Photo by Michael Talley)

The next day when the storyteller returned, the children wore their vests and began to retell variations of the Ukrainian tale. At first, they thought of farm animals, zoo animals, desert animals, and tropical animals. Then they decided that the desert animals and the tropical animals would not be getting into a mitten to keep warm. How could they change the story if they included tropical animals? They decided to have the tropical animals get under a straw hat to shade them from the hot desert sun and a rain hat to shield them from the rain in the tropics. This provided opportunities for the children to elaborate on an idea and be flexible in their thinking as they used art and drama in their activities.

As an extension of the story, the artist-in-residence asked the children if they would like to act out the story of *The Lost Mitten With Tiny, Shiny Beads*. He encouraged them to discuss all the different events that occurred. They decided that a tablecloth could serve as a prop to represent the mitten. A child could enter the imaginary mitten by crawling under the tablecloth. The children selected the parts they wanted to play in the reenactment. The first child was the field mouse. Then came the frog, an owl, rabbit, fox, wolf, wild boar, bear, and finally the cricket. Then they exploded out of the mitten.

The drama and art were connected to the Ukrainian folktale. However, the richness of the experience was in the children's recreation of the story. Using flannel board pieces, the children retold the story in their own special ways. After several days of interest in *The Lost Mitten With Tiny, Shiny Beads*, the teacher brought in two different versions of the folktale. Until this time, the story was the one told by the storyteller. The children were anxious to compare the animals in the two versions to the ones in the storyteller's tale, and to find out if any animals from their stories were included. They compared Jan Brett's (1989) *The Mitten* and Alvin Tresselt's (1990) version of *The Mitten*. They discovered similarities and differences as they identified the characteristics of the stories. Their creative problem-solving and the generation of ideas lead them into an expanded study of other folktales.

A Creative Project from a Reggio Emilia Inspired Classroom

Cheryl Breig-Allen, Jill Hill, Lori Geismar-Ryan, and Louise Boyd Cadwell wrote about their experiences in the Clayton Schools' Family Center in St. Louis (1998). They were inspired by their observations of one child who noticed that his riding toy produced lines when he drove it through water and onto the pavement. This became the basis of an investigation of lines. The teachers followed this interest by providing many different materials and opportunities to create lines. The teachers asked provocative questions as the children experimented. Children drew, painted, rolled trucks through paint, created lines, and observed lines in nature. They experimented with making long lines and big lines, and connecting objects to make lines of pipe cleaners, shreds of paper, and Cuisenaire rods (solid rectangular bars of various sizes and colors). At first, their lines were straight. Then they discovered curves, squiggles, and lines that appear in nature. They played with lines, connected lines, and displayed lines. The teachers used the children's interest to spark a project, provided the materials, trusted their questions, and provided a few provocations that the children would use to investigate the concept of lines. While the project may seem like a small one, for two- and three-year-olds, the powerful observation of lines lead them to create in new ways.

Teacher and children playing with pig puppets. (Photos by Michael Talley)

Following the child's interests, for example "lines," as a topic of study is based on the view of the emerging curriculum that may include the project approach. Often, children work in pairs, solve problems, and develop the habit of improving by systematically documenting their explorations of a topic (Wright, 1997). The teachers are participant-observers in what the children are learning. They talk with them as a means to provoke additional learning, but the questioning and interactions are background for what the child is doing. They are not directive in their interactions: they are resources for the learners.

Summary

All curriculum and content areas contain opportunities for creative thinking. The creative arts are recognized as being extremely important for young children's artistic expression, divergent thinking, and affective development. Recently, curriculum developers and early childhood educators have reappraised the value of the arts. They state that all children have the right to be involved in the arts and have begun to look for ways to make this a reality. The creative process involves cognitive events that include making choices, investigating interest, exploring materials, and collaborating with others. These experiences can occur in themes, units, projects, classroom environments, and in content areas where the arts are integrated into the total curriculum. This design helps children learn to see the arts as an essential part of their lives and a way of unifying a community of learners.

Key Terms

little-intervention orientation

product-oriented orientation

guided-exploration orientation

Artist-in-Residence

Reflection

1. The teacher provided many colors for painting, but the children primarily used yellow, white, and green. Why do you think the children made these choices? Discuss your ideas with a classmate.

2. From your observations, describe a creative episode such as the dandelion event in an early childhood classroom, where the teacher seized an opportunity to inspire children's creativity.

3. Read Bresler's article on three orientations to arts education. Compare the little-intervention, product-orientation, and guided-exploration orientations. Give examples, from your experience as a student or from your observations.

4. Consider your experiences in the expressive arts. Which art form gives you the most pleasure? Recall a time from your childhood and one as an adult. Discuss how you experienced the pleasure of artistic or creative expression.

Thinking about the Creative Episode

1. What are some of the reasons the preschoolers picked the dandelions?

2. How did the chart help the children think in a new way about the dandelions?

3. Can you explain why young children categorized the dandelion as a flower instead of a weed?

Possibilities for Adult Learners

Activity: Bringing It Together

Goal: To relate content to the real world of children.

Materials: Graph paper, camera and film, measuring tape, pencil, and paper.

Procedure:

1. Visit a pre-K, kindergarten, or primary classroom.

2. Diagram at least two of the following: the art area, blocks, music, storytelling, puppetry, or dramatic play.

3. Share your drawing with members of the class.

4. Discuss your observations of the different centers, children's participation, and the materials in each area.

Activity: Artist-in-Residence

Goal: To talk with an artist about his work with children.

Materials: Tape recorder, pencil or pen, and a note pad.

Procedure:

1. Interview an artist-in-residence.

2. Find out how he is funded, favorite ages of children, and how teachers can help the artists be more successful.

3. Answer any questions about the age of children you teach.

Activity: A Creative Unit

Goal: To develop a unit on a unique topic that would interest young children.

Materials: Paper, and pencil or pen to record ideas and possibilities.

Procedure:

1. Work with a partner.

2. Brainstorm possible topics and continue to identify units that you have not seen.

3. Together, make your choice.

4. Brainstorm ideas that connect art, music, and drama to integrate the arts into the unit.

5. Research the topic.

6. Write down your ideas and share with the members of your class.

Activity: Tell a Story

Goal: To develop your ability to tell a story without the use of a book.

Materials: Collection of stories, index cards to write the story outline, and tape recorder or video camera.

Procedure:

1. Select five stories from a collection of stories for young children.

2. Study, outline, and practice telling each story to friends and classmates.

3. Volunteer to tell the stories to children (see Raines & Isbell, 1999; Isbell & Raines, 2000).

4. Share your experiences with other students.

Open-ended Activities for Young Children

Pre-K–K

Activity: Smell the Roses

Goal: To develop an awareness of the world around you.

Materials: Note pad, sketch pad, or camera.

Procedure:

1. Enjoy a sensory walk.

2. Focus on the sights, sounds, and smells of your environment.

3. Plan a creative way to tell, show, or perform your feelings related to your sensory walk.

Primary grades

Activity: A Collection of Beautiful Things

Goal: To find a creative way to represent objects that you appreciate.

Materials: A collection of favorite items, and the materials for creating a display such as fabric, photos, and drawings.

Procedure:

1. Collect several favorite beautiful objects from around your house.

2. Determine how to demonstrate their significance to yourself.

3. Draw, photograph, or write about the collection, and your feelings related to the objects.

Notes

[1]Caldwell, L. B. (1997). *Bringing Reggio Emilia home.* New York: Teachers College Press.

[2]Fitzhenry, R. I. (Ed.) (1993). *The Harper book of quotations* (3rd ed.). New York: Harper Collins Books.

[3]Applewhite, A., Evans, W. R, III, & Frothingham, A. (Eds.). (1992). *And I quote.* New York: St. Martin's Press.

References

Bredekamp, S., & Copple, C. (1987). *Developmentally appropriate practice in early childhood education.* Washington, DC: National Association for the Education of Young Children.

Breig-Allen, C., Hill, J., Geismar-Ryan, L., & Cadwell, L. B. (1998). The language of lines. *Young Children, 53*(4), 64–66.

Bresler, L. (1993). Three orientations to arts in the primary grades: Implications for curriculum reform. *Arts Education Policy Review, 94*(6), 29–34.

Brett, J. (1989). *The mitten: A Ukrainian folktale.* New York: The Putnam Publishing Group.

Dixon, G. T., & Chalmers, F. G. (1990). The expressive arts in education. *Childhood Education, 67*(1), 12–17.

Edwards, C., Gandini, L., & Forman, G. (1993). *The hundred languages of children: The Reggio Emilia approach to early childhood education.* Norwood, NJ: Ablex.

Egan, K.(1988). The origins of imagination. In K. Egan & D. Nadaner (Eds.), *Imagination and education* (pp. 91–127). New York: Teachers College Press.

Egan, K. (1997). The arts as the basic of education. *Childhood Education, 73*(6), 341–345.

Getty Center for Education in the Arts. (1985). *Beyond creating: The place for art in America's schools.* Los Angeles: J. Paul Getty Trust.

Hansen, K. (1986). *The self-imagined.* London: Routledge & Kegan Paul.

Himmelman, J. (1990). *Ibis: A true whale story.* New York: Scholastic, Inc.

Hoffman, H. (1968). *The green grass grows all around.* New York: Macmillan Publishing Company.

Hoffman, S., & Lamme, L. L. (Eds.). (1989). *Learning from the inside out: The expressive arts.* Wheaton, MD: Association for Childhood Education International.

Isbell, R. T., & Raines, S. C. (2000). *Tell it again 2: Easy-to-tell stories with activities for young children.* Beltsville, MD: Gryphon House.

Jalongo, M. (1990). The child's right to the expressive arts: Nurturing the imagination as well as the intellect. *Childhood Education, 66*(4), 195–201.

Malaguzzi, L. (1993). History, ideas, and basic philosophy. In C. Edwards, L. Gandini, & G. Forman (Eds.), *The hundred languages of children: The Reggio Emilia approach to early childhood education* (pp. 41–89). Norwood, NJ: Ablex.

Moyer, J., Egertson, H., & Isenberg, J. (1987). The child-centered kindergarten. *Childhood Education, 63*(4), 235–242.

Raines, S. C., & Canady, R. J. (1989). *Story s-t-r-e-t-c-h-e-r-s: Activities to expand children's favorite books.* Mt. Rainier, MD: Gryphon House.

Raines, S. C., & Canady, R. J. (1990). *The whole language kindergarten.* New York: Teachers College Press.

Raines, S. C., & Canady, R. J. (1992). *Story s-t-r-e-t-c-h-e-r-s for the primary grades: Activities to expand children's favorite books.* Mt. Rainier, MD: Gryphon House.

Raines, S. C., & Isbell, R. T. (1999). *Tell it again: Easy-to-tell stories with activities for young children.* Beltsville, MD: Gryphon House.

Smith, B. O., Stanley, W. O., & Shores, J. H. (1957). *Fundamentals of curriculum development.* New York: Harcourt Brace Jovanovich.

Stake, R., Bresler, L., & Mabry, L. (1991). *Customs and cherishing: Art education in the United States.* Urbana, IL: Council of Research in Music Education.

Tresselt, A. R. (1990). *The mitten: An old Ukrainian folktale.* New York: William Morrow and Company.

Wright, S. (1997). Learning how to learn: The arts as core in an emergent curriculum. *Childhood Education, 73*(6), 361–365.

Additional Reading

Arnold, A. (1997). Stories & art: Creating multiple levels of meaning. *School Arts, 96*(8), 22.

Ascbacher, P. (1996). A FLARE for the arts. *Educational Leadership, 53*(8), 40–44.

Balke, E. (1997). Play and the arts: The importance of the "unimportant." *Childhood Education, 73*(6), 355–360.

Barrentine, S. J. (1996). Engaging with reading through interactive readalouds. *The Reading Teacher, 50*(1), 37–43.

Bolen, L. (1989). The importance of the arts in early childhood curriculum. *Dimensions of Early Childhood, 18*(1), 11–14.

Bouleris, J. (1991). Measuring up: Teaching geometry through art. *School Arts, 91*(3), 22–24.

Bresler, L. (1995). Introduction to the symposium on the integration of the arts into the curriculum reform. *Arts Education Policy Review, 97*(1), 9–10.

Cameron, L. (1997). Draw a story . . . write a picture. *School Arts, 96*(8), 20–22.

Demetrulais, D. M. (1992). Developing intellectual creativity through children's literature for preschoolers through third grade. *Education 112*(3), 464–469.

Dunn, P. C. (1995). Integrating the arts: Renaissance and reformation in arts education. *Arts Education Policy Review, 96*(4), 32–37.

Fauth, B. (1990). Linking visual arts with drama, movement, and dance for the young child. In W. Stinson (Ed.), *Moving and learning for the young child.* Reston, VA: American Alliance for Health, Physical Education, Recreation, and Dance.

Giles, C., Andre, C. D., & Pfanneenstiel, V. (1998). Talking about books: Connections through literature using art, music, and drama. *Language Arts, 76*(1), 67–75.

Irwin, R. L., & Reynolds, J. K. (1995). Integration as a strategy for teaching the arts as disciplines. *Arts Education Policy Review, 96*(4), 13–19.

McCall, A. L. (1999). Speaking through cloth: Teaching Hmong history and culture through textile art. *The Social Studies, 90*(5), 230–235.

Mills, H., & Clyde, J. A. (1992). Using art and mathematics to tell a story. *Dimensions of Early Childhood, 20*(3), 28–29, 40.

Nevinskas, N., & Pizer, C. H. (1998). Art in motion. *School Arts, 97*(9), 40–42.

Nicholas, R. A. (1992). Drawing from life: Helping children preserve culture through art. *Dimensions of Early Childhood, 20*(3), 5–7.

Parr, N. C., Radford, J., & Snyder, S. (1998). Kaleidoscope: Building an arts-infused elementary curriculum. *Early Childhood Education Journal, 25*(3), 181–188.

Pinciotti, P. (1993). Creative drama and young children: The dramatic learning connection. *Arts Education Policy Review, 94*(6), 24–29.

Reimer, B. (1989). A comprehensive arts curriculum model. *Design for Arts Education, 90*(6), 2–16.

Schon, D. A. (1983). *The reflective practitioner.* New York: Basic Books.

Seefeldt, C. (1993). *Social studies for the pre-school primary child.* New York: Macmillan Publishing Company.

Stinson, W. J. (Ed.). (1990). *Moving and learning for the young child.* Reston, VA: American Alliance for Health, Physical Education, Recreation, and Dance.

Walczak, J. (1994). Escher tesselations. *School Arts, 93*(7), 29–31.

Children's Literature Connection

Alexander, M. (1983). *How my library grew.* New York: H. W. Wilson Company.

Neither Dinah nor her Teddy Bear have ever been to the library, but when one is built, just down the street, she looks forward to the opening day and works to complete a special present for the new library. (Pre-K–1)

Anderson, J. (1990). *Harry's helicopter.* New York: Morrow Junior Books.

One day, Harry's bright red cardboard helicopter takes off with him in a gust of wind, and gives him a thrilling ride. (Pre-K–1)

Cooney, B. (1990). *Roxaboxen.* New York: Lothrop, Lee & Shepard.
A hill covered with rocks and wooden boxes becomes an imaginary town for Marian, her sisters, and their friends. (Primary)

Engel, D. (1988). *Josephina the great collector.* New York: Morrow Junior Books.
Josephina's passion for collecting anything and everything finally drives her sister out of the room they share. Josephina develops a creative plan to reconcile with her sister. (Pre-K–2)

Himmelman, J. (1990). *Ibis: A true whale story.* New York: Scholastic, Inc.
A survival story of two friendly whales. (Primary)

Helpful Web Sites

The addresses and corresponding agencies below are taken from the Web sites. Due to the dynamic nature of the Internet, please remember that Web sites are subject to change at any time.

http://www.project-approach.com/   Project Approach—Provides readers with resources to enable them to carry out projects wherever they may work with children.

http://www.aee.org/   The Association for Experiential Education—The Association is committed to support professional development, theoretical advancement, and evaluation of experiential education worldwide.

http://pblmm.k12.ca.us/   The Challenge 2000 Multimedia Project—An innovative program that harnesses the power of multimedia to engage students in challenging learning activities.

http://www.galstar.com/~davii/jilllink.html   A Web site of information links on Early Childhood Education.—A forum for articles, ideas, and resources for educators and parents of children in early childhood (three to eight).

For additional resources involving creativity and the arts with young children, visit our Web site at **http://www.earlychilded.delmar.com**

The Child's Right to the Expressive Arts: Nurturing the Imagination As Well As the Intellect

A Position Paper of the Association for Childhood Education International by Mary Renck Jalongo. Mary Renck Jalongo is Professor of Education, Indiana University of Pennsylvania, Indiana.

When we describe someone as "imaginative," we usually mean the person can formulate rich and varied mental images, see beyond the obvious, or draw upon experience in inventive and effective ways. Most of us believe that childhood is the wellspring of adult imagination (Cobb, 1977). But have our schools really nurtured children's imagination? In 1935, Lois Meek observed:

> . . . we have recognized that young children are active and free in imaginative play, that as they grow older they become more stereotyped in their behavior, and that in adult life, only the unusual person displays the ability to put old ideas and experiences into new forms (p. vii).

Contemporary educators have arrived at much the same conclusion (Klein, 1984; Lindberg, 1980; Sutton-Smith, 1988). "What happened to imagination?" Greene (1988) wonders. "It has been discouraged by literalism, by complacency, by technical rationality, by obsessions with predictable results . . . [we need] to break through the fixities of our age . . . to look at things as they could truly be otherwise" (p. 55).

In response to these concerns about the child's right to creative expression, this Association for Childhood Education International position paper will:

- examine the contributions of creativity and imagination to the total learning of the child.
- offer counter arguments to myths that de-emphasize the arts in the curriculum.
- recommend ways of refashioning our schools to promote the expressive arts.

A Rationale for Imagination and Creativity

Contrary to popular opinion, imagination is not wild, irrational or self-indulgent (Degenhardt & McKay, 1988; Johnson, 1987; Vandenberg, 1983). The products of imagination are unusual, but they must also be effective (Barrow, 1988). As one of the leading educators of this century explained, imagination without knowledge is foolishness and knowledge without imagination is pedantry (Whitehead, 1929). It is useful to think of imagination in action as a kaleidoscope: knowledge is comparable to the bits and pieces in the kaleidoscope; imagination is what enables us to turn the drum and create new patterns (Parnes, 1963). Imagination "gives rationality life, color and meaning" (Egan, 1988, p. 118). Thinking imaginatively engages learners in "as-if" thinking, "if-then" thinking and empathic thinking (Tamburrini, 1984). Furthermore, imaginative thought functions simultaneously at three levels: as a stimulus, a material and a companion (Furlong, 1961).

The expressive arts—music, art, drama, dance, writing—are important because they are the means of communicating our creative productivity and imaginative thinking. Some of the benefits associated with an expanded role for the expressive arts in schools include:

- The expressive arts foster "learning from the inside out," authentic learning that changes behavior and encourages reflection (Heathcote, 1984; Hoffman & Lamme, 1989).

- The expressive arts enhance the child's ability to interpret symbols. It is the "symbolic ability of the child on which everything which is distinctly human will develop" (Smith, 1984, p. 28).

- The expressive arts are associated with growth in all areas of development, including academics (Courtney, 1982; Sylva, 1984; Wagner, 1988).

- The expressive arts regard the child as a meaning-maker and constructor, a discoverer and an embodiment of knowledge rather than a passive recipient of someone else's ready-made answers (Bruner, 1986; McLaren, 1986; Wells, 1986).

When imagination, creative productivity and the expressive arts are fostered in schools, we find children who are

. . . becoming sensitive to or aware of problems, deficiencies, gaps in knowledge, missing elements, disharmonies, and so on; bringing to-

gether in new relationships available information; defining the difficulty or identifying the missing elements, searching for solutions, making guesses or formulating hypotheses about the problem or deficiencies, testing and retesting them; perfecting them and finally communicating results (Torrance, 1969, p. vi).

Why Are the Expressive Arts Undervalued in Our Culture?

At least five popular myths are used to justify neglecting the expressive arts in classrooms.

1. First, some adults dichotomize children's academic achievement and artistic achievement, as if the former were nutritious vegetables and the latter, a rich dessert. But human beings must balance their need for objective truth with their need for aesthetic truth (McLaren, 1988), because facts stripped of images and feelings cannot be said to have meaning (Landau, 1985). The expressive arts complement academics; they are what makes knowing academics worthwhile. Educators must lead others to abandon this sort of either/or thinking. It is a major deterrent to innovation, not only in schools but also in society at large (Rickards, 1985).

2. A second explanation for reducing the importance of the arts is insufficient time in an already overburdened curriculum. But if teachers get caught in a mad race to "cover" everything, they may literally do just that—conceal the real purposes of learning from the child (Duckworth, 1972).

3. Third, it is sometimes argued that only a small percentage of children have exceptional artistic talent, so education in the arts is more expendable than education in other areas of development. But it is not our purpose in the expressive arts to be elitist to "discover" stars. Adults have the responsibility of affirming and nurturing every talent in every child and giving all children opportunities to participate in authentic artistic experiences (Lamme, 1989; Treffinger, 1989).

4. A fourth common misconception is that parents will not support programs that emphasize the expressive arts. Ironically, parents flock to programs that highlight children's achievements in the arts, whether it is a single event (such as a school play) or an entire school curriculum with an arts curriculum (such as the Settlement House School or St. Augustine's in the South Bronx). Even those parents who are skeptical of the value of "nonacademic" subjects become converts when they see their children expressing themselves through the arts instead of racing through activities completely conceived and controlled by misguided adults. As one music educator remarked, school concerts that "elicit nothing more than remarks from parents that the performance was 'cute' are not good enough." Authentic experiences in the performing arts ". . . inspire children to actively pursue music as performers and consumers throughout their lives" (Moriarity, 1988, p. 22).

5. The fifth and final myth is that because there are socially trained teachers for at least some of the expressive arts (such as art, music and

movement), they have complete responsibility for the expressive arts. But when regular classroom teachers delegate this authority to others, they are relinquishing a powerful educational and motivational tool. Most of the things we now use as motivational devices—tests, grades, privileges, the promise of future jobs—are "alienated from the act of learning now" (Shor & Freire, 1987, p. 5). The opportunity to participate in the expressive arts gives children a reason to learn today. And those opportunities will be far too limited if they are reserved for one class period per week.

ACEI Position

The Association for Childhood Education International believes that, in order to reaffirm the importance of the expressive arts in schools, educators must accept the following precepts:

Every Child has a Right to Opportunities for Imaginative Expression. Imaginative expression is not the exclusive province of special programs for the gifted and talented. It is not a curricular "frill" to be deleted when time is limited. Nor is imagination synonymous with enrichment, something reserved for those children who have already completed their "work." Rather, imagination is a capacity in every child that should be nurtured. "If we think of imagination as part of our intelligence, then we must be ready to admit that, like the rest of human intelligence, it needs education" (Warnock, 1977, p. 202).

Educating the Child's Imagination is Education for the Future. As we look ahead to the future, what will be required of tomorrow's children? Minuchin (1987) predicts they will need "resilience and flexibility, a creative and integrative way of thinking, and a certain psychological sturdiness in the way they face new circumstances in the company of other people" (p. 254). One thing we can be certain about in our culture is change. The "personal inclinations required by the arts" are well suited to the demands of a rapidly changing society. These include play with images, ideas and feelings, recognizing and constructing the multiple meanings of events, looking at things from different perspectives and functioning as risk-takers (Eisner, 1976).

The Educated Imagination is the Key to Equity and Intercultural Understanding. Creative productivity can be social rather than isolationist and its outcomes need not be money-saving, labor-saving or even artistic. Imagination dramatizes the inner workings of our minds and is the undercurrent of human interaction (Rosen, 1980). As we gain insight into ourselves, we can use imaginative powers to identify with others (Hanson 1986). We can empathize with their situations, envision possibilities and enact creative solutions to social problems. These connections with others, forged by imagination, are the basis for intercultural understanding.

Children's Creative Productivity is Qualitatively Different from Adults. We must resist "childism," the tendency for adults to look condescendingly upon children's ideas and feelings, to regard them as less real or important than their own (Lightfoot, 1978). One of the great assets of childhood is that young children are less constrained by convention, less literal in their thinking, less restricted by boundaries between and among subject areas (Gardner, 1983). "We don't really see what we take for granted," and children's creative productivity is no exception (Silberstein-Storfer & Jones, 1982). If adults overlook children's imaginative processes, then children are deprived of an authentic voice, both in the arts and in traditional subject areas.

Consider, for example, children's drawing. Too often, adults demand realism in art. But if we push this prejudice to its logical extreme, the essence of art is lost. Individuality is replaced by conformity and our "artists" are inferior to our copy machines. Likewise, if we insist on hurrying children into using the conventions of print, meaning is sacrificed to form. Eventually, the child's composing process functions like computer software designed to locate mistakes, rather than as a vehicle for creative expression. Children's imagination is just that: it belongs to children, not to miniature adults.

Creative Expression Should Permeate the Entire Curriculum. When we speak of basics in education, people immediately think of reading, writing and arithmetic. But is that what is basic? If basic means something that is fundamental to the experience of all children, then other things would surely be basic. Play would certainly be "basic" (Isenberg & Quisenberry, 1988). Telling and enacting stories would be "basic" (Nelms, 1988). Drawing, painting, and sculpting surely would be "basic" because, even before children can read, write, or calculate, they are using these ways to communicate their ideas, emotions, and individuality. Music and dance are "basic" because even before children can speak, they can listen and move to music.

Clearly, a rigid, lackluster curriculum is an environment inimical to the basic expressive arts. Under regimented conditions, teachers become walking contradictions, like the teacher in a cartoon who announces to the class: "I expect you all to be independent, innovative, critical thinkers who will do exactly as I say" (Warren, 1989, p. 38).

Imagination is the Key to Artistry in Teaching and Excellence in Our Schools. We keep searching for the panacea in education by creating artificial dichotomies. The 60s gave us the humanistic movement which was countered with back-to-basics. When the basics failed to improve schools, an excellence-or-else approach was lauded as the answer. Education may have traveled far, but the course has been a series of zigzags between opposites instead of straight and steady progress toward quality and equality.

Teachers are jaded by these bandwagons, tired of legislative mandates, weary of standardized tests that dictate the curriculum. What is worse, our schools have been sapped of their surprisingness—so much so that the overwhelming impression after thousands of hours of observation in classrooms is that they are routinized, predictable and "emotionally flat" (Goodlad, 1984).

Where does the solution lie? Many prominent educators state that our schools need artistry, creativity, intuition, insight, inspiration and reflection (Rubin, 1985; Schon, 1983; Sizer, 1984)—all intimately connected with imagination.

We Must Refashion Our Schools for the 21st Century. School reform must, in the view of the National Education Association, recognize that the Industrial Model is obsolescent in our Information Age (Futrell, 1989). We need to shut off the rapid assembly line of textbooks, tests, schedules and paper work in favor of "circles of learning" (Johnson et al., 1984) and projects (Katz & Chard, 1989). As a society, we must go beyond tolerating imagination, and begin to value and educate it. In schools of the 21st century, children will learn to make decisions, to reflect upon experience, and to understand their own imaginative processes as well as those of others (Ayers, 1989; Hatcher, 1987; Hoffman & Lamme, 1989; Paley, 1981).

Conclusion

A belief in the child's right to imaginative expression transforms the classroom. For too long, education has operated like a pupil postal system—we spend most of our time sorting and determining destinations. And, like the post office, we operate on the premise that environmental conditions should be ignored, that "the mail must go through." Never mind that junk mail addressed to "occupant"—the postal equivalent of a developmentally inappropriate curriculum—also gets delivered.

In a school committed to the expressive arts, children are active participants. They learn how to bring order out of chaos, to use their frames of mind, to interpret symbols, to be open to feelings, to develop a tolerance for ambiguity and to seek problems as well as solutions. If a school nurtures children's imagination and creativity, it means that children function more autonomously as they meet challenges in a supportive environment (Kamii, 1988). It means that teachers function as enablers who share their power and wisdom—inviting children to manage their own learning processes and giving them time to revise their tentative notions about the world (Isaksen & Treffinger, 1985), deferring judgment until children are satisfied with their work (Klein, 1984).

As Egan (1988) stated, developing the imagination "is not an alternative educational activity to be argued for in competition with other claims; it is a prerequisite to making any activity education" (p. ix). In the past, in the present and in the future, our most enlightened educational visions will be connected by the common thread of imagination, creativity and the expressive arts.

References

Ayers, W. (1989). *The good preschool teacher: Six teachers reflect on their lives.* New York: Teachers College Press.

Barrow, R. (1988). Some observations on the concept of imagination. In K. Egan & D. Nadaner (Eds.), *Imagination and education* (pp. 79–90). New York: Teachers College Press.

Bruner, J. S. (1986). *Actual minds, possible worlds.* Cambridge, MA: Harvard University.

Cobb, E. (1977). *The ecology of imagination.* New York: Columbia University.

Courtney, R. (1982). *Re-play: Studies in human drama and education.* Toronto: OISE Press.

Degenhardt, M., & McKay, E. (1988). Imagination and education for cultural understanding. In K. Egan & D. Nadaner (Eds.), *Imagination and education* (pp. 237–255). New York: Teachers College Press.

Duckworth, E. (1972). The having of wonderful ideas. *Harvard Educational Review, 42,* 217–232.

Egan, K. (1988). The origins of imagination. In K. Egan & D. Nadaner (Eds.), *Imagination and education* (pp. 91–127). New York: Teachers College Press.

Eisner, E. (1976). *The arts, human development and education.* Berkeley, CA: McCuthen.

Furlong, E. J. (1961). *Imagination.* London: George Allen & Unwin.

Futrell, M. H. (1989). Mission not accomplished: Education reform in retrospect. *Phi Delta Kappan, 71*(1), 8–14.

Gardner, H. (1983). *Frames of mind: The theory of multiple intelligences.* New York: Basic Books.

Goodlad, J. (1984). *A place called school: Prospects for the future.* New York: McGraw Hill.

Greene, M. (1988). What happened to imagination? In K. Egan & D. Nadaner (Eds.), *Imagination and education* (pp. 45–56). New York: Teachers College Press.

Hanson, K. (1986). *The self imagined.* London: Routledge & Kegan Paul.

Hatcher, B. (Ed.). (1987). *Learning opportunities beyond school.* Wheaton, MD: Association for Childhood Education International.

Heathcote, D. (1984). In L. Johnson & C. O'Neil (Eds.), *Dorothy Heathcote: Collected writings on education and drama* (p. 104). London: Hutchinson.

Hoffman, S., & Lamme, L. L. (Eds.). (1989). *Learning from the inside out: The expressive arts.* Wheaton, MD: Association for Childhood Education International.

Isaksen, S. G., & Teffinger, D. J. (1985). *Creative problem solving: The basic course.* Buffalo, NY: Bearly Ltd.

Isenberg, J., & Quisenberry, N. (1988). Play: A necessity for all children. *Childhood Education, 64,* 138–145.

Johnson, M. (1987). *The body in the mind: The bodily basis of meaning, imagination, and reason.* Chicago: University of Chicago Press.

Johnson, D. W., Johnson, R. T., Holubec, E. J., & Roy, P. (1984). *Circles of learning: Cooperation in the classroom.* Alexandria, VA: Association for Supervision and Curriculum Development.

Kamii, C. (1988). Autonomy of heteronomy: Our choices of goals. In G. F. Roberson & M. A. Johnson (Eds.), Leaders in Education: Their views on controversial issues. Lanham, MD: University Press of America.

Katz, L., & Chard, S. C. (1989). *Enaging children's minds: The project approach.* Norwood, NJ: Ablex.

Klein, B. (1984). Power and control, praise and deferred judgment. *Journal of Creative Behavior, 17,* 9–17.

Lamme, L. L. (1989). Illustratorship: A key facet of whole language instruction. *Childhood Education, 66,* 83–86.

Landau, J. (1985). The necessity of art in education. *World Futures, 21,* 29–51.

Lightfoot, S. L. (1978). *Worlds apart: Relationships between families and schools.* New York: Basic Books.

Lindberg, L. (1980). Child development and the arts. In *Proceedings of the ACEI Summer Seminar July 9–11* (pp. 74–77). Taipei, Taiwan, Republic of China: Association for Childhood Education International of the Republic of China. (ERIC Document Reproduction Service No. ED 231 499).

McLaren, P. (1986). *Schooling as a ritual performance: Towards a political economy of educational symbols and gestures.* London: Routledge & Kegan Paul.

McLaren, P. (1988). The limited servant and the ritual roots of critical pedagogy. *Language Arts, 65,* 164–179.

Meek, L. H. (1935). Forward. In F. V. Markey, *The imaginative behavior of preschool children* (p. vii). New York: Teachers College Press.

Minuchin, P. (1987). Schools, families and the development of young children. *Early Childhood Research Quarterly, 2,* 245–254.

Moriarity, K. (1988). Learning by doing: Lessons of a summer arts program. *Music Educators Journal, 75,* 18–22.

Nelms, B. (1988). *Literature in the classroom: Readers, texts and contexts.* Urbana, IL: National Council of Teachers of English.

Paley, V. (1981). *Wally's stories.* Cambridge, MA: Cambridge University Press.

Parnes, S. J. (1963). In C. W. Taylor & F. Barron (Eds.), *The identification of creativity and scientific talent* (pp. 225–255). New York: Wiley.

Rickards, T. (1985). *Stimulating innovation.* London: Frances Pinter.

Rosen, H. (1980). The dramatic mode. In P. Salmon (Ed.), *Coming to know* (pp. 152–169). London: Routledge & Kegan Paul.

Rubin, L. (1985). *Artistry in teaching.* New York: Random House.

Schon, D. A. (1983). *The reflective practitioner.* New York: Basic.

Shor, I., & Freire, P. (1987). *A pedagogy for liberation: Dialogues on transforming education.* South Hadley, MA: Bergin & Garvey.

Silberstein-Storfer, M., & Jones, M. (1982). *Doing art together.* New York: Simon & Schuster.

Sizer, T. (1984). *Horace's compromise.* Boston, MA: Houghton Mifflin.

Smith, P. K. (1984). The relevance of fantasy play. In H. Cowie (Ed.), The development of children's imaginative writing (pp. 12–31). New York: St. Martin's Press.

Sutton-Smith, B. (1988). In search of the imagination. In K. Egan & D. Nadaner (Eds.), *Imagination and education* (pp. 3–29). New York: Teachers College Press.

Sylva, K. (1984). A hard-headed look at the fruits of play. *Early Child Development and Care, 15,* 171–184.

Tamburrini, J. (1984). The development of representational imagination. In H. Cowie (Ed.), *The development of children's imaginative writing* (pp. 32–48). New York: St. Martin's Press.

Torrance, E. P. (1969). *Dimensions in early learning: Creativity.* Sioux Falls, SD: Adaptation Press.

Treffinger, D. J. (1989). The potentials of productivity: Designing the journey to 2000. *Gifted Child Today, 12*(12), 17–21.

Vandenberg, B. (1983). Play, logic and reality. Imagination, Cognition, and Personality, 3, 353–361.

Wagner, B. J. (1988). Research currents: Does classroom drama affect the arts of language? *Language Arts, 65,* 46–55.

Warnock, M. (1977). *Schools of thought.* London: Faber & Faber.

Warren. (1989). Cartoon. *Phi Delta Kappan, 71*(1), 38.

Wells, G. (1986). *The meaning makers: Children learning language and using language to learn.* Portsmouth, NH: Heinemann.

Whitehead, A. N. (1929). *The aims of education and other essays.* New York: Macmillan.

The National Standards for Arts Education

These standards describe "what every young American should know and be able to do in the arts." They were developed by the Consortium of National Arts Education Associations which includes the National Association for Music Education (MENC).

Dance/Movement (K–4)

1. identifying and demonstrating movement elements and skills in performing dance

2. understanding choreographic principles, processes, and structures

3. understanding dance as a way to create and communicate meaning

4. applying and demonstrating critical and creative thinking skills in dance

5. demonstrating and understanding dance in various cultures and historical periods

6. making connections between dance and healthful living

7. making connections between dance and other disciplines

Music (K–4)

1. singing a varied repertoire of music, alone and with others

2. performing a varied repertoire of music on instruments, alone and with others

3. improvising melodies, variations, and accompaniments

4. composing and arranging music within specified guidelines

5. reading and notating music

6. listening to, analyzing, and describing music

7. evaluating music and musical performances

8. understanding relationships between music, the other arts, and disciplines outside the arts

9. understanding music in relation to history and culture

Dramatic Arts (K–4)

1. script-writing by planning and recording improvisations based on personal experience and heritage, imagination, literature, and history

2. acting by assuming roles and interacting in improvisations

3. designing by visualizing and arranging environments for classroom dramatizations

4. directing by planning classroom dramatizations

5. researching by finding information to support classroom dramatizations

6. comparing and connecting art forms by describing dramatic arts, dramatic media (film, television, and electronic media), and other art forms

7. analyzing and explaining personal preferences, and constructing meanings from classroom dramatizations and from the dramatic arts, film, television, and electronic media productions

8. understanding context by recognizing the role of the dramatic arts, film, television, and electronic media in daily life

Visual Arts (K–4)

1. understanding and applying media, techniques, and processes

2. using knowledge of structures and functions

3. choosing and evaluating a range of subject matter, symbols, and ideas

4. understanding the visual arts in relation to history and cultures

5. reflecting on and assessing the characteristics and merits of their work, and the work of others

6. making connections between visual arts and other disciplines

From *National Standards for Arts Education*, published by Music Educators National Conference (MENC). Copyright (c) 1994 by MENC. Used by permission. The complete National Arts Standards and additional materials relating to the Standards are available from MENC, The National Association for Music Education, 1806 Robert Fulton Drive, Reston, VA 20191. Telephone: 800-336-3768.

The Ducks That Could Not Swim

Once there was a little old man and a little old woman who lived in a big house at the top of a hill. Every day, when they finished their work, they would sit on their porch and relax. They enjoyed looking at the big beautiful pond in the valley below. They enjoyed the reflection of the setting sun on the water and watched the trees at the edge sway with the breeze.

One evening, as they were enjoying the pond, they decided that their view would be more beautiful if they had some white ducks to swim in the pond. They began to check the newspaper for ads of ducks to be purchased. One day they found an advertisement, "Ducks for Sale." They called and got directions to the place where the ducks were for sale. All the while, they imagined how beautiful the white ducks would be swimming in their pond.

The little old man and little old woman drove their truck up into the mountains, around curvy roads, higher and higher. At last, they reached the place where the white ducks were for sale. The owner took them to a big chicken house where the ducks had lived their entire life. The couple was thrilled with the beautiful white ducks and bought five of them. They lifted them into a cage in their truck. They drove home, over the mountains and around the curves with the ducks quacking all the way.

When the little old man and woman arrived at their home, they couldn't wait to take their five white ducks to the pond. They drove their truck to the edge of the pond and unloaded the cage. The white ducks ran out of the cage, but did not go into the water. They stood at the edge and walked around the pond, but, they did not go in the water. The little old man began to shoo the five white ducks toward the pond. The ducks only circled the edge of the water. They did not place their webbed feet in the pond. The ducks looked at the water but made no attempt to swim in the pond.

The little old man and the little old woman were very puzzled. Why were the ducks afraid of the water? Of course ducks know how to swim? Each day the man and woman would walk to the pond and try to get the ducks to swim in the water. Each time the ducks would simply walk around and around the pond, but they never entered the water. Once, the man ran a duck to the edge of the water. The duck's foot touched the water but he quickly removed it - almost like the water was hot. Months passed and the white ducks never swam in the pond, they simply walked around and around the edge of the water. The ducks never swam in the pond. And to this day, these five white ducks do not know that they can swim. They simply walk around and around the edge of the beautiful pond.

Based on a true story by Rebecca Isbell.

Basic Rules for Brainstorming

1. Quantity of ideas is important. Later, possibilities can be evaluated.

2. Do not criticize your own ideas or the ideas of others.

3. The combination of ideas is encouraged; one idea can spark another.

4. Wild and imaginative ideas are valued in brainstorming.

5. It is okay for the group to have times of silence.

6. The group leader or facilitator is responsible for establishing and maintaining the basic rules.

7. Brainstorming works best in small groups of three to eight children or adults.

Young children are very good at brainstorming. They abide by the rules involved in the idea-generating session.

Adapted from the work of Osborn, A. F. (1963). *Applied imagination*. New York: Charles Scribner's Sons.

Clay and Play Dough Recipes and Tools

COLLECTED BY STACY LARSEN

When children learn to mix and make their own materials, many avenues of creative expression open up to them. This is a collection of quality clay and play dough recipes that offer a variety of textures, ingredients, and uses. Most of the materials used in these recipes are inexpensive and found in the home. A few items must be purchased at a grocery store. In either case, the finished media will be less expensive than the ready-made products and certainly more rewarding. It is recommended that children be supervised during activities.

Helpful Hints Before You Begin

Use an electric skillet whenever possible to keep heat low. Provide plenty of cooling time for clay or play dough that has been cooked. Use more drops of food coloring to create bright and intense colors. To prevent sticky fingers while kneading cooled clay or dough, spray hands with cooking oil. Provide steady tables with enough space for children to explore the media. For easy clean up, place sheets of heavy plastic on top of the working surface. Store finished product in an airtight container in a cool place.

Recipes

Play Clay

Ingredients

$^1/_2$ c. salt	$^1/_4$ c. cold water
$^1/_2$ c. hot water	$^1/_2$ c. cornstarch

Procedure

In a saucepan, mix salt and hot water. Bring mixture to a boil. In a small bowl, stir cold water into cornstarch until well blended. Add cornstarch mixture to boiling water. Stir vigorously to break up lumps. Cook over low heat and let cool on breadboard. When cooled, knead until smooth. Store in an airtight container.

Optional: Food coloring can be added after adding cornstarch to boiling water. This clay has a unique and wonderful texture.

Salt Modeling Clay

Ingredients

1 c. nonself-rising flour (do not substitute)	$1/3$ to $1/2$ c. water
$1/2$ c. salt	food coloring (optional)
1 tsp. powdered alum	

Procedure

Combine flour, salt, and alum in a bowl. Add water, a little at a time, and stir until it is like pie dough. Knead until dough is thoroughly mixed. Add food coloring and knead until blended well. Store in an airtight container. This clay has a grainy texture and dries well. And this is a good recipe for projects that require painting dried clay.

Used Coffee Ground Dough (a great way to recycle)

Ingredients

2 c. used, dry, coffee grounds	1 1/2 c. cornmeal
$1/2$ c. of salt	Warm water

Procedure

Mix dry ingredients together. Add enough warm water to moisten. Store in an airtight container. The dough has a unique texture and is good to roll, pat, and pound.

Clay and Play Dough Tools

Add these fun tools to your play area.

forks	string
cookie cutters	spoons
garlic press	sponges
rolling pin	combs
tea strainer	paints
sifter	glue
toothpicks	water
tooth brushes	craft sticks
spatula	safe scissors
safe knifes	ceramic tools

Traditional Children's Songs for Guitar and Autoharp

THE CHORDING FOR GUITAR AND AUTOHARP HAS BEEN ADDED BY REBECCA ISBELL.

The Bear Went over the Mountain

      G   D7   G
Oh, the bear went over the mountain, the bear went over the mountain,
                         C   D7   G
The bear went over the mountain, to see what he could see.
           C   C   C   G
To see what he could see, to see what he could see.
                                     D7   G
Oh, the bear went over the mountain, the bear went over the mountain,
                       C   D7
The bear went over the mountain, to see what he could see.

(Glazer, 1973, p. 12)

The More We Get Together

     D   A7   D
The more we get together, together, together,
                            A7   D
The more we get together, the happier we'll be.
 A7   D   A7   D
Your friends are my friends, and my friends are your friends,
                     E   A7   D
The more we get together, the happier we'll be.

(The more we sing together . . . For your song is my song . . .)

(Glazer, 1973, pp. 48–49)

Old MacDonald

G   C   G   D7 G
Old MacDonald had a farm, E-I-E-I-O.
                              C   G   D7 G
And on that farm he had a duck, E-I-E-I-O.
          G   G
With a quack-quack here, and a quack-quack there,

Here a quack, there a quack; Everywhere a quack-quack.
                 C   G   D7 G
Old MacDonald had a farm, E-I-E-I-O.

(Old MacDonald had a dog, cat, horse, cow, chicken, pig, sheep, etc.)

(Glazer, 1973, pp. 56–57)

Johnny Works with One Hammer

   C   G7   C
Johnny works with one hammer, one hammer, one hammer,
(*Beat right fist on right knee.*)
                            G7   C
Johnny works with one hammer, then he works with two.
   C   G7   C
Johnny works with two hammers, two hammers, two hammers,
(*Beat left fist on left knee.*)
                            G7   C
Johnny works with two hammers, then he works with three.
   C   G7   C
Johnny works with three hammers, three hammers, three hammers,
(*Tap right foot on floor.*)
                            G7   C
Johnny works with three hammers, then he works with four.
   C   G7   C
Johnny works with four hammers, four hammers, four hammers,
(*Tap left foot on floor.*)
                            G7   C
Johnny works with four hammers, then he works with five.
   C   G7   C
Johnny works with five hammers, five hammers, five hammers,
(*Move head back and forth.*)
                            G7   C
Johnny works with five hammers, then he goes to sleep.

(Glazer, 1973, p. 61)

This Old Man

  F
This old man, he played one,

```
        C7   F   C7 F   C7
```
He played nick-nack on my thumb (*tap thumb*).
```
   F
```
Nick nack, paddy-wack, give a dog a bone,
```
 C7            F   C7     F
```
This old man came roll-ing home.

Next verses, each followed by the chorus: two-shoe; three-knee; four-door
(*forehead*); five-hive (*shoo bees away*); six-sticks (*tap two fingers together*);
seven-up in heaven (*fly*); eight-pate; nine-spine; ten-once again. Finish chorus
with "Now we'll all go running home."

(Glazer, 1973, pp. 82–83)

If You're Happy!

```
            C                          G7
```
If you're happy and you know it, clap your hands,
```
                                    C
```
If you're happy and you know it, clap your hands,
```
              F                     C
```
If you're happy and you know it, then your face will surely show it,
```
            G7                      C
```
If you're happy and you know it, clap your hands.

Other ideas: tap your toe, nod your head, snap your fingers, scratch your head,
blink your eyes, and click your teeth.

(Fowke, 1969, pp. 44–45)

The Farmer in the Dell (English Folk Song)

```
     G
```
The farmer in the dell!
```
     G
```
The farmer in the dell,

Hi-ho, the derry oh!
```
     D7        G
```
The farmer in the dell!

Where, Oh Where is Dear Little Mary? (American Folk Song)

```
   G
```
Where, oh where is dear little Mary?
```
   D7
```
Where, oh where is dear little Mary?
```
   G
```
Where, oh where is dear little Mary?
```
 D7                  G
```
Way down yonder in the paw-paw patch.

References

Fowke, E. (Ed.). (1969). *Sally Go Round the Sun.* Garden City, NY: Doubleday & Company, Inc.

Glazer, T. (Ed.). (1973). *Eye Winker Tom Tinker Chin Chopper.* Garden City, NY: Doubleday & Company, Inc.

Rhymes and Finger Plays

All By Myself (Adapted Traditional)

There are many things I can do
All by myself. (*point to self*)
I can comb my hair and lace my shoe
All by myself. (*pretend to comb hair and lace shoe*)
I can wash my hands and wash my face
All by myself. (*pretend to wash hands and face*)
I can put my toys and blocks in place
All by myself. (*pretend to arrange objects*)

My Friends (Adapted Traditional)

My friends are gaily waving, (*have everyone wave*)
Waving, waving.
My friends are gaily waving,
And I will wave at them. (*wave back*)
My friends are sweetly smiling, (*have everyone smile*)
Smiling, smiling.
My friends are sweetly smiling,
And I will smile at them. (*smile back*)

Floppy Rag Doll (Adapted Traditional)

Flop your arms, flop your feet, (*do action as rhyme indicates*)
Let your hands go free.
Be the floppiest rag doll
You ever did see.

Reach for the Ceiling (Adapted Traditional)

Reach for the ceiling. (*do actions as rhyme indicates*)
Touch the floor.
Stand up again,
Let's do some more.

Nod your head,
Bend your knee.
Shrug your shoulders
Like this, you see?

Reach for the ceiling,
Touch the floor.
That's all now,
There isn't anymore.

Jack-in-the-Box (Author Unknown)

Jack, Jack, down you go,
Down in your box, down so low. (*crouch down*)
Jack, Jack, there goes the top.
Quickly now, up you pop! (*jump up*)

Magic Feet (Adapted Traditional)

Have you seen my magic feet, (*do the action as rhyme indicates*)
Dancing down the magic street?
Sometimes fast, sometimes slow,
Sometimes high, sometimes low.

Come and dance along with me,
Dance just like my feet you see.
First we'll slide and then we'll hop,
Then we'll spin and then we'll stop.

Dig a Little Hole (Traditional)

Dig a little hole, plant a little seed,
Pour a little water, pull a little weed.
Chase a little bug—Heigh ho, there he goes!
Give a little sunshine, grow a little rose.

Five Little Babies (Traditional)

One little baby rocking in a tree.
Two little babies splashing in the sea.
Three little babies crawling on the floor.
Four little babies banging on the door.
Five little babies playing hide and seek.
Keep your eyes closed tight, now,
Until I say . . . PEEK!

Stories to Dramatize with Young Children

Three Billy Goats Gruff (A Norwegian folktale adapted by Raines & Isbell, 1999)

Once upon a time, there were three billy goats whose family name was Gruff. The three brothers were Little Billy Goat Gruff, Middle-Sized Billy Goat Gruff, and Great Big Billy Goat Gruff. They grazed on the lush green grass that grew on the hillsides. Middle-Sized Billy Goat and Great Big Billy Goat often warned Little Billy Goat not to wander far from home.

"Don't go across the bridge. There is a mean old troll who lives under the bridge. He eats little billy goats. Always stay on this side of the bridge."

Little Billy Goat, being an obedient little brother, always listened to the advice of Middle-Sized Billy Goat and Great Big Billy Goat Gruff. But one day, he grazed all the green grass on the little hillside near their home. He nibbled the grass on the little hillside near their home. He nibbled the grass right up to the edge of the wooden bridge.

When he looked across the bridge, there on the other side was a grassy hillside with green, green grass. He thought to himself, "If I could just graze on that green, green grass, I could grow big and strong like my middle-sized brother, maybe even as big and strong as my great big brother." He looked longingly across to the hillside and glanced down under the bridge. He didn't see the troll, so he decided to cross the bridge.

Trip-trap, trip-trap, trip-trap. Little Billy Goat Gruff came trip-trapping across the wooden bridge.

Suddenly, he heard the troll say, "Who is that trip-trapping across my bridge?"

"It is Little Billy Goat Gruff."

The troll replied, "Little Billy Goat Gruff, I love to eat little Billy goats and I am going to eat you up!"

Little Billy Goat Gruff, being a smart little goat, answered, "Oh, Mr. Troll, you don't want to eat me. I am just a little billy goat. Wait for my brother, who is much bigger than I am. Then, you would have more to eat."

The troll, thinking how nice it would be to have a big meal of billy goat, replied, "But, how do you know your brother will come to my bridge?"

"Mr. Troll, when my brother cannot find me, he will come looking for me. When he sees me eating the green, green grass across this bridge, he will come to fetch me home."

And so Mr. Troll waited while Little Billy Goat Gruff trip-trapped, trip-trapped, trip-trapped across the wooden bridge and up the hill to the green, green grass on the other side.

Soon, Middle-Sized Billy Goat Gruff spotted his little brother eating the green, green grass across the bridge. He decided to go get his little brother, to bring him home.

Trip-trap, trip-trap, trip-trap, Middle-Sized Billy Goat Gruff came trip-trapping across the wooden bridge.

Suddenly, he heard the mean old troll say, "Who is that trip-trapping across my bridge?"

"It is Middle-Sized Billy Goat Gruff."

The troll growled, "Middle-Sized Billy Goat Gruff, I love to eat middle-sized goats and I am going to eat you up!"

Middle-Sized Billy Goat Gruff, being a smart middle-sized goat, answered, "Oh, Mr. Troll, you don't want to eat me. I am just a middle-sized billy goat. Wait for my brother, who is much bigger than I am. Then, you would have more to eat."

The troll, thinking how nice it would be to have a great big meal of billy goat, said, "But how do you know your brother will come to my bridge?"

"Mr. Troll, when my brother cannot find me, he will come looking for me. When he sees me eating the green, green grass on the hillside across the bridge, he will come fetch me home."

And so Mr. Troll waited and waited, while Middle-Sized Billy Goat Gruff trip-trapped, trip-trapped across the wooden bridge and up the hill to join his little brother and eat the green, green grass on the other side.

Soon, Great Big Billy Goat Gruff, spotting his two brothers grazing on the green, green grass across the bridge, decided to go get his little brothers to bring them home.

Trip-trap, trip-trap, trip-trap, Great Big Billy Goat Gruff came trip-trapping across the wooden bridge.

As expected, the troll growled, "Who is that trip-trapping across my bridge?"

"It is Great Big Billy Goat Gruff."

The troll growled, "Great Big Billy Goat Gruff, I love to eat great big billy goats and I am going to eat you up!"

Great Big Billy Goat Gruff, being a quick-thinking great big billy goat, answered, "Oh, Mr. Troll, I don't think you are going to eat me. Just come up and see how big I am and how tough I would be to eat."

The mean old troll crept up the banks of the creek and over the edge of the bridge. Great Big Billy Goat Gruff stood in the middle of the wooden bridge and lowered his head. He butted the mean old troll off the bridge, up into the air, and far, far down the river.

When the troll landed, he ran off to another bridge and another hillside.

Now, every day, the three Billy Goats Gruff cross the wooden bridge to graze on the green, green grass on the hillside.

I can just hear them now, crossing the bridge.

Trip-trap, trip-trap, trip-trap, trip-trap, trip-trap, trip-trap, trip-trap, trip-trap.

The Lost Mitten With Tiny, Shiny Beads (An old Ukrainian folktale adapted by Raines & Isbell, 1999)

Once upon a time, a grandmother and her grandson lived together in a little house beside a great wood. One cold winter morning, the grandmother said, "Grandson, please go and find some kindling for the fire, so that I might make some porridge."

The boy, being an obedient boy, dressed in his warmest winter snowsuit. He pulled on his fur-lined boots. He wrapped his warm scarf around his neck. He pulled his warm hat over his ears. Then he put on his mittens.

The mittens were ones his grandmother had made him. She knitted them, stitched in warm fur, and sewed tiny, tiny beads on the outside. The boy loved his beautiful mittens.

He planned to fill his sled with kindling from the forest. Even with the howling wind, the swirling snow, and the gray skies, he liked walking in the woods.

The snow was so deep that it was difficult to find the little broken branches or to find the spot where the woodcutters often left scraps of wood. The boy pulled his sled deeper and deeper into the forest, searching for the kindling. Each piece of kindling he found he put on his little sled.

Once, when the boy stopped to pick up a piece of kindling, he saw a beautiful icicle hanging from the bough of a majestic evergreen tree. The boy took off one of his mittens and laid it carefully on the sled. He touched the icicle and a few drops of water melted onto his hand.

The icicle glistened in his hand. Just ahead, he spotted a place where the woodcutter had worked. There would be some kindling there. He rushed ahead, pulling his sled behind him. The little boy did not notice that his beautiful furry mitten, with tiny, shiny beads stitched on the outside, dropped from the sled and fell onto the snow.

When the boy reached the clearing, he picked up the small pieces of kindling the woodcutter had left behind. He was so busy that he did not notice that his beautiful furry mitten, with tiny, shiny beads stitched on the outside, was missing.

When the sled was loaded, he started back home. His hand felt cold. He stopped to get his mitten from the sled, but he could not find it. He looked under each stick of kindling on the sled, but he could not find his beautiful furry mitten, with tiny, shiny beads stitched on the outside.

The boy looked for the beautiful mitten everywhere. The wind continued to howl, and the blowing snow made it hard to see. He could not even see the tracks from his sled. With a heavy heart, he realized that he could not find his beautiful furry mitten, with tiny, shiny beads stitched on the outside.

So, the little boy put his cold hand into his pocket and started for home. With the swirling snow and his search for the mitten, he had gotten off the path and did not know which way was home. He was so cold and getting more frightened by the minute. Then he remembered some advice the woodcutter had given him: follow the tall row of evergreens that line the path. The little boy searched until he found the evergreens that lined the path and made his way back to the little house beside a great wood.

Meanwhile, his beautiful furry mitten, with tiny, shiny beads stitched on the outside, lay upon the snow. It seems that the little boy was not the only one who was cold that morning. Field Mouse had been out searching for dried seeds, and he became so cold. He spied the beautiful furry mitten, with tiny, shiny beads stitched on the outside. Field Mouse wiggled inside and felt the warm fur. He decided that he would wait out the snowstorm inside this beautiful furry mitten, with tiny, shiny beads stitched on the outside. Just as Field Mouse was about to take a little nap, he heard someone outside the mitten. "Croak, croak, it is so cold outside. Please, may I come in?"

"Who is that croaking voice outside in the cold?" the warm field mouse asked. "It is I, Frog, and I am so cold." Field Mouse, recognizing the croaking voice of Frog, said, "Yes, of course, there is always room for one more." So, Frog hopped inside the beautiful furry mitten, with tiny, shiny beads stitched on the outside.

Just as Field Mouse and Frog were about to take a little nap, they heard someone outside the mitten. "Hoot, hoot, it is so cold outside. Please may I come in?"

"Who is that hooting voice outside in the cold?" the warm field mouse and frog asked. "It is I, Owl, and I am so cold." Field Mouse and Frog, recognizing the hooting voice of Owl, said, "Yes, of course, there is always room for one more." So, Owl flew inside the beautiful furry mitten, with tiny, shiny beads stitched on the outside.

Just as Field Mouse, Frog, and Owl were about to take a little nap, they heard someone outside the mitten. "Sniff, sniff, it is so cold outside. Please may I come in?"

"Who is that sniffing voice outside in the cold?" asked the warm friends. "It is I, Rabbit, and I am so cold." Field Mouse, Frog, and Owl, recognizing the sniffing voice as Rabbit, said, "Yes, of course, there is always room for one more." So, Rabbit hopped inside the beautiful furry mitten, with tiny, shiny beads stitched on the outside.

Just as Field Mouse, Frog, Owl, and Rabbit were snuggling up to take a little nap, they heard someone outside the mitten. "Growl, growl, it is so cold outside. Please may I come in?"

"Who is that growling voice outside in the cold?" asked the warm friends. "It is I, Fox, and I am so cold." Field Mouse, Frog, Owl, and Rabbit thought it was getting very crowded inside. But, recognizing the growling voice of Fox, said, "Yes, of course, there is always room for one more." So, Fox crowded inside the beautiful furry mitten, with tiny, shiny beads stitched on the outside.

Just as Field Mouse, Frog, Owl, Rabbit, and Fox were settling down and trying to make room for each other inside the tight space, they heard another voice. "Snarl, snarl, it is so cold outside. Please may I come in?"

"Who is that snarling voice outside in the cold?" asked the warm friends. "It is I, Mountain Lion, and I am so cold." Field Mouse, Frog, Owl, Rabbit, and Fox yelled back, "No! It is too crowded in here. We can barely move. Mountain Lion, you are too big. You cannot come in."

Mountain Lion was so cold and he began to snarl, cry, and shiver. "Friends," he begged. "Please make room for me. It is so cold outside that my paws are freezing." So the warm friends crunched closer and said, "Yes, of course, there is always room for one more." So Mountain Lion crawled inside. The mitten was stretching, and stretching, and stretching. Finally, he was inside. The beautiful furry mitten had stretched so big that most of the tiny, shiny beads had popped off the outside, but the friends were warm inside the very tight space.

Just as they were settling down in close company inside the mitten, they heard another voice. "Chirp, chirp, it is so cold outside. Please may I come in?"

"Who is that chirping voice outside in the cold?" asked the warm friends stuffed inside. "It is I, Cricket, and I am so cold." Field Mouse, Frog, Owl, Rabbit, Fox, and Mountain Lion thought, if we can get a great big mountain lion inside this beautiful fur-lined mitten, we can stretch it a little more to get a tiny cricket inside. So they said, "Yes, of course, there is always room for one more." So Field Mouse, Frog, Owl, Rabbit, Fox, and Mountain Lion drew in their breaths to make room for Cricket.

The beautiful fur-lined mitten stretched and stretched. This time, it stretched so far that the stitches holding it together broke, and the beautiful fur-lined mitten burst open.

Field Mouse, Frog, Owl, Rabbit, Fox, and Mountain Lion tumbled out onto the cold snow. While they had been inside, the wind had stopped blowing, and the sun was peeking through the clouds. So Field Mouse, Frog, Owl, Rabbit, Fox, and Mountain Lion felt the warmth of the sun and rushed back to their homes in the great woods.

Only Cricket was left. Finding a piece of the beautiful furry mitten, with one tiny, shiny bead left on the outside, Cricket said, "This will make me a nice, warm home, to wait out the winter, until spring comes." And so he did.

One day, the following spring, the little boy was playing along the path where the evergreens lead into the big woods, when he found a scrap of woven cloth. It reminded him of his beautiful furry mitten, with tiny, shiny beads stitched to the outside. In fact, there was one tiny, shiny bead stitched on the scrap of woven cloth. When he picked it up, he heard a voice inside.

"Chirp, chirp, who is moving my warm house?"

"It is I, Little Boy, who lives in the house beside the big woods. How did you come to have this scrap of woven cloth for your house?" asked the boy.

"Chirp, chirp, now that is quite a story, chirp, chirp. Sit here on this stack of kindling and let me tell you about a cold day last winter."

So, Cricket hopped upon the shoulder of the little boy and told the story of how the beautiful furry mitten, with tiny, shiny beads stitched on the outside became his home for the winter.

The Great Lion and the Tiny Mouse (An Aesop's fable adapted by Isbell & Raines, 2000)

Once upon a time, a Great Lion was king of the jungle. He ran where he wanted to run. He ate what he wanted to eat. And he slept where he wanted to sleep.

No one bothered Great Lion. The monkeys did not bother him. The zebras did not bother him. The water buffalos did not bother him. The giraffes did not bother him. Even the elephants did not bother the Great Lion.

One day, Tiny Mouse was hurrying home to his tiny burrow. Because he was in a hurry, he was not looking where he was going. He ran over the paw of Great Lion while he was sleeping. Tiny Mouse tickled Great Lion's paw as he ran over it, and Great Lion awoke. He slapped his huge paw down and caught Tiny Mouse by the tail.

"Well, what do we have here?" Great Lion said in a huge booming voice.

"Oh, please, Great Lion, please let me go. Do not hurt me. I am just a tiny little mouse."

"Just a nice little afternoon snack for me, I should think," boomed Great Lion.

"Oh please, Great Lion, please let me go. If you let me go, some day I will do a favor for you," squeaked Tiny Mouse.

"A favor, a favor for me? You will do something good for me some day?" laughed Great Lion. "Well, I don't think a great strong lion like me will ever need a little mouse like you to do me a favor, but I'm not very hungry, so I'll let you go." And Great Lion lifted his great paw.

Tiny Mouse ran away, as fast as he could, but he yelled back to the lion, "I always keep my promises. Some day, I will do something good for you. I will do you a favor."

But Great Lion was already sleeping, making great snoring sounds. He did-n't even hear Tiny Mouse. From that day on, tiny Mouse was careful to stay away from sleeping lions.

Not long after Great Lion spared Tiny Mouse's life, Tiny Mouse thought he heard something in the far distance. It sounded like the Great Lion's roar. Sure enough, Great Lion was roaring. He was roaring and clawing, stretching and straining, trying to get loose. Great Lion had been caught in a trap. Some trappers had rigged a net to fall on Great Lion. The more Great Lion stretched and strained, rolled and tumbled, the more he became entangled in the ropes of the net.

Great Lion roared and roared, calling for other animals to help him. The monkeys came to see what all the commotion was about. But they just stared at Great Lion, laughed at him caught in the ropes, and swung back into the trees, chattering all the while.

Great Lion roared and roared, calling for the other animals to help him. The zebras came to see what all the commotion was about. But they just stared at Great Lion, laughed at him caught in the ropes, and trotted on back to their grazing.

Great Lion roared and roared, calling for the other animals to help him. The water buffalos came to see what all the commotion was about. But they just stared at Great Lion, laughed at him caught in the ropes, and went on down to the watering hole to drink.

Great Lion roared and roared, calling for the other animals to help him. The giraffes came to see what all the commotion was about. But they just stared at Great Lion, laughed at him caught in the ropes, and went back to nibbling leaves from the treetops.

Great Lion roared and roared, calling for the other animals to help him. The elephants came to see what all the commotion was about. But they just stared at Great Lion, laughed at him caught in the ropes, and went back to swinging their trunks and herding their babies along the path.

Tiny Mouse was rushing, as fast as he could, in the direction of the roaring lion. He passed the monkeys swinging in the trees. He passed the zebras grazing on the grass. He passed the water buffalos by the watering hole. He passed the giraffes nibbling leaves from the treetops. He passed the elephants herding their babies along the path.

Finally, Tiny Mouse reached Great Lion. He saw him caught in the ropes, but Tiny Mouse did not laugh at Great Lion. He told him to be still and rest. Then, Tiny Mouse gnawed and chewed, chewed and gnawed, until he gnawed right through one rope. Then he gnawed right through another rope. Finally, he gnawed a hole in the ropes big enough for Great Lion to escape.

Tiny Mouse said, "I always keep my promises. I promised you that one day I would do something good for you. I promised you that if you let me go, I would do you a favor."

Great Lion lay his great paw down on the ground gently. Tiny Mouse stepped on it. Great Lion lifted Tiny Mouse up to his great strong back and they walked away. And, to this day, if you ever see a great sleeping lion, look for a tiny mouse. He is sure to be close by.

References

Raines, S. C., & Isbell, R. T. (1999). Three Billy Goats Gruff. *Tell it again: Easy-to-tell stories with activities for young children* (pp. 36–40). Beltsville, MD: Gryphon House.

Raines, S. C., & Isbell, R. T. (1999). The lost mitten with tiny, shiny beads. *Tell it again: Easy-to-tell stories with activities for young children* (pp. 120–126). Beltsville, MD: Gryphon House.

Isbell, R. T., & Raines, S. C. (2000). The great lion and the tiny mouse. *Tell it again 2: Easy-to-tell stories with activities for young children* (pp. 48–52). Beltsville, MD: Gryphon House.

Primary Thematic Unit: Icky Sticky Fun!

DEVELOPED BY STACY LARSEN, AMY CARMICHAEL,
CAROLYN KENT, AND SHELLEY NOTTER

Overview

Children will learn about "stickiness" through art, music, movement, dramatic arts, creative thinking, literature, and a "sticky" learning center.

List of Lesson Plans

1. Design: Turning Mud Pies into Houses

2. Dramatics: Pretendo

3. Creative Problem-solving: What's This Sticky Stuff?

4. Movement: Don't Get Stuck in the Human Pretzel

5. Art: Sticky Recipes

Goals

We believe children learn best through meaningful activities and hands-on experiences. The "sticky" learning center and many "sticky" activities in the areas of art, music, movement, dramatics, literature, and problem-solving will provide open-minded, experiential, and creative activities to assist children in constructing their understanding of the properties of stickiness.

The sticky center will consist of a wide variety of sticky and non-sticky materials that students can explore. Additional materials will be provided for constructing creative objects as children practice using glue, tape, contact paper, and other sticky materials. The center will contain choices of activities allowing students to explore their interests at their own pace.

Additional Activities

Additional activities will provide support for the student developing understanding of stickiness. Each activity and the learning center will be described in full detail within this unit plan. We also want to provide flexibility within the unit to accommodate children's ideas and projects.

Introduction

We suggest the use of a K-W-L as an introductory activity for this learning center and unit. Using either a chalkboard, paper, or dry erase board, create three categories with the word STICKY across the top. The first category is What We Know. The second category is What We Want to Know and the third is What We Learned. Begin by asking the children to tell you what they know about the word sticky. Record every response by writing it in category one on the chart. Talk about their responses and ask them to share their ideas about what they would like to learn about sticky. Record these responses in the second category. At the end of the unit, revisit the K-W-L to record what has been learned.

Follow up this activity by asking the children to look around the room for anything that is sticky. Supply them with post-it-notes to "tag" the sticky items they found. Record these items on an additional sheet or section of the board. In addition, send a letter home to parents to introduce the new sticky learning center and unit. Ask the patents to look around the house with their child and create a list of sticky things at home. Allow everyone to share his list with the entire class the following day. The letter is also a good time to ask for sticky donations, if needed.

Letter to Parents

Dear Parents,

In class today, we discussed the word "sticky." We made a list of everything sticky we know and identified sticky things in our classroom. As you can probably tell, we will be spending some time in class exploring things that are sticky, finding out why they are sticky, and discovering what sticky things can do.

Please take some time to look around your house, and with your child's help, create a list of the sticky things you found. The bathroom and kitchen are a good place to start. We will share this list on Wednesday during morning meeting.

If you have anything sticky to add to our learning center, we would appreciate it. Please feel free to call with any questions or drop by to see the sticky learning center.

Thank you.

Art Center

Purpose.   To allow children to question, discover, explore, and learn about the properties of things that are sticky.

Materials.   Sticky things such as all sorts of glue and tape, Post-It® note pads, Velcro®, honey, molasses, syrups, food coloring, contact paper, sugar, vanilla, oil, paints, Kool-Aid®, Jell-O®, and bubbles. Nonsticky things such as water, cornstarch, soap shavings, paper, markers, scissors, stapler, rubber bands, material, sponges, brushes, containers, wood pieces, sand, magnets, and straws.

Set-up.   The art center can be available for the children to explore every day. The materials can be changed periodically and the children can bring items from home to contribute. This center will have a facilitator on hand at all times for safety purposes and the proper handling of potentially harmful materials (when applicable). This center provides materials and space for any creative endeavors the children construct throughout the day pertaining to sticky stuff, and should remain free and open-ended for their discoveries and interests.

Lesson Plan 1. Design: Turning Sticky Mud Pies into Houses

Goal.   A long time ago, house builders throughout the world discovered that soil mixed with straw and water would harden into bricks with the sun's help. Mud could be used to hold the bricks together for building long-lasting homes. This technique is still used today and can be replicated in the classroom. Aside from the fun of approved mud clay, the children will learn about evaporation, building construction, and the creative use of natural resources.

Materials.   The items needed for this project include plastic quart bags, empty pint milk cartons trimmed to about one inch high, dirt (with clay base helps), dried straw or grass from the yard, water, and a large tub for mixing. This project is great for outdoor play.

Procedure
1. In the mixing tub, mix the soil with water until it is the consistency of pancake batter. Add the dried grass clippings or straw. It will pour better if the straw is cut into small pieces before mixing.

2. As you mix, talk about the importance of the water as a mixing agent, and that dirt and water can be poured. Why do you mix the dirt and grass? The grass holds dirt together.

3. Where does the water go? Place a plastic quart bag over one carton of adobe. Water should collect at the top of the bag, showing it escaped the mud by means of evaporation.

4. Place a similar bag, though not completely, over the carton. No water should appear. Would the adobe be a good way to build a house in your area? Why or why not?

5. After mixing, spoon the mixture into the milk cartons. Tamp the container so that the mud slides down. That way, the surface of the brick will be flat for later stacking.

6. Place the containers in the sun to bake and dry. This will take several days depending on the humidity. You may remove the bricks from their

molds (cartons) as soon as the mixture sets in order to reuse the containers.

7. Build a simple adobe structure using mud as your mortar (glue). Plaster it with more mud for smooth walls. A wet sponge can be used to smooth stacked blocks. Let the structure dry thoroughly before using for play.

Extension

1. Other substances can be used to make different structures. Make concrete in the cartons using cement, gravel, and water. The proper proportions for mixing should be listed on the bag of cement. This shows how water mixes with a solid to form another solid. Concrete, like bricks, will require mortar to keep things in place.

2. Ice cubes can be frozen into blocks that later can be turned into an icehouse. For an ice structure, you will need a day with temperatures around freezing, and a wet sponge or sprayer filled with water to help form a solid structure from ice blocks. Packing snow into containers would provide another building material.

Vocabulary

solid	adobe
liquid	straw
evaporation	construct
mix	architecture
mixture	design

Connections to Art

1. Have the children create blueprints of what they want their structure to look like. Use real examples, invite architects to speak about design, take walks to look at buildings in the neighborhood, and bring in construction workers to discuss building procedures and safety. Visit a building or home that is currently under construction.

2. Provide magazines and books about homes and building for reference and reading materials.

3. Allow children to really explore the properties of mud. Let them play.

Literature Connections

Barton, B. (1981). *Building a house.* Boston: Greenwillow.

Burton, V. (1942). *The little house.* Boston: Houghton.

Crosbie, M., & Rosenthal, S. (1993). *Architecture shapes.* Washington, DC: The Preservation Press.

Devlin, H. (1964). *To grandfather's house we go: A roadside tour of American homes.* New York: Parent's Magazine Press.

Lillegard, D. (1986). *I can be a carpenter.* Chicago: Children's Press.

Malone, N. (1988). *A home.* New York: Bradbury Press.

Martin, C. (1984). *Island winter.* Boston: Greenwillow.

Penner, F. (1985). *A house for me.* Boston: Greenwillow.

Lesson Plan 2. Dramatics: Pretendo

Goal. Children will use their imagination in this game of pantomime charades.

Materials. Imagination, children, and idea cards in a bag.

Procedure

1. Make several sticky idea cards before starting to play. Ask students to help. Examples may include some of the following ideas.

   You have just stepped on a piece of gum that is sticking to the bottom of your shoe.

   Your hands have been glued together and won't come apart.

   Someone put glue on your chair and now you can't get up.

   Your lips have been glued shut and you are trying to order a meal at the drive through.

   You are eating something really sticky like honey, marshmallow fluff, taffy, or the like.

2. Ask everyone to make a big circle and sit down.

3. Ask for a volunteer and let him pick a sticky idea card from the bag.

4. Everyone in the circle can chant the volunteer's name until they start to pantomime their sticky idea.

5. The volunteer begins his pantomime, and the first person to guess what is going on gets to go next.

6. If nobody guesses correctly, allow the volunteer to tell the audience what he was acting out and let him pick the next person.

Lesson Plan 3. Creative Problem-solving: What's This Sticky Stuff?

Goal. Children will use their sensory perceptions to identify sticky materials.

Materials. Containers to hold sticky stuff, scarves, wet wipes, and a number of sticky items such as honey, saran wrap, hair mousse, liquid soap, maple syrup, contact paper, tree sap, molasses, marshmallows, hair gel, bubbles, peanut butter, tooth paste, chewing gum, cotton candy, shaving cream, sugary water, taffy, Velcro®, fruit juice, Jell-O®, pudding, tape, and glue.

Procedure

1. Have parents assist with this activity or have children participate in this activity during center time in small groups.

2. Place the materials into plastic containers ahead of time.

3. Blindfold the children and allow them ample time to inspect and explore the various materials as they try to guess what it is. Encourage them to use their senses. "What does it smell like?" "How does it feel?"

4. Record the children's responses and share their answers with them afterwards. This information can be tallied and graphed by the children.

Lesson Plan 4. Movement: Don't Get Stuck in the Human Pretzel

Goal. This movement activity will strengthen problem-solving skills and understanding of spatial relationships.

Materials. A large, open space.

Procedure

1. Have the children stand in a circle and join hands with people in the circle, either across the circle or beside them.

2. The only rule of this game is that they cannot join both hands with the same person. They must join one hand with one person and the other with another person.

3. After everyone has joined both of their hands, ask the children to try and untangle themselves and get into one circle again, with everyone still holding hands.

4. This requires a great deal of teamwork, spatial understanding, and trial and error problem-solving. The first time you use this activity, break the children into small groups and let them practice before attempting to do it with the entire class.

Lesson Plan 5. Art: Sticky Recipes (The following recipes are really sticky!)

Fingerpaint

Ingredients

$^1/_2$ c. cornstarch   2 c. boiling water
1 c. cold water   food coloring or poster paint
1 package unflavored gelatin

Procedure

In a saucepan, mix cornstarch with $^3/_4$ cup cold water to a smooth paste. Soak gelatin in $^1/_4$ cup cold water. Set aside. Pour boiling water slowly over cornstarch mixture, stirring. Cook over medium heat, stirring constantly, until mixture boils and clears. Remove. Stir in gelatin. Cool and divide into separate, small, screw-top jars. Add color and use. Refrigerate to store. Paint is transparent, strong, and durable with a high-gloss finish. May be used on dry and wet paper.

Silly Putty

Ingredients

$^1/_2$ c. liquid starch $^1/_2$ c. Elmer's® glue

Procedure

Mix the starch and glue together until it feels like silly putty. Store in an air-tight container in the refrigerator.

Classroom Paste

Ingredients

1 c. nonself-rising wheat flour   4 c. boiling water

1 c. sugar   1 tbsp. powdered alum

1 c. cold water

Procedure

Combine flour and sugar in a large pot. Slowly stir in cold water to form paste. Slowly add boiling water, stirring vigorously to break up clumps. Bring mixture to a boil, stirring constantly, until thick and clear. Remove from heat and add alum. Stir until mixed well. Store in airtight container Makes about $1^1/_2$ quarts. Classroom paste is a good, all-purpose paste, especially appropriate for work with children. This paste will keep for several weeks. If it gets too thick, it can be thinned with hot water for easy spreading.

Decoupage Glue

Ingredients

3 parts white household glue   1 part warm water

Procedure

Combine glue with water in a jar or bottle with a screw-top lid. Shake until mixed well. To make a collage, brush a thin layer of glue on the back surface of paper scraps or pictures. Smooth them onto a piece of cardboard. Brush on a thin layer of glue to coat the surface.

Literature Connection

Bennet, S., & Bennet, R. (1993). *365 outdoor activities you can do with your child.* Holbrook, MA: Adams Media Corporation.

Bently, D. (1999). *The icky sticky frog.* New York: Piggy Toes Press.

Bree, L. T., & Bree, M. (1993). *Kids squish book: Slimy, squishy, sticky things to do that should only be done when wearing your oldest clothes.* New York: NTC/Contemporary Publishing.

Carle, E. (1981). *The honeybee and the robber.* New York: Putnam Publishing Group.

Matthews, M. (1997). *Icky sticky gloop.* New York: Troll.

Miller, R. (1999). *Sloppy, slimy, sticky, soggy, dripping, moving science.* New York: Scholastic.

Numeroff, L. (1998). *If you give a pig a pancake.* New York: Harper Collins.

Sattler, H. R. (1987). *Recipes for art and craft materials.* New York: Morrow, William and Company.

Stevens, C. (1996). *Paper craft school.* New York: Reader's Digest.

Warbrick, S. (1996). *What is sticky?* Portsmouth, NH: Heinemann.

Wilt, J. (1977). *Touch! 48 tactile experiences for children, plus 34 art media recipes to make and use.* Waco, TX: Creative Resources.

Pre-K–K Thematic Unit: The Bubble Factory

DEVELOPED BY CAREN FULLER, MARCIE KING, KRIS JUSTICE, TRACY PANNELL, AND ROBIN MCCLELLAN

Overview

Young children are fascinated with bubbles. This unit provides opportunities to explore bubbles through art, music, creative drama, movement, literature activities, and recipes.

List of Lesson Plans

1. Art: Bubble Surprise

2. Creative Drama: Carefree Cruising

3. Movement: Tug of Bubbles

4. Art: Bubble Recipes

Lesson Plan 1. Art: Bubble Surprise

Materials. Various colors of tempera paint, $1/2$ gallon bubble solution, tag board or white construction paper, $1/4$ cup measuring cup, large bubble wands.

Procedure

1. Have students measure $1/4$ cup of paint color into the bubble solution.

2. Divide the class into small groups.

3. Have the teacher, aide, or students themselves blow bubbles using the wand; students can "catch" the bubbles on their paper.

4. Be sure students wear protective clothing and a paint tarp is laid on the floor.

Lesson Plan 2. Creative Drama: Carefree Cruising

Materials. One glove for each student, Velcro®, and small styrofoam balls.

Procedure

1. The children participate in the following finger play as they wear their glove and flip "bubbles" (Styrofoam balls) off of each finger at the end of the play.

2. Perform the following finger play and actions.

Five little bubbles cruising through the air. (*hold up all five fingers then close fist*)
The first bubble said, "I haven't a care!" (*hold up index finger*)
The second bubble said, "It's warm in the sun." (*hold up middle finger*)
The third bubble said, "I'm having such fun!" (*hold up ring finger*)
The fourth bubble said, "It's great to be free." (*hold up little finger*)
The fifth bubble said, "I'm happy as can be!" (*hold up thumb*)
A bird flies by. (*flap hands*)
Its wings go flop.
Five little bubbles go Pop! Pop! Pop! Pop! Pop! (*hold up hand and flip bubbles off*)

Lesson Plan 3. Movement: Tug of Bubbles

Materials. Bubble wands, bubble solution, and masking tape.

Procedure

1. Divide class into teams of four people.

2. Position masking tape fifteen feet from the starting line.

3. Have one team member blow bubbles for the entire two minutes.

4. Instruct the other team members to take turns trying to blow their team's bubbles over the finish line.

5. Have the children appoint a scorekeeper to keep track of each team's bubbles blown over the line. If a team member's bubble pops, she must go back to the end of the line to blow a new bubble.

Lesson Plan 4. Art: Bubble Recipes

Simple Solution

Ingredients

2 Tbsp. dishwashing liquid $^1/_2$ c. water

Procedure

Gently mix the dishwashing liquid and water together. Makes about 4 ounces.

Super-Sized Solution

Ingredients

$1^3/_4$ c. dishwashing liquid   14 c. water

Procedure

Mix the dishwashing liquid and water together. Makes about one gallon.

The Best Bubble Brew

Ingredients

1 qt. water   measuring cup
1 clean 2-qt. bottle with a tight lid   3 Tbsp. glycerin (also called glycerol)
4 ozs. dishwashing liquid   bowl

Procedure

Place the water into the bowl. Add the soap. Swish the liquids together and pour them into the empty bottle. Add the glycerin. Cap the bottle tightly and shake the liquids together.

Literature Connection

Bell, J. L. (1993). *Soap science.* New York: Addison-Wesley.

Berger, M., & Kuhn, D. (1994). *Bubbles, bubbles, everywhere.* New York: Newsbridge Educational Publishing.

Dalton, S. (1992). *Bubblemania!* Victoria, BC: Orca Books.

DePaola, T. (1996). *The bubble factory.* New York: Grosset & Dunlap.

Meyer, M. (1992). *Bubble, bubble.* New York: Rainbird Productions.

Moore, S. (1998). A bounty of bubbles. *The Mailbox,* 38–41.

Noddy, T. (1998). *Tom Noddy's bubble magic.* Philadelphia: Running Press.

Rhodes, M. (1996). Billions of bubbles. *The Mailbox,* 31–35.

Robinson, K. (1991). *Thematic unit: Bubbles.* Hunington Beach, CA: Teacher Crafted Materials.

Schubert, I., & Schubert, D. (1985). *Magic bubble trip.* New York: Kane/Miller Book Publishers.

Woodruff, E. (1991). *Show and tell.* New York: Holiday House.

Glossary

A

accommodation   The part of adaptation in which new schemas are created and old ones are adjusted to produce a better fit with the environment.

action songs   The combination of melody and movement.

active listening   The act of responding to sounds that are heard.

aesthetics   An area of art concerned with feelings and responses to color, form, and design.

appreciation   This refers to the listener enjoying the sounds of music.

art center   A specific area of the classroom designed to serve as the hub of artistic creation.

art education   Art curriculum with specific goals and standards taught by art educators who have specialized training related to the content of art.

Artist-in-Residence   Practicing artists, often supported by school districts or community arts councils, who agree to spend some of their time demonstrating their art, facilitating lessons, and helping children understand their profession.

assimilation   That part of adaptation in which the external world is interpreted in terms of current schemas.

associative play   A form of social participation in which children are engaged in separate activities, but they may interact briefly by exchanging toys and commenting on one another's behavior.

atelier   A workshop, or studio, furnished with a variety of resource materials, used by all the children and adults in a school.

atelierista   A teacher trained in art education, in charge of the atelier, who supports teachers in curriculum development and documentation. The art specialist who provides the catalyst for artistic expression in the Reggio Emilia schools of Northern Italy.

atmosphere   The prevailing tone of a place or classroom.

auditory awareness   Being conscious of sounds in the environment.

auditory discrimination   The ability to distinguish between sounds.

auditory sequencing   The ability to remember the order of sounds heard.

autocasmic play   A type of play defined by Erikson as involving self, people, and things.

Autoharp   A stringed instrument that produces chords by pressing buttons. Can be used to accompany children's singing.

axial movements   Those movements that involve twisting, turning, and extending from the trunk of the body.

B

basic form stage   At three to four years of age, a child's drawing begins to exhibit form and organization. Repeated patterns, and the use of basic forms and lines, define this stage of art development.

behaviorist theory   An approach that views directly observable events such as the focus of study and the development of behavior, as taking place through classical and operant conditioning.

bodily-kinesthetic intelligence   An intelligence that includes physical movement, and awareness or wisdom of the body. The body is used to solve problems, make things, and convey ideas and emotions.

body awareness   Recognition of how much space the body occupies and how to control movements.

brainstorming   A technique widely used as a way of producing many ideas.

C

cephalocaudal   The usual pattern of physical development that progresses from the head down to the toes.

chant   the repetition of phrases and/or words in a rhythmic pattern.

characters   The people who carry out the story and action. Often, the characters use dialogue as they communicate with each other.

children's theater   Performances by actors for children. Scripts and staging are included in the production.

collaboration   A tool used to assist children or adults in working together on projects, sharing ideas, clarifying thinking, and mediating problems.

collage   A combination of different elements that can be either two- or three-dimensional.

color   Primary and secondary hues created by light and pigments.

composition   Arrangement of the design and space.

construction play   Play in which children manipulate and/or combine objects to build something.

constructivist theory   The position, based on Piaget's theory, that people interpret objects and events that surround them in terms of what they already know so that one's current state of knowledge guides processing.

controlled scribble   The second step of the scribble stage of artistic development that occurs approximately between birth and two years of age. This step demonstrates the beginning awareness of cause and effect as children begin to experiment with the different marks they can make such as zigzags, lines, circles, and suns.

convergent thinking   The generation of a single correct answer to a problem.

cooperative play   A form of true social participation in which children's actions are directed toward working together.

cooperative work   Being able to work with a group of people and adjusting personal ideas during the process.

creative drama   An informal technique that includes spontaneous acting without rehearsals and props.

creative movement   Using one's body to move in nondirected ways to express feelings and thoughts.

Creative Problem Solving (CPS) model   Developed by Osborn and Parnes, this model focuses on the generation of creative ideas with an emphasis on divergent thinking.

creative process   The creative act, and the methods or procedures used during the process.

creativity training   A planned training program to increase the production of creative ideas.

creativity   The production of novel thoughts, solutions, and/or products based on previous experience and knowledge.

critical periods   Times when the brain is primed for certain types of learning to take place.

culminating activity   A celebration, event, or product that occurs at the end of a project to represent what was learned.

cultural creativity   An act, idea, or product that impacts the world or how it is viewed. This type of creativity is rare and happens infrequently.

D

Developmentally Appropriate Practice (DAP)   Education that is based on both typical development and the unique characteristics of a given child.

display   An attractive arrangement of products for others to view.

divergent thinking   The generation of multiple and unusual possibilities when faced with a task or problem.

duets   Two people or two instruments performing together.

dynamic balance   Maintaining equilibrium while moving.

dynamics   The volume of sounds: soft or loud.

E

egocentric speculation   Thinking that does not take into account the viewpoints of others.

elaboration   A component of the creative process identified by Torrance. Elaboration is taking an idea and expanding it to make it more intriguing and complex.

emerging curriculum   Curriculum based on the child's interests and exploration of a topic.

energy   The force that is used to show intentions. This can include smooth or sharp, and sudden or sustained.

environment   Refers to the physical space in which the teacher and children live.

F

fine motor skills   The use of small muscles such as those in the hands and fingers.

finger play   Song, story, or chant accompanied by the movement of hands and fingers.

flexibility   A component of the creative process identified by Torrance. Flexibility is the ability to change directions or think in another way.

fluency   A component of the creative process identified by Torrance. Fluency is the generation of many different ideas.

focus   Concentrating on the drama and staying involved in the process.

folk art   Art produced by folk artists who rarely have formal training, but have learned their craft from elders or peers in their family or community.

form   Three-dimensional quality that includes height, width, and depth.

G

gross motor skills   The use of large muscles such as those in the arms, legs, and trunk. Also referred to as large motor skills.

group process   A group of people working together to solve an identified problem.

group projects   Projects done by a group of children working together to plan, discuss, and create work.

guided-exploration orientation   An orientation to the art curriculum in which children are taught about art form and aesthetic qualities.

guitar   A stringed instrument that can be used to play chords or melody.

H

harmony   The blending of sounds These may be produced by two or more sounds performed at the same time.

High/Scope   An early childhood program that focuses on the development of cognition through key experiences.

holistic   A term used to refer to the development of the whole child physically, cognitively, emotionally, socially, and creatively.

human impulses   Children's desire to construct when provided with multiple opportunities for learning.

humanistic theory   The theory that contends that people have a natural capacity to make decisions about their lives and control their behavior while striving to be a self-actualized person.

I

illumination   The third step in the creative process defined by Wallas. This step is often described as the moment of "aha," or "eureka!" because a new idea or combination appears that meets the requirements of the problem.

imagination   The ability to form rich and varied images or concepts of people, places, things, and situations, when they are not present.

incubation   The second step in the creative process defined by Wallas. This step involves a period of abstinence when the problem is not considered.

initiating activities   Teacher-initiated activities used to generate an interest in an event, project, or unit.

interpersonal intelligence   An intelligence that deals with person-to-person relationships and communication, working effectively with others, understanding people, and recognizing their goals, motivations, and intentions.

intrapersonal intelligence   An intelligence that involves self-reflection and metacognition, or the understanding of one's own emotions, goals, and intentions.

J

junior theater   In junior theater, young actors perform well-rehearsed productions for an audience.

K

keyboard   A musical instrument that can be used to play a melody such as a piano, organ, or synthesizer.

kinesthetics   Use of the body to gain control and learn about physical capabilities, develop body awareness, and gain understanding of the world. It is another way of knowing and feeling.

L

learning centers   A way of organizing the classroom into areas designed for specific learning to occur. Provides opportunities for small groups to work together.

left hemisphere   The left portion of the brain that specializes in logical operations.

line   A mark made by using a tool across a surface (can be vertical, horizontal, diagonal, or curved).

little-intervention orientation   An orientation to art curriculum most often associated with the belief that if one provides the materials for artistic expression, time in the schedule, and the expectation that children will engage the materials, then the children will express themselves creatively.

locomotion skills   Body motion such as walking, running, jumping, hopping, galloping, and skipping.

locomotor   This is movement through space, and includes walking, marching, jumping, and skipping.

logical-mathematical intelligence   An intelligence that includes deductive or inductive reasoning, and recognizing and manipulating abstract reasoning.

M

macrosphere play   A form of play identified by Erikson that involves sharing play with others.

manipulative abilities   Skills that include reaching, grasping, releasing, throwing, catching, and striking.

melody   The tune of music and the pattern of sound that makes up a musical composition.

microsphere play   Using small items to represent the world in play (for example, small plastic family dolls).

mobile   Three-dimensional art that moves when suspended in space.

motor development   The development and coordination of large and small muscles for movement purposes.

multicultural education   A form of education in which the goal is to develop an understanding of original cultures.

multi-sensory   The use of several different ways of learning combined into an experience.

musical intelligence   An intelligence that deals with the recognition of tonal patterns, environmental noise, sensitivity to rhythm and beats, and responsiveness to the emotional implications and elements of music.

N

National Association for the Education of Young Children (NAEYC)   A professional organization for people who work with young children from infancy through age eight.

naturalistic intelligence   An intelligence with the capacity to recognize flora and fauna, make distinctions in the natural world, and use this ability productively.

nonlocomotion   Stationary actions that include stretching, bending, swaying, and shaking.

novel   An object that is new, unique, and different.

O

onlooker play   Action in which children simply watch others at play but do not actually participate themselves.

open-ended   An activity that allows for many different responses to a problem; divergent thinking is needed.

oral language   Language that is expressed verbally.

originality   A component of the creative process identified by Torrance. In order for something to be original, the idea truly must be unique.

P-Q

painting   The use of tempera, watercolor, oil, or acrylic paint to produce a creative product.

pantomime   The use of movement and gestures to express ideas or feelings.

parallel play   A form of limited social participation in which the child plays near other children with similar materials but does not interact with them.

pattern   The repeat of design, lines, or shapes in the artwork.

perceptual theory   A theory based on the assumption that children draw what they see.

percussion instruments   An instrument that is played by striking.

personal creativity   Doing something new for the individual, something he has never done before. This type of creativity can be seen in everyday happenings and accomplished by ordinary people.

personal experimentation   An individual's exploration.

personal space   The personal or shared area that is used by the body during movement. This includes the levels of high and low, and directions such as forward, backward, up, and down.

perspective   Point of view created by techniques such as size and overlapping.

pictorial stage   When drawings are recognizable to the viewer and artist.

pitch   The highs and lows of musical sound patterns.

play   The spontaneous activity of young children that is enjoyable to them.

playfulness   The ability to play with ideas, to experiment, and try interesting things.

pleasure principle   The primary reason for an activity is the enjoyment it brings to the participants.

plot   The sequence of events in a drama that creates the meaning. Setting the place where the action occurs.

practice theory   A theory developed by Gross, who believed play was an intrinsic activity that continues to develop as the child matures.

preoperational play   The second stage of Piaget's constructivist theory. It is dominated by the development of symbolic representation.

preparation   The first step in the creative process defined by Wallas. This step involves exploration, gathering information, finding available resources, and getting acquainted with the "problem" or "issue."

preschematic stage   The third stage of artistic development that occurs at approximately four to seven years of age. Children begin to use symbols in an attempt to represent objects in their own perspective.

process   Exploring and playing with tools, techniques, and materials throughout the creative process.

product   The final result of the creative process.

product-oriented orientation   An orientation to the art curriculum in which children are expected to produce a product with little self-expression or independence.

project approach   A curriculum approach that allows children to study a topic of interest for an extended period of time.

proximodistal   Expected physical growth that progresses from the center of the body outward.

psychoanalytic theory   An approach to personality development introduced by Freud that assumes children move through a series of stages in which they confront conflicts between biological drives and social expectations. The way these conflicts are resolved determines psychological adjustment.

psychologically safe environment   An environment that meets the child's basic needs, supports ideas, and provides respect for individual differences.

puppetry   A drama technique that allows children to take on the role of another with the use of a prop.

R

readers' theater   Children read scripts of a story or play with rehearsal and props.

realism   The fifth stage of artistic development that occurs from approximately nine to twelve years of age. Children become more concerned about realism in their art through size, proportion, placement, shape, color, and perspective. This stage is characterized by a loss of individuality and creative freedom.

Reggio Emilia   city in Italy with early childhood programs that have received international attention for their excellent practices.

rehearsal   Practicing a presentation, story, or song until it can be performed at a higher level.

relaxation theory   Developed by Patrick who believed play was a way to recover from fatigue or hard work.

resonator bells   A set of bells, arranged by the musical scale, with soundboards under each to produce a beautiful tone.

rhythm instruments   A group of instruments such as rhythm sticks, bells, and tambourines used to play the rhythm.

rhythm   The beat of music, including tempo and meter.

right hemisphere   The right hemisphere is the visual-spatial portion of the brain.

rounds   A musical composition played or sung, with groups beginning and ending at different times.

rubbing   Paper is placed on an object. Then, a crayon, charcoal, or marker is used to rub the paper and reproduce the outline of the object.

S

schemas   In Piaget's theory, a specific structure, or organized way of making sense of experience that changes with age.

schematic stage   The fourth stage of artistic development that occurs approximately from seven to nine years of age. Children continue to develop symbols to represent the world "realistically," and experiment with detail, placement, and materials.

scribble stage   The early stage of artistic development that includes scribbles produced by a young child.

sculpture   Three-dimensional art made from wood, clay, metal, and/or found objects.

self-actualized   Maslow defines the self-actualized person as one who has become all that he is capable of being.

self-assessment   The process of evaluating one's own work.

sensorimotor development   Using the five senses and motor development in a coordinated way.

sensory development   Seeing, hearing, touching, tasting, and smelling.

sensory exploration   The use of the senses to examine an object or experience.

sensory-motor play   The first stage of Piaget's cognitive theory. In infancy the young child learns by acting on his world through his senses.

shape   Configuration, contours, or outline.

small motor coordination   The use of the eye and hand to complete a task (for example, putting together a puzzle).

social competencies   The collection of social skills that permit individuals to perform successfully in social settings.

social constructivist theory   Vygotsky's interpretation of constructivism that sees the process as influenced by the social world.

social play   Participating with others in play activities.

social skills   The ability to work with others using techniques such as sharing or collaboration.

sociodramatic play   Make-believe play with peers that first appears around two-and-one-half years, and increases rapidly until four to five years.

solitary play   Play on one's own: others are not involved in the activity.

space awareness   The recognition of near, far, over, under, up, down, and proximity and distance between objects and/or one's body.

static balance   Staying balanced while remaining still.

story dramatization   Creating an improvised play based on a story or piece of literature.

story line   The events and conclusions that make up the form of the story.

storytelling   The sharing of a story without the use of a book.

subject area   A content area of the curriculum such as science or mathematics.

surplus energy theory   Earliest theory of play; developed by Spencer who thought children release their excess energy through play.

T

teachable moment   Spontaneous opportunity for teachers to expand on a child's interests.

texture   The way an object feels or how the grain might feel when touched.

thematic unit   A curriculum approach that focuses on a specific topic, and includes an integration of content areas and the arts.

theme   A concept or idea that is used to organize curriculum and activities in an early childhood classroom.

three-dimensional   A product that is not flat, and has dimensions of length, width, and height and/or depth.

timbre   The tone of the sound (for example, the uniquely different qualities produced by a log drum or steel drum).

time   Time includes rhythm, speed, emphasis, and duration of the movement.

two-dimensional   A product that is flat, and has dimensions of length and width.

U

uncontrolled scribble   First step in the scribble stage of artistic development that occurs between the ages of birth and two. These first marks are typically uncontrolled, unrefined, and show little concern for the final product.

unoccupied play   Not involved in any play.

use of body   The coordination of the body to communicate in drama such as gestures, facial expressions, and movement.

V

verbal expression   Speaking clearly and effectively, using volume, tone, pitch, and pauses. It includes the ability to improvise dialogue.

verbal-linguistic intelligence   A form of intelligence related to words and language that produces language with sensitivity to the nuances, order, and rhythm of words.

verification   This is the fourth step in the creative process, as defined by Wallas. Trying out the solution and determining if the ideas will work occurs during this step.

visual-spatial intelligence   An intelligence that relies on the sense of sight and being able to visualize an object. It also involves creating visual-spatial representations of the world, and transferring them mentally or concretely.

W-X-Y

whole child   A theory of child development that focuses on the emotional, social, physical, creative, and cognitive growth of a child.

Z

zone of proximal development   In Vygotsky's social construction theory, a range of tasks that the child cannot yet handle alone, but can do with the help of an adult or more skilled partner.

Index

A

C

Omni Chord (electronic), 160

percussion, 145, 157

physical accompaniments, 157

recorder, 146

resonator bells, 159

rhythm, 145, 158–159

step bells (xylophone), 159

zither, 146

Intelligence

bodily-kinesthetic, 17, 175

interpersonal, 17

intrapersonal, 17

logical-mathematical, 17, 176

musical, 17

naturalistic, 17

spatial, 100

theory of multiple intelligences, 16–18

verbal-linguistic, 17

visual-spatial, 17

Interpersonal intelligence, 17

Intrapersonal intelligence, 17

Isbell, Rebecca T., 269, 290

adapted stories to dramatize, 301–307

Music (*continued*)

    selected recordings, 167–169

    songbooks, 166–167

Musical intelligence, 17

Mustard, F., 19

N

National Art Education Association, components of a quality art program for young children, 114–115

National Association for the Education of Young Children (NAEYC), 25

    on curriculum, 229

    Developmentally Appropriate Practice (DAP), 262

    position statement on play, 71

National Education Association, 284

Native American saying, 230

Naturalistic intelligence, 17

Novel toys and ideas, 41

Nursery rhymes, 153

O

O'Keefe, Georgia, books for young children, 117

Originality, 10

P

Painting, 6

Parents, in understanding importance of play, 88

Paste recipe, 315

Perceptual theory, of art development, 100

Perkins, David, 6

Personal development, 26

Personal experimentation, 74

Physical development principles, 176–178

Physical spontaneity, 73

Piaget, Jean

    constructivist theory, 14–16

        of art development, 99

        and movement, 176

    stages of play, 66–69

        construction play, 68

        games with rules, 69

        preoperational play, 67–68

        sensory-motor play (functional play), 67

Pica, Rae, 180

Planting a Rainbow, 35

Play

    benefits of in the curriculum, 72

    brain development, 70–71

    children's literature connection, 95–96

    children with special needs, 86–87

    creative episode, 63

    environment

        play materials, 78

        time and space for, 78

    historical perspective, 64–65

    importance of, 71–72

    learning (play) centers, 78–83

        blocks, 80–81

        items to enrich play, 82

        long-term and special centers, 82–83

        water and sand play, 81–82

    modern theories

        autocasmic play, 66

        constructivist theory, 66–69

            construction play, 68

            games with rules, 69

            preoperational play, 67–68

            sensory-motor play (functional play), 67

        macrosphere play, 66

of art development, 99–100

Psychologically safe environment, 13

Puppets and puppetry, 206–207

    puppet junk box, 221

    puppet stages, 222–223

    resources for masks and puppets, 221

R

Raines, S. C., 269

    adapted stories to dramatize, 301–307

Recipes

    bubbles, 319

    clay

        ground coffee dough, 294

        play clay, 122, 293–294

        salt modeling clay, 294

    decoupage glue, 315

    fingerpaint, 314

    paste, 315

    Play-Doh®, 122

    Silly Putty, 314

    three-dimensional, 122

Reggio Emilia programs, 25, 41

    approach to art, 127–128

    atelier and the atelierista in, 263–264

    a creative project from, 271–272

    the emerging curriculum and, 236–238

    nine beliefs that guide the program, 264

Relaxation theory, 65

Rhymes, 153, 155–156, 299–300

Risk-taking, 40

Rogers, Carl, 13, 14

Role models, 13

Rosegrant, T., on curriculum, 229

Rote memory, 37

Round Trip, 40

Rousseau, J. J., 64

S

Scaffolding of learning experiences, 99, 214

Schema, 15

Schirrmacher, R., on aesthetics in the classroom, 117

Self-actualized person, 14

Sense of humor, 73

Sensitivity to world around you, 39

Sensorimotor development, 176

Sensory development, 176

Sensory exploration, 74

Shore, R., link between play and brain development, 70

Silly putty recipe, 314

Simplicio, J.S.C., 42

Singing, 151–152

    selected songs for

        chants, 154

        finger play and action, 154–155

        folk and traditional, 153–154

        jump rope rhymes and street chants, 155–156

        lullabies, 153

        nursery rhymes, 153

Skinner, B. F., 12

Slovak, Sidney, 126

Small, D., 40

Smilansky, Sarah, sociodramatic play, 76

Smith, Patty Hill, 24–25

Social competencies, 147

Social constructivist theory, 16. *See also*

Tresselt, Alvin, 271

V

Verbal-linguistic intelligence, 17

Verification, step in the creative process, 8

Visual-spatial intelligence, 17

Vygotsky, L.S.

    constructivist theory, and movement, 176

    on importance of play, 72

    social constructivist theory, 16

        of art development, 99

        of play, 69–70, 71

W

Wallas Model, steps in the Creative Process, 8–9

Ward, W., 205

Web sites

    art, 140

    creative movement, 194

    creativity, 33, 62

    curriculum, 255

    drama, 225

    Expressive Arts, 277

    music, 171

    play, 96

    teachers, 62

What I Like, 40

Williams, F. E., 20

Window, 40